D1827493

DEVELOPING EDUCATIONAL LEADERS

INTERNATIONAL INTERVISITATION PROGRAMME 1990

9

Edited by Peter Ribbins, Ron Glatter, Tim Simkins and Len Watson

)

Longman

In association with
The British Educational Management

Longman Industry and Public Service Management,
Longman Group UK Limited,
The High, Harlow, Essex, CM20 1 YR, England
and Associated Companies Throughout the World.
Telephone Harlow (0279) 442601; Fax Harlow (0279) 444501;
Telex 81491 Padlog

First published 1991

A catalogue record for this book is available from the British Library

ISBN 0-582-08386-9

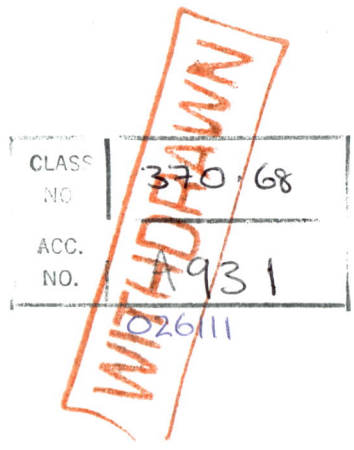

Typeset by Indah Photosetting Centre Sdn. Bhd.

Printed in Great Britain by Bell and Bain Ltd., Glasgow

CONTENTS

INTRODUCTION

Developing Educational Leaders: Sharing Ideas

Peter Ribbins, Ron Glatter, Tim Simkins and Len Watson

Preface

For eight days in late April 1990, following four years of planning and preparation, a major international conference was held in Manchester. Its theme was 'The Development of Educational Managers for the Future' and it was designed to enable practitioners and scholars in educational management and administration to meet and to share and explore ideas and approaches on an issue currently attracting worldwide attention. The conference was attended by some 150 members drawn from almost 30 countries including Australia, Barbados, Canada, Fiji, France, Germany, Hong Kong, India, Italy, Japan, Kenya, Malaysia, Mauritius, New Zealand, Nigeria, Norway, Singapore, South Africa, Sri Lanka, Sweden, The Netherlands, Tonga, USA, USSR along with a significant, but not overwhelming, representation from England, Northern Ireland, Southern Ireland and Scotland.

The conference was the seventh in a series of similar events known as the *International Intervisitation Programme* or, more usually, the IIP. In these introductory remarks, we shall begin with an account of the concept of the IIP, follow this with a description of the IIP in Manchester and end with a survey of the contents of the book. We stress that *Developing Educational Leaders* is not intended as a conventional report of proceedings but rather as a means of recording for a wider audience the thinking of key contributors to the conference.

The idea of the International Intervisitation Programme

The International Intervisitation Programme is widely regarded as the most important international conference of its kind on the study and practice of administration and management in education. It had been held at four yearly intervals since 1966 when the first IIP, developed by the University Council of Educational Administration (UCEA) and sponsored in part by the Kellog Foundation, was held at the Universities of Michigan and Alberta. The Commonwealth Council for Educational Administration (CCEA), which came into existence during the second IIP in Australia became joint sponsor with UCEA for subsequent IIPs.

After many years in which the IIP was managed by the groups responsible for organizing individual conferences, in 1978 a Standing Committee was established. Since then it has been chaired by Robin Farquhar, Dan Griffiths, Meredydd Hughes and, currently, Richard Rossmiller. Membership of the Standing Committee now includes representation from the Inter-American Society for Educational Administration and the European Forum for Educational Administration. The Standing Committee and the individual Planning Committees, to which it delegates detailed responsibility for the organization of individual IIPs, work to three main stated purposes:

1. to open new channels of communication among leaders interested in the study and practice of educational administration and policy;
2. to provide opportunities to share and examine ideas within an international perspective, thus both stimulating participants and enabling them to examine their own values, concepts and attitudes as they communicate with fellow professionals;
3. to provide opportunities to explore the potential, and follow up endeavours, in areas of research, development, dissemination and training, for those who are interested in the study and practice of educational management and administration. It can be assumed that motivation among leaders in various countries for follow-up action and communication is strong, and that the potential for individual stimulation and growth, as well as for collective professional accomplishment is marked.

Successive programmes, following the first, have been held in Australia, the UK, Canada, Nigeria, Hawaii, Fiji and New Zealand and again in the UK. The next IIP is planned for 1994 in the United States (Buffalo) and Canada (Toronto) on the theme of 'Centralization-Decentralization: Implications for Administrator Preparation'.

Past programmes have addressed a wide variety of themes:

- international perspectives on educational administration and management, identifying trends, exploring issues, and giving consideration to the encouragement of teaching and research;
- analyses and challenges in Australia and elsewhere, concentrating on planning and systems analysis, on teacher participation and negotiating in policy making;
- educational management and administration as an international challenge, discussing new directions in practice and theory;
- a review of Canadian and comparative educational administration and management;
- educational administration and planning at the crossroads; and
- equity and diversity: challenges for educational administrators.

So much for the IIP in general, what of the IIP in Manchester?

Preparing educational managers for the future

IIP 1990's theme was *Developing Educational Managers for the Future*. The conference was devised for an international gathering of experienced educational planners, managers and other practitioners, scholars and researchers. Experience of earlier IIPs suggested many participants would hold senior positions and some would exercise considerable influence over education in their own countries. The aim was to explore key themes through keynote and other invited lectures, group discussions and workshops and related visits.

From the main theme, four key components were identified:

1. What would the world look like in the future? With what effect on the relationship between education and its social environment?
2. How can schools and other educational institutions be prepared best over the next decade to meet these changes and how can they be helped to be more responsive to the society of the future?
3. What skills, knowledge, abilities and characteristics will the effective educational manager of the future need and require?
4. What strategies and methods can be used for effective management development for education in the future?

The programme addressed these issues in five main ways. First, by providing *background documentation* in the form of DES descriptions of aspects of the education system – *Education in Britain* – and of recent educational reform – *Education Reform in Britain* – and supporting papers from Ray Bolam, Ron Glatter and Torsten

Husen. Revised versions of the papers by Bolam and Glatter are included in this book. We were unable to add Husen's generous contribution 'Observations on a future orientated education' because it was a chapter taken from a book published elsewhere (Husen, 1990). Second and third, the exploration of issues related to the conference theme in *working groups* and in *visits* designed to provide a balanced opportunity for conference members in multi-national groups to consider developments in the rapidly changing English educational system. The fourth and fifth elements took the form of *keynote lectures* and *invited papers* in which contributors were requested to offer complementary perspectives on the themes identified above. In all more than 40 papers were presented. Many were illuminating, although a few were not as directly related to the central themes of the IIP as our screening arrangements had fondly led us to anticipate. It is from the many fine papers that were relevant that the 25 included in this book were selected. We have had some hard choices to make.

Developing educational leaders: four themes

We have grouped the papers in four main themes as follows: 'New Directions in Education and its Management', 'The Study and Practice of Educational Management', 'Leadership in Education', and 'The Development of Educational Leaders'. This was no easy task given that many of the chapters contribute significantly to two or more themes.

Before turning to an account of content, there is an issue which may need some preliminary clarification. It will be noted that some contributors refer to 'managers' and 'management' and others to 'administrators' and 'administration'. Does anything important turn on this? Wilson and Macintosh suggest not. In a note to their title, which refers to 'educational administrators', they comment that 'educational managers is the more common term in Europe' (see Chapter 4.3). This implies that whilst there may be two terms they refer to the same concept. Such a view would square with a well established tradition in the United Kingdom in which, as Ron Glatter (1972) has pointed out, 'we see no difference in practice between "administration" and "management"' (p5). On this view the terms may be used interchangeably as, indeed, they are in much of the literature. From such a perspective, we may take them both to mean 'the process of securing decisions about what activities the organization (or unit of an organization) will undertake, and mobilizing the human and material resources to undertake them'.

However, this issue may not be quite so easily resolved. As Glatter has observed, such a definition seems to entail two different levels of activity. This is a notion shared by Hodgkinson (1980) who examines in some detail what follows from such a distinction. However, theorists are not the only ones who adopt such a view. On the contrary, the notion of such a division is well entrenched in the public consciousness, within which the terms 'management' and 'administration' are used to represent different activities. Which term relates to which activity is less resolved. Glatter found that 'sometimes "management" and sometimes "administration" carries the implication of directing or policy making functions, with the other word implying more routine work. In the private sector, though, "management" generally has the connotation of higher level work'. To add to the potential confusion, there is a tendency to use 'administration' to describe higher level work in central and local government with 'management' more often applied to the direction of institutions.

Most who tackle this issue feel it necessary to have a single generic term to cover both sets of activities. Several of our contributors, like Hodgkinson, plump for 'administration', others for 'management' and one or two for both terms. As editors we have compromised. We have settled for the term 'management' but accept that others are happy with 'administration'.

Part one: New directions in education and its management

To illustrate the rapidly changing social, economic and political contexts which have shaped recent developments and may determine possible future alternatives for education we have selected diverse studies from four very different parts of the world.

Kariyawasam, from her perspective as academic and practitioner, sets out to examine some of the many and enormous challenges faced by the developing world. These include economic stagnation, rising external debt, civil strife, war, inter-racial conflict, drugs, environmental degredation and rapid population growth. A key social factor influencing education and its provision has been an explosion of aspiration. At the same time, there has been a significant reduction in levels of investment in education in most low income countries. She argues that the evidence suggests that such countries have been less successful at improving quality than quantity. All this is in the context of a growing recognition that investment in education is essential and productive both socially and economically. Much of this chapter is concerned with an attempt to identify the major issues currently facing education in the developing world and with suggestions as to how some of these might be tackled.

In comparison with the world which Kariyawasam describes, the scale and seriousness of the problems Abbott and Hewlett address are modest if deeply ingrained. 'Education 2000' set out to radically challenge cherished and long held assumptions about education in the UK. Its origins can be traced back to 1982 and the publication of the Finniston Report (a study of the engineering industry). From its outset it has questioned aspects of schools, including their reliance on academic subjects, didactic teaching methods and rudimentary technology, on the grounds that such an approach could not hope to meet contemporary educational needs at a time of rapid economic and social change. What is required is more attention to the support and professional development of teachers, a far higher level of learning resource and a greater emphasis on the role of pupil as active learner. In their chapter Abbott and Hewlett describe the work of the Education 2000 Trust and examine the implications for educational managers of the introduction of the ideas which it espouses. Their many years experience of secondary headship in the United Kingdom make them well qualified to do this.

Chan's is one of several chapters in this symposium which consider the role of education and educational managers in the management of change in the developing world. There is good news. He opens his analysis with a brief account of Hong Kong's spectacular social and economic achievements but warns of the problems which might accompany the transfer of sovereignty to China in 1997. One such problem may well be the flight from teaching which is currently taking place amongst teachers and principals. This, and other considerations, raises a number of dilemmas for the many principals who remain. The Government, he suggests must take positive steps designed to equip both experienced, and the growing numbers of new, school administrators with an appropriate range of survival and other skills for the future.

Ken Rae is a Senior Policy Analyst in the Ministry of Education in New Zealand. Much of the first part of his chapter takes the form of an account of the antecedents of what he claims is 'a radical new model of school-based management' which has recently been introduced within New Zealand. He discusses the terms of reference, work, findings and recommendations of the Picot Task Force and its report *Administering for Excellence* and the incorporation of its main proposals within a government policy statement published under the title of *Tomorrow's Schools*. The implementation of these proposals has entailed significant change in the governance and management of schools and in the role and responsibilities of educational leaders of all kinds. He concludes that 'Principals, teachers and trustees in New Zealand schools will need to be equipped to function as participants in a wider learning community' and to do so within a context in which the curriculum in terms of purpose and delivery is seen as the central educational task.

Part two: The study and practice of educational management

What we mean by the term 'educational management' (or 'educational administration') and how we can interpret it in study and practice are the main themes of this set of papers.

In his keynote lecture to the Conference, Meredydd Hughes advanced the idea that educational managers have a crucial role to play in the achievement of educational advance. Accordingly, there is an urgent need across the world for the provision of relevant preparation and development for educational leaders of all levels and kinds. In this chapter, Hughes considers a number of contrasting approaches to educational management from traditional structural and processual modes to the development of new models including the concept of multi perspectives. He argues that 'In different ways and with different assumptions, each of these approaches provides a basis for purposeful practitioner activity and for the preparation of educational leaders. As such this paper offers a remarkably broad yet economical overview of the current state of thinking on "educational management" and "management development for education"'.

Bolam's chapter is a revised and updated version of a paper first presented at an International Conference on *Development Through Education: Learning from Experience*, held at the University of Oxford, in September 1989. In this wide-ranging contribution Bolam claims that there are good grounds for thinking that recent developments in the UK (and possibly Australia and New Zealand) have taken a distinctive character which generates a series of new questions on management and the quality of schooling. In the context of a study of the implications of the Education Reform Act, 1988 he argues that in the longer term, LEAs and schools must base their management training strategies on a policy-based approach. This would entail giving appropriate weighting to the three main components of management development – management training, management education and management support.

Evers and Lakomski offer an introduction to a number of key contemporary theoretical and methodological controversies in study and research in educational administration. In doing so they point to the paradox that whilst the place of science in the study of educational administration seems to have been increasingly challenged in recent times, the natural sciences seem to be going from strength to strength. They argue that this paradox has been sustained as a result of a confused equation between *positivism* and *science* at a time when the most plausible current developments in the philosophy of science and theory of knowledge reflect *post-positivist* views. In their chapter they begin to sketch out the case in favour of a *coherentist* approach which is made fully and powerfully in their recent book *Knowing Educational Administration*.

The context of Manley-Casimir's chapter is the *Greenfield-Griffiths Debate* on theory in educational administration, the nature of the field and the character of appropriate research. The antecedents of this debate, he claims, can be traced back to a seminar on the role of theory in educational administration convened in 1957 by the University Council for Educational Administration and held at the University of Chicago. At this seminar the field took the road of positivist social science – a consensus not seriously challenged until Greenfield's attack delivered at an earlier IIP. Manley-Casimir argues that another road, one which would have placed the exercise of *discretion* or *judgement* at the heart of any worthwhile understanding of administrative behaviour, was identified by Griffiths but not followed. In his chapter, he reviews the substantial literature on administrative discretion in decision making which, he claims, the study of educational administration has largely and mistakenly ignored. In doing so he identifies points of contact between this literature and the work of Greenfield and Hodgkinson. It is, he proposes, time for the study of educational administration to take this 'new' road.

Part three: Leadership in education

There is some overlap between the papers included below and those which are contained in the previous section. Both are concerned with aspects of the management of education but the five papers in this part of the book focus more on aspects of the specific case of leadership in education. They deal successively with what headteachers need to be good at, with their need for strategic skills, with the relationship between leadership and quality in teaching and learning, with the predicament of new principals and with the recruitment of new educational leaders. In this last study Jacobson stresses the problems faced in the United States. Significant as they are they seem modest when contrasted with the account which Sapra gives of India's requirements (Ch 4.9).

Cave and Wilson report on the first of what is planned to be a two phase research project investigating the concept of managerial capability in the context of educational institutions. They review existing analyses of managerial work, particularly that of head-teachers. In doing so they offer a critical assessment of compe-tence-based approaches in general, comment on the *Management Charter Initiative* in the UK in particular, and present their own findings based on a 'focus group' methodology. Four key concepts are seen to be especially significant; reading the situation, balanced judgement, intuition and political acumen. The authors stress the interconnected nature of managerial activities.

Guthrie, in the context of an examination of the rapidly evolving sets of international forces which are currently dramatically altering the external environments and internal dynamics of educational organizations, seeks to examine the characteristics of the effective modern executive. Such an executive, he argues, must be able to: (1) assess a changing external environment; (2) interpret these changes and deduce their consequences for the organization; (3) co-operate with others in the organization to determine appropri-ate new directions; (4) Motivate others; and (5) Appraise the orga-nization's progress in meeting its developing objectives – in short to engage in *strategic leadership*. He stresses that successful strategic executives need not be superhuman but they do need help in the form of appropriate strategic leadership development to under-stand what is involved in the exercise of effective strategic leader-ship.

At the centre of Mulford, Fisher and Grady's analysis and pro-posals is the claim that 'Leadership preparation programmes have, in the past, tended not to focus upon curriculum and instruction'. They identify and review literature which emphasises the impor-tance of the links between leadership and quality teaching and learning, and suggest a number of priorities for action designed to strengthen and develop this critical relationship. In doing so they develop a functional view of leadership and affirm Duke's (1987) view that 'If school leaders are to help others to find meaning in the school experience, they themselves must be clear about what the school experience means'.

Thomas argues that there is a need for a great deal more research focussing upon 'arriving' or newly appointed principals as well as on those who have already 'weathered the storm'. He pre-sents a specific case drawn from an Australian study of beginning principals and identifies four main issues which they face – estab-lishing credibility, establishing relationships, introducing change, and shifts in values – which seem to account for much of the experience of arrival. As such, this is a useful addition to the small number of studies which have been conducted within the UK and elsewhere on the early years of headship.

Jacobson suggests that the demand for educational administrators will grow sharply in the next few years. What of supply? Should the proposals of the National Commission on Excellence in Educational Administration which reported in 1987 be implemented, there will be a significant reduction of preparation programmes and, presumably, fewer administrators in training at a time when growing numbers are needed. Even if this does not happen, there are reasons to predict that conventional methods will be unable to produce the numbers of educational administrators required. In this context, the author examines the potential of relatively untapped sources of supply of educational leaders. As such, his ideas will be of interest in other countries facing similar shortfalls from traditional sources of supply.

Part four: The development of educational leaders

Part Four contains 12 chapters. They consider how educational leaders and managers can be prepared and developed to take on the roles which they face in a fast changing world. These 12 papers are sub-divided into four sections which offer a general overview of management development in educational and other contexts, sets of papers on management development in the developed and developing world and a final overview of IIP 1990 from the leader of the Government's Task Force on School Management Development and Training in the United Kingdom.

1. Management development in education and elsewhere: three overviews

Stewart's chapter is based on her keynote addresses. From a perspective of general management training and research, she considers current approaches to management development and the competences that are needed in times of rapid change. She stresses a need to develop not just competent individual managers but to generate 'learning organizations' – an idea which has much in common with the influential notion of the 'learning school' advanced by a number of contemporary writers in the UK – and asks if institutions dedicated to education in the UK can always be accurately described in these terms.

Glatter draws on an international project which looked at the work of school leaders and their professional development in ten

OECD countries. He discusses some of the requirements of school leadership for educational improvement, suggests some implications for national policies relating to the development of school leaders and indicates a number of key issues on which further work both within and across national boundaries would be valuable. Although the discussion focusses explicitly on school leaders, it is claimed that the analysis and proposals seem applicable to management in other educational contexts as well.

Wilson and Macintosh take the view that perhaps more has been written and said about the preparation of educational administrators than many would care to know. Even so, practice falls continually short of purpose. Given this, the purpose of this chapter is to review some of the major criticisms of existing forms of preparation programme and to suggest a rapprochement based upon an enriched understanding of what the authors describe as 'the stuff' of educational administration and derived from the premise that much greater account should be taken of the kinds of perspective such administrators-in-training already have or may need to experience.

2. Developing educational leaders in the developed world

As with several other chapters, Earthman's contribution is set within the context of the debate on the perceived inadequacy of administrator preparation programmes – in this case the United States. He claims that these 'simply give a person a licence to obtain a job; the programmes do not really prepare them for the challenges and problems they will face in that position'. He describes and explains the design of an innovative off-campus programme which is intended to address the criticisms he makes of current practice. This programme seeks to implement a number of the reform proposals which have been made in recent reports on education and education administrations. As such, his case study might well have relevance to the needs of educational administrators and those responsible for their development and training, well beyond the state of Virginia.

Internships are a common component of training programmes in educational administration in Canada and elsewhere and have been so for many years. Given this, it is remarkable that no substantial body of literature exists which describes the variety of internship experience, explores problems associated with the provisions of these experiences or considers the impact of internship on practice. In their chapter, Hickcox and House report on a survey of internship programmes in Canadian universities and school systems and review the literature related to this theme. They attempt to offer some clarification of the general notion of internship in terms of models and critically examine issues surrounding its development and use.

Clark describes an approach to leadership development for the next century from her perspective as the Director of a Catholic school system based in Parramatta, Australia. The area covered by the Diocese of Parramatta is the fastest growing in Australia in terms of population. It caters currently for 72 schools and 37,000 pupils with a projection of 90 schools and 60,000 pupils by the year 2001. Against this background, Clark identifies relevant challenges and goals, sets out a strategic model for school development planning and review and describes an integrated, system-wide approach to staff training.

Johnson identifies three reasons for the growing interest in the training of educational administrators in Australia – the growing influence of the certification movement, the increasing devolution of administrative decision to the local or institutional level and the developing enthusiasm in higher education to offer training relevant to practice which is intellectually demanding and flexible. In the context of a detailed examination of the review and redesign of one such course, the author identifies three needs – periodic review, clarification of purpose and examination of content – which he suggests course designers must engage in if they are to play a worthwhile role in the preparation of educational managers for the 1990s and beyond.

It is only in the last few years that the predicament of the new principal has begun to attract the attention of field researchers in educational administration (for another examination of aspects of this theme see Thomas, Ch 3.4). In their chapter, Schwartz and Harvey examine some of the pressures experienced by 'fledgling principals' in the context of a close study of the first year in office of ten newly appointed principals in Western Australia. In doing so they explore the transition from teacher to principal in terms of such questions as, 'What is it which confronts new principals? What are the more common coping strategies they use? What skills and knowledge do they need? How can they be helped by agencies which carry responsibilities for the supervision and professional development of new and aspiring principals?'

3.   Developing educational leaders in the developing world
Olatunji, discusses the political, economic, religious and socio-cultural developments which may influence the nature and character of education in Nigeria over the next decade. In doing so she seeks to identify the way in which developments in education will interact with these developments to bring further change. Much of the chapter focuses upon the implications which these developments

might have for the role of educational leaders and on the kind of preparation and training which, in consequence, they will require. In her final section, Olatunji emphasises the urgent need to make the best use of trained administrators and stresses that this will only be achieve when appointments to administrative posts go to professionals. By professionals she means those who have received and completed appropriate training.

Sapra suggests that the tasks facing educational managers in India and in other developing countries have increased in complexity over recent times and are set to become much more complex still in the future. He stresses that any worthwhile long-range consideration of the educational sector needs to be underpinned by a clear understanding of the direction in which a society wishes to move. India, he argues, aspires to a society shaped by the national goals of socialism, secularism and democracy. Following an examination of how far India still is from achieving these goals, he considers the extent to which the statement on *National Policy on Education* of 1986 stresses the importance of education in every aspect of life and re-emphasizes a commitment to the above-mentioned goals. In the context of this discussion, Sapra examines the challenges which his analysis entails for educational managers and says something about how they might be prepared. His estimate that there will be a need for almost 1,800,000 managers in India by the turn of the millenium may help many of the rest of us to view our own national problems in this area in a new light.

For Velayuthan the preparation and training of educational managers in the South Pacific countries presents problems and prospects which in some respects are similar to those found elsewhere and in others are peculiar to the region. From his perspective as an experienced trainer of educational managers in the South Pacific, and especially within its 11 English speaking countries, Velayuthan comments on aspects of the training which are and which might be offered to educational managers within the region. He stresses that it is not enough to prepare responsive managers. Rather, if educational managers are to help young people to fulfil their dreams, they will need to learn to anticipate future needs and trends and develop a capacity to shape the future.

4. Postscript: reflections

Styan was asked by the organizers of IIP 1990 to respond, from his perspective as an experienced teacher, headteacher, consultant, trainer in educational management and leader of the School Management Task Force, to the deliberations of the conference. This he did with rare skill and much enthusiasm. In his chapter he draws upon the recommendations of the report of the Task Force and the reports of the conference's working groups to comment upon contemporary issues in educational management and on their implications for management development for schools and school leaders. In his 'Response' to the Conference David Styan commented that:

> 'It is often by seeing the way others tackle issues that we can see more clearly our own predicament. It is this process of travelling to other situations in order to more precisely recognise where you are at home that is . . . the value of such international conferences.'

This will serve excellently as a pithy statement of the philosophy of the International Intervisitation Programme and of the central purpose of this book. In reading it, we hope that you travel well and find the journey as enlightening as we have.

References

Duke, D 1987 *School Leadership and Instructional Improvement*, New York: Random House.

Evers, C and Lakomski, G 1991 *Knowing Educational Administration*, Oxford: Pergamon Press.

Glatter, R 1972 *Management Development for the Education Profession*, London: Harrap.

Hodgkinson, C 1980 'A new taxonomy of administrative process'. Paper presented to the *Canadian Association for the Study of Educational Administration, Congress of Learned Societies*, Montreal, June.

Husen, T 1990 *Education and the Global Concern*, Oxford: Pergamon Press.

PART I
NEW DIRECTIONS IN EDUCATION AND ITS MANAGEMENT

1.1 The Developing World: Education for the 1990s and Beyond

Tilokasundari Kariyawasam

As we enter the 1990s the developing world faces major global challenges, including the threat of economic stagnation and decline, wars, civil strife, inter-racial conflict, the menace of drugs and crime, environmental degradation and rapid population growth. The social factors influencing education find expression in the 'demand' for education. The explosion of 'educational aspiration' is one of the striking features of the social scene in developing countries. These challenges pose constraints to the development of individuals and society.

Human beings are both the end of and the means to all economic enterprise. Acceptance of this statement leads us away from a view of development which has ever-increasing levels of gross domestic product (GDP) as its primary aim. High GDP and quality of human life are not necessarily correlated.

Rising external debt burdens, adverse terms of trade and foreign exchange scarcity are putting the educational improvements of the last 20 years at risk. The result is that lower income countries are 42 per cent more in debt than in 1980. Africa has more than twice the debt it had in 1982. Increased expenditure on defence, rapid population growth, and fiscal policies have created a cut in the resources available for the development. Central government expenditure on the social sectors have proved to be particularly vulnerable in cost-cutting exercises. Between 1972 and 1983 investment in education dropped from 13.2 per cent to 7.6 per cent of the total budget of all low income countries except India and China.

Armed conflicts and civil disorder have uprooted more than 14 million people from their homelands. Of these, about 13 million live in the most improverished countries of Africa, the Middle East and South Asia. There are even greater numbers of internal refugees who are displaced within their own countries, while increased urbanization and illegal drug use have created further problems for millions of people the world over.

Population growth adversely affects economic, social and environmental problems. In 1987 the world population was more than 5 billion. In less than fifteen years the population had risen by one billion. Ninety per cent of this growth took place in Asia, Africa and Latin America.

Rapid population growth, dislocation of population and various other factors have resulted in exploitation of the natural environment. Deforestation is rampant. Improper waste disposal, use of toxic chemicals and industrial expansion have caused environmental pollution in many areas.

The problems posed for economic and social development by the rapid population growth is the wide disparity of the projected future shifts in demographic patterns and growth among countries. The forecasted average annual population growth rates for the 1990s, for example, vary from 0.94 per cent for China to 2.45 per cent for Bangladesh and 2.71 per cent for Afghanistan. This large and growing population is 'young' in its age composition. According to United Nations projections, over two-fifths of the population in Afghanistan, Bangladesh, Iran, Laos PDR, Nepal, Pakistan and Papua New Guinea will be under 14 years of age during the 1990s. About one-third of the population in Fiji, Indonesia, India, Malaysia will be in this age group during the same period. The developed countries of the Region (such as Australia, Japan and New Zealand) will have only about 20 per cent of their population in this age-group. This provides a good indication of the amount of effort and resources required of the adult population and the educational burden that it will have to shoulder.

An analysis of the world's educational conditions reveal that 965 million people are illiterate, including 105 million children (World Conference on Education for All 1990). Of these nearly 70 per cent are in developing countries and 60 per cent are girls. A third of adults are unable to read and therefore unable to gain the knowledge and skills to cope with change.

Primary education has witnessed rapid growth in the 20 years since 1960, from 157 million to 325 million in 1990. The size of the unenrolled primary school-age population stands at some 54 million for the Asian region as a whole. It is projected that this unenrolled population will drop to only 26 million by the end of the century. The bulk of the unenrolled are girls, and children of disadvantaged groups – people living in remote and isolated areas, ethnic and religious minorities, nomadic tribes, poor and low-income groups, and slum dwellers. The countries with the widest gap in enrolment between boys and girls are also the ones with low overall enrolment.

The issue of quality and quantity are inextricably related. Quality enhancement improves the efficiency of an education system because it enables students to complete schooling in a shorter period of time with the same or better results. The available evidence suggests that underdeveloped countries have been far less successful in improving quality than quantity. The schools have failed to prepare students either for living or for making a living.

The recognition of the contribution of education to social and economic development is supported by several World Bank researches. A study of over 100 countries indicated that nations that have invested heavily in primary education – and especially where goals are reached – have achieved higher economic productivity, high mobility, lower infant and maternal mortality, higher life expectancy and lower fertility rates. There is ample literature to indicate that acquisition of education has an important bearing on such widely diverse areas of human activity, on the ability of people to innovate, to make an intelligent choice, about the kind of existence which will bring greater benefits. As Grant (1990) claim the 'Literacy of women is the most important single factor in the reduction of mortality of children. The children of more educated mothers have a greater chance of survival and of healthy growth than those of less educated and illiterate'. Literacy generally increases the capability and efficiency of women and enhances intergenerational educational benefits. We have to recognise the contribution of education to our civilisation, culture and economies.

Education is the key to development. Development means improving the quality of life and eradicating deprivation of all kinds. It enables an individual to cope with life situations and the environment. It also contributes to the freedom of expression and action, decision making, self reliance and self-respect. It provides opportunities for fulfilment and many other qualities of life. Fulfilling every-

one's right to education is now a bigger task than it was 40 years
ago when the nations of the world agreed on the Universal
Declaration of Human Rights.

The lesson emerging from both the developing as well as the
industrial world is that investment in education is essential and productive both socially and economically. The number and proportion
of children in the developing world still without the benefit of primary education and of adults without access to basic learning opportunities is simply alarming. Education is a basic human right. Strong
correlation between basic education and birth rates and child mortality rates, and between achievement of literacy, numeracy and
basic life knowledge and economic growth is now recognised. But
to achieve the full benefits of education, countries have to take into
account both quantitative and qualitative issues. Many developing
countries have impressive figures for enrolment which often mask a
deterioration in the quality of education.

These changes define new needs, knowledge, skills, values and
attitudes and special training for the 1990s. There should be comprehensive systems of education, both formal and non-formal and
they should be formulated to respond flexibly to the development of
the country concerned. This implies the development of the potential of every citizen and the social, cultural and economic development of the country.

Ensuring mass participation in education and development is
considered as vital in a comprehensive national education system.
To improve the quality and efficiency of the primary system and to
increase its relevance for the majority of school learners who will
join the labour force, development of basic skills during the first
cycle of the education system, and the provision of a minimum education as a necessary condition for the effective participation of the
masses in target groups are proposed.

(a) Basic learning needs are knowledge, skills, values and attitudes.
    People need to survive, to live in dignity, to continue learning,
    to improve the quality of their own lives and those of their com-
    munities and nations.

(b) Efforts should be made to provide more educational opportuni-
    ties to meet the diverse learning needs of youths and adults, in
    many different ways, including literacy programmes, skills
    training and specialized education on such topics as health,
    nutrition, safe water, child care and family life.

(c) It is necessary to achieve parity between male and female
    literacy rates. Commitment should be made to groups
    disadvantaged because of gender, economic status, geo-
    graphical location, physical and intellectual disability. Basic
    education must be provided equitably so that all children,

youths and adults can attain a necessary level of learning achievement.

(d) All available channels of information, communication and social action should be utilized to educate people in knowledge and skills for life, and for participation in social and economic development.

Basic learning needs have to be met through channels.

The first is for all children of primary school age, and consists of formal primary schooling. Children who complete this channel successfully should possess essential life skills and the capability to benefit from further education. Achieving universal primary education will be the goal for many countries in the 1990s. For a large number of developing countries, it is unlikely that enough schools can be built, equipped and staffed at a quality level. Other vehicles for primary education, such as religious and community-based education; radio, television and learning activities in clubs and libraries can assist to meet basic learning needs.

The second channel for basic education is for youths and adults, who have not achieved an adequate minimum through the formal route. For minimum learning skills the system can utilize night schools, study circles, libraries, community development societies, apprentice boards and service organizations.

The primary stage would provide the foundation for all children. The two years following should be for children who wish to proceed to junior secondary schools. These would be organized with courses to cover the full general education course. The senior secondary stage would provide different secondary and vocational institutions, allowing entry to those at several levels from primary via non-formal, or after the junior secondary stage. A wide variety of tertiary level institutions, community schools, further education institutions and technical colleges should be established and developed.

The kind of learning provided in the formal system is unsuited to transforming the rural sector. Among the approaches that can be tried in the developing countries are an open access to education with diversified and varied learning systems, non-formal schemes and parallel and alternative programmes, formal education and functional literacy programmes. The rural sector through the many kinds of influence must be given an opportunity to become active participants in development. Their attitudes have to be changed, new values inculcated and a general climate created, based on the fuller and more productive utilization of human resources.

The minimum learning needs required for efficient participation in economic, social and political activities are functional literacy and numeracy, knowledge for productive activity, family planning and health, child care, nutrition, sanitation and knowledge required for civic participation (Coombs et al, 1975).

Enhanced efficiency is also important. There is the problem of irrelevance of curriculum and the difficulty in recruiting and retaining good teachers. There is the need to strengthen efforts to promote an integrated approach to pre-service and in-service training programmes

There is also the presupposed range of analytical and management capabilities, from policy analysis and planning through administration and financial management of programmes and institutions, to design and implementation of educational development projects. All the management functions require reliable, up-to-date information. A large number of professionals covering a wide range of expertise are needed to analyse policy options, plan improvements and manage day-to-day operations. These management skills are indispensable to any nation.

Even skilled managers will encounter problems from outmoded administrative structures. Innovative methods and structures will also be needed for developing and managing flexible programmes for alternative primary education, for the training of youths and adults, and for education using the information and community skills required by Information Technology.

While there is the need for diversified educational opportunities for both non-formal and informal education, primary schooling will continue to occupy the dominant position in all efforts to promote basic education in each country. However, a major task facing most countries will be to effectively adjust to the tremendous backlog of over-age children and out-of-school youth who are illiterate.

The large annual addition to the out-of-school population warrants serious attention in the 1990s. It may necessitate the amount of effort required of the education systems to double or even triple, in order to cater for the educational needs of both illiterate and out-of-school youths. Class repetition and school dropouts result in wastage of educational resources – facility investment, learning materials, teacher-time and effort, all may fail to produce even an adequately acceptable learning outcome. A large number of dropouts represent a massive wastage in education and should be a source of major concern as regards the internal efficiency of education systems in Asia and the Pacific.

Continuous assessment of the size, disparity patterns and causes of wastage; identification of salient innovative strategies and measures to combat wastage; and adapting ways and means to combat the different patterns and causes of wastage; are some of the measures that can be adopted to tackle this problem.

Success of education for all in the 1990s will hinge on the creation of a better, more efficient and more effective learning environment. There will be a close link between literacy and universal primary education. Those countries having low literacy rates are also the ones with low access to, and retention in, basic education. This calls for co-ordinated and integrated action.

To meet the major issues facing the education system the main focal points for articulation will be:

- new administrative structures;
- research;
- development of varied skills;
- equity;
- efficiency;
- teacher education;
- evaluation;
- planning and management.

The main aim will be the taking of responsibility for developing the education system in a way which makes it capable of transforming human potential into human productivity that will supply new momentum to economic, social and humanitarian life. The success of education in the 1990s rests on the ability of teachers. The key to educational progress is the quality of the teaching force.

In the implementation of these proposals, a massive decentralisation of decision-making processes is necessary. The whole process of change involves changes in courses, structure, curricula, text books, learning materials and training of teachers, and the development of their varied skills.

Each country will need to adopt new targets for meeting these needs and define definite implementation strategies to attain them in the context of the country's larger societal goals and priorities.

In improving quality, student characteristics, educational inputs, processes, outputs and outcomes should be taken into account. Promoting equity is equally important. Steps have to be taken to avoid inequalities related to poverty, gender, location, religion or ethnic identification on the part of government and society. Helping to incorporate disadvantaged groups into the larger society should be one of the explicit goals of primary education.

The post-basic primary stage should be reoriented to match the changes made at other levels. It should serve to provide education in teaching skills, in practical learning situations, especially for youth in agriculture, health, literacy, pre-school education, family planning, occupational skills, co-operative and many aspects of community development. Entry to secondary schools should be voluntary so that aspirations, ability and industriousness would be the decisive factor. This system would provide a network of opportunities at specific ages, within the range of non-formal provision for secondary education.

Primary tasks for the future will be to pinpoint the size and distribution of the disadvantaged groups in a country, study the patterns and causes which prevent them from accessing education, identify more effective ways to cater for their educational needs, and initiate a concerned effort to improve the predicted course of development; one way would be to increase the provision of educational opportunities to all disadvantaged children through both formal and non-formal educational channels. Primary schooling will undoubtedly continue to occupy a predominant position in the overall endeavour to promote basic education in each country.

Universal access, retention and complete and qualitative improvement of learning achievement are the main problem areas. Of those who are not enrolled, many belong to disadvantaged groups. Especial attention will have to be devoted to these educationally disadvantaged. In many countries of the Asian and Pacific region, the combined population of these groups constitutes the majority of the population.

These goals can be achieved by:

1. Provision of special services – textbooks, uniforms, mid-day meals, transport and hostel accommodation.
2. Provision of essential facilities such as school buildings, toilets, drinking water.
3. Provision of minimal learning facilities – blackboards, playgrounds, games materials and learning materials.
4. Use of non-formal and informal learning approaches.
5. Enhancement of teacher living standards.

In most developing countries there is a growing imbalance in society, because they cannot afford education for all. They have an overdeveloped system of formal education which fails to meet the needs of its large rural population. The need for developing alternative kinds of education is of prime importance.

Agriculture is, and will continue to be in the coming decade, the important activity in the developing countries of the region. Priorities for educational development in the next decade, therefore, have to be related to the need to provide education in rural areas on a scale and of a quality that will contribute to rural transformation.

The transmission and enrichment of common cultural and moral values are equally important. It is in these values that the individual and society find their identity and worth.

References

Coombs, P H and Ahmed M 1974, *Attacking Rural Poverty*, John Hopkins Press.

Coombs, P H, Presser, N C and Ahmed M 1975, *New Paths to Learning for Rural Children and Youth*, International Council Education Development.

World Conference on *Education for All: A Global initiation to meet basic learning needs*: Jomten, Thailand, 5–9 March 1990.

1.2 The Education 2000 Project in the UK and its Implications for Educational Managers

John Abbott and Mark Hewlett

Introduction

Education 2000 is a distinctive attempt to reform British education (Fisher, 1990). Its distinctive features include:

1. Changing the way learners learn – away from the traditional classroom teacher as instructor' model towards independent self-learning supported by teachers in which learners take greater responsibility for their own learning, and can learn at their own maximum pace.
2. Changing the resource mix of education, in particular shifting the balance of resource inputs towards material resources, especially new information technologies, needed to enable the achievement of (1).
3. Increasing the use of learning opportunities outside the school.
4. Obtaining a high degree of support for education from the whole local community to create an 'educative community' in which everyone feels that they have responsibility for education.
5. Bringing state and independent schools together in active collaboration.

6. Achieving large scale reform in the state sector through inde-
    pendent initiative. No project of this size has been undertaken
    in the state sector other than through statutory local and
    national Government channels.

The project has attracted wide interest in the UK and promises, we
believe, to offer a likely model of education in the future not only in
the UK but throughout the world.

What is Education 2000?

Origin and aims

Education 2000 is a private charitable trust established in the UK
in 1982. From the outset, the Trust expressed concern that the
traditional organisation of schools – particularly their heavy dependence on learning based on academic subjects, their over-didactive
teaching methods and rudimentary technology – was failing to meet
people's educational needs, particularly at a time of rapid technological and social change. These defects reflected the schools' tenuous relationships with the communities they were intended to
serve.

The Trust considered that, though there existed many interesting
and positive educational initiatives in the UK, their impact was
slight because they were scattered, piecemeal and incoherent.
Moreover, it recognised that educators had not succeeded in
capturing public confidence, certainly not its enthusiasm, and that
the public had little idea of changes which could greatly improve
and possibly revolutionise education. (The same applies to many
teachers.) If education were to mount a successful programme
of reform which would engage public interest, attract political
support and win resources, it had to demonstrate that schools
themselves recognised possibilities for improvement and were willing to make the necessary changes in working practices.
Additionally the Trust wished to raise awareness that formal learning in school is only part of education. Therefore, it has emphasised learning opportunities outside school, acknowledging
particularly that the information-rich age in which we now live creates a wealth of such opportunities for those who wish to manage
their own learning.

Essentially the Trust set out to show how, through giving greater
attention to supporting the professional development of teachers
and ensuring far higher levels of learning resources (eg books,

electronic technologies and the community), a fundamental and beneficial shift in pedagogic practice can be achieved. It believed that achieving these ideas and convincing the public of their value required the creation of exemplars where groups of schools, in partnership with their communities, could demonstrate what can be achieved when major innovations are brought together in a coherent way and are properly resourced. It assumed that people would not listen to educational philosophy – but they *might* take notice of a successful practical experiment.

Location, financing and management

The Education 2000 experiment was started in Letchworth Garden City, a town of 35,000 people 40 miles north of London. Initially designed as a 'self-contained, planned community', it now has many people commuting mainly to London, but has retained a strong sense of local community. The Garden City Corporation, a public body with no statutory educational responsibility but with considerable influence, gave the Project its support.

There are four 11–18 maintained secondary schools and two smaller independent boarding schools in Letchworth. In 1985 the pupil population was 3,500; in 1990 it had fallen to 3,000 and is expected to bottom out at approximately 2,800 in 1993. There are approximately 250 teachers in the six schools.

The original programme was costed at £2 million – but in fact it became necessary for the Trustees to raise over £2.5 million. That the Trust has been sole provider of funds to the Project has been a major limitation throughout; despite enormous efforts, the Trust has never been able to find all the funds needed to fit the Project's objectives.

The Project is managed by a Management Committee representing both education and the community, advised by a professional Steering Group of headteachers and County officers. Serving this group is the Central Project Management Team (CPMT) run by the Director. In addition to the Director and Project Manager, separate Co-ordinators were appointed for the four components of the programme: 1) needs for the young person, 2) curriculum development, 3) the educative community, and 4) information technology. To ensure effective linkage with the schools, each school then appointed four co-ordinators from its own staff: that for information technology was on a half-time basis, the others varied from half a day per week to two days per week. Two external Project Consultants – one for community education and one for technology – were employed on a part time basis.

The components of the Project

Fundamental to the whole programme was the pervasive thrust of the Project towards the *Needs of the Young Person* and the *Curriculum Development* components. The major purpose of this thrust was to make the curriculum responsive and applicable to the perceived needs of young people in their future lives.

Perhaps the most distinctive aspect of the Project is the *Educative Community* component. The Project believes that it is essential to develop ways in which schools and community become far more supportive of each other, recognising that young people – if motivated and encouraged – will find learning opportunities anywhere within their experience.

In the Project's search to determine the most effective learning strategies for young people, it was essential that it addressed three questions:

1. What kind of society do we wish to create – or expect to be created?
2. How can the education system help us to realise such a society?
3. To what extent will formal structures of education be changed by the impact of the new technologies, and by social changes within society itself?

It was considered vital that an attempt be made (at the *local* level) to engage schools and the communities which they served in direct discussion of these matters. In 1986 a series of breakfast meetings were set up at two to three week intervals. Many of these meetings were followed by community members shadowing teachers for half a day. Individually these were relatively low-key activities – but their number and frequency combined to make the interaction between community and school a significant large-scale operation.

In 1987 the first of twelve special interest study groups was set up. These were made up of 8–10 representatives from different organisations (such as Rotarians, Council of Churches, Chamber of Trade, school governors) along with an equal number of teachers, and met for 8 to 10 sessions over a two term period. During the course of these meetings the groups explored a wide range of issues relatng to education and answered three particular questions:

1. What does your interest group define as the objectives for secondary education in the town?
2. What can your group do to support the teachers in achieving these objectives?
3. What could your group do to provide richer opportunities within the community to support these objectives?

The other major element of the Educative Community component was the secondment of up to 15 per cent of the teachers each year (for two week periods) into local industry and commerce so that up to half the teachers in a three year period would be able to consider in depth the skills expected of young people in the first two years after leaving school, how particular organisations manage their own in-house professional development programmes, and how various organisations seek to exploit new technology to their own advantage.

The Trust sees the fourth component *Information Technology* as providing great opportunities for more effective learning. A major factor here is the motivation of the student. Information technology involves the students, makes them responsible for their own learning and has been shown to be effective in enabling learners to work in a more focused, intensive way. Information technology is a powerful learning tool in the home; and the potential for its use outside educational institutions is increasing rapidly.

The Open University, a British pioneering innovation, has brought formal higher education into our living rooms. Now broadcast information is no longer restricted to fixed times, thanks to video recording systems; and it need not be monopolised by broadcasting authorities as local video sale or rental shops will increasingly take material from a variety of sources as this market matures. Interactive video systems such as videotext (Prestel) which link homes to a vast and growing range of databases are forecast to increase their penetration by AD 2000. Techniques of computer-aided instruction and experiments in distance learning are being pioneered under such Government-backed schemes as Open Tech, the Department of Trade and Industry grants for distance-learning course developments, and Alvey's Interactive Knowledge Base Systems. Many private sector correspondence course schools and educational publishers are beginning to recognise the commercial potential of IT-based learning materials.

The motivated individual, whether in Letchworth or elsewhere, can now therefore acquire powerful learning tools without resort to formal education. The reserve and hesitancy that prevents some people from attending night school or college is avoided when they can buy their own learning equipment and work at home. The potential impact of these changes is little recognised. It is interesting to note that about a quarter of all homes in Letchworth now have a computer, often purchased for educational purposes.

The opportunities for secondary education are obvious. However, despite information technology's power as a learning aid and motivator, it is essentially a tool and facilitator. Its development must go hand-in-hand with curriculum development and staff training. Teachers must be enabled to use information technology as a means of developing skills and competences in their pupils rather than as an end in itself. They must also be brought to understand and master it and see its full potential, enabling them to drive the revolution rather than seeing it simply as an adjunct to a teacher-centred view of learning.

The Project's aim was, over a period of three or four years, to install 500 computers (one to every seven pupils) in the schools, along with the software and peripherals necessary to make full use of them. It succeeded, with very significant effects on the nature and effectiveness of education in the Project schools.

The Trust's long term strategy

The first phase of the Project in Letchworth is now two-thirds complete; it has allowed the Trust's ideas to be developed initially within a compact, coherent and largely supportive community.

The second phase consists of four projects, starting in the Autumn of 1990, in deprived urban areas in the North of England. In parallel with this, the Trust is working a 'franchise' arrangement with a financially autonomous project in Ipswich, and is exploring further ways of working with other areas.

A third group of projects may eventually be set up to test such ideas in suburban/rural communities in the mid 1990s.

Management implications of the Project

The management of the curriculum and pedagogy

In the UK there has arguably been a persistent mis-match between educational aims and the curricula ostensibly designed to achieve them. The immediately striking feature of Education 2000, therefore, is the clear articulation of a philosophy and set of prioritised aims allied to a strong systematic drive to achieve them.

Hewlett (1986) argues that the main aim of education.

> is to help learners acquire and develop (i) knowledge and conceptual understanding, (ii) skills, (iii) personal qualities and attitudes so that they will be able (iv) to take advantage of opportunities and cope with challenges in the various circumstances of their present and future lives – to enable and encourage them to contribute responsibly and constructively to society (in its various facets) and so that their personal lives may be enriched.

The fourth and critical element is frequently ignored or treated only casually, rather than being the focus of a curriculum whose essential purpose is to develop people's abilities in order that they may be 'applied' in the various circumstances of their lives, which need to be specifically identified. Education 2000's specific identification (in its Curriculum Development component) of real life scenarios identified by the communities for analysis and problem-solving, and the carefully planned incorporation of cross-curricular themes into coherent inter-related programmes of study are notable examples of a curriculum initiative specifically and directly designed to achieve such specified aims.

But none of these elements would be considered by the Trust to be as important as the task of developing universally applicable learning skills so that learners will be able to gain access, through a variety of media, to what they will need to know in the real world of escalating change. Few educationalists would dispute the central importance of developing general skills and, even more important, the inculcation of positive habits of self-learning.

If these lessons are fully learned, the implications for education in the next century are immense, raising basic educational management questions, including a very fundamental one: what role should schools have (if any) in the pattern of educational provision in the future?

The second notable feature of Education 2000 is the active inter-relationship between school and community through the 'educative community' component exemplifying ideals of community education, ie education *about* the community, and *by* the community. The active seeking of support from the whole community, particularly the business community, in order to acquire significant additional resources in kind (expertise, direct educational experience) and finance has added a new dimension to community education as it has been experienced in the UK.

The management of material and human resources

Education 2000 has addressed the question of how to raise significantly greater resources for state education other than through existing bureaucratic mechanisms and marginal private fund-raising. It has also argued the case for significantly changing the existing resource mix, particularly by increasing the proportion of resources devoted to material and self-learning resources.

Although the £2.5 million raised from major UK business organisations is small in relation to the national educational budget, this independent resource-raising feat is remarkable and has had a notable effect on the quality of education offered in a locality. How far this is replicable remains to be seen, but the idea of an individual or small group approaching business firms and saying in effect: 'The government isn't doing enough to provide what the nation wants; it's time you took your responsibilities seriously and invested in good quality state education', is unique. Educators might blanch at the thought of engaging in this sort of educational selling and resource-raising, but who else is going to do it? The eventual aim is to form an effective lobby to persuade national government to invest more in education.

By resource generation is meant not only the raising of resources in cash and kind, though this has been notable enough, but the development of resources in the form of staff skills (arguably the major resource) through significant investment in staff development. The professional development programme follows from the radical shift envisaged in learning methods. The move towards learners handling their own learning through IT systems means that teachers have to assimilate different skills and attitudes: the teacher's role is changed to that of facilitator and exemplar. The Trust's decision to allocate 10 per cent of the teacher budget to professional development was a bold move, putting conventional staff development budgets (even those in Government-sponsored initiatives where staff development has been particularly emphasised) in a new light. The size of the staff development programme, its precise relationship to curricular priorities, and its planning (as carefully planned and timetabled as the pupils' timetable) contrast markedly to much in-service training and staff development which is small in quantity and superficial in impact.

In shifting the balance from teacher numbers towards professional development and material resources, the Trust's work challenges the conventional assumption that increases in staffing and reduced pupil:teacher ratios is the pre-eminent requirement for high quality learning. While there is no argument that, other things being equal, the more staff the better, the Trust believes that political, including Union, pressure to allocate additional resources overwhelmingly to increased staffing has had the consequence of reducing expenditure on other learning resources (books, audio-visual aids, information technology etc), all too often forcing teachers into didactic modes of teaching and thus reducing the quality of learning. At the same time the sheer shortage of material resources and equipment has made self-directed learning very difficult if not impossible to develop. By increasing teaching establishments out of proportion to other resources, education has been stuck with ineffectual teaching/learning methods which have ironically held back progress that most teachers would advocate.

Shifts in resource mix have major implications for future approaches to educational resourcing. Pilot schemes of local management have so far seen only small shifts of resources through virement. But the logic of a major shift of resources towards self-learning based on high quality programmed resources has obvious implications for school management. (Again the future role of schools comes into question.)

The management of communication and decision making

Three particular changes have affected the *internal* structure of communication and decision making within the schools: the development of cross-curricular themes, the emphasis on general skills across the curriculum, and the developing professional interdependence of staff. Traditional vertical structures have not disappeared: certain types of decision require them. But intra-school links have greatly strengthened lateral communication especially where teams of teachers from different departments have been working together. Such developments have led increasingly to a management structure which might be called 'fibrous' (as strong in lateral as in vertical threads) and 'dispersed' (reflecting the development of semi-autonomous teams of teachers).

The most notable *external* linkages are associated with the marketing of the schools in the community. The dynamic outward thrust of Education 2000 has opened new territory in terms of the extent and success of such activity. The implications for other schools are obvious. How far and to what purpose should they devote resources to ascertaining what their clients need and want? To the extent that schools consider they have something worth selling, it is a moral obligation. The returns obtained by Education 2000 – in terms of finance, active support in kind and moral support – suggest that the efforts are worthwhile.

The concept of the 'educative community' in Education 2000 implies a much greater involvement of the community with its schools. The Project has had significant effects in the ways in which the community *thinks* about education, *gets involved* in education and *actively supports* education. It has increased the understanding of local employers, making them more realistic in their expectations of young recruits and more anxious to help in what they now see, less simplistically than before, is a complex process.

The community in Letchworth has identified with all its schools. The realisation that a firm's employees may come from any school changes potential criticism about low standards into a desire to actively support schools and raise standards. It has also led to an understanding that schools' reputations are frequently ill-founded. The Project has developed a community of interest not just between schools and their communities but between the schools themselves (even to the extent that fellow colleagues put pressure on a school not to opt out of local education authority control).

However, despite this example of collective loyalty to the local education authority, it is clear that the forging of close bonds within local communities could be seen as a threat to their authorities. An increased sense of ownership of education by the schools and by the local community and the consequent confidence in self management, the experience of strong professional support of colleagues in neighbouring schools, and extensive experience of running in-service training and professional development programmes, has inevitably cast doubt on the need for a larger organising body especially where talent is spread evenly throughout the system and where benefits available from the 'centre' are questionable. Substantial resources are at stake and the downward thrust of independent responsibility to staff, to pupils and to parents inevitably leads to critical questions being raised about the need for overlying layers of bureaucracy; layers that absorb resources which would, along with power and independence, be profitably given to the schools directly to assist pupils' learning.

Developing management training

The Education 2000 Project, in raising questions on all aspects of education management inevitably raises questions on all aspects of education management training. Such questions are not new but they need asking again more carefully in the light of the Education 2000 experience.

Management development trainers should devote more attention to examining radical alternatives to established local authority and school-based systems in the search for more effective working practices. The answers to fundamental questions should not be taken for granted. Are the basic purposes and priorities clear? Have they been articulated clearly to all concerned? Is the curriculum deliberately and specifically designed to achieve agreed aims in the most effective way? Does resourcing match curricular priorities?

Examination of current British practice suggests there is a general and significant mis-match between aims and practice which Education 2000 has sought to rectify. For example if it is agreed that the curriculum is a service for the benefit of its users – society and its individual members – has marketing (or at least some careful reflection) revealed what its users really need and want? Patronising assumptions that 'professionals know best' about education will no longer do.

The overall purpose of trainers questioning current practice in the light of the Education 2000 experience is to encourage trainees to adopt a more searching critical approach to their working environment and to engender in them a confidence that management *can* be improved.

References

Fisher, P 1990 *Education 2000: educational change with consent*, London, Cassell.
Hewlett, M 1986 *Curriculum to Serve Society: how schools can work for people*, Loughborough, Newstead Publishing.

1.3 Challenges for School Managers in a Fast-changing Society: the Case of Hong Kong

Benjamin Chan

Hong Kong as a thriving metropolis is well-placed in the world; its economic and social achievements are widely recognized. It is probably the largest container port in terms of tonnage of goods passing through it. Comparable to New York and London, Hong Kong is among the top three financial centres. It also ranks first in export values in textile goods, toys and electronic watches (Lee, 1990). With a growing market in, and the potential for, export and re-export with the People's Republic of China, the prospect of greater economic and social development is foreseeable: that is, if the uncertainties related to the transfer of sovereignty in 1997 from the British Crown to China can be dispelled.

The uncertainties emerged when the British Prime Minister, Mrs Margaret Thatcher, visited Beijing in 1983 to discuss with the Chinese authorities the transfer of Hong Kong in 1997. The Chinese government persuaded the British government to agree to the city's return of sovereignty with a pledge to allow the people there a high degree of autonomy, in their words, 'Hong Kong people governing Hong Kong'. In order to facilitate continuity and to ensure stability and prosperity, Mr Deng Hsiao-ping came up with the slogan 'one country two systems'. Both governments agreed that post-1997 Hong Kong should be governed by a Basic Law within the purview of the Chinese constitution, to be approved by the National People's Congress. To ensure smooth transition a Joint Liaison Group would be set up, under the provision of the Joint Declaration which was signed in the following year with the prime ministers of both countries present.

Confidence crisis in the making

Several events in particular have complicated the sovereignty issue and eroded the confidence of the people of Hong Kong over the future prospects of their city. The first of these is the ensuing argument between the more progressive members of the Basic Law Drafting Committee from Hong Kong and their Chinese counterparts over the question of the structure of the legislature after 1997. The final version of the Basic Law, although representing a practical compromise of different views, nonetheless caused great disappointments for certain segments of the community (Hong Kong Foundation 1990).

The people's confidence might have been maintained had there not been the sensational Tian-an-men massacres of 4 June 1989. The presumed atrocities had the unfortunate effect of confirming the views of those who did not have much faith in the promises and goodwill of the Chinese government. Asked about whether they are confident of Hong Kong's future after 1997, among a systematic sample of 535 respondents aged 20 to 30, a staggering 66.2 per cent gave a negative answer. The stream of emigrants to such foreign countries as Australia, Canada, the United States and the UK steadily increased from 30,000 in 1988 to 45,000 in 1989 (Patrikeef, 1990).

The response from educators

Educators in Hong Kong are particularly sensitive to the 1997 issue since, as individuals engaged in the instruction and discussion of controversial issues, they are vulnerable to external pressures. Teachers of social subjects such as history, public affairs, government, civic education and social studies are most affected in this regard. Headteachers and principals as well as education officers supervising the schools are not immune.

A survey conducted by the Hong Kong Subsidized Secondary Schools Council after the Tian-an-men incidents indicated that turnover among teachers in this type of secondary school was 15.4 per cent in the year 1988–9 (Wong 1989). Among these, 23.6 per cent changed to non-teaching jobs. Another 15.7 per cent emigrated overseas. An even larger number, 33.8 per cent moved from one type of school to another, with the option to draw out their share of the superannuation fund.

There are no statistics available for turnover among principals and heads of schools. But any conjecture in this direction would put the figure considerably higher than that of the teachers. One secondary school teacher with an extended period of service in a government school, who is also an active union man, when asked what might be the proportion of secondary school principals leaving the Territory before 1997 put the figure as 'at least 50 per cent'.[1] Two well-informed secondary school principals privately confided that this figure is not overstated. Another reliable source told this author that all secondary school principals of a large sponsoring body have expressed the wish to emigrate.[2] The high percentage of principals and heads of schools intending departure may be one reason why the Right of Abode Scheme, which aims at boosting confidence levels, includes them under a separate category.

School principals' dilemmas during the run-up to 1997 and beyond

The principal's job is considered one of the best-paid jobs in the Hong Kong occupational hierarchy. In a local study the secondary school principal ranks second only to medical doctors (Tsang, 1990). It is also a job which carries much social status. Many heads of primary and secondary schools hold seats in the local constituencies, or the district boards. At a higher level the Vice-Chairman of the Regional Council is a secondary school principal. In the Legislative Council, the highest consultative body responsible for law-making and territory-wide financial appropriations, two secondary school principals and one primary school head hold their seats either through election or by government appointment.

Inside the school, the principal supervises the work of several dozens of teachers and a dozen or more clerical and other support staff. In turn he or she is overseen by a group of school governors who represent the sponsoring body and who normally carry out no more than ceremonial duties. The government education department also keeps a watchful eye on the principal, but its function is basically regulatory. The advisory inspectorate pays attention to subject teaching and related matters and seldom ventures into general school administration. The principal in Hong Kong is therefore left with virtually all decision-making prerogatives.

It can be said then that the school principal has in the past enjoyed a high degree of social recognition and influence. Indeed during the past half a century since the Second World War the schools in Hong Kong have been relatively calm and peaceful. It is conceivable, however, that this may not be the case in the future. The incident at the Madame Lau Kam Lung Secondary School in 1989 is revelatory.

The issue in this case was the settlement of students' donations in support of the university students demonstrating in Beijing in the months of April to June of that year. In the process of deciding what to do with the money which could not be delivered, some misunderstanding between the principal and a member of staff evolved, leading to the dismissal of the teacher. Eventually through the intervention of the teachers' union, the board of governors was persuaded into a compromise in which the teacher was merely transferred to another school with full benefits guaranteed.

The Lau Kam Lung case should be looked at as the precursor of things to come. For as conflicts between China and Britain, China and Hong Kong, Hong Kong and Britain over the issues of transition continue to multiply as they have in the last five years, the principal will certainly face various dilemmas over teacher employment, curriculum, discipline of students and other issues which have a bearing on ideological thinking. Many of these conflicts must be dealt with and settled within the school, by the school administrator.

An appeal and some thoughts on management development needs

The authority must have the courage and wisdom to recognize that something really serious is worrying the school administrators to the extent that great numbers would be quitting their job in the coming years. This issue is seldom brought up in open discussion, let alone in the agenda of government meetings. Perhaps the government would do more good than harm if it were to face this issue. For many principals who are worried about the future the government should reassure these people that the government is doing what it can to guarantee certain types of freedom in the post-1997 Hong Kong.

For those principals who stay in their jobs the government must take positive steps to equip them with survival skills needed for their jobs. Such training programmes must be thorough and vigorous, comprehensive and penetrating. They should not be equated with the thirty-hour crash course designed for vice-principals. Some of the skills which should receive immediate attention are conflict resolution skills, skills in negotiation, the art of team management and of flexible leadership. It is hoped that efforts in this direction may also help to slow down the tide of attrition of principals.

Accompanying a high degree of turnover is the need for increased recruitment of new principals. Exactly how are these to be recruited, and what type of individuals are we looking for? Do we still maintain the current practice of promoting from the rank and file, or can we recruit beyond the confines of the teaching profession?

If the new breed of school administrators have to face an uncertain future and be confronted with an array of political or ideological strands, it may be to his or her advantage to have gained experience beyond the classroom, such as in business or government. Notwithstanding, future school administrators should still be a highly professional group who uphold standards and ethical values of the profession.

It is difficult or even impossible to predict what is going to happen in 1997. But one thing is sure: if we can maintain the quality of education through the assurance of quality of teaching, the prospect for the future is still bright. And can we have quality teaching unless we have quality administration?

Notes

[1] Personal conversation on 7 April 1990.
[2] Personal conversation on 11 April 1990.

References

Hong Kong Foundation 1990, Newsletter.

Lee, A 1990, Talk at Chung Chi College Chapel, 23 February 1990.

Milstein, M (ed) 1980, *Schools, Conflict and Change*. Teachers' College Press.

Patrikeef, F. 1989, *Hong Kong at the Crossroads: Mouldering Pearl*. Hodder and Stoughton.

Tsang, W K 1989, Unpublished material. School of Education, The Chinese University of Hong Kong.

Wong, A. 1989, 'Turnover among Hong Kong subsidized secondary school teachers', *Ming Pao* (December).

1.4 Te Ao Hurihuri – 'Tomorrow's Schools': Administrative Change in New Zealand and the Consequences for Educational Administration and Supervision

Kenneth Rae

Ka pu te ruha; ka hao te rangitahi – the old net is cast aside; the new net goes fishing – whakatauki Maori

New Zealand schools in the last six months have moved to a radical new model of school-based management. They are now each under the governance of a board of trustees, operating since 1 October 1989 in terms of a charter drawn up in conformity to national guidelines. Old linkages in the State education system have been knocked away and new networks of services and communication are not yet fully discernible. The transition has not been achieved without pain, and politicians' claims notwithstanding, students as well as parents and teachers are noticing the difference in administrators' responsibilities and workloads, and in available finance.

The transition is currently incomplete, in that bulk funding has been achieved for an operations grant but not for the larger input, the grant for salaries. It can be said with confidence, however, that certain constants for educational managers to the year 2000 are very apparent – there will be ongoing political and economic crisis, reflecting into ongoing social and educational stress. The nature of this crisis has only recently been adequately theorised. Major contributions have now been made by a paper from Nash (1989), which draws on the concept of 'legitimation crisis' (Habermas, 1976), and in the collection of papers in the fields of education policy and politics edited by Middleton, Codd and Jones (1990).

Today there is a search in New Zealand for a new bicultural identity, 150 years after the signing of the Trearty of Waitangi – there is a search also for a human resource base for economic change and new relationships to the world economy. These will place conflicting demands on schools. The managers of schools will be increasingly exposed and held accountable by a range of masters, community and national, both formal and self-appointed.

From the Education Act of 1877, New Zealand has had a national system of primary education with limited local management by school committees elected by householders, and district management by education boards elected by those committee members. From 1903 a national pattern of secondary education was provided for, and universal entry into secondary schools achieved in 1945, after major curriculum reform which introduced the 'core curriculum' still current and the raising of the school leaving age to 15. Secondary school governance had been, from even earlier than 1877, generally in the hands of single-school boards, many created last century by their own acts of provincial or national parliament. From about 1960 they usually had a majority of elected parent representatives. In matters of buildings and staffing entitlements until 1989 they worked to three regional offices of the Department of Education. Department inspectors reported regularly on the programmes offered in both primary and secondary schools, and in 1989 were still grading some primary school teachers.

The drive for educational change

After the election of 1987 returned New Zealand's fourth Labour Government for a second term, the education portfolio was taken by the prime minister, David Lange. He had chosen to campaign in 1987 on the need to effect changes in the subsequent three years in the areas of social administration – health, education and social welfare – which would match the changes in economic management, fiscal policy and monetary policy achieved by his government in the face of financial crisis in its initial three-year term. The emphasis on 'efficiency' in the first term was however to be supplemented in the second by an emphasis on 'equity'.

In July 1987 a Task Force to Review Educational Administration, chaired by Mr Brian Picot (a prominent businessman and member of the Council of the University of Auckland) was given the following terms of reference by the Government:

To examine:

- the functions of the Head Office of the Department of Education with a view to focusing them more sharply and delegating responsibilities as far as is practical;
- the work of polytechnic and community college councils, teachers college councils, secondary school boards and school committees with a view to increasing their powers and responsibilities;
- the Department's role in relation to other educational services;
- changes in the terrritorial organisation of public education with reference to the future roles of education boards, other education authorities, and the regional offices of the Department of Education;
- any other aspects that warrant review (Task Force Report 1988, p1).

The Task Force was also charged with ensuring that proposed structures were flexible and responsive to community needs and government objectives, with identifying the costs and benefits of its recommendations and with making recommendations on transitional arrangements. The review signalled a shift of the new minister away from the Curriculum Review pursued over three years by his predecessor. The terms of reference focus on administration as distinct from curriculum, and have posed considerable difficulty for those who believe educational administration is about administration of a curriculum, about its appropriateness, and about evaluation of change in the learners. The terms of reference reflected advice to the Government on education from its 'control departments', the Treasury and the State Services Commission.

The Task Force reported its findings as *Administering for Excellence*. The recommendations reflected its terms of reference. Not surprisingly, but in contradiction of OECD reviewers of only five years earlier, who had commented on the degree of satisfaction in New Zealand with the education system (OECD, 1983, p10), it

found that substantial changes were required, that present structures were 'creaking and cumbersome', and without overall plan or
design, the result of 'increments and accretion'. It concluded (page
36), 'The time has come for quite radical change, particularly to
reduce the number of decision points between the central provision
of policy funding and service, and the education delivered by the
schools or institutions'.

The changes to be noted in the proposed new structures were:

- the establishing throughout the land of single-school boards
  elected by parents with powers of governance and the appointment of staff, a structure long known in secondary education but
  a bold initiative in the primary sector, the more so given the
  small size of a majority of primary schools;
- the bulk funding of the boards, with responsibility on them to
  adopt a budget on the recommendation of the principal, who as
  a member of the board in the role of manager enters into a new
  relationship with staff;
- the passing to the board of responsibility within nationally negotiated industrial awards for setting up a personnel policy which
  conforms to the 'good employer' and 'equal opportunity' criteria
  of state sector industrial relations legislation;
- the charging of each board with responsibility for maintenance
  and minor capital works;
- the complete removal therefore of property supervision, personnel, finance and professional guidance roles of education boards
  and regional offices of the department and their removal from
  the scence;
- at the centre a fined-down ministry, and clear separation of policy makers from deliverers of 'services';
- the knitting together of centre and periphery, to meet concerns
  for national comparability and equity for disadvantaged groups, by
  the device of the charter, a schedule of agreed school objectives
  within national guidelines, seen by the task force as a 'lynch pin';
- the achievement of quality assurance by an independent review
  and audit agency, charged with measuring the educational and
  managerial achievements of schools against their charter objectives by school visits every two years; and
- two safety nets to allow discussion and negotiation without fall-
  out – at district level Community Education Forums, convened as
  required, and able to make representations to the Ministry; and
  at national level a Parents' Advocacy Council able to report to
  the Minister on the one hand or advise parents on issues such as
  home schooling on the other.

Amended in some details in the light of the public response
invited over the next six weeks, the task force proposals were

incorporated in a policy document prepared by government officials from a range of departments including Education, signed by the minister in August 1988, and published as *Tomorrow's Schools* (Lange 1988).

Through early 1989, after installation (on an 18-month contract) of a change-agent director-general, a compact Implementation Unit recruited from within the department and a range of working parties completed their follow-up to the policy statements of *Tomorrow's Schools*. Attention then focused in turn on the election of boards of trustees, accomplished with the help of massive television publicity in April; development of charter material, especially the national guidelines component, delivered to the new boards in May; and creation of the appropriate block-funding formulae for an operating grant and a salaries grant, the former delivered in preliminary form to boards in June. The grant included loadings for equity concerns – to support work with Maori pupils and in support of Maori language, and to support schools with pupils disadvantaged by socio-economic factors. Because of difficulties of implementation, bulk funding of salaries was put on hold for at least one year, and has now been delayed for at least a further twelve months.

At the centre, in May 1989 a combined briefing by the Implementation Unit of the Department of Education and by the State Services Commission revealed to state education employees and to board members the new structures of the national network – a reshaped Ministry of Education (with a significant district presence); a new Education Review and Audit Agency (with ministerial approval renamed and reshaped by its new chief executive after one month as the Education Review Office); two new quangos, the Special Education Service and the Early Childhood Development Unit; and in outline the Teachers Registration Board and the Parents Advocacy Council.

Administering for Excellence and *Tomorrow's Schools* had been paralleled in the early childhood field by *Education to be More* (ECCWG 1989) and *Before Five* (Lange 1988). In the tertiary and allied fields the *Report of the Working Party on Post-Compulsory Education and Training* (Hawke 1988) was to be followed by *Learning for Life I* and later *Learning for Life II* (Gott 1989). Changes in the early childhood field were built into the structures to operate from 1 October 1989. Decisions by the government and subsequent legislation are scheduled for 1990 in the tertiary field of PSET (post-school education and training), although the initial appointments in advance of legislation have been made to a National Education Qualifications Authority, while the University Grants Committee is set down for dissolution.

The new model of education's reviews of effectiveness

Administering for Excellence in May 1988 proposed that a Review and Audit Agency would make judgements on both local and national concerns, the ministry as well as the boards, as it was responsible for:

- the review and audit of every institution's performance in terms of its charter;
- the provision of independent comment on the quality of policy advice, and on how well policies are implemented at national level in their local impact on schools.

At the school level the review was to have as its purpose 'helping the institution assess its own progress towards achieving its objectives' (a catalyst role) and providing 'a public audit of performance in the public interest' (an audit role).

Reviews in the proposals of the task force would be undertaken at two-year intervals by a 'multi-disciplinary team' consisting of one or more 'curriculum specialists', a co-opted principal, a community representative, and a financial/property/management support officer. Preliminary data-gathering would be followed by a visit to produce a report on strengths and weaknesses, which would make recommendations for improvement. The review was capable of being a 'co-operative attempt to improve the quality of education being provided...an impartial and informed assessment...able to be incorporated in the institution's staff development programme'. This report in preliminary form would be left with the school to allow comment and/or changes in school practice. After a second visit one term later the final report would be made public and referred to the minister. One outcome for the board of trustees of the school could be a requirement to ensure change – failing which there could be dismissal by the minister and replacement by a commissioner. For the review team, there was a prohibition against further advice and guidance outside of the report, to ensure autonomy in their audit function. In the subsequent negotiations of the officials groups, stress fell increasingly on the audit role, but the emphasis shifted back in the Education Review Office subsequently created.

Negotiations had to incorporate the later reports on educational restructuring. The parallel report on early childhood education recommended annual 'developmental' visits for such institutions and services, to be provided by the Office. The other report, on post-school education and training, recommended audit of the performance of tertiary institutions with regard only to the equity and equal employment objectives of the charters which from 1990 they are required to draw up. School visits are being fitted, in the light of these requirements, to a three-year cycle – which matches the term of office of the boards of trustees but is a target the former inspectorates found difficult to achieve.

The Office has come into existence with a central office, four regional managers and eleven district teams. Personnel are grouped for each review visit according to the planning of the district manager from among the total district corps of available reviewers. One reviewer in each district has been recruited for expertise in financial management, one for expertise in property management, and one to report on development in institutions of policies of equal employment opportunities. One officer has been appointed in each region to co-ordinate oversight of issues of Maori education and to knit together those officers identifying a Maori or supporters of Maori interests.

The reshaping of the department to a 'Ministry of Education' has seen the shedding of some functions to other agencies – the advisory services to teachers' colleges and special education support and early childhood support to new quangos. These agencies, like the Ministry, are subject to comment from the Education Review Office on their efficiency and effectiveness in their impact on schools.

Gianotti, the chief executive, was formerly secretary to the Picot Committee, after a career in education spanning primary teaching up to district senior inspector of primary schools, and service in national and regional offices of the former Department of Education. He has stated clearly his belief (1989) that the Office can fill its role of guarantor of educational standards only if it wins confidence by recruiting reviewers of proved experience in management, ie officers drawn from traditional inspectorate sources of principalships in the larger primary schools and from senior head of department and above in secondary schools. Guiding principles for reviews being developed by managers of the Education Review Office have reinforced the shift from processes of external audit to internal appraisal and review. Improved education for learners is posited as the central goal and a review is to be consultative and to build on the institution's own review processes – to encourage all places of learning to develop mechanisms of self-evaluation. Snook (1989) has observed that 'the Review and Audit Agency has been reclaimed by the profession'.

Discussion

The dominant energising 'myth' (Beeby, 1986; Renwick, 1987) of New Zealand education for forty years was that of 'equality of opportunity'. By the 1980s, under the sponsorship of Renwick as director-general, increasingly the discourse was of 'equity' as measured by educational outcomes. From the first report in 1970 of the National Advisory Committee on Maori Education, and especially in the major report of 1980, *He Huarahi*, it was evident that such equity of outcomes had not been achieved for Maori students through a generation of rapidly expanding educational provision. The social debate has broadened the discussion of equity issues through the 1980s to incorporate women and girls, learners with special abilities, and New Zealand's other ethnic minorities.

In line with the government's strategy for its second term and in the lead-up to 1990, a year of commemoration and a further election, the new structures of education administration were frequently praised by prime minister Lange because they 'empowered' the trustees of boards of the 2,700 schools of the nation in the common search for equity. The final section of the paper suggests a turning point in the debate on equity, and the tensions that will persist for those charged with supervision of education in New Zealand and the training of the leaders in the schools. Whether the tensions will be dynamic or satisfying will depend on management decisions taken at both national and local levels. They will test the judgement in particular of education reviewers appraising school managements in the performance of charter responsibilities negotiated with or imposed by the ministry.

Equity issues

Government policy statements of 1988–89 proposed achievement of equity for the new structures as a criterion – but linked to effectiveness, efficiency and economy, so giving at least two strikes to those whose concern for change was in the direction of closer financial management. Financial flows were to be 'targeted', and the laying of equity responsibilities on boards of trustees in the model charter objectives was accompanied by the setting up of an Education Review and Audit Agency to measure outcomes. However, in the May 1989 recruitment handout, to staff moving to the new structures, 'equity' was defined as 'distribution of resources to promote *equality of opportunities*, even if this means unequal distribution' (my emphasis). This appears a move back from the goal of equity *of outcomes*, as proposed in past years by Renwick.

Equity as a matter of informed educational choice and of mere logistics of targeted resource flows is however an inadequate concept. It requires deeper analysis in the light of the concepts of 'habitus' and of schooling as 'cultural reproduction', derived from

Bourdieu. Such perspectives have been advanced in a critique of New Zealand Maori education policies by Harker and McConnochie (1985) and more extensively applied by Codd, Harker and Nash (1985, pp10–12) in establishing 'strategies of family reproduction' in a class-society as the driving force behind persisting educational and social inequality within New Zealand's system of State-sponsored education. Both Lauder *et al.* (1988) and Snook (1989) have even gone so far as to doubt the genuineness of those in the control departments in their propounding of the principle of 'equity' in tandem with 'efficiency'.

Equity is a matter of values, efficiency a matter of technique, equity a matter of ends, efficiency a matter of means. They are of different orders of consideration, and their achievements are not necessarily linked. Snook concluded (page 10),

> A free market economic system as advocated by the Treasury cannot deliver equity; at every step of the way it operates against equity. The invocation of the term 'equity' is a blatant appeal to local concerns and is in no way a genuine feature of the reforms. To be cynical 'equity' is the dogma used to sell free-market policies to New Zealand.

Objectives and community-based charters

The new structures propose clarity of objectives as the path to clarity of evaluation of educational outcomes. Education however is about growth and change. More fundamentally, educational objectives spring from values, about which there will be contention and debate. It is to be expected therefore that ambiguity and tension concerning objectives will persist, especially in issues thrown up by the evolving policy of the government concerning the Treaty of Waitangi and a bicultural New Zealand, and imposed by model objectives on boards in some cases reluctant to accept this lead.

Tension will also persist between the centre and the periphery, especially if the centre views education as mere service delivery, and the periphery sees schools as learning communities. There will be tension between accountability of the minister in parliament to questions on a centrally-funded system, and a different accountability of each board and school to its community. In these communities social inequalities have been increased in recent years as a consequence of policies of economic restructuring. Changing patterns of incomes and heightened levels of unemployment, especially youth unemployment, have struck communities differentially across New Zealand, initially hitting the regions rather than the cities. Their stress has focused also on the Maori and Pacific Island communities in particular.

The charter as 'lynch pin', as outcome of three-way negotiation between minister, board of trustees and community, in the process of the initial implementation has been flawed. Debate over delayed funding of schools raised doubts in late 1989 for many boards on the nature of the agreement they were being asked to reach. The drive to produce guidelines early in 1989 produced not performance objectives but blanket demands on schools, in some cases achievements beyond the ability of the state with all its resources in the past to provide (for example, management training and development for principals, staff *and* trustees – and access to education in Maori for all students whose parents so desire).

As a management tool and a basis for review, a charter composed of the present compulsory components is not an adequate starting point. The charter and the guidelines require further development, preferably out of negotiation in a partnership relationship with schools as learning communities, and out of consideration of ethics and values as well as of administrative techniques. In early 1990 the debate was moved to new ground with the wording of charters amended by the ministry to replace 'agreement' with the word 'undertaking' – a commitment laid not on all parties, but now on one only, the trustees. In April the minister however announced further modifications, accepted by the School Trustees Association. The Education Review Office will be required to comment on such issues, as they impact on schools.

Support for schools

Support services in times of change are vital to sustain the teachers and especially the principals. The changes occurring in New Zealand have been based on the thesis, however, of reallocation of existing resources and 'efficiency savings' of $93 million. So resources that could have been devoted to consultancy in school development and community consultation, or a network of district superintendents of schools, alternative models of development and supervision, have not become available because of policy decisions in favour of close monitoring of an accountability laid directly on the local schools, its trustees and the principal.

Tensions will persist because of the pressures of the time-scale imposed on the total change in educational administration. There is evidence in New Zealand especially from Ramsay (1984, p224) that schools in touch with their communities do meet their students' needs more effectively. Schools, however, need time to establish ongoing and self-sustaining procedures of consultation. The current changes in New Zealand were a process of cultural interruption in 'the education family', marked by break-neck speed and observed symptoms of 'future shock' among teachers and administrators (CRRISP, 1989, p37).

Education Service Centres, free-standing client-driven supporters of schools in the Picot design, had a difficult and belated birth, fraught with political charge and counter-charge. They are unique to New Zealand in their provision of support for schools in all areas except the core business of curriculum. They may in fact develop in this area, and so come into competition with the colleges of education, to whom are currently assigned the Advisory Services of the former department.

The crowded playing field

The Picot Report in 1988 presented administrative structures elegant in their simplicity, on first approach. The reality for schools in 1990 is not simplified relationships but multiplying relationships. Former communication pathways disappeared on 1 October 1989. Communication pathways within, as well as between, the organisations at the centre have yet to be fully established. Building networks across the education family is a priority in 1990. Sallis (1988) from England is quite clear that partnership between the professionals and the governors is vital to the restored health of a state education system under conditions of devolved responsibility. Such a perception could be the motivation for the State Services Commission to maintain a participation in annual salary negotiations that is impacting at the level of personnel relationships in the individual school as it continues its educational agenda, promoting a narrowly technical concept of efficiency with direct impact on pay structures and pay fixing at the local level of the individual school.

From the perspective of the players, the 1990 playing field does not appear too level. It certainly appears crowded. The problem is that the Ministry is charged with marking the field for the precision plays of netball in its directive charter requirements, the Review Office prefers the fluid and close associations of rugby in its proposed co-operative reviews, and the Commission is likely to determine that the game for this month is not hockey but hurling as it assumes the role of employers' advocate in the annual rounds of award negotiations.

The state and state-schooling

At a deeper level, tensions discussed above will be confounding to the extent that concepts of 'community' and 'the state' remain untheorized. The substantial normative overlay of the concept of community has already been referred to in passing. The 'reform' of educational administration was presented in 1988 as desirable because it returned 'power' to the community from the bureaucracy. The locus of 'control' on the other hand is yet to be established by practice, as schools present charters locally developed for approval by the new ministry for the first time in 1990.

A powerful analysis from within New Zealand of contesting theories of the state was advanced by Wilkes (1982), who in the context of issues of community development critiqued the pluralist state of the Weberian tradition, driven by the purposes of serving 'the common good' as an 'instrument of reason'. Drawing on Habermas he posed by way of contras t the structuralist analysis of the role of the state in a developed capitalist economy like New Zealand, engaged of necessity in functions of class production and class reproduction, resultant ambiguities providing contestable locations for those seeking social reform. Only very recently have such perspectives been introduced from the educationist side into the New Zealand debate on state-sponsored education, by Codd (1990, pp197 – 9) drawing on the analysis of the Welfare State of Offa (1984) and O'Connor (1987), and by Nash (1986).

The development of school managers

Funding was made available in 1989 for a Schools Management Development Project. The Implementation Unit invited the six teacher training colleges to join as a network and resourced them to provide training opportunities for principals and trustees of 'clusters' of schools, each with a principal as cluster leader. A decision at national level invited Brian Caldwell and Jim Spinks from Tasmania to address district seminars on their model of the 'self-managing school'. The dominant rubric for the project was however 'response to expressed needs'. So much of the restructuring had been driven from outside education and so much had to be put in place by 1 October that no centrally designed blueprint of development and training was attempted.

A range of development tasks faced school principals and the newly elected trustees. Between April and October trustees had to make themselves ready as teams to assume legal responsibilities for school management, to consult with their communities in developing charters within the national guidelines, and to build management, personnel and financial plans for the 1990 school year. They had to do this in advance of the passage of legislation (achieved on

29 September), amidst continuing uncertainty on budget allocations, and in the face of a sequence of administrative memoranda
from the centre, sometimes conflicting and contradictory, as rules
were adjusted.

Principals were faced with significant new learning in establishing
relationships with the trustees and distinguishing their respective
spheres of 'management' and 'governance'. They had to open
school goals and programmes to community debate, accept
responsibility for budgetary advice to their board and manage the
flow of administrative information from the centre to the boards
and teachers. As they assumed the role of executive officer to the
board, overload was their common experience. This was especially
the case of the principal of any primary school of seven teachers or
less, who retained responsibility for the teaching programme of a
class (67 per cent of New Zealand's primary schools). Their release
from the classroom for 2.5 to 7.5 hours per week was confirmed in
the 1989 Budget.

There were, however, strengths to build on to carry through
these daunting development tasks. Mainstream education thinking
in New Zealand on effective schools had emphasised the recruitment of a qualified and trained teaching force. Principals had been
encouraged to work in a collegial manner with the staff to develop
school schemes of work. By regulation these had to be appropriate
to the needs of the student population and their community, and to
the skills of the staff. At secondary school a model existed of boards
who had always had responsibilities of governance and appointments, and significant financial responsibilities. At primary level the
concept of the neighbourhood school was firmly established and
parent-teacher associations were a standard feature of school life.
With 'integration' of the Catholic schools into the State system
from 1978, there was no significant private school sector, and 95
per cent of children attended the State schools.

To a considerable extent these strengths of the educational family
were discounted by the rhetoric and the practice of the restructuring process. Close financial accountability, management focussed
by objective setting, and initiation of contracts for senior staff
(imposed by legislation for secondary principals during 1989),
reflected a technical results-oriented management ethos favoured
by the advisers to the government in the 'control departments'.
This was promoted at the expense of an emphasis on 'organisation
development', an orientation recognising process and factors of
culture and school climate, which educationists would have found
more congenial. This they would have been able to relate to the
'School Development' model (Stewart and Prebble, 1985) promoted in education administration programmes by the Department of

Education from 1978, and by New Zealand's one Master of Education Administration course, offered by Massey University.

The funding of the Schools Management Development Project ceased on 1 October 1989. For the schools' financial year commencing 1 February 1990 all in-service funding previously managed at district level by the Department of Education was incorporated in the Operations Grant dispersed to school boards of trustees, for local decisions on training expenditure. Colleges of education had their six months relationships with cluster groups to build on, and from 1 October had assumed responsibility for the Schools Advisory Service, and for the network of teacher resource centres developed over the years by Department or Education Board initiatives. The tertiary sector, including the colleges, had in 1990 however to face their round of restructuring, and the shift to be instituted from 1991 to funding on a student-related base.

The colleges have, in fact, maintained their contacts to varying degrees in 1990 with the 'clusters' of schools. Private consultants have entered the field. There has been significant growth in the programmes of the principals' associations, secondary and primary, and the secondary association has instituted programmes to meet training needs of deputy principals. The New Zealand Educational Administration Society has expanded to seven branches in 1990, and at its biennial conference in January 1990 provided common ground for principals, academics, teachers and officers of the new government agencies, to meet as the education family and reflect on the restructuring, and on the development tasks ahead.

The Society at a national level links in the publication of its journal with the Principals' Centre in Auckland. This functions under the aegis of the Centre for Continuing Education of the University. The Otago branch of the Society has worked with the School Trustees' Association district organisation to publish a programme of all the training opportunities available to principals and trustees.

That schools have survived the new requirements laid on them in 1990 is a tribute to skills of adaptability, survival and leadership exhibited by their managers, in particular the principals, and the commitment of teachers and trustees. That schools will flourish under the new regime requires a shift of focus from matters of technique to issues of educational goals for the learners in New Zealand schools, and appropriate relationships of the schools to the needs of New Zealanders and of New Zealand. New Zealand's society is increasingly differentiated by factors of geography, ethnicity and class, and relationships to the Pacific, Asia, America and Europe are being redefined. The real issues in education management lie in the realms of values and of ethical choice.

Principals, teachers and trustees in New Zealand schools will need to be equipped to function in these realms as participants in a learning community, in addition to showing mastery of the details of technique emphasized by handbooks and flows of memoranda through the restructuring to 1 October 1989. At the centre, the talk is now of finding a new focus on curriculum. It is likely however that the shift of focus to the issues at the heart of educational administration will be driven by 'caring professionals' at work as the managers of learning and instruction, and culture and climate, in their schools (Jenkins, 1989).

Nau te rourou, naku te rourou
Ka ora ai te manuhiri.
With your food basket, and with mine,
the guests will be well fed.

References

Beby, C E 1986, in W L Renwick's *Moving Targets: Six essays on educational policy*. Wellington: New Zealand Council for Educational Research.

Codd, J, Harker, R and Nash, R 1985, *Political Issues in New Zealand Education*. Palmerston North: Dunmore. Second edition, 1990.

Curriculum Review Research in Schools Project 1989, *The Initial Impact of the Curriculum Review Exploratory Project*. CRRISP Occasional Paper No 3, Hamilton: University of Waikato.

Curriculum Review Research in Schools Project 1989, *Effecting Change in Schools: Some Implications of the Initial Phase of the Curriculum Review Exploratory Project*. CRRISP Occasional Paper No 4, Hamilton: University of Waikato.

Department of Education 1982, *Education Policies in New Zealand. Report Prepared for the OECD Examiners by the Department of Education in March 1982*. Wellington: Government Printer.

Department of Education 1989, *The Reform of Education Administration in New Zealand: Information for Employees*. Wellington: Department of Education (mimeo).

Department of Education 1989, *Governing Schools: a practical handbook for school trustees*. Wellington: Department of Education.

Early Childhood Care Working Group 1988, *Education to be More*. Wellington: Government Printer.

Gianotti, M 1989, *Education Review Office*. Wellington: Department of Education (mimeo).

Goff, P 1988, *Learning for Life: One. Education and training beyond the age of fifteen*. Wellington: Government Printer.

Goff P 1989, *Learning for Life: Two. Education and training beyond the age of fifteen*. Wellington: Government Printer.

Habermas 1976, *Legitimation Crisis*. London: Heinemann.

Harker, R K and McConnochie, K R 1985, *Education as Cultural Artefact: Studies in Maori and Aboriginal Education*. Palmerston North: Dunmore.

Hawke, G R 1988, *Report of the Working Party on Post-Compulsory Education and Training in New Zealand*. Wellington: Government Printer.

Jenkins, H O 1989, *Education Managers – Paradigms Lost*. Armidale, Australia: Commonwealth Council for Educational Administration (Studies in Educational Administration No.51).

Lange, D 1988, *Before Five: Early Childhood Care and Education in New Zealand*. Wellington: Government Printer.

Lange, D 1988, *Tomorrow's Schools: The Reform of Education Administration in New Zealand*. Wellington: Government Printer.

Lauder, H, Middleton, S, Boston, J and Wylie, C 1988, 'The third wave: critique for the New Zealand Treasury's Report on Education', *New Zealand Journal of Educational Studies*, 23(1): 15–34 and 23(2): 115–114.

McKenzie, D 1988, 'Responses to Picot: Education after the Picot Report', *New Zealand Journal of Educational Administration*, 3:1–9.

Macpherson, R J S 1989, 'Why politicians intervened in the Administration of Education in New Zealand', *Unicorn*, 15(1):38–43.

Middleton, S, Codd, J and Jones, A (eds) 1990, *New Zealand Education Policy Today: Critical Perspectives*. Wellington: Allen and Unwin and Port Nicholson Press.

Nash, R 1986, 'Education and social inequality: the theories of Bourdieu and Bourdon with reference to class and ethnic differences in New Zealand', *New Zealand Sociology*, 1(2): 121–137.

Nash, R 1989, 'Tomorrow's Schools: state power and parent participation'', *New Zealand Journal of Educational Studies*, 24(2): 113–128.

National Advisory Committee on Maori Education 1980, *He Huarahi*. Wellington: Department of Education.

O'Connor, J 1987, *The Meaning of Crisis*. Oxford: Blackwell.

OECD 1983, *Review of National Policies of Education: New Zealand*. Paris: EECD.

Rae, K A 1988, 'Rural education in New Zealand: A case study in provision and policy making', *New Zealand Journal of Educational Administration*, 3: 29–38.

Rae, K A 1989, 'New principles and models for reviewing New Zealand education: a critique', *New Zealand Journal of Educational Administration*, 4: 1–10.

Ramsay, P D K (ed) 1984, *Family, School and Community Perspectives in the Sociology of New Zealand Education*. Sydney: George, Allen and Uniwn.

Renwick, W L 1986, *Moving Targets: Six essays on educational policy with an introduction by C E Beeby*. Wellington: New Zealand Council for Educational Research.

Renwick, W L 1987, 'Forty years on in New Zealand: a new net goes fishing', *New Zealand Journal of Educational Administration*, 2: 1–12.

Sallis, J 1988, *Schools, Parents and Governors: A New Approach to Accountability*. London: Routledge.

Snook, I 1989, *Education Reform in New Zealand: What is Going On?* Paper presented to a conference of the NZ Association for Research in Education, Wellington (mimeo).

Stewart, D and Prebble, T 1985, *Making it Happen: A School Development Process*. Palmerston North: Dunmore.

Task Force to Review Educational Administration 1988, *Administering for Excellence: Effective Administration in Education*. Wellington: The Task Force.

Treasury, The 1987, *Government Management: Brief to the Incoming Government, Vol.II. Education Issues*. Wellington: The Treasury.

Wilkes, C 1982, 'Development as practice: the Instrument of Reason' in I Shirley (ed), *Development Tracks: The Theory and Practice of Community Development*. Palmerston North: Dunmore.

PART II
THE STUDY AND PRACTICE OF EDUCATIONAL MANAGEMENT

2.1 Advancing Education: International Challenge

Meredydd G Hughes

In any enterprise, significant advance is unlikely to occur by chance: it has to be organised and co-ordinated, and requires careful preparation. To achieve educational advance there will, therefore, be an important role for those educational managers at all levels who have responsibilities in developing and encouraging new initiatives, and for facilitating their joint implementation. Correspondingly, there will be an urgent need across the world for relevant initial preparation and in-service training for all facing new and challenging situations in the field of action in which change is endemic. Fresh insights and better understanding are likely to be of critical importance to educational managers worldwide in achieving educational advance.

In this chapter a number of contrasting approaches to educational management will be considered. We begin with the basic structural and processual modes of thinking about organisations which have been found helpful in ordering the complexity of corporate endeavours, and then note the emergence of new perspectives and of the concept of multiple perspectives. In different ways and with different assumptions, each of these approaches provides a basis for purposeful practitioner activity and for the preparation and development of those in the vanguard of educational advance.

Accepting that much current thinking in the worldwide educational management community, at least in the nations represented at the IIP, can be accommodated within a multiple perspectives approach, a number of issues will be discussed and related to the relevance and adequacy of the approach. A final overview leads to a speculative comment on the possible direction of future development.

A structural approach

It is an intriguing paradox that, though bureaucratic administration is universally castigated, the classical concept of bureaucracy as expounded by Max Weber (1947) continues to have a powerful and pervasive influence on governmental and non-governmental organisation, and notably on educational administration in the public sector. As a means of bringing order where there would otherwise be chaos, well-defined structure is an attractive idea, and there is instant appeal in the key concept of rational decision-making which is neither arbitrary, nor compromised by inappropriate or unethical considerations. A number of papers at this conference, and those delivered on similar occasions since the first UCEA-sponsored International Intervisitation Programme in 1966, implicitly recognise the conceptual power of the 'ideal type' proposed by Weber and perpetuated in management texts across the world.

Over the years there has also been wide recognition of the dysfunctional consequences of bureaucracy, and of the limitations of tight, monolithic, hierarchical structures. Various manifestations of 'structural relativism' have been proposed, including contingency models, loosely-coupled systems and organized anarchies, which have been discussed on a number of occasions (eg Bush 1986; Hughes 1987). Of particular relevance in an international context is a critique of the colonial legacy in educational administration (Marshall and Newton 1983) which examines formalism in bureaucracies, broadly described as the extent of discrepancy or congruence between the formally prescribed and the effectively practised. Such formalism is, of course, by no means confined to Third world countries.

In adopting a structural model, a major problem for education systems is to accommodate the conflict between centralising and decentralising tendencies, as Dr Kariyawasam's chapter (1.1) makes clear. The widening of participation through various models of decentralisation is an important issue in both developing and more developed countries.

Structural issues within educational bureaucracies have been explored in IIP and CCEA conferences on a number of occasions. Thus Ben Ukeje drew on Nigerian experience at the 1974 IIP in Britain to examine critically the variable roles of central, regional and local government in educational decision-making. He drew attention to problems which are created in most developing countries by 'the rapid multiplication of new administrative units which have to be co-ordinated with each other and with the existing departments' (Ukeje 1975, p104). It is a theme to which he returned at the 1982 IIP in Nigeria, in a paper which identified rapid socio-economic and socio-political change as major determinants of the 'structural fluidity' which he perceived as endemic in multi-level administration (Ukeje 1986, p165).

A related issue provided the theme of the 1980 CCEA Regional Conference in Cyprus, namely the significant leadership role within educational bureaucracies of the headteacher or school principal (Cyprus Educational Administration Society 1980). Andreas Anastassiades, Inspector-General of Primary Education in Cyprus, was critical of the rigidity which a central bureaucracy can involve, and saw it as the cause of reluctance by heads to lead and to innovate:

> In a centralised system of education all decision-making on matters of importance and direction come from the top. For the heads the problem is not ability to show initiative and leadership to solve the problems of the school but rather a lack of the administrative framework and structure in which the head will be able to function properly and fully (Anastassiades 1980, p35).

The greater flexibility of structure which Anastassiades favoured makes it possible for a degree of discrepancy between the formally prescribed and the effectively practiced to be seen as an opportunity rather than as a problem. This was a point subsequently taken up at the Cyprus conference by Professor Len Watson in a paper in which he advocated managerial discretion as a key concept for the principal (Watson 1980).

A processual approach

A processual approach sees management as a series of linked events over a period of time, and may be conceptualized in terms of an ordered sequence of managerial tasks such as Fayol's fundamental elements, 'to forecast and plan, to organise, to command, to co-ordinate and to control' (Fayol, 1916). There have been countless subsequent reformulations, but they can all broadly be characterised as involving three essential stages: preparation and planning, implementation, and evaluation. Later formulations are often expressed in terms of input-output models of increasing sophistication. The resulting imagery of black boxes, control loops and trigger mechanisms is liable to conjure up a cybernetic nightmare of management fit for robots, the control mechanism being computerised or exercised mechanically as in a thermostat (Beer 1966).

Also within the processual mode, but in marked contrast to the technically sophisticated computerised systems now available, are management approaches which are essentially people-related. These draw on well-known studies of human relations and human resources, open and adaptive systems, group dynamics, management by objectives, organisation development and leadership theory. While some writers in this tradition have justifiably been criticised for tending to ignore genuine conflicts of interest between managers and their subordinates (Clegg and Dunkerley 1980, p134), it remains true that human relations approaches, by directing attention to important personal variables in organisations can significantly contribute to understanding educational organisations and to the professional development of their members.

The contributions to this volume by Professor Guthrie and Dr Stewart may aptly be cited as providing support for this view. Both of them broadly adopt a processual approach, but without exclusive commitment to management conceived primarily in terms of cybernetic control loops. Guthrie describes strategic leadership as 'a new and enlarged executive framework into which conventional management activities fit' (Ch 3.2), and places emphasis on the possession of a vision. This requires 'a sense of purpose' and an ability 'to assist all parts of an organisation in acquiring such a sense'. This may be achieved by modelling, by inspiration, or by co-optation, but it is noteworthy that a further tactic in the arsenal of leadership is identified as power, confirming that an element of control is retained, as a last resort presumably, in the new executive framework.

Dr Stewart's initial emphasis is on dependence rather than on power, achieving objectives through other people being an enduring characteristic of managerial work: 'A manager is dependent upon others to achieve his or her objectives...The more senior you are the more your work is done by influencing others' (Ch 4.1).

Among other competencies this requires leadership and vision, the word 'vision' implying a need 'to encourage leaders to think boldly about what they want to accomplish'. There is a corresponding need for managers to deploy human resources more effectively by becoming 'more involved themselves, for example, in appraising the performance of their staff'. We are thus reminded that the concept of managerial dependence in no way diminishes the very potent dependence of staff on management. Dependence is clearly a two-way phenomenon.

A multiple perspectives approach

Over the last two decades a number of new perspectives have been developed which challenge fundamentally the tenets and assumptions of mainstream structural and processual approaches to organisation theory. For the purposes of this chapter, I confine attention to developments in the educational management field, but it is interesting to note in passing that during the same period a similar critical awakening and challenge to traditional theory has occurred in the public administration literature, as I have discussed elsewhere (Hughes 1988).

In retrospect two significant milestones may be identified as doubts and some disenchantment with traditional approaches became a stimulus to new thinking:

Firstly, the publication in 1971 of Victor Baldridge's seminal book *Power and Conflict in the University*. Baldridge drew on interest group and community power studies to develop a political theory perspective on university government and administration. This was intended to replace both bureaucratic theory and the claimed collegiality of an academic community, neither of which appeared adequately to illuminate and pull together his empirical studies of American universities.

> When we look at the complex and dynamic processes that explode on the modern campus today, we see neither the rigid, formal aspects of bureaucracy nor the calm, consensus-directed elements of an academic collegium. On the contrary . . . policies are shaped, reshaped and forged out of the competing claims of multiple groups (Baldridge 1971, pp19–20).

Secondly, T B Greenfield's devastating attack on conventional organisation theory at the 1974 IIP in Bristol (Greenfield 1975). Two contributions to the recent *Handbook of Research into Educational Administration* include interesting references to the occasion. Jack Culbertson (1988, p20) writes of Greenfield's historic paper:

> Speaking to those attending the Third International Intervisitation

Programme in Bristol, England, in 1974, he fired a shot at the Theory Movement that was heard around the world.

According to Dan Griffiths (1988, p30) who – like the present writer – was actually present, the occasion was even more dramatic.

> The demise [of the theory movement] came at the 1974 meeting of the IIP in Bristol, England. The *coup de grace* was delivered by Greenfield, who made an across the board denunciation of every aspect of the theory movement.

Such picturesque accounts may be exaggerated, but there can be little doubt of the lasting impact of Greenfield's proposal to replace traditional theory by a subjectivist perspective. Claiming that 'organisations are invented socially reality' he gave primacy to the interpretations and beliefs of organisational paticipants, rather than to organisational structures and processes governed by immutable laws.

If 1971 and 1974 proved to be significant milestones, there was an interesting development some years later in relation to each of these new approaches. Both Baldridge and Greenfield published expositions of their views in significantly less exclusive terms than previously. Whereas Baldridge (1971) had stressed the severe limitations of the bureaucratic model, Baldridge et al (1978) were prepared to see the political and bureaucratic perspectives as complementary.

> ...our original political model probably underestimated the impact of routine bureaucratic processes. Many decisions are made not in the heat of political controversy but because standard operating procedures dominate in most organisations (pp42–43).

The new emphasis was on the partial nature of any one approach: 'the search for an all-encompassing model is simplistic, for no one model can delineate the intricacies of decision processes in complex organisations such as universities and colleges' (p28).

Greenfield (1979) similarly, in a paper delivered at a 1977 UCEA seminar, called for tolerance of the existence of different viewpoints. He recommended 'research that attempts to look at social reality from a variety of perspectives' (p179), and concluded by advocating a pluralist, multiple perspectives approach:

> The attempt to reach an encompassing and consistent set of theories that explain social reality and order all its so-called facts is a mistaken path... From this dilemma we should conclude that we should permit and encourage alternative and even conflicting theories. From these premises, it follows that methodologies must also be open and eclectic (p187).

At the 1978 IIP, held in Canada, reference to such issues was peripheral and somewhat muted, but new perspectives and methodologies were keenly discussed at the 1982 IIP in Nigeria. Dan Griffiths (1986) announced that 'the era of paradigm diversity is already upon us and will be more in evidence in the near future' (p269). Referring to the fourfold typology of paradigms of social change developed by Burrell and Morgan (1979), he predicted that 'looking at organisations through the assumption of four different paradigms will produce far more and different questions than we have yet dealt with' (p269).

Also at the 1982 IIP, Benno Sander (1986) drew on the rich diversity of the South American context to argue a need to conceive of 'multi-dimensional options', and proceeded to outline a model of four interactive categories or dimensions: anthropological, political, pedagogical and economic (pp300–306). Crucial to the model is an 'analysis of the confluences and contradictions between the different dimensions of the paradigm' (p306). Such analysis is intended to take account of differences of perspective and evaluative criteria, but is not explained in detail.

In a book for American managers, Bolman and Deal (1984) developed further the theme of multiple perspectives. Their concern was to develop a broader range of options for managerial action:

> Managers in all organisations – large or small, public or private – can increase their effectiveness and their freedom through the use of multiple vantage points. To be locked into a single path is likely to produce error and self-imprisonment (p4).

Four perspectives or 'frames' are again identified, designated respectively as natural system, human resource, political and symbolical. Corresponding to Sander's analysis of confluences and contradictions, 're-framing' is proposed as a means 'to generate new insights and options for managerial action' (p255). The book is written from the viewpoint of managers rather than of the managed, and tends to be somewhat top-down in its approach. The 'switching across frames' (p240), which is advocated, would however enable practitioners at all levels to 'diagnose the multiple realities of the people with whom we interact daily' (p255).

While the Bolman and Deal volume demonstrates practitioner relevance, two volumes may be cited in support of Greenfield's point concerning the research potential of alternative perspectives and open and eclectic methodologies. A University of New England teaching monograph (Macpherson 1987) is intended to demonstrate, in the words of its editor, that research in the field 'has, diversified in the last decade to straddle a range of philosophical, strategic, cultural and political questions in education' (p11). Greenfield's interpretative approach is adopted, for instance, to illuminate Macpherson's own study of Australian regional directors of education (Macpherson 1987a). Watkins (1987) gives an account of a team ethnographic approach to a critical theory standpoint at Deakin University, Gronn's (1987) chapter on leader watching also placing emphasis on critical observation. A New Zealand school development project, reported by Prebble (1987), draws eclecticly on new perspectives, while two elegant philosophical contributions (Evers 1987; Lakomski 1987) provide rigorous critiques of perspectives, old and new.

The second reference is a recent British Educational Management and Administration (BEMAS) volume (Saran and Trafford 1990), which includes papers on research and methodology in education management in the United Kingdom. Its research reports, case studies and discussions of methodological issues, together with overviews of the literature of the past decade, provide confirmation, in a different setting, of the power and insight of multiple perspectives and eclectic methodologies.

Some critical issues

In preparing strategies for further advance a variety of issues arise for consideration in relation to the approaches and trends which have been briefly described. I propose to offer personal comments on four of these issues:

- relevance for practice;
- theoretical adequacy;
- management ideology;
- applicability across cultures.

Relevance for practice

In the heyday of the so-called 'Theory Movement' in the United States it was confidently claimed that it is theory which gives meaning and coherence to practice. According to Griffiths (1959),

> Facts, to be of value, must bear a relationship to one another. The use of theory in the gathering of facts provides the relationship . . . But over and above the search for new facts is the concept that theory gives meaning to the facts that are uncovered (p26).

A spatial metaphor developed by Getzels (1960), which depicted theory as a mapping, aptly illustrates the standpoint. At an appropriate level of detail a good map gives an accurate representation of a particular territory which will permit a prospective traveller to vary the route according to circumstances. eg traffic holdups and broken bridges. Administrative theory similarly, according to Getzels, makes evident the pattern of structures and relationships underlying practice, to which a wise administrator will be sensitive. Theory and practice, though inter-related, are thus seen as separate and entirely distinguishable activities. The practitioner has the joys and tribulations of travel. The theorist is essentially a cartographer, producing an ever more accurate representation of the world out there, which will tell the practitioner where he/she has been and may even suggest where he/she might go next.

By the time of the 1966 IIP the dominance of theory was beginning to be questioned, as the resulting publication (Baron, Cooper and Walker 1969) makes clear. It was at this occasion that Griffiths (1969, p166) advised that 'the search for one encompassing theory (if anyone is searching) should be abandoned...We have learned that a modest approach to theory pays off'. At subsequent IIPs achieving a fruitful relationship between theory and practice has been a quadrennial challenge to an ever-widening international circle of conference participants, as IIP volumes demonstrate (Thomas, Farquhar and Taylor 1974; Hughes 1975; Farquhar and Housego 1980; Ukeje, Ocho and Fagbamiye 1986; Edwards 1986). Increasingly it has been appreciated that theory has to be relevant for practice, and not the other way around.

In contrast to the Getzels mapping metaphor which emphasises separateness, a contemporary image in the management literature suggests a more interactive relationship between theory and practice (Hughes and Bush 1991). The practitioner and the theorist/researcher are now to be seen side by side in a helicopter, travelling together to investigate the territory of operation from different angles and perspectives, touching down as necessary to have a close look, but lifting off again to have a different view. As they work together and they share their expertise, the roles of the practitioner and the theorist/researcher appear to merge, and any precise division of responsibilities would be arbitrary and artificial.

In similar vein Everard (1984) has claimed, quoting industrial research in support, that 'helicopter quality is a major determinant of success for the practitioner'. He defined helicopter quality as 'the statesmanlike attribute that enabled a manager easily to shift position between the particular and the general and abstract, so that he/she could relate seemingly unrelated experiences in his/her day-to-day work and make a coherent pattern of them (seeing both the wood and the trees and how they relate)' (pp17–18; gender neutrality added). So defined, helicopter quality is clearly as enabling for the theorist/researcher as for the practitioner, and relevance for practice is seen by both as an important common objective.

Theoretical adequacy
As different perspectives are, by definition, incommensurable with one another, the theoretical legitimacy of a multiple perspectives approach is a question which has to be faced. Switching frames, as advocated by Bolman and Deal, if hopefully adopted as a labour-saving device to avoid the hassle of rigorous thinking within a particular perspective, is liable – at the very least – to lead to blurred vision and superficiality. Used crudely and simplistically, a multiple perspectives approach can be tantamount to asserting two or more contradictory propositions simultaneously. One is reminded of the passage in Lewis Carroll's *Alice in Wonderland* in which the Red Queen advises Alice to practise believing a dozen impossible things before breakfast every day. Perhaps paradigm diversity needs a label to say that it should be handled with care!

The crazy and unpredictable logic of Alice's Wonderland is thankfully not the only alternative possible to the uncompromising purity of a single disciplinary mode. If educational management is accepted as an applied rather than a pure science, there is a corresponding recognition that it is a field of application of several disciplines rather than a mode of learning structured in terms of a single type of truth criterion (Hughes 1978). As with other applied sciences, ground rules have to be developed for a critical, detached and eclectic examination of the complex issues of practice. Judgement is required as one draws circumspectly on a number of different and disparate perspectives.

The value of a discriminating eclecticism was appreciated many years ago by Joseph Schwab, who may be regarded as a prescient precursor of a multiple perspectives approach. Warning against the pursuit of one sufficing model as 'an uncritical aping of the wrong model', Schwab observed that 'a sophisticated and cynical grasp of about a dozen separate distinct bodies of "theory" are indispensable to deliberately good, intelligent administration' (Schwab 1964, pp59–60). His use of the term 'cynical' is, perhaps, unfortunate, seeming to suggest that the catholicity of approach which is 'indispensable' for good practice is intellectually suspect. To that extent Schwab was acknowledging the dominant theoretical orientation of his time.

It is of interest that twenty years later Everard (1984) similarly advocated a multiple perspectives approach to practitioners, but without any implication that it was cynical to do so:

> Any situation that needs managing is many-sided, and while there will usually be a dominant framework of thought in which it is most appropriately and conveniently construed, the manager should always try to apply various templates to the situation in order to size it up fully (pp7–8).

In the context of highly skilled metalwork the template is the pattern or example, which is the original meaning, but in a different context, of the term 'paradigm'. To obtain a good result, it may be noted, different templates have to be fitted and they have to be used with great care and accuracy. In applying particular templates or perspectives to a management situation, it is similarly desirable to ensure that the analysis is rigorous and that the reasoning is precise. One needs to be clear, for instance, concerning one's assumptions, stated and implicit, and their mutual compatibility.

Avoiding contradiction is not, however, the only issue, or indeed the main issue. Perhaps I may be allowed to illustrate this by reference to my undergraduate days at Cambridge, where I read mathematics and theoretical physics. That was half a century or so ago in the heady, exciting days when relativity was a new and unfamiliar concept. In lectures and tutorials our imagination was fired by the elegant simplicity and generality of Einstein's equations, which magically replaced the seeming need for continual *ad hoc* adjustments to latter-day Newtonian mechanics to take account of the latest astronomical discoveries. We called ourselves 'New Phythagoreans' and sought to impress each other with knowledgeable talk of Occam's razor!

In similar vein today, seeking for theoretical adequacy in education management, I find the concept of criteria of coherence as developed by Colin Evers and Gabrielle Lakomski (Ch 2.2) highly attractive as a new approach to paradigm diversity. Their emphasis, like that of the new generation of applied mathematicians of over half a century ago, is on achieving broad generality of scope, which avoids a continual need to adjust theory to unanticipated empirical evidence. Their unity thesis has clear relevance to the issue of the legitimacy of a multiple perspectives approach, and it is my expectation that it will stimulate further creative developments in this area (Evers and Lakomski 1990).

Management ideology

It is sometimes argued that the ethos and general standpoint of the educational management community is not managerial enough, and that a more wholehearted acceptance of traditional management concepts would be beneficial. In the UK, for instance, educational management is diagnosed by Squire (1987, p75) to be 'in skew to the mainstream of management theory and practice', the remedy recommended being a corporate strategy based on management by objectives techniques as practised in industry. Others from a general management background have been less comprehensively critical (e.g. Everard 1984, 1986; Handy 1984), but have called for 'learning bridges' between education and industry.

Later developments in the UK may also be of interest. There has been lively discussion of the extent to which the theory and practice of industrial management are applicable to schools (Maw et al. 1984; Everard and Morris 1985). Recent government legislation has resulted in a significant measure of localisation of decision-making, but accompanied by a contrary tendency towards increased centralisation of policy and key resource decisions. Implications for educational management at school level are a concern of the School Management Task Force established in 1989, which hopes to encourage management development initiatives from both public and private sectors, as explained by David Styan (1990).

Educational management is a matter of public concern in other countries also, and development activities of any magnitude usually require governmental approval and support. A precise ideology of control may not necessarily be explicitly articulated, but effectiveness and efficiency are likely to be emphasised as obligatory considerations. In most developing countries firm support for the prevailing national system of administrative structures is understandably expected, and this is sometimes formalised in the requirements that a national association of educational administrators has to be registered and approved before it can officially come into existence. In such circumstances the external pressures on members of the education service may be considerable, but it would be unwise to assume that similar constraints, sometimes operating in more subtle ways, do not also apply within other nations.

Subject to a variety of external pressures, could it be that the education management community is sometimes too managerially minded, in the sense of being deeply involved in manipulation and social control? Such criticism has long been commonplace of classical management texts drawing on the writings of Taylor, Fayol and their successors. There may be grounds for similarly criticising some human relations formulations, including those advocating schemes of organisation development. The OD approach works well when participants see themselves as the undisputed 'owners' of the programme and its outcomes (Milstein 1982), but can be a disaster when those involved consider themselves to be manipulated (Wolcott 1977), or under threat because of contracting resources (Cyert 1978).

In contrast to the hostility which human relations exercises engender if they are perceived to be inauthentic, a multiple perspectives management approach, through its openness and flexibility, has potential for making educational management a genuinely collaborative and democratic process. In particular I consider that we should welcome the contribution which radical perspectives, such as Greenfield's subjectivist approach and critical theory as applied to educational systems by Richard Bates (1982) and others, have made by focussing attention on the perceptions of the West and underprivileged, and the strategies available to them. It is therefore regrettable and somewhat ironic that the term 'management' is sometimes used perjoratively, as though all management approaches necessarily involve a top-down ideology and are therefore to be rejected as instruments of domination and coercion.

Such a view has recently been advanced by Stephen Ball (1989), who argues that the lack of an adequate sociology of school organisation has led to the area 'being claimed and colonised by the prescriptive ideology of management theory' (p218). He perceived a 'micropolitical versus management' dichotomy and claims that 'writers like Hoyle (1986), locked into a management perspective, tend to see micropolitics as pre-eminently a top-dog strategy' (pp232–3). Interestingly Ball's own perceptive and stimulating analysis of school headship in Britain (Ball 1987) is fast gaining recognition as a valued contribution to the educational management literature, side by side with Hoyle's work.

Ball accepts that the systems perspective is no longer unchallenged within management theory. He argues, however, that 'for the most part the insights and possibilities of subjective theory . . . have been incorporated into the existing "knowledge" of the management perspective' (1989, p226), citing in support a book edited by Peter Ribbins, Hywel Thomas and myself (Hughes et al. 1987). The multiple perspectives approach of the book, it seems, is not defence and may even be an aggravation of the alleged office:

> In a sense such theoretical diversity and willingness to accommodate criticism only strengthens the claims to scientific status of management theorists, consultants and practitioners . . . An understanding of contrasting or multi-theoretical perspectives is, it is claimed, a development of the skills of the manager and management theorist. It further extends the possibilities of and the repertoire of control . . . The basis ideology of management remains unbreached – indeed it is enhanced and re-legitimated' (pp226–7).

The last assertion is supported with a quotation from our final editorial chapter which claims that management becomes 'more purposeful and more effective' (p475) through the adoption of a multiple perspectives approach.

It would appear that Ball underestimates the cataclysmic and liberating power of new perspectives as they penetrate fixed positions of whatever ideological persuasion, exposing them to the challenge of alternative ways of seeing. If it is true, as he claims, that new insight 'further enhances and extends the possibilities and the repertoire of control', it is surely equally true that it enhances and extends the possibilities and the repertoire of participation and co-operation and indeed of 'more purposeful and more effective' (if I may be permitted to use the phrase) resistance to autocratic and arbitrary control. Books such as *Managing Education* are not aimed exclusively at top management, but are intended for practitioners at different levels, bearing in mind that all educational personnel are managers who need to organise their work purposefully and effectively.

Our discussion of management ideology began with Squire's attack on contemporary educational management from a traditionalist management viewpoint. We have finally noted the powerful contrary critique of Ball, for whom 'management' appears to be synonymous with 'control', which he interprets as invariably top-down and oppressive. Between these two extremes it is claimed that a multiple perspectives approach can be developed which offers a promising means of sustaining co-operative endeavour to achieve educational advance.

Applicability across cultures

This is a topic which received scant attention in the classical management literature. It seems to have been assumed as self-evident that structures, techniques and principals are universally applicable without regard to national or cultural differences. Successful management practices and systems can then simply be picked up and transported across the world without modification.

An interesting example of this way of thinking is provided by a celebrated 1887 paper by Woodrow Wilson, later President of the United States of America. Wilson drew extensively from European experience, but had some qualms about advocating ideas and procedures from political systems of which he disapproved. He justified his borrowings in the following terms:

> If I see a murderous fellow sharpening a knife cleverly, I can borrow his way of sharpening the knife without borrowing his probable intention to commit murder with it; and so if I see a monarchist dyed in the wood managing a public bureau well, I can learn his business methods without changing one of my republican spots (Wilson 1887, p220).

He went on to observe that so long as administration is studied 'as a means of putting our own politics into convenient practice . . . we are on perfectly safe ground, and can learn without error what foreign systems have to teach us'. Administrative structures, according to Wilson, are independent of politics and culture, and can travel without regard to contextual constraints.

In a chapter on comparative educational administration in a recent AERA Handbook (Hughes 1988), attention is drawn to the vastly different ideas being expressed in the public administration literature half a century later. According to Robert Dahl (1947), for instance, writing in the aftermath of World War II and its unrivalled opportunities for international travel:

> . . . as long as the study of public administration is not comparative, claims for a 'science of public administration' sound rather hollow . . . The study . . . must become a much more broadly based discipline, resting not on a narrowly defined knowledge of techniques and processes, but rather extending to the varying historical, sociological, economic and other conditioning factors that give public administration its peculiar stamp in each country (pp8–11).

In educational management a correspondent broadening of interest came considerably later. Comparative study had no place in the early literature of the Theory Movement, which was mainly concerned with the development of research on the correlates of administrative behaviour and the personal characteristics of administrators, regardless of context. The emphasis reflected the disciplinary interests, mainly psychological, of leading proponents such as Getzels (1952) and Halpin (1956).

The first major sign of a recognition of wider international horizons was the 1966 IIP in the United States and Canada. At the final session Fred Enns of the University of Alberta made a powerful plea for intercultural research. He called for careful design and conceptual clarity, and claimed that the resulting studies 'would have a generally stimulating effect on local researchers generally, and would help to jolt them out of commonly held parochial views' (Enns 1969, p316). To a considerable extent this has happened, and it can fairly be claimed that successive IIPs have contributed significantly to greater understanding within the educational management movement worldwide of the crucial importance of cultural and contextual factors.

In particular it has come to be appreciated that the instant transfer of techniques and modes of thought from Western industrial to developing countries may not necessarily be desirable without careful scrutiny. As John Weeks (1988, p384) has cautioned in a perceptive review of his own wide experience, 'Sometimes models urged upon Third World educational administrators do not fit comfortably into the alien environment'.

Over the years the literature of the Commonwealth Council for Educational Administration has consistently provided support, sometimes in vivid terms, for such warnings. Premadasa Udagama (1986, p5), writing of educational administration in the small island states of the South Pacific, was scathing of perspectives on administration 'with no politics, no economics and no culture'. In an analysis of educational reform attempts in Zambia, Gatian Lungu (1986, p6) observed that a reform programme in a developing country, however well planned in the systems terms of the traditional management textbook, fails to take off 'if objectives are not linked to the cultures, norms, structures and resources of the target group'. In such circumstances, he concluded, even 'to be an advocate of reform is to be a voice in the wilderness, or, more appropriately, a poorly armed African hunter confronting an infuriated wild elephant'.

While the assumption of general applicability associated with traditional management models has frequently been criticised, it has been appreciated that newer perspectives pay closer attention to context and can therefore be described as more culturally sensitive. At the 1982 IIP in Nigeria, for instance, Ukeje (1986, p164) put forward the concept of 'a culture-loaded theory of organisation', and developed his argument by quoting Greenfield's view of organisations 'not as structures subject to universal laws but as cultural artefacts dependent upon the specific meaning and intention of people within them' (Greenfield 1975, p74).

The applicability of different models for the professional development of educational administrators in developing areas was the theme of a CCEA symposium in Barbados (Marshall and Newton 1985). Differential cultural sensitivity was a recurring issue, the training needs of female administrators receiving particular attention. Traditional perspectives were again considered to be of limited value, but Earle Newton (1985) was able to demonstrate that critical theory, loose coupling and Greenfield's critique had considerable potential for providing insight on management development in different cultural contexts.

It may be concluded that there is growing recognition of the differential applicability of perspectives on management across nations and cultures. It is a diversity which the International Intervisitation Programmes and its organisations, with their broad international membership, both academic and practitioner, are well placed to explore.

Concluding remarks

Our survey of approaches to educational management began with the application to organisations of the classic concepts of 'structure' and 'process'. These are universal constructs whose clarity and precision, often exemplified in diagrams and figures, have an appeal to practitioners as well as to theorists. The former are usually looking for help to smooth out the complexities of real-life situations, the latter want to develop models which combine generality and simplicity. The structural approach is, of course, most vividly demonstrated in Weberian bureaucratic theory. Over the years it has come to be recognised that there are limitations, as well as advantages, in a tight hierarchical structure, and a succession of more differentiated and increasingly flexible forms of organisation have been proposed. Such manifestations of 'structural relativism' may not retain the austere grandeur of the original conceptualization, but they come close to the realities of schools and education offices.

The processual approach, as conceived by Fayol, essentially defined the elements of a management control loop, a closed system consisting of successive management stages. Later formulations provided greater flexibility and differentiation, either technically in terms of more sophisticated cybernetic automation or, alternatively, by proposing an open systems approach, which both takes account of environmental constraints and permits a human relations or organisational development standpoint to be adopted. Such flexibility, however, seldom poses a fundamental challenge to the top-down assumptions of traditional management thinking.

Over the last twenty years or so a dramatic change in the situation has occurred, as I have sought to show in this chapter. Pioneering contributions were made in the early seventies by Victor Baldridge and Thom Greenfield, and the view has gradually gained acceptance that it is legitimate, both in undertaking research and in practical application, to draw on different and disparate perspectives. A multiple perspectives approach is claimed to provide fresh insights and to open up new opportunities for advance. It also presents problems and renews old controversies, some of which were discussed in the latter part of the chapter.

Relevance for practice and theoretical adequacy are perennial issues which have to be addressed. Relevance is rightly seen as an essential concern for administrators and their training course tutors, but it is sometimes less readily accepted that theoretical adequacy is an integrally related, and equally important, concept. If the theory is weak and incoherent, application to practice is uncertain and unpredictable and may even be dangerous. Granted that access to different perspectives, as from a helicopter, gives promise of a better understanding of practice than traditional theory permitted, acceptable criteria have yet to be developed to legitimize and guide the simultaneous drawing on disparate perspectives which, as Schwab (1964) observed, is an essential part of 'deliberately good, intelligent administration'. There is clearly work to be done in this area.

The ideological orientation of educational management studies is another area which merits re-appraisal. While the disfavour of the more traditionalist general management theorists is not surprising, recent critiques from a sociological viewpoint may prove to be more stimulating and fruitful. Though the intriguing proposition that a multiple perspectives standpoint is simply a clever disguise for a prescriptive control ideology is manifestly untenable, there may still be danger that, without the safeguard of explicit criteria of relevance, a multi-perspective stance could be deliberately manipulated to lessen the impact of a particular perspective, whether traditionalist or radical.

Finally there is the challenging issue of applicability across nations and cultures, which becomes more insistent with the increasing appreciation internationally that educational advance requires more and better management preparation and training (World Bank 1985, p53). A trial training programme, recently prepared for Unesco (Hughes and Rodwell 1988), may be cited as an example of a multi-perspective course developed for international use. Such a course, using distance learning techniques as appropriate, needs to be complemented and reinforced by locally-based action-learning methods and materials which are largely culture-specific.

Looking to the future one may speculate that general acceptance of a multiple perspectives standpoint may not persist indefinitely. It could well prove to be a transitional phase, a staging post *en route* to a more comprehensive and coherent paradigm in the longer term. For many of us, the magic of a musical masterpiece is that it introduces a number of disparate themes, tunes and rhythmic patterns, developing, modifying and interweaving them to create a new work of deeper significance. Perhaps our long-term aim in educational management should likewise be to create a unitary paradigm which incorporates the distinctive insights, while transcending the limitations, of conflicting perspectives. It may be that such a theory is an ideal which cannot wholly be achieved, but the attempt which would be involved, across national, cultural and ideological boundaries, to combine creativity with coherence and concern for people, would surely be worthwhile. It is a challenge which, in some form or another, educational management practitioners have to face every working day.

References

Anastassiades, A 1980 'Background to school management in Cyprus', in Cyprus Educational Administration Society, *Managing the School of the Future: Focus on Principals*. Nicosia, Cyprus: CEAS.

Baldridge, J V 1971 *Power and Conflict in the University*. New York: Wiley.

Baldridge, J V et al. 1978 *Policy Making and Effective Leadership*. San Francisco: Jossey-Bass.

Ball, S J 1987 *The Micro-Politics of the School: Towards a Theory of School Organisation*. London: Methuen.

Ball, S J 1989 'Micropolitics versus management: towards a sociology of school organisation' in S Walker and L Barton (eds), *Politics and Processes of Schooling*. Milton Keynes: The Open University Press.

Baron, G, Cooper, D H and Walker, W G (eds) 1986, *Educational Administration: International Perspectives*. Chicago: Rand McNally.

Bates, R J 1982 'Towards a critical practice of educational administration', *CCEA Studies in Educational Administration*, 27: 1–15.

Beer, S 1966 *Decision and Control*. London: John Wiley.

Bolman, L G and Deal, T E 1984 *Modern Approaches to Understanding and Managing Organizations*. San Francisco: Jossey-Bass.

Burrell, G and G Morgan 1979 *Sociological Paradigms and Organisational Analysis*. London: Heinemann.

Bush T 1986 *Theories of Educational Management*. London: Harper and Row.

Clegg, S and Dunkerley, D 1980 *Organisation, Class and Control*. London: Routledge and Kegan Paul.

Culbertson, J A 1988 'A century's quest for a knowledge base' in N J Boyan (ed), *Handbook of Research on Educational Administration*. New York: Longman.

Cyert, R M 1978 'The management of universities of constant or decreasing size', *Public Administration Review*, 38(4): 344–349.

Cyprus Educational Administration Society 1980 *Managing the Schools of the Future: Focus on Principals*. Nicosia, Cyprus: CEAS.

Dahl, R A 1947 'The science of public administration: three problems', *Public Administration Review*, 7(1): 1–11.

Edwards, W L (ed) 1986 *Equity and Diversity: Challenge for Educational Administrators*, Record of Sixth International Intervisitation Programme in Educational Administration, Palmerston North, New Zealand: Massey University.

Enns, F 1969 'The promise of international co-operation in the preparation of educational administrators', in Baron G, Cooper, D and

Walker, W G (eds) *Educational Administration: International Perspectives*, Chicago: Rand McNally.

Everard, K B 1984 *Management in Comprehensive Schools – What can be Learned from Industry?*, 2nd Ed, York: Centre for the Study of Comprehensive Schools, University of York.

Everard, K B 1986 *Developing Management in Schools*, Oxford: Blackwell.

Everard, K B and Morris, G 1985 *Effective School Management*, London: Harper and Row.

Evers, C W 1987 'Philosophical research in educational administration', in Macpherson, R J S (ed) *Ways and Meanings of Research in Educational Administration*, Armidale, Australia: University of New England.

Evers, C and Lakomski, G 1990 *Knowing Educational Administration: Contemporary Methodological Controversies in Educational Administration Research*, Oxford: Pergamon Press.

Farquhar, R H and Housego, I E (eds) 1980 *Canadian and Comparative Educational Administration*, Vancouver: University of British Columbia.

Fayol, H 1916 *Administration Industrielle et General*, translated by Storrs, C 1949 as *General and Industrial Management*, London: Pitman.

Getzels, J W 1952, 'A psycho-sociological framework for the study of educational administration', *Harvard Educational Review*, 22, 235–246.

Getzels, J W 1960 'Theory and practice in educational administration: an old question revisited', in Campbell, R F and Lipham, J M (eds), *Administrative Theory as a Guide to Action*, Chicago: Midwest Administration Centre, University of Chicago.

Greenfield, T B 1975 'Theory about organisations: a new perspective and its implications for schools', in Hughes, M G (ed), *Administering Education: International Challenge*, London: Athlone.

Greenfield, T B 1979 'Ideas versus data: how can the data speak for themselves?', in Immegart, G L and Boyd, W L (eds), *Problem-finding in Educational Administration*, Lexington, Massachusetts: Lexington Books.

Griffiths, D E 1959 *Administrative Theory*, New York: Appleton-Century-Crofts.

Griffiths, D E 1969 'Theory in educational administration: 1966', in Baron, G, Cooper, D H and Walker, W G (eds) *Educational Administration: International Perspectives*, Chicago: Rand McNally.

Griffiths, D E 1986 'Theories in educational administration: past, present and future', in Ukeje, B O, Ocho, L O and Fagbamiye, E O (eds), *Issues and Concerns in Educational Administration*, Lagos: Macmillan Nigeria.

Griffiths, D E 1988 'Administrative theory', in Boyan N (ed) *Handbook of Research on Educational Administration*, New York: Longman.

Gronn, P C 1987 'Notes on leader watching', in Macpherson, R J S (ed), *Ways and Meanings of Research in Educational Administration*, Armidale, Australia: University of New England.

Halpin, A W 1956 *The Leadership Behavior of School Superintendents,* Columbus, Ohio: Ohio State University Press.

Handy, C 1984 *Taken for Granted? Understanding Schools as Organisations,* London: Longman for Schools Council.

Hoyle, E 1986 *The Politics of School Management,* London: Hodder and Stoughton.

Hughes, M G (ed) 1975 *Administering Education: International Challenge,* London: Athlone Press.

Hughes, M G 1978 'Educational administration: pure or applied?', Inaugural Lecture, Birmingham: University of Birmingham. Reprinted in *CCEA Studies in Educational Administration,* 27, 1–10.

Hughes, M G 1987 'Theory and practice in educational management', in Hughes, M G, Ribbins, P and Thomas, H (eds), *Managing Education: The System and the Institution,* London: Cassell.

Hughes, M G 1988 'Comparative educational administration', in Boyan, N J (ed) *Handbook of Research on Educational Administration,* New York: Longman.

Hughes, M and Bush, T 1991 'Theory and research as catalysts of change', in Walker, W, Farquhar, R and Hughes, M (eds), *Advancing Education: School Leadership in Action,* Lewes, Sussex: Falmer Press.

Hughes, M G and Rodwell, S 1988 *A Modular Training Programme: Educational Administration and Management,* Paris: Unesco Division of Educational Policy and Planning. Spanish version, Programa Modular de Formacion: Administracion y Gestion de la Educacion, 1989.

Hughes, M, Ribbins, P and Thomas, H (eds) 1987 *Managing Education: The System and the Institution,* London: Cassell.

Lakomski, G (1987) 'The cultural perspective in educational administration', in Macpherson, R J S (ed), *Ways and Meanings of Research in Educational Administration,* Armidale, Australia: University of New England.

Lungu, G F 1986 'Attacking the elephant: reforming educational administration in Zambia', *CCEA Studies in Educational Administration,* 40, 1–12.

Macpherson, R J S (ed) 1987 *Ways and Meanings of Research in Educational Administration,* Armidale, Australia: University of New England.

Macpherson, R J S 1987a 'System and structure man, politician and philosopher: being a Regional Director of Education', in Macpherson, R J S (ed), *Ways and Meanings of Research in Educational Administration,* Armidale, Australia. University of New England.

Marshall D and Newton, E 1983 'The professional preparation of school administrators in developing countries: some critical issues for decision-making', *Department of Educational Foundations Centre for International Education and Development Occasional Paper* Series No 3, Edmonton, Alberta: University of Alberta.

Marshall, D G and Newton, E H (eds) (1985) *The Professional Preparation and Development of Educational Administrators in*

Developing Areas: The Caribbean, North Bay, Ontario: Nipissing University College, on behalf of CCEA.

Maw, J et al. 1984 *Education plc?*, London: Heinemann for London University Institute of Education.

Milstein, M M 1982 'Training internal change agents for schools', in Gray, H L (ed), *The Management of Educational Institutions*, Lewes, Sussex: Falmer Press.

Newton, E H 1985 'Critical issues in the professional preparations and development of educational administrators in developing areas', in Marshall, D G and Newton, E H (eds) *The Professional Preparation and Development of Educational Administrators in Developing Areas: The Caribbean*, North Bay Ontario: Nipissing University College, on behalf of CCEA.

Prebble, T 1987 'School research: action research for the whole school, in Macpherson, RJS (ed), *Ways and Meanings of Research in Educational Administration*, Armidale, Australia: University of New England.

Sander, B 1986 'Educational administration: challenge, prospects and options', in Ukeje, B O, Ocho, L O and Fagbamiye, E O (eds), *Issues and Concerns in Educational Administration: The Nigerian Case in International Perspective*, Lagos, Nigeria: Macmillan Nigeria.

Saran, R and Trafford, V (eds) 1990 *Research in Education Management and Policy: Retrospect and Prospect*, Lewes, Sussex: Falmer Press.

Schwab, J J 1964 'The professorship in educational administration: theory-art-practice', in Willower, D J and Culbertson, J A (eds) *The Professorship in Educational Administration*, Columbus. Ohio: University Council for Educational Administration.

Squire, W H 1987 *Education Management in the UK*, Aldershot, Hants: Gower.

Styan, D 1990 'Better managers: better management', *Management in Education*, 4.2, 28–33.

Thomas, A R, Farquhar, R H and Taylor, W (eds) 1974 *Educational Administration in Australia and Abroad: Analyses and Challenges*, University of Queensland Press, St. Lucia, Queensland.

Udagama, P 1986 'Educational administration in small island states: success or failure?', *CCEA Studies in Educational Administration*, 42, 1–8.

Ukeje, B O 1975 'Structure and educational decision-making: the roles of central, regional and local authorities', in Hughes, M G (ed), *Administering Education: International Challenge*, London: Athlone Press.

Ukeje, B O 1986 'Educational administration and planning at the crossroads: a general overview', in Ukeje, B O et al (eds) *Issues and Concerns in Educational Administration*, Lagos: Macmillan Nigeria.

Ukeje, B O, Ocho, L O and Fagbamiye, E O (eds) 1986 *Issues and Concerns in Educational Administration: The Nigerian Case in International Perspective*, Lagos: Macmillan Nigeria.

Watkins, P 1987 'Collective research strategies in studying the devolution and restructuring of the Victorian Education Department', in Macpherson R J S (ed), *Ways and Meanings of Research in Educational Administration*, Armidale, Australia: University of New England.

Watson, L E 1980 'Managerial discretion: a key concept for the principal', in Cyprus Educational Administration Society *Managing The Schools of the Future: Focus on Principals*, Nicosia, Cyprus: CEAS. Also in *CCEA Studies in Educational Administration*, 24, 1–9.

Weber, M 1947 *The Theory of Social and Economic Organisation*, Translated by Henderson, AM and Parsons, T, Glencoe, Illinois: The Free Press.

Weeks, J 1988 'Current issues in professional development in developing countries: a personal view', *Journal of Educational Administration*, 26.3, 382–392.

Wilson, W 1887 'The study of administration', *Political Science Quarterly*, 2, 197–222.

Wolcott, H F 1977 *Teachers Versus Technocrats*, Eugene, Oregon: Centre for Educational Policy and Management, University of Oregon.

World Bank 1985 *Education Sector Policy Paper*, Washington DC, USA: World Bank.

2.2 Management and the Quality of Schooling: Some Implications of Research and Experience in England and Wales

Ray Bolam

According to a recent account of educational reforms in the USA and Canada '. . . . all major reform efforts to date have failed' (Fullan et al 1989, p1). In justifying and explaining this conclusion they distinguish between four roughly chronological themes in the reform movement. The first two, which they call the adoption and implementation themes, characterised the 1960s and 1970s respectively and were concerned with the technicalities of effective innovations. The third theme – the standardization and testing of students and teachers – emerged in the early 1980s and the fourth one, in the late 1980s, emphasised the upgrading of teacher education and the restructuring of teachers' roles, careers and conditions in the workplace. Although similar strategies and outcomes are evident in other developed countries (*see* Miles et al 1987, and Beare et al 1989) there are good grounds for thinking that recent developments in the UK (and possibly in Australia and New Zealand) have taken on a distinctive character which generates a whole series of new questions about management and the quality of schooling.

School management and effective schools

In England and Wales, headteachers, deputy headteachers, heads of subject departments and other staff have formal school management responsibilities – for achieving the school's aims by working through and with other professional teachers – which are separate and different from their classroom management responsibilities, and for which they are paid additional salary rewards. These managerial responsibilities may include: overall policy and aims; communication and decision making structures and roles; curriculum, teaching methods and examinations; staff and staff development; pupils and pupil learning; financial and material resources; external relations; monitoring and evaluation of the school's performance; school improvement; and self-development. There are at least 130,000 staff with such management functions in primary, middle, secondary and special schools in England and Wales. They include approximately 30,000 headteachers, 40,000 deputy headteachers, and 70,000 department or section heads.

Four further notable features of the situation in England and Wales are:

- appointments to headships and deputy headships are made by school governors, some of whom represent political parties, following a process of advertising in the professional journals and press;
- applicants for such posts are not required to have completed an accredited course in school management and administration (since accredited courses, as such, do not exist), but are judged on the basis of their previous experience and performance in a selection interview;
- there is a tendency towards management by teams of senior staff, including the head, particularly in secondary schools, which affects job specifications and training needs;
- women are significantly under represented in senior positions in all types of schools.

Progress has been made on the question of 'What constitutes effective school management?' by UK researchers. Hughes (1983, 1990) provides a good summary and analysis of recent British research, from which one may reasonably conclude that role theory has been the main theoretical orientation, that secondary headteachers have received most attention, and that little has been published on other managerial roles. The tasks of secondary heads have been studied directly or indirectly by several researchers (eg Lyons 1976; Webb and Lyons 1982; Morgan et al 1984; Jenkins 1983; Hall et al 1986; and Weindling and Earley 1987). The tasks of primary heads have not been directly researched to the same extent, though one study has filled some gaps in our knowledge of primary school relationships (Nias et al 1989) and another of the distinctive tasks of heads in small schools (Wallace and Butterworth 1987). On the vexed question of school effectiveness, some encouragement and illumination are now forthcoming from the two major research studies carried out in Inner London Education Authority secondary schools (Rutter et al 1979) and, most recently, primary schools (Mortimore et al 1988).

The main relevant findings about effective school management processes from these two ILEA studies are as follows. The secondary schools study (Rutter et al 1979) concluded that the following factors were important:

- strong positive leadership: decisions are taken at senior level, but teachers' views are represented. Expectations are high and the school has a recognised set of discipline standards, as well as an emphasis on reward, praise and appreciation. Checks are made that staff set homework and there is an awareness of staff punctuality;
- staff involvement: joint planning occurs in departments and there is consistency of aims and values. Teachers share high expectations, and know that their views are considered before senior management makes decisions;
- positive school ethos: an amalgam of all the above effective processes, plus care and decoration of the school, availability of drinks and telephones for pupils, and pupil participation in assemblies and meetings.

The junior schools study (Mortimore et al 1988) concluded that the following factors were important:

- purposeful leadership: heads are involved in curriculum planning, and request that teachers keep records, which they discuss with teachers. They intervene selectively to influence teaching strategies, and plan teacher attendance on in-service courses to meet the school's needs;
- involvement of deputy heads: in policy decisions, the allocation of classes and budget;
- consistency among teachers: all teachers follow curriculum guidelines in the same way, demonstrating unity of approach;
- parental involvement: the school is an open-door establishment, where parents feel welcome, help in classes, on outings and with fund-raising and attend meetings;

- positive climate: the school's atmosphere is pleasant, with greater emphasis on praise and less on punishment. Clubs and outings are organised for pupils. The climate is also positive for teachers, who have non-teaching periods for planning.

Broadly speaking, these findings are consistent with those from other developed countries, particularly the USA, Canada and Australia (see Beare et al 1989) but one major caveat applies to all such findings. The scope for headteachers and other school managers to make an impact appears to be limited: most input-output style research studies have concluded that schools account for a small (eg 10 per cent) proportion in school achievement compared to social class factors (Bossert 1988). Nevertheless, between-school differences are large enough to warrant giving serious consideration to their implications for school management and headteacher training.

A further problem, 'What is effective teaching and learning in schools?', is implicit in the first question but it is worth considering separately. Here again the ILEA studies, which confirm and extend US and other foreign research, are instructive. The secondary school study (Rutter et al 1979) identified the following factors as being associated with effective teaching and learning: an 'academic' emphasis (for example on homework, high expectations, work display, teaching time and the use of the library) and a purposeful approach to classroom work (for example, a high proportion of time on subject matter, work with the whole class, periods of quiet work, few disciplinary interventions and careful timing of lessons). The primary school study (Mortimore et al 1988) identified the following teaching factors: well structured teaching sequences, intellectually challenging teaching, a work-centred classroom environment, a focus upon a limited number of subjects at one time, maximum communication with children, careful record keeping and a positive climate.

The Government's reform strategy

Profound changes in the context of school management have resulted from the Government's commitment to the achievement of its policy goals of improved teaching quality (DES 1983) and better schools (DES 1985) via an education reform programme which is embodied in the 1986 and 1988 Education Acts. The main components of this programme include:
- a national curriculum plus national testing and examinations;
- headteachers and school governors to be responsible for the

local management of schools, including the budget and the hiring and firing of staff;

- the opportunity for schools to opt out of local education authority (LEA) control;
- Government-imposed national salaries, conditions of service and career-ladders for all teachers;
- a national teacher appraisal scheme which includes classroom observation;
- school-level budgets for staff development plus five school closure days available for training each year.
- regular monitoring and evaluation of school performance by LEA inspectors.

These changes have the following features:

- the establishment, for the first time, of a framework of national objectives, standards and priorities, hitherto the responsibility of schools and LEAs;
- the redistribution of power by decentralising as many decisions (eg on finance and the hiring and firing of staff) as possible to the school level and by requiring local education authorities to act as 'enabling' implementation agencies and evaluation of the outcomes of school level decision-making within the framework of national objectives and standards;
- the creation of a market-oriented culture for schools whereby clients (parents) are empowered (via governors, open enrolment, published assessment scores and the possibility of opting out of LEA control), to choose which schools to support and whereby schools are compelled to compete with each other for their clients and thus, in theory, to raise their teaching and learning standards by using their financial, human and physical resources most cost-effectively;
- the requirement that LEAs should hold school heads and governors accountable for the planning and delivery of the national objectives and standards by evaluating and inspecting their work according to specified performance indicators.

It is beyond the scope of this paper to trace the genesis and development of the Government's reform strategy but some key points are worth highlighting. Although it is by no means inconsistent with the professional practitioners' and researchers' more technical approaches to effective school management, it is evident that the Goverment's approach is at once more political and ideological (*vide* Simon, 1988). At the heart of the reforms are the creation of a social market in education and the promotion of both customer choice and of competition between schools – notions derived directly from industry and commerce rather than research. Many of the management techniques being advocated also come from the same source, eg de-regulation within a framework of national standards, staff appraisal and development, market-research, site-level decision-making and inspection on the basis of performance indicators. The applicability of the social market concept to schooling is, of course, highly problematic and controversial (*vide* Tomlinson, 1989) but it is undeniable that it is novel, if not unique in Europe and, because it is centrally driven and 'framed' by the national Government, most unusual in developed countries.

Managing multiple change

The reform programme is due to be phased in over a five year period and hence a key task facing all education managers is to implement a complex package of radical changes simultaneously while maintaining ongoing work. The core changes are those relating to the national curriculum and testing, which are management tasks rather than techniques and which in any case are in the early stages of implementation. This section deals briefly with several supporting changes which are, in themselves, new management approaches and techniques and which are already being implemented, at least in a pilot scheme context.

Strategic self-management in schools

Schools are now having to adopt several strategic management techniques as part of the reform programme. The most fundamental of these arises from the introduction of financial delegation to schools and of the new powers for governors, together known as 'Local Management of Schools (LMS)'. The headteacher and governors will, under this scheme, be responsible for the school's budget and for the recruitment, appointment, payment and dismissal of the staff. Other responsibilities include staff travel expenses, funding external examinations, paying for books, equipment, furniture, stationery, postage, telephones, energy costs, internal maintenance and the community 'poll' tax. In turn, the school can charge for the provision of such services as hire of the building to adult education, sports groups and voluntary organisations. Although LEAs have some discretion in interpreting the formula for calculating school budgets, one key element has to be present: 75 per cent of the aggregated schools' budget in the LEA must be allocated on the basis of age-weighted pupil numbers, which is specifically designed to promote competition between schools in attracting and retaining pupils (see Hill et al 1990).

The technical and administrative issues raised by this innovation (eg should all schools appoint a registrar or bursar, how much additional secretarial support is needed and what are the particular implications for small primary schools?) are all, of course, very important but our concern here is to consider some of the broader management issues. Although LMS is still in the early stages of implementation with many problems still to be resolved, headteachers appear to be generally supportive of the increased opportunities it offers for making school-level decisions about priorities and policies. One set of techniques which is finding favour goes under the general heading 'School Self-Management' and has been widely disseminated in a book of that name (Caldwell and Spinks 1988). The main purposes of school self-management are: to relate resource allocation to learning and teaching priorities; to facilitate shared decision-making by governors, professionals, parents, pupils and other interested groups to make clear links between management tasks and information; to provide simple, quick management methods (eg for evaluation and review). A key feature is the distinction between the tasks and responsibilities involved in strategic policy and operational programmes. The Caldwell and Spinks book includes a wide range of practical methods, requiring the minimum of time which are very appealing, but are, as yet, largely untried.

A second set of methods for 'School Self-Review and Development' has been widely used in England and Wales. The original GRIDS materials (McMahon et al 1984) aimed to help schools to carry out a general review of their present strengths and weaknesses, to identify priority areas for intensive review and development work and to promote the adoption of collaborative, rigorous and systematic methods. The materials have now been extended to include departmental review, working with governors and the use of external consultants (Abbott et al 1988). They clearly have considerable appeal for schools and LEAs and have been subjected to limited evaluation (Constable et al 1988). They do not deal directly with financial delegation.

A third approach has been generated by the Government's requirement that each school should produce an annual curriculum development plan. Given that schools have also to manage the implementation of several other innovations, many LEAs have extended this to require schools to produce an annual Institutional Development Plan (IDP) which embraces the curriculum plan. IDPs are at the piloting stage in most LEAs but their main components include: a mission statement; long term aims and action plans; medium term aims and action plans; arrangements for monitoring, evaluation and review of the implementation and effectiveness of the plan. The action plans include consideration of the resource implications and hence relate directly to LMS (see Wallace 1989; Holly and Southworth 1989).

A fourth approach involves the use of Performance Indicators to monitor and evaluate progress. The background to this approach is well described by Hopkins and Leask (1989), who relate it directly to IDPs and a growing trend towards public accountability. They offer the following definition:

> A performance indicator is a statement against which achievement in an area or activity can be assessed; they are also useful for setting goals and clarifying objectives. For some performance indicators, a brief statement is sufficient; for others, the statement should be more specific and refer to supplementary processes which would give a measure of depth, quality and/or commitment in the particular area. In our view there is a place for both quantitative and qualitative indicators. For the purposes of school improvement, performance indicators should reflect a synthesis of LEA, national and local aims and be constructed in such a way as to provide signposts for development. (Hopkins and Leaske 1989, pp6–7)

Teacher development and appraisal

The application of the Government's concept of the social market to education in general was preceded by its application to the in-service education and training (INSET) system for teachers. Prior to 1987, LEAs could claim from a national 'pool' substantial sums to cover the costs of sending their teachers on long, award-bearing courses, but this is no longer the case. Since 1987, each LEA has been required to submit to the DES an annual plan showing how their INSET policy aims are to be achieved and their planned expenditure both on designated national priority areas and on their own selected local priority areas (the latter have recently been excluded from central support). The following April, LEAs receive their national Training Grants and then allocate a proportion to schools. All schools, therefore, now have a staff development budget as well as five annual 'closure' days available for INSET. Accordingly, both LEAs and schools now purchase their INSET from higher education institutions and commercial trainers on the open market. There has thus been a significant shift from the pre-1987 situation, when it was essentially a seller's market controlled by HE institutions, to the present position of a buyer's market controlled by LEAs and schools.

The impact on provision in HE institutions has been considerable and controversial but is beyond the scope of this paper (see Bolam 1988 and Turner 1989). The impact upon school management

has also been considerable but it has not been particularly controversial, mainly because the new system confirmed and extended
what was already in place. Most secondary schools have long had a
designated senior post (eg a deputy head) carrying staff development responsibilities and most primary heads take on this role
themselves. There is also a long tradition of school-based and
school-focused INSET (eg Baker 1980; Oldroyd et al 1984) in
England and Wales and much of the associated technical knowledge has now been codified and presented in the form of training
materials (eg Oldroyd and Hall 1987). One central principle is that
staff development is more than external training courses and should
include a wide range of off-the-job, close-to-the-job and on-the-job
activities.

The new INSET system exemplifies well some important features
of the Government's educational strategy as it is put into practice.
Its basic goal is to improve the quality of teaching. At the ideological or policy level, the system is based upon a form of social market
which is governed and restricted by a framework of national regulations and national priority areas and within which LEAs (and, in
some cases, schools) are held accountable for their annual plans. At
the technical level, the system draws upon a mixture of educational
and industrial ideas and practices, one of which is teacher
appraisal.

The Government has argued in favour of teacher appraisal for
several years (DES 1983 and 1985) and enabling legislation which
could be used to make appraisal mandatory was included in the
Education No. 2 Act 1986. The conditions of service for teachers
which were introduced in 1987 refer to their participating in
appraisal 'according to an agreed framework'. A provisional framework already exists in the form of the ACAS (Advisory, Conciliation
and Arbitration Service) agreement, drawn up in 1986, between
the teacher associations, the local authority employers and the
DES. The DES subsequently funded six LEAs to pilot schemes for
teacher appraisal which embody the ACAS principles. This pilot
work ended in July 1989, and the National Steering Group for
appraisal consequently put forward its recommendations to ministers for a national framework (DES, 1989).

The intended purposes of teacher appraisal were clearly stated in
the ACAS document. Principle 3 states that appraisal should be a
tool for professional development but also recognises its potential
contribution to the management of the teacher force.

> The Working Group understands appraisal not as a series of
> perfunctory periodic events, but as a continuous systematic pro-
> cess intended to help individual teachers with their professional
> development and career planning, and to help ensure that the

in-service training and deployment of teachers matches the complementary needs of individual teachers and schools. An appraisal system will take into account the following matters:

- Planning the participation of individual teachers in in-service training.
- Helping individual teachers, their headteachers and their employers to see when a new or modified assignment would help the professional development of individual teachers and improve their career prospects.
- Identifying the potential of teachers for career development, with an eye to their being helped by appropriate in-service training.
- Recognition of teachers experiencing performance difficulty, the purpose being to provide help through appropriate guidance, counselling and training. Disciplinary procedures would remain quite separate, but might need to draw on relevant information from the appraisal records.
- Staff appointment procedures. The relevant elements of appraisal should be available to better inform those charged with the responsibility for providing references.

It will be seen that what the Working Group has in mind is a positive process, intended to raise the quality of education in schools by providing teachers with better job satisfaction, more appropriate in-service training and better planned career development based upon more informed decisions. (ACAS 1986)

Any national framework for appraisal will have to set out what should be the key components in a teacher appraisal process but, in addition, it will have to address the issues of purposes and policy which are dealt with in the ACAS report and have arisen in other countries including the USA. For instance, Darling-Hammond et al (1983) distinguish between four basic purposes for appraisal, two for the individuals and two for the organisation, as indicated in Figure 2.2.1.

Purpose	Individual level	Organisational level
Improvement (formative information)	1A Individual staff development	2A School improvement
Accountability (summative)	1B Individual personnel (job status) decisions	2B School status (eg certification decisions)

Figure 2.2.1 The purposes of appraisal (*adapted from Darling-Hammond et al* 1983)

They argue that 'though many teacher evaluation systems are nominally intended to accomplish all four of these purposes, different processes and methods are better suited to one or another of these objectives'. The purposes of appraisal as set out in the ACAS agreement covered purposes 1A, 1B and 2A. Problems might arise if key interest groups in LEAs and schools disagree about the priority that should be given to these different purposes. For example, the National Association of Governors and Managers believe that Governors should play an active part in appraisal whereas the teacher unions and the LEA employers believe that only professionals should engage directly in the appraisal process. This debate now has a sharper focus since under the terms of the 1988 Education Reform Act school governors have responsibility for hiring and firing staff.

The purely technical issues associated with appraisal are still problematic but the pilot schemes have resulted in a widely supported approach which is based upon the four-stage process outlined in Figure 2.2.2.

The broader policy issues are still far from being resolved. At the time of writing the position is as follows. The Secretary of State announced on 10 December, 1990 that he intended to introduce Regulations under section 49 of the Education (No. 2) Act 1986 to make teacher appraisal compulsory. LEAs and governing bodies of grant maintained schools will be required to arrange for all the teachers whom they employ to have a first appraisal by the end of the 1994–95 school year. The Regulations will be accompanied by a Circular covering similar ground to the supplementary guidance issued with the draft National Framework in September 1990. The local authority and teacher associations will be consulted about the Regulations in advance. The DES has proposed that the teachers' conditions of service document be amended to include a requirement that teachers participate in appraisal not within an 'agreed national framework', as at present, but in compliance with the Regulations.

The initial response of several of the teacher associations to the Secretary of State's announcement was mixed. They generally welcomed the proposal to introduce Regulations on appraisal but were highly critical of the low level of funding and expressed concern about the possible use of appraisal statements in salary discussions and disciplinary procedures. It remains to be seen what position the teacher associations will finally take and the possibility that they might oppose appraisal cannot be ruled out.

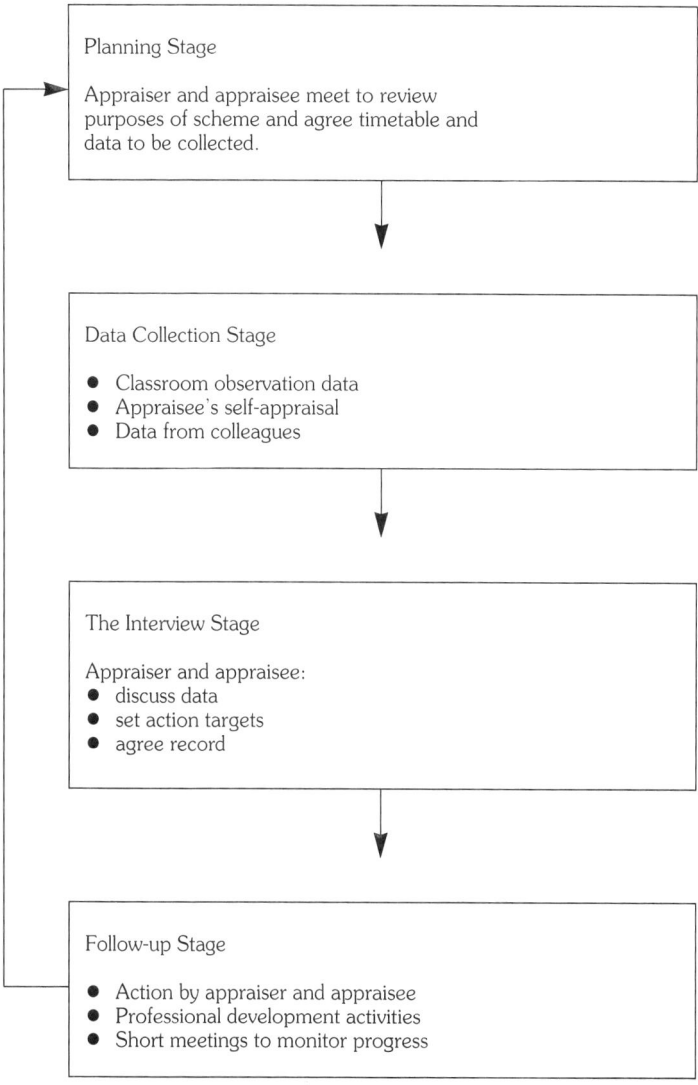

Figure 2.2.2 The appraisal process

LEAs and school management

The main focus of this chapter is on the school level but it is, of course, recognised that LEAs have a crucially important role in the management of schools. (Although it should be noted that the Government's policy of decentralising so many decision-making powers to schools has been interpreted by some (eg Simon 1988) as an attack on LEAs and indeed on local government in general.) In brief, LEAs continue to be responsible for ensuring that schools implement the national curriculum and the other components of the Reform Act and for the appraisal and development of staff. Thus, they also continue to have a dual function: to support and advise upon school improvement and to monitor and inspect the implementation process and its outcomes. This duality of function is reflected in the changes and developments now occurring in LEAs.

Most LEAs are re-structuring their advisory and support services to give much greater prominence to inspection roles and procedures (SCIA 1988), including the operation of LMS schemes. However, as the projected national scheme of appraisal is introduced, demands on the workload of inspectors, advisers and officers is bound to increase: it is likely that every headteacher appraisal will involve several days of their time each year.

Many LEAs are appointing more advisers and inspectors to cope with these new demands and all such staff are learning new managerial techniques to deal with the effective use of information derived from, for example, institutional development plans and educational audits (see FEU 1989).

One major dilemma remains to be clarified and resolved. On the one hand, it is clear that Government policy will require all LEAs to maintain a substantial number of central staff to carry out monitoring and inspection. On the other hand, it is much less clear to what extent schools will be empowered via LMS to buy in advice and support from the LEA. Thus LEA staff will not entirely escape the pressures of the market and the implications for the size and functions of LEA teams will only emerge as the Reforms are implemented.

School management training

In the 1980s there were important developments in school management training: from 1983–7 the Government-funded 50-day and 20-day courses for 6,000 headteachers and deputy heads; monitored and supported by a small National Development Centre.

From 1987 school management training was established as a national priority in the Government's Training Grants Scheme.

A great deal was learned about the nature of effective management training and learning both from practical experience and research but it is still difficult to put this knowledge into practice. Needs analysis is tackled in a variety of ways, two important methods being individual appraisal interviews and questionnaire surveys. New methods and training techniques are being used, especially those which are close-to-the-job and on-the-job. Industrial training techniques are being tried, including action learning and team-building. Many more courses and activities are now systematically evaluated but a great deal remains to be done on the evaluation of impact.

Management training and development is now an even higher priority because the sheer scale and pace of the current educational reform means that the main task facing headteachers and teachers is the management and implementation of multiple change. The Government has acknowledged this by, first, setting up a Task Force to identify the implications for management training and development (DES, 1990) and, second, by requiring each LEA to adopt a systematic approach to management development (Circular 5/89) along lines advocated by the NDC (McMahon and Bolam 1990). A key short-term aim for LEAs is to ensure that the numerous and diverse activities which make up their training programme to support the implementation of the various components of the Education Reform Acts have coherent and consistent aims and methods, avoid duplication of content and are delivered as cost effectively as possible. At present, this aim is proving difficult to achieve although a number of techniques are being developed including the use of in-house training teams, open-learning packages and modules and annual development plans at LEA and school levels.

The longer term aim for LEAs and schools is to base their management training strategies upon their institutional development plans, ie to adopt a policy-based approach. This would involve giving appropriate weighting to the three main components of management development:

1. 'Management Training', which refers to short conferences, courses and workshops which emphasise practical information and skills, which do not normally lead to an award or qualification and which may be run by LEAs, schools or by external trainers and consultants from higher education or elsewhere.

2. 'Management Education', which refers mainly to secondment and to long, external courses which often emphasise theory

and research-based knowledge, and which lead to higher education and professional qualifications (eg specialist school management Diplomas and MEds).

3. 'Management Support', which refers to those job-embedded arrangements and procedures for, for example, selection, promotion and career development, appraisal, job rotation, job enhancement, on-the-job assistance and coaching, team building, retirement, re-deployment, and equal opportunities, and which are the responsibility of the LEA and the school.

References

Abbott, R (ed) 1988, *GRIDS Handbooks* (2nd edition). York: Longman for the SCDC.

Advisory, Conciliation and Arbitration Service (ACAS) 1986, *Teachers' Dispute ACAS Independent Panel: Report of the Appraisal/Training Working Group* in DES 1989.

Baker, K 1980, 'Planning school policies for INSET: the SITE Project' in E Hoyle and J Megarry (eds), *World Yearbook of Education 1980: Professional Development of Teachers*, London: Kogan Page.

Beare, H, B J Caldwell and R H Millikan 1989, *Creating an Excellent School: Some New Management Techniques*. London: Routledge.

Bolam, R 1988, 'What is effective INSET?' in National Foundation for Educational Research (ed), *Professional Development and INSET: Proceedings of the 1987 NFER Members Conference*. Slough: NFER.

Bossert, S 1988, 'School effects' in N J Boyan (ed), *Handbook of Research on Educational Administration*. pp341–354. London: Longman.

Caldwell, B and J Spinks 1988, The Self-Managing School. Lewes: Falmer Press.

Circular 5/89 1989, *The LEA Training Grant Scheme 1990–91*. London: DES.

Constable, H, R Brown and R Williams 1988, 'An evaluation of the implementation of GRIDS in one LEA'. *Educational Management and Administration*, 16 (1), pp43–58.

Coopers and Lybrand 1988, *Local Management of Schools: a Report to the DES*. London: HMSO.

Darling-Hammond, L, E A Wise and S R Pease 1983, 'Teacher evaluation in the organisational context: a review of the literature'. *Review of Educational Research*, 53 (3) pp285–328.

Department of Education and Science and the Welsh Office 1983, *Teaching Quality*. Cmnd 8836 London: HMSO.

Department of Education and Science and the Welsh Office 1985, *Better Schools*. Cmnd 9496 London: HMSO.

Department of Education and Science 1989, *School Teacher Appraisal: a national framework*. HMSO.

Department of Education and Science 1990 *Developing School Management: the way forward*, London: HMSO.

Fullan, M G, Bennett, B, Rolheiser-Bennett, C 1989, *Linking Classroom and School Improvement*. (Unpublished, invited address to the American Educational Research Association) Toronto: University of Toronto, School of Education.

Further Education Unit 1989, *Towards an Educational Audit*. London: FEU.

Hall, V, Mackay, H and Morgan, C 1986, *Headteachers at Work*. Milton Keynes: Open University Press.

Hill, D, Spinks, J and Oakley Smith, B 1990, *Local Management of Schools*. London: Paul Chapman.

Holly, P and G Southworth 1989, *The Developing School*. Lewes: Falmer Press.

Hopkins, D and M Leask 1989, 'Performance indicators and school development', *School Organisation*, 9(1), pp3–20.

Hughes, M G 1983, 'The role and tasks of heads of school in England and Wales: research studies and professional development provision' in S Hegarty (ed), *Training for Management in Schools*. Windsor: NFER.

Hughes, M G 1990, 'Institutional Leadership: Issues and Challenges' in R Saran and V Trafford (eds), *Research in Education Management and Policy: retrospect and prospect*. Falmer Press.

Jenkins, H O 1983, *Job Perceptions of Senior Managers in Schools and Manufacturing Industry*. PhD thesis. Birmingham: University of Birmingham, Faculty of Education.

Lyons, G 1976, *Heads' Tasks: A Handbook of Secondary Administration*. Windsor, Berks: NFER.

McMahon, A and R Bolam 1990, *School Management Development and Educational Reform: a Handbook for LEAs*. London: Paul Chapman.

McMahon, A, Bolam, R, Abbott, R and Holly, P 1984, *Guidelines for Review and International Development in Schools: Primary and Secondary School Handbooks*. York: Longman for the Schools Council.

Miles, M B, Ekholm, M and Vandenberghe, R (eds) 1987, *Lasting School Improvement*. Leuven, Amersfoot: ACCO.

Morgan, C, Hall, V and Mackay, H 1984, *A Handbook on Selecting Senior Staff for Schools*. Milton Keynes: Open University Press.

Mortimore, P, Sammons, P, Stolle, L, Lewis, D and Ecob, R 1988, *School Matters: the Junior Years*. Wells, Somerset: Open Books.

Nias, J, Southworth, G and Yeomans, R 1989, *Staff Relationships in the Primary School*. Cassell.

Oldroyd, D and V Hall 1987, *Managing Professional Development and INSET: A Handbook for Schools and Colleges*. Bristol: NDCSMT, Bristol University School of Education.

Oldroyd, D, Smith, K and Lee, J 1984, *School-Based Staff Development Activities: A Handbook for Secondary Schools*. York: Longmans for the Schools Council.

Rutter, M, Maughan, B, Mortimore, P and Ouston, J 1979, *Fifteen*

Thousand Hours: Secondary Schools and their Effects on Children.
   London: Open Books.
Simon, B 1988, *Bending the Rules: the Baker Reform of Education.*
   London: Lawrence-Wishart.
Society of Chief Inspectors and Advisers 1988, *LEA Advisory Services
   and the Education Reform Act: a Discussion Document*, London:
   SCIA.
Tomlinson, J 1989, 'The Education Reform Bill – 44 years of progress?'
   Journal of Education Policy. 4(3) pp275–280.
Turner, J 1989, 'The open market in higher education: the universities
   and the future', *British Journal of Educational Studies.* 37(2)
   pp99–110.
Wallace, M 1989, 'Planning for multiple change in primary schools'.
   Education 3–13, 17(3).
Wallace, M and B Butterworth 1987, *Management Development in
   Small Primary Schools.* Bristol: NDCSMT.
Webb, P C and G Lyons 1982, 'The nature of managerial activities in
   education' in Gray, H L (ed), *The Management of Educational
   Institutions: Theory Research and Counsultancy.* Lewes, Sussex:
   Falmer Press.
Weindling, R and P Earley 1987, *Secondary Headship: the First Years.*
   Windsor: NFER-Nelson.

2.3 Educational Administration as Science: A Post-positivist Proposal[1]

Colin Evers and Gabriele Lakomski

Introduction

Recent debates in educational administration have often focussed on purported limits to scientific views of administration and on the provision of alternatives. For example, scientific approaches are said to be incapable of dealing with ethical issues; yet the practice of administrators, managers and policy analysts is irreducibly value-laden, being routinely concerned with questions of what *ought* to be done or what is the *right* course of action to advise or follow. Or, since organisational behaviour involves vast networks of intentional human activity, no adequate understanding of organisations seems possible without some appeal to human subjectivity, to the *interpretations* people place on their own actions and those of others. Yet scientific models of administrative behaviour in the name of objectivity, seek to eschew interpretations, intentions and the inner life of agents in general. In the realm of research too, case studies, cultural studies and ethnographic methods seem able to deliver important detailed knowledge about administrative processes. But again, these are methodologies that are hard to place within a scientific tradition of controlled experiment or statistically significant reproducible results.

Such major differences between the orientation of traditional scientific approaches to educational administration on the one hand and the focus and direction of often quite systematic rivals or alternatives on the other, clearly lie behind much of the perceived intellectual turmoil in the field. Educational administration, in common with most of the applied social sciences, has experienced a growing appreciation of the methodological weaknesses inherent in positivist construals of science and its methods. Ironically, however, the natural sciences go from strength to strength and hardly any part of modern life remains untouched by the application or use of some aspect of natural science: for example, medicine, transport and communications, to name just a few. So at a time when natural science has never been more successful in explaining and predicting phenomena and in enhancing our understanding of the world, paradoxically its methods and content are increasingly being questioned or even denied in the social sciences.

We suggest a resolution of this paradox as it arises in educational administration. In our view, the paradox is generated principally by the still widespread but mistaken belief that *positivism*, in its many varieties, can be equated with *science*. But in philosophy positivism, in all its main forms, is now regarded as false, its key tenets clearly refutable. The most plausible current developments in philosophy of science and theory of knowledge reflect post-positivist views. Our point, therefore, is that while many of the criticisms of administrative science in educational administration are sound, they are directed at a narrow target. They discredit only positivist versions of administrative science. An alternative post-positivist science of educational administration, we believe, is not only possible but theoretically and practically desirable. The argument we employ for this conclusion has the following broad structure. First, we acknowledge the importance theoretical writers have attached to epistemology or theory of knowledge, by arguing that the weaknesses critics have identified in traditional administrative science flow from *foundationalist* epistemological assumptions embedded in traditional views. Instead, we claim that the proper justification of knowledge is structured by *coherentist* considerations such as theoretical simplicity, consistency, comprehensiveness, conservativeness and fecundity. If the justification of scientific claims, including administrative claims, proceeds according to the coherentist canons of our holistic epistemology, then the scope of science is very much broader than is usually conceived and will fail to sustain significant distinctions between fact and value, the subjective and the objective, and the alleged 'paradigms' of educational research.

Second, we note that major recent criticisms of traditional administrative theory assume theories that in turn share foundationalist epistemological structures. Critics tend to argue for more or different foundations for knowledge to supplement the deficiencies of positivist science. We advance our case here by offering some coherentist epistemological criticism of the Theory Movement, critical theory, and administrative decision-making.

Educational administration and the theory of knowledge

Since the mid 1970s, educational administration, as an area of study has undergone a fundamental transformation. Although traditional views of science still dominate understandings of theory, research and administrative practice, there are now systematic alternatives to this approach. As a result, educational administration is now theoretically much richer, more diverse and complex than at any other time in its short history.

These developments have not occurred without controversy. For example, following a relatively brief period of intense, indeed unprecedented, academic debate in journals, books and conferences, Daniel Griffiths (1979, p43) remarked, in 1979, that, 'if educational administration is not in a state of intellectual turmoil, it should be, because its parent, the field of organisational theory, certainly is'.

Griffiths could well have added a number of related areas of applied social science to make his point such as policy analysis (Garson 1986), educational studies and educational research methodology, (Phillips 1987) and social theory (Giddens 1982). These areas, too, were in turmoil, and for much the same reason. The traditional scientific view of knowledge was increasingly perceived to be inadequate as a basis for social science because it ignored values, human subjectivity, and the social and political context in which organisations exist and in which administrative practices occur.

It is unlikely that objections such as these would have been so effective in reshaping the agenda of educational administration were it not for the existence of alternative philosophical perspectives on the nature of knowledge which could function as frameworks for rival systematic conceptions of administration. And in our view, what has made the alternatives seem credible is the work done in the 1960s by Thomas Kuhn (especially his 1962), Paul Feyerabend (1981) and other philosophers of science which showed, successfully, that traditional views of scientific knowledge are inadequate even for the physical sciences.

The importance for administrative theory of philosophy in general and theories of knowledge, or epistemologies, in particular has been widely acknowledged by writers such as Greenfield (1975), Griffiths (1979) and Willower (1981). In a recent analysis of the state of educational administration conducted as part of a review of contributions to the *Handbook of Research on Educational Administration*, Willower (1988, pp730–1) identifies six trends representing '... directions in which educational administration as field of inquiry appears to be moving', and he completes the list by remarking: 'The sixth trend is a turn towards philosophy, and especially towards epistemological questions'. In our view, Willower is perfectly correct. The only caveat we would want to enter – and one with which we expect he would entirely agree – is that philosophy, especially epistemology, has *always* been significant, though perhaps not widely recognised as such until of late.

Epistemology and administrative knowledge

We argue that *all* major developments in educational administration, from the rise of the Theory Movement (see Culbertson 1981) in the late 1940s onward, have been driven by philosophical considerations. Although the reasons for this are complex and vary with the particular developments in question, the general pattern is clear enough. For *any* set of organised interrelated claims that purports to be knowledge, such as a theory of administration, is subject to constraints that apply to all knowledge claims. However, within philosophy it is epistemology that deals with questions concerning the nature of knowledge, what makes claims knowable, and how they may be justified. Our central argument is that what epistemology counts as a satisfactory justification imposes powerful constraints on the content and structure of administrative theory. Or, in other words, the structure of justification, as specified by epistemology, determines much of the overall framework in which theorising in administration is conducted.

Three major developments in epistemology may be cited to illustrate this point. *Logical empiricism*, which developed out of, and partly in opposition to, the logical positivism of the Vienna Circle provided the first systematic philosophical influence. (For an overview, see Achinstein and Barker 1969.) In particular, it is Herbert Feigl's version of logical empiricism which has been critical in the development of the Theory Movement (Feigl 1974) which in turn has shaped much of mainstream educational administration throughout the 1960s, 1970s, and the 1980s. In it may be found the bases for separating fact from value and observation from theory, for employing the methodological constraint of operational definitions, and for seeing administration theory as a classical hypothetico-deductive structure with laws at the top and facts at the bottom. (See Feigl 1953.)

The second development is the *paradigms approach* associated with the work of Kuhn and Feyerabend. Originally formulated as a systematic critique of logical empiricist views of scientific knowledge, their work – and especially Kuhn's since it is written in nontechnical language – has functioned increasingly to underwrite attacks on objectivity in the social sciences, and to promote varieties of relativism and subjectivism. It has been able to do this because, crucially, a paradigm is supposed to contain within itself the standards for its own assessment. (See Kuhn 1962, pp109–110.) In this intellectual climate, if alternative views of administration are construed as either different paradigms, or as developing within different paradigms, then they are presumed to enjoy some methodological immunity from objections arising from one particular paradigm, say a systems scientific view. At the extreme, different paradigms are said to be incommensurable, or unable to be compared or adjudicated (Kuhn 1962, p150).

Two important results of the Kuhn-Feyerabend critique of logical empiricism are alleged to support this extreme view as well as a number of other familiar subjectivist conclusions. The first result is that empirical adequacy is not a sufficient criterion for deciding the merits of competing theories: the same empirical foundation may adequately confirm any number of different theories. The second is that what counts as empirical evidence is partly determined by theory. Observations are said to be theory laden, mainly because the vocabulary used to describe observations is also part of a wider theoretical vocabulary.

Consistent with the paradigms approach, a further conclusion drawn from these results is that science is significantly non-empirical, that considerations of empirical adequacy place no essential constraints on the construction of scientific theories. Thomas Greenfield (1978, p8), whose writings have been largely responsible for the subjectivist turn in educational administration, needs to presume something as strong as this in order to say:

> The process of truth making in the academic world ... does not differ materially from what goes into truth making in the world at large. Truth is what scientists agree on or what the right scientists agree on. It is also what they can get others to believe in.

And this, in turn, yields talk of reality being mind-dependent, of us inhabiting different worlds or their being multiple realities all of which outrun any empirical evidence for distinguishing them. It also suggests a certain methodological infirmity when it comes to the question of evidence for adjudicating the merits of different interpretations of human behaviour, the stuff of hermeneutics, ethnographies and cultural studies of organisational life. (See Evers 1988.)

The third, most recent approach, and the one we prefer, acknowledges the soundness of certain key results arising out of the 1960s critiques of logical empiricism; notably the underdetermination of theory by observation and the theory ladenness of observation. However, the correct conclusion to be drawn from these results is not a flight from objectivity and realism. Rather, it is the admission that there is more to evidence than observation or the establishing of mere empirical adequacy (Churchland 1985). After all, any theory can be made to square with empirical findings if we are prepared just to go on adding statements to it. What is more, a contradictory theory will square with any finding whatsoever. On this third approach, which we endorse, theory choice needs to be guided by a consideration of the extra-empirical virtues possessed by theories. These virtues of system include simplicity, consistency, coherence, comprehensiveness, conservativeness and fecundity, though they are often referred to collectively as coherence considerations or as the elements in a coherentist account of epistemic justification (Quine and Ullian 1978; Williams 1977).

In the following, we want to demonstrate briefly, how the constraints on justification imposed by our preferred coherentist or holistic epistemology can be used to reshape and redefine the substantive content of educational administration in the direction of a new science of administration.

Foundational epistemologies and coherence justification

Since coherentist epistemologies are best seen as responses to the problems of foundational theories of justification it will be useful to begin by sketching a classical solution to the problem of knowledge. How do we know anything at all?? What is knowledge and what makes it possible?

Within the classical empiricist tradition the candidates for immediate knowledge – the foundations – have been, in decreasing order of strictness, sense data, first person sensory reports, and observation statements (Hooker 1975). However, as the history of philosophy readily attests, the hope of justifying all knowledge in this way is fraught with difficulty, especially in view of some of its consequence for science. For example, many of the objects posited by physics are unobservable, at least directly – such things as time, curved space, electrons and quanta – and are known only through economical theorising about more gross observable consequences. Worse still, the law-like universal generalisations characteristic of our best theories, seem to require as evidence an infinite number of observations. Yet only a finite range of observations is ever available for justifying claims of the form 'all X are Y'. It would be nice if we had some sound principle of induction that would enable us reliably to infer from a finite set of observations to an infinite set of past, present and future events of the sort that scientific laws can delimit; but no such principle has ever been forthcoming (Popper 1963, especially Ch 1). Because so little of what ordinarily passes for reliable knowledge can be deduced from empirical foundations, classical empiricism functioned more as an attack on knowledge, with scepticism the end result, rather than a rational reconstruction.

The crucial methodological worry here is that the knowledge claims ruled out appear more reliable than the epistemology that rules them out. This is because an epistemology, in specifying conditions for claims to count as knowledge, also embodies a theory of the powers of the mind (Churchland 1987). For what we can know will depend, to some extent, on our cognitive capacities, our skills for learning and, in general, what sort of creature we are. One weakness of classsical empiricism is that it embodies a singularly implausible empirical psychology of learning. For example, the process of learning from perception is not one in which a passive mind more or less faithfully records copies of sensory images, permuting them (or their decomposable components) according only to the laws of logic. Our current most sophisticated neurological theories of sensory information processing tell a vastly more complex story of human knowledge acquisition (Churchland 1986).

A further methodological worry with the classical view is that it appears to be unknowable on its own account of itself. To see this recall that the epistemology makes general or universal claims concerning all (human) knowing. On its own terms, either these are known directly or indirectly. But classical empiricist epistemology in all its generality cannot itself be a sensory experience, that is, part of the foundations, if for no other reasons that only a limited number of relevant observations are ever possible. Nor can it count as derived knowledge because of the problem of induction, the problem of using finite observational evidence to infer a general claim. On our view, these methodological problems suggest that the epistemology is *incoherent*.

In response, logical empiricism, in common with twentieth century varieties of positivism, reversed the earlier classical relationship between theory and foundational evidence. For logical empiricists like Hempel (1965) or Feigl (1974) observation statements are deduced from theories rather than the other way around. That is, logically, theories imply observations. The relationship between theory and observation is therefore one of *testability*.

Roughly speaking, theories, as networks of general and particular empirical statements, are supported by evidence to the degree that the observation statements they imply are *confirmed* or the tests are successful. As a method for testing hypotheses by matching deduced observation statements against actual observations, logical empiricism is sometimes identified with the hypothetico-deductive method.

For present purposes, two clear difficulties which lead to revisions along coherentist lines, may be briefly noted. The first, mentioned earlier, is that the same finite observational base may equally confirm different theories, as pointed out by Karl Popper (1959, p266). Piling up more and more confirming instances, he argued, is of little value when it takes only one disconfirming observation to falsify a theory. It is falsification that is crucial for promoting the growth of knowledge, for improving our theories, not confirmation. Theory change is driven by counter-examples, unexpected observations and predictions that are shown to be false. And our best theories are those that have been subject to the most severe testing but have not been falsified.

However, more is required for excellence of theory than just passing severe tests, for it is never individual hypotheses that are tested but, rather, whole networks of statements (Hesse 1970). And if networks or conjunctions of statements are needed to deduce observation statements for testing, a counter-example, or unexpected observation, shows at most only that one or more statements in the network are faulty. It does not, by itself, show which *particular* statements are in need of revision, as Quine (1951, p43) has argued. We can even adjust the troublesome observation statement if we feel that those parts of our theory under threat are more reliable than the theory implicit in making the observation.

How then are we to choose the best theory from among an infinite number of empirically adequate alternatives, all equally supported by whatever they deem to be a foundation for knowledge? Our suggestion is to choose the most *coherent* theory, that is, the one that enjoys more than any other the extra-empirical virtues of system. (See Lycan 1988; Bonjour 1985.) To see how a coherence approach can work over the question of choosing theories of knowledge, consider again the two methodological weaknesses we noted in classical empiricism. One was that the epistemology could not explain how it could ever be known. It failed to be comprehensive over the matter of self-reference. In seeking to adjudicate on the status of all knowledge claims it assumed an external vantage point which it could never know to be true. Other things being equal, therefore, we would prefer an epistemology that was truly comprehensive; one whose embodied psychology of knowledge acquisition renders it knowable.

Once we see an epistemology as itself a set of knowledge claims, we can ask whether the claims it rules out as knowledge are more reasonable or plausible than the epistemology that rules them out. For classical empiricism this is an acute methodological issue since it attempts to disqualify all of the most characteristic features of good science on the strength of a very modest empirical psychology used to select foundations for knowledge. It renders this particular programme of foundational justification incoherent by robbing it of its point. The way to avoid the problem is to require an epistemology to embody our most powerful and sophisticated theories of knowledge acquisition. But if we are appealing to our best natural science of human learning to justify knowledge there is no need to bother with foundations. We just appeal to science outright to justify and explain how scientific knowledge is possible. In our view, there is no knowable epistemically secure and privileged vantage point from which the whole of knowledge can be adjudicated. There is just our most coherent scientific practice. Epistemology becomes naturalised, as Quine (1969) suggests, and falls into place as a part of psychology.

How then can we apply coherence criteria to theories of educational administration? In general we require consistency; we would aim for more comprehensive theories – those able to explain more phenomena rather than fewer, and with fewer anomalies, counter-examples and falsifying instances rather than more. We would prefer simplicity to complexity in the sense of using the least amount of explanatory apparatus to account for the largest range of phenomena. We prefer theories that do not outrun their own explanatory resources, that do not posit distinctions for which there is, on their own terms, no evidence. Finally, we require that administrative theories be *learnable* in the sense that they meet the following two demands that were applied specifically to epistemologies: first, that they cohere with the broad demands of our best naturalistc accounts of human learning and second, that they are not inconsistent with more reliable bodies of knowledge elsewhere in our total or global world view. The net effect of these demands is to require administrative theory to be a part of the most coherent global theory we can construct. We end up with a science of administration to the extent that this global theory also includes our most reliable scientific knowledge (Evers 1988).

Applying these general considerations is always a matter of detailed critique of particular issues. Coherence justification, because of its global character, is just a more intricate and difficult business than foundational justification. However, since foundationalism is mistaken, there is really no serious alternative. The following applications, because of their brevity, are only methodological guides. Nevertheless, they do go some way towards illustrating the use of a coherentist methodology.

The theory movement

In the late 1940s an increasing number of scholars doing research in educational administration, sought to develop a more systematic and rigorous basis for their work and findings. (For a historical overview, see Moore 1964.) As an antidote to the so-called 'naked empiricism' (Halpin 1958, p1) of fact finding and anecdote collection assumed typical of the field, a number of attempts were made to establish a theoretical structure for administrative theory as it was then being applied in educational studies. The notion of theory that found favour, as we noted earlier, was Herbert Feigl's logical empiricist account of scientific theory, and so what became characteristic of the Theory Movement was the attempt to structure administrative theory and research according to the strictures of Feigl's vision of science and its methods. The results, always energetically pursued, met with varying degrees of success. We here consider one.

Of the many ways in which the epistemological doctrines of logical empiricism shaped the early development of the movement, none is perhaps so counter-intuitive and unrepresentative of ordinary administrative thought and practice as the removal of values from the scope of administrative theory. Administrative theories that disqualify themselves from addressing the value question have, however, a theory/practice problem: theory fails to be relevant for a large part of administrative practice.

This methodological infirmity arises if it is believed that *every* empirically significant term in a theory is meaningful because it corresponds to some specific range of sensory experience. Terms like 'chair' and 'table' readily satisfy this condition; terms like 'good' or 'just' appear problematic. Similarly, we have a fair idea of what counts as favourable or unfavourable evidence for testing the claim 'there is a chair in my office'; for a claim like 'that person was treated unjustly' there is a difficulty. Essentially the difficulty is this. All the sensory evidence we may ever gather for the claim will merely describe how the person was in fact treated, the facts of the matter, as it were. But the injustice is not a fact there to be observed. It is not some kind of object that produces sensations of injustice. Rather, so the story goes, the basis for our judgment of injustice resides in our subjective response to the observational evidence. So if cognitive significance resides in term by term correspondence with specific sensory experiences, or even in testability then, as Hooker (1975, p191) remarks in his critique of empiricism's theory of language, '...empiricists, like positivists, offer no cognitive content to ethics, aesthetics, religion, metaphysics, or indeed to philosophy...' Stripped of its cognitive content, moral deliberation and judgement collapse down into mere affective preference.

We will outline here just one line of response to this argument. We can begin by noting that if the argument is sound our knowledge of scientific concepts like electron or quantum is as problematic as our knowledge of moral concepts since neither many of the theoretical terms of science nor the sentences in which they figure correspond to any definite range of observations. The demand that all concepts be operationally defined – that is, defined as the operations to be performed in some test – is the traditional way of meeting this difficulty (Hempel 1966, pp88–97). Hence the common practice of attempting to give operational definitions in traditional science of administration. (See Griffiths 1959, pp75–91, for examples.) However, strictly speaking, every purported definition admits of an infinite number of alternative possible operations, which would make a scientific vocabulary potentially limitless, and hence unlearn-able. To be sure, many of the differences would seem trivial; for example distinguishing 'length[1]' as measurement with a wood rule from 'length' as measurement with a plastic rule. But the distinction between trivial and non-trivial differences is a *theoretical* distinction, drawn with the aid of an antecedent grasp of the concept to be operationally defined. This is an instance of a logical empiricist epis-temological procedure outrunning its posited resources.

The source of this difficulty is the belief that a specific range of sensory experience exhausts the meaning of a term. Once we need to use theory (as turns out to be the case in foundational justification) to *select* the relevant sensory experiences, we end up blurring the distinction between observation and theory. Since the portions of theory being used are assumed to be cognitively significant, in our view it is more reasonable to suppose that the significance of more theoretical terms like 'electron' or 'quantum' resides in their *conceptual role* within the theory rather than in any immediate connections with experience.

The view we wish to defend is that moral terms like 'good' or 'right' are significant in the same way that the most theoretical terms of science are. In realist fashion, we assume the unobservables of science exist because they are posited by the most coherent global account we can give of our interpreted experience (Quine 1960). Similarly, we suppose a moral theory and its associated judgments to be warranted to the extent that they also are part of the same global theory. On a coherentist approach to scientific knowledge there is therefore no sharp epistemological boundary to be drawn between administrative theory on the one hand and a large class of naturalistic moral theories and their normative claims on the other.

Critical theory and administration

Among the many critics of traditional science of administration are those who have been influenced by the writings of Jürgens Habermas. There is now a considerable body of literature in educational administration that might be regarded as falling within the critical theory perspective. (See Foster 1986, for an overview.) Although critical theory approaches to administration are complex and multi-faceted, covering ethical, political, social, linguistic and personal dimensions, at least one strand of Habermas's thought that has been developed and applied to administrative contexts is uncompromisingly epistemological and lends itself readily to some brief coherentist remarks here.

We have in mind Richard Bates's thesis that a science of administration is essentially manipulative and concerned with social control (Bates 1980, 1983). In developing this claim Bates draws on a reading of the early work of Habermas for an understanding of science; particularly the epistemological theses of *Knowledge and Human Interests* and the 'General Perspective' lecture published as the Appendix to the English translation (Habermas 1972). In this work, Habermas (1972, p308) identifies three 'knowledge-constitutive' interests: the *technical* presumed by the empirical analytic sciences; the *practical* underlying the historical-hermeneutic sciences, and the *emancipatory* represented by critical social science. Traditional (so called positivist) science which Bates, following Habermas, identifies with empirical-analytic science, is seen as hypothetico-deductive after the Nagel/Hempel empiricist model, with predictive success a measure of technical exploitability. For Habermas (1972, p309)

> . . . theories of the empirical sciences disclose reality subject to the consti-

tutive interest in the possible securing and expansion, through informa-tion, of feedback-monitored action. This is the cognitive interest in tech-nical control over objectified processes.

In Bates's view, the technical scientific definitions of knowledge and rationality are far too narrow for social science and need to be sup-plemented by critical discourse. A suitable broadening, he suggests,

> ... is argued at length by Habermas, who contends that the annexation of rationality by dominant scientific, technical, manipulative interests has prevented the continuation of an historical discourse directed towards a rational administration of the world ... (Bates 1980, p68).

He goes further, asserting that: 'as currently conceived by professor and professional alike, educational administration is a technology of controls' (Bates 1983, p46).

And finally, in summarising a robust and systematic indictment of poor philosophy for this state of affairs, he declares:

> The inadequacies of the hypothetico-deductive model of positivist sci-ence and the positivist, apolitical model of society were argued to be intellectual products that provided the illusions necessary for the contin-ued employment of techniques of hierarchical administrative control that perpetuate the injustices of an unequal society. (Bates 1983, p30)

There are a number of things that are puzzling about this account of science and administration, especially in view of the fact that Bates thinks traditional empiricist accounts of the practice and con-duct of science are mistaken. For if the traditional view of science is wrong, and we know that it is thanks to the work of Quine, Kuhn, Feyerabend, Hesse and others, then the story Habermas tells of empirical science being *constituted* by technical interests of control and manipulation is also wrong. This is because Habermas's account of empirical-analytic science is as much dependent on tra-ditional empiricist theories of science as the traditional science of administration that Bates is using Habermas's machinery to criti-cise. In more recent work Habermas recognises some of these difficulties. (*See* Hesse 1982.)

One attempt at avoiding the major incoherence threatening knowledge constitutive interests is worth briefly noting. The key move would involve distinguishing between traditional accounts of science being wrong on the one hand and people *acting* as though these wrong accounts are true on the other. A revised Habermasian argument might then run as follows:

> If traditional views of science (positivism, logical empiricism and the like) were true then technical control and manipulation would occur. Therefore, it everyone (professor and practitioner alike) acted as though they were true then technical control and manipulation would occur.

The missing premise in this argument is a subjectivist claim to the effect that my having a particular theory of the world somehow *makes* the world that way, or brings it into line with my theory. This is perhaps an extravagant extension of the reasonable epistemological thesis that all observation is theory laden. To see the limits of the thesis, however, consider another example. Suppose, for the moment, that the dominant orthodoxy concerning water says that if flows uphill. We know that the orthodoxy is wrong but we also know that if water did flow uphill it would require a special form of technical handling. It does not follow that if everyone *acted* as though water flowed uphill it would *require* a special form of technical handling. Presumably, water would continue to defy orthodoxy in a range of ways.

Critical theorists may be sympathetic to certain subjectivist theses since bad theory may influence humans more than it influences water. But they cannot be too sympathetic to this one without undermining the reality of human suffering and injustice, or the objectivity of the class and political analyses that underwrite their approaches to human emancipation.

Administrative decision making

The last two examples of epistemological critique were directed mainly at views of the content and structure of administrative theorising. Our final example will draw attention to the importance of epistemological views for organisational design.

The classic work in the field of administration is undoubtedly Herbert Simon's *Administrative Behavior*, first published in 1945. In that work Simon identifies rational decision-making as the locus of administrative theory. As against the prescription to make *optimal* decisions, the cornerstone of Simon's theory of decision-making is the *bounded* or limited nature of human rationality. We satisfice rather than optimise. He identifies three sources of limitation that organisational structures would need to address to enhance decision-making. First, an individual is limited in skills: dexterity, reaction times, powers of computation, thought and understanding. A second limitation concerns individual values and the understanding of organisational values and goals. Finally, there are limits to relevant knowledge, both knowledge of theory and knowledge of all the conditions that must obtain for a sound application of theory (Simon 1976, pp34–41).

Simon is reluctant to endorse any 'principles of administration' for enhancing administrative efficiency in advance of specific analyses of case by case administrative arrangements for reducing these limitations. Nevertheless, a particular approach to administrative reform is suggested by his theory. For example, if the growth of knowledge is a matter of *accumulating* more and more information, as the empiricism behind *Administrative Behavior* implies, a satisficing strategy will have a characteristic emphasis. For if optimal decision-making requires optimal initial information inputs to best theory, a less than optimal or second best approach will involve not a difference in kind but a difference in degree of ambition. Resulting administrative arrangements will place a premium on ensuring the highest practicable quality of *initial input* into the actual point of decision-making. Depending on cases, reforms may focus on ensuring suitable concentrations of expertise, communications structures aimed at enhancing the availability of that expertise, and so on.

But on a coherentist epistemology, very large changes in knowledge are seen to occur through the promotion of a systematic virtue like simplicity in a theory network that includes among its statements a number of theory laden contrary observations. For the big gains in knowledge appear to flow more from the theoretical resolution of error than the incremental accumulation of data. Given that the existence of limitations to our knowledge is likely to promote the occurrance of *error*, a case by case analysis of decision making may show greater gains to be had by the promotion of *error correction* at the expense – given only finite resources – of extensive attention to *error prevention*. Of course, in any administrative design for sound long term decision making there is always some trade-off, in the allocation of resources, between error prevention and error correction. But a theory of learning, the core of which conceives knowledge as growing through a process of conjecture and refutation, is more sensitive to the possibility of learning through mistakes. The option of securing efficiencies in decision making through the rapid correction of error becomes, on this approach, a more explicit methodological guide to defining a suitable prevention/correction trade-off. Empirical studies by Chris Argyris and co-workers (Argyris 1982; Argyris and Schon 1978) show some of the conditions under which error correction by administrative feedback loop structures is more valuable. Not surprisingly, these are where the organisational environment is unstable or undergoing rapid change; where organisational knowledge and expectations are most likely to be falsified, and where there is a greater premium on more rapid acquisition or growth of knowledge.

This epistemological consideration suggests that theories of organisational *learning* can impose important constraints on the administrative structures of decision-making. Simon's position in *Administrative Behavior* does not deny this. However, in noting the relevance of epistemology for administrative theory it is sufficient to observe, for our purposes, that significant differences in organisational consequences can flow from adopting divergent theories of human knowledge acquisition.

Summing up, in applying coherentist considerations very briefly to some issues concerning the Theory Movement, critical theory, and a view of decision making, we suggested a number of conclusions. Since our holistic epistemology places severe limits on attempts to partition knowledge into different compartments, we challenged both the fact/value distinction posited by logical empiricism and the three-fold division in knowledge posited by Bates's use of the earlier work of Habermas. Both challenges have extensive consequences for the administrative theories that employ these partitions in knowledge. Finally, we explored some organisational consequences of different views of the growth of knowledge on the question of enhancing structures for decision making.

Notes

[1] This chapter is based on parts of the Preface and Chapter One of CW Evers and G Lakomski 1991 *Knowing Educational Administration*, Oxford: Pergamon Press.

References

Achinstein P and Barker F, 1969 eds *The Legacy of Logical Positivism*. Baltimore: Johns Hopkins Press.

Argyris C 1982 *Reasoning, Learning and Action*. San Francisco: Jossey-Bass.

Argyris C, and Schon D 1978 *Organisational Learning: A Theory of Action Perspective*. Menlo Park: Addison-Wesley.

Bates R J 1980 'New developments in the new sociology of education', *British Journal of Sociology of Education*, 1(1), pp67–79.

Bates R J 1983 *Educational Administration and the Management of Knowledge*. Geelong: Deakin University Press.

Bonjour L 1985 *The Structure of Empirical Knowledge*. Cambridge, Mass: Harvard University Press.

Churchland P M 1985 'The ontological statues of observables: in praise of the superempirical virtues' in Churchland P M and Hooker C A (eds.) *Images of Science*. Chicago: University of Chicago Press.

Churchland P S 1986 *Neurophilosophy: Towards a Unified Science of the Mind-Brain*. Cambridge, Mass: MIT Press.

Churchland P S 1987 'Epistemology in the age of neuroscience', *Journal of Philosophy* 84 (10), pp544–553.

Culbertson J A 1981 'Antecedents of the Theory Movement', *Educational Administration Quarterly*, 17 (1), pp25–47.

Evers C W 1988 'Educational administration and the new philosophy of science', *Journal of Educational Administration*, 26(1), pp3–22.

Feigl H 1953 'The scientific outlook: naturalism and humanism' in Feigl H and Brodbeck M (eds) *Readings in the Philosophy of Science*. New York: Appleton-Century-Crofts. Also reprinted in Feigl, Inquiries and Provocations.

Feigl H 1974 *Inquiries and Provocations: Selected Writings 1929–1974*. Boston: Reidel.

Feyerabend P K 1981 *Philosophical Papers*, Vols. 1 and 2. Cambridge: Cambridge University Press.

Foster W 1986 *Paradigms and Promises*. New York: Prometheus Books.

Garson G D 1986 'From policy science to policy analyses: a quarter century of progress' in Dunn W M (ed.) *Policy Analysis: Perspectives, Concepts and Methods*. London: JAI Press Inc.

Giddens A 1982 *Sociology: A Brief but Critical Introduction*. London: Macmillan.

Greenfield T B 1975 'Theory about organisation: a new perspective for schools' in Hughes M G 1975 (ed.) *Administering Education: International Challenge*. London: Athlone Press.

Greenfield T B 1978 'Reflections on organisation theory and the truths of irreconcilable realities', *Educational Administration Quarterly*, 14 (2), pp1–23.

Griffiths D E 1959 *Administrative Theory*. New York: Appleton-Century-Crofts.

Griffiths D E 1979 'Intellectual turmoil in educational administration', *Educational Administration Quarterly*, 15 (3), pp43–65.

Habermas J 1972 *Knowledge and Human Interests*. London: Heinemann.

Halpin A W 1958 'The development of theory in educational administration' in Halpin A W (ed) *Administrative Theory in Education*. Chicago: Midwest Administration Centre.

Hempel C G 1965 *Aspects of Scientific Explanation*. New York: The Free Press.

Hempel C G Hempel 1966 *Philosophy of Natural Science*. Englewood Cliffs: Prentice-Hall.

Hesse M 1970 'Duhem, Quine and a new empiricism' in Vesey G N A (ed.) *Knowledge and Necessity*. (London: Macmillan.)

Hesse M 1982 'Science and objectivity' in Thompson J B and Held D (eds) *Habermas: Critical Debates*. London: Macmillan.

Hooker C A 1975 'Philosophy and meta-philosophy of science: empiricism, popperianism and realism', *Synthese*, 32, pp177–231.

Kuhn T 1962 *The Structure of Scientific Revolutions*. Chicago: University of Chicago Press.

Lycan W G 1988 *Judgement and Justification*. Cambridge: Cambridge University Press.

Moore H A 1964 'The ferment in school administration' in Griffiths D E (ed.) *Behavioral Science and Educational Administration*. Chicago: University of Chicago Press.

Phillips D C 1987 *Philsophy, Science and Social Inquiry*. Oxford: Pergamon Press.

Popper K R 1959 *The Logic of Scientific Discovery*. London: Hutchinson.

Popper K R 1963 *Conjectures and Refutations*. London: Routledge and Kegan Paul.

Quine W V (1951) 'Two dogmas of empiricism', *Philosophical Review*, 60 pp20–43. Cited as reprinted in Quine W V 1961 *From a Logical Point of View*. Cambridge, Mass.: Harvard University Press.

Quine W V 1960 'Posits and reality' in Uyeda S (ed), *Basis of the Contemporary Philosophy*, Vol 5. Tokyo: Waseda University Press. Reprinted in Quine W V 1976 *The Ways of Paradox and Other Essays*. Cambridge, Mass.: Harvard University Press, revised and enlarged edition.

Quine W V 1969 'Epistemology naturalised' in Quine W V *Ontological Relativity and Other Essays*. New York: Columbia University Press.

Quine W V and Ullian J S 1978 *The Web of Belief*. New York: Random House, second edition.

Simon H A 1976 *Administrative Behavior*. New York: The Free Press, 3rd edition revised and enlarged.

Williams M 1977 *Groundless Belief: An essay on the possibility of epistemology*. Oxford: Blackwell.

Willower D J 1981 'Educational administration: some philosophical and other considerations', *Journal of Educational Administration*, 19 (2), pp115–139.

Willower D J 1988 'Synthesis and projection' in Boyan N J (ed) *Handbook of Research on Educational Administration*. New York: Longman.

2.4 Taking the Road not Taken: Reframing Educational Administration for Another Day – a Critique and Proposal

Michael Manley-Casimir

The Road Not Taken

Two roads diverged in a yellow wood,
And sorry I could not travel both
And be one traveler, long I stood
And looked down one as far as I could
To where it bent in the undergrowth;

Then took the other, as just as fair,
And having perhaps the better claim,
Because it was grassy and wanted wear;
Though as for that, the passing there
Had worn them really about the same,

And both that morning equally lay
In leaves no step had todden black.
Oh, I kept the first for another day!

Yet knowing how way leads on to way,
I doubted if I should ever come back.

I shall be telling this with a sigh
Somewhere ages and ages hence:
Two roads diverged in a wood, and I –
I took the one less traveled by,
And that has made all the difference.

Robert Frost (1916)

Preface

In 1957 when the University Council for Educational Administration convened a seminar on the role of theory in educational administration at the Midwest Administration Center, University of Chicago, the field of educational administration had a choice of two roads much as the traveller in Frost's poem. Strongly influenced by the papers and people at this seminar and related developments, the field of educational administration took the road of positivistic social science, '. . . having perhaps the better claim'; a claim based on the perception that positivistic social science had '. . . already served to foster modern progress, enlightenment, and "successful" science generally' (Greenfield 1990). This road led to adoption of a social scientific conception of inquiry in educational administration, a conception endorsing organization theory as the parent discipline, a commitment to 'value free' inquiry as the research ideal, associated research methodologies, and a belief in the logico-deductive method as the preferred method of theory development. With these came a focus on organizations as the *sine qua non* of administrative study, the development of distinctive concepts relating to organizational properties and administrative situations, and the gradual reification of administrative study into an impersonal, 'objectified' field, one many found experientially irrelevant and existentially distant from the everyday world of administrative action.

I have, perhaps, overstated and oversimplified the case. Still, in general, such a view of educational administration was what prompted Professor Greenfield[1] at IIP in 1974 to challenge the governing assumptions of the field and to spark the 'debate' that has come to be known as the Greenfield-Griffiths debate about theory in educational administration, the nature of the field, and the character of research appropriate to the field, *inter alia*. It is not my intention here to review the arguments at issue in that 'debate'; that is most ably and comprehensively done elsewhere (Gronn

1983; Greenfield 1986; Bates 1989). My purpose is to develop a counterpoint to the exchange between Greenfield-Griffiths; a contrast that is in no way new, that has its roots in much earlier work about administration (eg, Barnard 1938) and that runs as a thread through Griffith's work as well as Greenfield's. Such a counterpoint, or contrast, had it been adopted earlier would have represented the road that 'bent in the undergrowth'. Clearly, had the field taken this other road we would not now be where we are. I argue we would be closer to understanding the practice of educational administration, understanding that we, as those responsible – at least in part – for preparing the managers for the twenty-first century, need if we are to prepare such people effectively.

Personal starting point and premises

The origin of an idea is often hard to trace; harder yet is it to ascribe responsibility for the creation and development of the idea honestly and accurately to those who first articulated its elemental properties. In the case of this essay no such difficulty exists; the idea at the heart of this discussion is not new and the identities of scholars and theorists of administration who have worked with the idea are well known. The idea – the notion of discretion – is part of everyday life and language and the scholars and commentators are well established figures in their respective disciplines. It is indeed the very pervasiveness of discretion in administrative life that perhaps explains why students of administration have tended to neglect its study – perhaps we ignore what is under our noses in the search for some universal insight that is far distant on the intellectual horizon; or perhaps it is the inherently problematic character of discretion that resists satisfactory solution; or, again, perhaps it is the normative discourse invoked by the concept of discretion that resists the application of technical managerial approaches to administration – the human factor in administrative life, the factor replete with the full range of human foibles, passions and motives. More likely, however, is it that the character of the questions and issues raised by the problem of discretion are fundamentally antithetical to the assumptions and methods of positivism.

   For my part, the genesis of this essay is known. I have long wanted to write this particular essay. Its origin lies in my doctoral studies at the University of Chicago and, in particular, in my participation there in a seminar on 'discretionary justice' offered by Kenneth Culp Davis in the Law School (Davis 1969; Manley-Casimir 1971, 1974, 1976). The ideas presented here grew as I reflected on the flaws in Herbert Simon's analysis of decision-making in his landmark treatise on *Administrative Behavior* (1965) and as I developed and extended my interest in the intersection of law and education – both intrinsically normative undertakings. Ultimately, the impetus for writing this essay arises out of a set of personal premises about educational administration that undergird and encapsulate my argument here. I hold, for example, that:

1. The practice of administration is a normative enterprise because it, at its heart, deals with questions of value (Hodgkinson 1978); in this sense, the technical ·aspects of administration, which unfortunately tend to dominate much of the literature, should properly be secondary to the fundamentally important questions of the ends or purposes of the administrative endeavour (MacIntyre 1984, p26). In short, the argument is that the practice of administration should be concerned first with the defensibility of the value choices reflected in the 'ends' of action and, second, with the means of accomplishment (Manley-Casimir 1989).

2. The practice of education itself is inherently normative. Hence the relation of 'education' with 'administration' fuses two realms of knowledge and action that are normatively grounded (Manley-Casimir and Pitsula, 1988).

3. The process of decision-making is not appropriately dissected (except for limited heuristic purposes) into rational versus intuitive, fact versus value, objective versus subjective, but is more appropriately conceptualized as a holistic, unitary process requiring none of the above separations or contrasts.

4. The central element in decision-making is the exercise of judgement or discretion. It is judgement or, put another way, the exercise of discretion that links the rational with the ethical, the empirical with the normative (Manley-Casimir 1986, p357). Failure to acknowledge and discuss the centrality of discretion in the administrative process is a serious oversight. For, as Pound observes:

> Discretion is an authority conferred by law to act in certain conditions or situations in accordance with an official's or an official agency's own considered judgement and conscience. It is an idea of morals, belonging to the twilight zone between law and morals (Pound 1960, p926).

The heart of my argument, the 'thesis' presented here, is that 'discretion' or judgement' is the essence of decision-making. Discretion and its exercise is what we need to understand if we are to come to terms with administrative behavior; it is, in effect, the calculus of decision-making. By 'calculus' I mean that the exercise of discretion '...is not a branch of the science of quantity, but of the logic of relations...' (Boyer 1949, p299) between variables and factors considered seriously in making a decision. It is the purpose of this essay to highlight 'the logic of relations' between variables and factors involved in decision-making. Such an undertaking requires the elucidation of the problem of discretion in administrative life by clarifying the conceptual dimensions of discretion and related concepts – concepts like power, responsibility and justice. It also requires explication of the theoretical and empirical work on administrative decision-making from a variety of disciplinary perspectives.

Accordingly, I proceed in this paper first by pointing out how the field of educational administration had a choice of two roads and chose one 'because it was grassy, and wanted wear', leaving the other for another day. Then I review briefly the substantial literature on administrative discretion that the field of educational adminsitration has essentially ignored; this literature is both conceptual and empirical and is mainly drawn from fields of study outside education. Finally, I conclude by illustrating some of the points of contact between Greenfield and Hodgkinson's work and the literature on discretion in the context of suggesting that we go back to the first road and, having kept it for another day, proceed along it.

The road not taken

The 'road not taken' was available to the field in 1957. Indeed, in one of the major contributions to that seminar at the University of Chicago, Griffiths (1957) himself suggested its character. In his paper 'Administration as Decision-Making' Griffiths argued, correctly it seems to me, that indeed decision-making is the central process in administration. He went on in this paper, *inter alia*, to define decision-making as, 'a settling or terminating, as of a controversy, by giving judgement on the matter; also a conclusion arrived at after consideration'. Importantly, Griffiths characterized a decision as a *judicial* proceeding requiring a *judgement* about the state of affairs:

> Thus a decision is essentially a judicial proceeding; that is, a state of affairs is present, and a judgement is made about it. The judgement is such as to influence action which results from the decision. Action is implicit in a decision, and the judgement is made so that a course of action will be influenced (Griffiths 1957, pp122 –123).

Griffiths, furthermore, pointed out the serial or sequential nature of decision-making, likening it to the judicial process; he clearly connected decision-making to action and concluded that 'The term "decision" is to be applied to all *judgements which affect a course of action'* (1957, p123, emphasis in the original).

In my reading this reasoning lies at the heart of Griffiths' paper. However, in the rest of the paper he moves away somewhat from the focus on administrative decision-making and to a consideration of organizational properties that provide a context for decision-making, concluding with a set of propositions derived from the exposition and argument.

I mention this paper because Griffiths laid out here, in preliminary form, the character of the road, the one the field did not take in following decades. Griffiths further expanded this discussion in *Administrative Theory* (1959) including there a more elaborated characterization of decision-making. The irony is that both Greenfield and Griffiths are today calling for – each in his own way – a return to the focus on administrative 'behaviour,' to administrative experience as the basis for explanation and understanding. So, for example, Greenfield recently wrote:

> What is required now is a transformation of the administrative scientist's attitudes toward the reality he studies. Scientists inspired by positivism approach administrators with the conviction that their theories and methods enable them to know administration in a way mere practitioners never could. The reverse assumption now seems a better point of departure: administrators know administration; scientists don't. The point of such inquiry would be to enable scientists to come to know what administrators know and to bring a fresh and questioning perspective to it. To accomplish this purpose, we might well return to one of Simon's original starting points and seek to understand the logic and psychology of human choice. But that will require the study of decisions, will, and intention in all their depth, perplexity, and subjective uncertainty (Greenfield 1986, p75).

In part contrast, Griffiths calls for research into the actual practice of administration:

> [how administrators] function in their jobs; how they learn the 'territory'; what styles they develop; whether the styles are consistent throughout their careers or change as situations change; what makes them effective; indeed, what is effectiveness in educational administration: (Griffiths 1979, p43).

Lest I be criticized for seemingly failing to understand the gulf that separates Greenfield and Griffiths, let me say that I do indeed understand both the existence and the character of their differences. My sole purpose here is to use these points of contact as the basis for weaving the threads that seem to me to provide an approach to the study of administrative practice that is useful.

What does seem clear is that when the New Movement in educational administration began in the late 1950s, the swift embracing of positivistic social science as the new paradigm had the effect of throwing the proverbial baby out with the bathwater, so to speak. Both before and since that time scholars in a variety of fields have confronted the centrality of discretion in administrative life but their work has had relatively little impact on educational administration as a field of study.

The study of administrative discretion

The problem of administrative discretion has engaged the attention of scholars from a variety of fields including political theory, public administration and organizational theory, cognitive psychology, sociology, criminology and law. At first sight the published work on discretion reflects this diversity of viewpoints; it seems to form a patchwork quilt of separate and largely unrelated analyses rather than a systematic and coherent examination of the problem. Yet these various studies, reflecting different disciplinary perspectives and employing different terms and methods, possess a common concern with the problem of discretion.

The literature reveals three general approaches to the problem of administrative discretion. The first is the concern of political theorists with the question of 'discretionary power'[2] and its management; these treatments tend to be conceptual, discursive and prescriptive. The second is the interest of administrative theorists, cognitive psychologists and sociologists in the role and function of 'discretion' in organizations and in the way officials actually exercise discretion in day-to-day situations. Studies of the function of discretion in organizations are usually conceptual, while studies of the actual exercise of discretion are often descriptive case-studies, in which the dominant research strategy is participant-observation supplemented by interviews, or they are studies of decisions and judgement under simulated or manipulated experimental conditions. The third is the concern of criminologists and lawyers, particularly administrative lawyers, with the presence of discretion in the justice system and with the 'justice' that may or may not result from the exercise of discretion by a variety of justice officials; these discussions are sharply analytic, discursive and prescriptive. These three approaches are not, however, mutually exclusive; in fact, they overlap in many respects. Each focuses on one aspect of the problem of discretion – they differ largely in the way the problem is conceptualized and the emphasis that results.

Discretionary Power

John Locke provides a good starting point. Writing at the end of the seventeenth century, Locke, in his discussion of the royal prerogative, affirms the need for discretion at the highest level of government:

> This power to act according to discretion for the public good, without the prescription of the law, and sometimes even against it, is that which is called prerogative. For since in some governments the law-making power is not always in being, and is usually too numerous, and so too slow for the dispatch requisite to execution; and because also it is impossible to foresee, and so by laws to provide for all accidents and necessities that may concern the public, or make such laws as will do no harm if they are executed with an inflexible rigour on all occasions and upon all persons that may come in their way, therefore there is a latitude left to the executive power to do many things of choice which the laws do not prescribe (Locke 1965, p109).

Although Locke is discussing the royal prerogative, several features of his argument are noteworthy. Locke defines the prerogative as 'discretionary power', that is, as the power to act according to discretion for the public good. He makes clear that this power is used without the prescription of the law and sometimes even in contravention of the law where circumstances warrant. In other words, discretionary power is needed at the point where the law is inappropriate or non-existent – the edge of the law. This power is necessary to executive action first because the legislature is not always in session and is often too unwieldy and second because it is impossible to foresee events and legislate beforehand for all possible contingencies. The power to exercise discretion confers flexibility and a latitude for action in which choice is a crucial element. Subsequently, Locke points out that this power must be exercised wisely, not arbitrarily, else the power must be restrained for the public good (Locke 1965, pp110–114).

James Mill, father of John Stuart Mill, also notes the need to control the exercise of power and ensure its wise and just use:

> All the difficult questions of Government relate to the means of restraining those, in whose hands are lodged the powers necessary for the protection of all, from making a bad use of it (Mill, 1937, p6).

Difficult though the problem of controlling discretionary power was to Locke and Mill, the problem is infinitely more acute today and extends far beyond the highest level of government. The twentieth century has witnessed the proliferation of government bureaucracies as governments have sought to provide more and more services. This bureaucratic expansion has necessarily increased the number of administrators and government officials who need to exercise discretion in their daily activities, consequently, a gradual but inexorable devolution of discretionary power has occurred as government agencies multiplied.

In the mid 1930s Laski drew attention to this increasing transfer of discretionary power from the legislature to government bureaucracies in England. While Laski acknowledged the need for discretionary power in administration he warned against the dangers of conferring absolute discretionary power on administrative agencies and proposed safeguards to protect the citizen against the arbitrary and illegal use of that power by government officials. For Laski it was not the transfer of power to administrative agencies that was the real problem,

> The real problem is the need to invent safeguards against its abuse, for, clearly enough, grave difficulties may arise in any society either through the power of government over its subjects or the manner in which this may be exercised (Laski 1933; pp274–275).

Laski, however, while commenting adequately about the problem posed by the devolution of discretionary power through the higher echelons of government, did not penetrate the actual exercise of discretion in day-to-day administrative situations, nor did he confront the question of justice at this level.

The nature of discretion

Discussions of the nature of discretion (or judgement) are both conceptual and empirical. Sir Josiah Stamp provided an early conceptual analysis of the anatomy of judgement in a paper presented at McMaster University in February 1938. In the paper, conditioned somewhat by the gathering storm in Europe, Stamp identified the central problem of bias in judgement. 'The first step in every judgement, after giving facts a fair hearing, is to judge your own ideology, in relation to the issue' (Stamp 1938, p5). A further important step is to assess the backgrounds of the people affected by the judgement. Stamp also noted the often very great difficulty of discerning the factors affecting judgements and the related problem of inferring the causes of a judgement from its consequences.

Writing two decades later, Friedrich (1958) usefully analyzed the relations between authority, reason and discretion. His discussion permits the following characterization of discretion. First, that the concept of discretion includes the related notions of choice and judgement. When an individual exercises his discretion, he makes a choice between alternative courses of action – the choice includes the possibility of inaction or deferring action until a later date; and he uses his judgement in the choice-making process – ideally his choice is not wanton, arbitrary or capricious because he used 'good' or his 'best' judgement. Administrators exercise good judgement when they act '...in such a way that their reasoning could afterward be examined and found defensible' (Friedrich 1958, p44). In other words, discretion is responsibly exercised not only when the administrator takes into account the relevant considerations and not only when he can elaborate reasons for his choice of a particular course of action but when the reasons themselves are defensible. Where the reasons themselves are not defensible, then the action taken may be considered the arbitrary abuse of power. Thus the crucial aspect of the exercise of discretion is the basis upon which the decision is made.

Sir Geoffrey Vickers made major contributions to our understanding of judgement in the early sixties. In various papers (eg Vickers 1961) and later in his book, *The Art of Judgement* (1965), Vickers characterized judgement:

1. Judgement is a fundamental, continuous process, integral with our thinking.
2. It has three aspects – for simplicity, three kinds of judgement – value judgement, reality judgement, action judgement. The first two are the more fundamental and important. Action judgement is only called for by the interaction of value judgement and reality judgement, and is only selected by further use of the same criteria.
3. The aspects of the situation which are appreciated (reality judgement) and evaluated (value judgement) are determined by the interest of the judging mind. (Vickers 1961, p33)

His discussion proceeded to distinguish judgement, initiative and ingenuity as he worked through the three aspects of judgement. What is very clear from Vickers' work is his recognition that judgement in all its apsects is a quintessentially human process not reducible to the mechanical or mathematical models of decision-making that in the early sixties were becoming popular.

By contrast to these conceptual analyses, there is a considerable and growing body of literature in cognitive psychology focusing on decision-making and related constructs. Initially, my interest was drawn to particular studies of attribution in decision-making like Maselli and Altrocchi's (1969) paper on attribution of intent, a study I found clearly relevant to my own investigation of how disci-

plinarians exercised discretion; in turn, this led me to Landy and
Aronson's (1969) paper on the influence of the character of the
criminal and his victim on the decisions of simulated jurors, to
Jones and Aronson's (1973) study of the attribution of fault to a
rape victim as a function of victim respectability, and then to
Kelley's (1973) more broadly cast discussion of the process of
causal attribution.

Since then the literature on decision-making in cognitive
psychology has broadened and is reflected in such books as Caroll
and Payne (1976), Janis and Mann (1977), Hammond, McClelland
and Mumpower (1980) and Wallsten (1980) to mention but a
few; these treat studies of decision-making from a variety of
perspectives ranging from mathematical modelling and game
theory to studies of information processing, causal attribution and
social judgement theory. Much of this work is relevant to the
exercise of judgement, hence to the use of discretion by administrators.

Discretion in organizations

The interest of administrative theorists, sociologists, criminologists and lawyers in the problem of administrative discretion
appeared with the New Deal in the United States and the accompanying expansion of administrative agencies. Commenting on the
pervasiveness of discretion in administration, Gulick, for example,
noted:

> It is impossible to analyze the work of any public employee from the
> time he steps into his office in the morning until he leaves it at night
> without discovering that his every act is a seamless web of discretion and
> action. It is impossible to discover any position in government service,
> or in any other service for that matter, in which the element of discretion
> is absent except in the purely mechanical operations which will doubt-
> less in time be intrusted to machines. What we have in administration is
> a continual process of decision-action-decision-action, like a man run-
> ning after a high-batted ball (Gulick 1933, p61).

In addition to noting the ubiquity of discretion in the administrative
process, Gulick pointed out that while in theory there is a decrease
of discretionary action from the top to the bottom of an organization, in practice much of the discretion actually exercised is at the
bottom of the organization where the official of the organization
comes into contact with the citizen (Gulick 1933, p61). In his more
comprehensive discussion of the role of discretion in administration, Dimock makes this same point, observing that '[a]t the point
at which the official and the citizen frequently meet, large numbers

of discretionary questions are likely to arise' (Dimock 1936, p51). More recently yet, Thompson reiterated this point in his systematic conceptual analysis of the role of discretion in organizations (Thompson 1967, p118).

The importance of this observation about the locus of discretionary action in organizations is that frequently the kinds of decisions made at the bottom of the organizational hierarchy have grave consequences for the individual concerned. For example, ward attendants in state mental hospitals '. . . may tell the nurses and doctors which patients need shock treatment and which one is ready for discharge; they can often put a patient in restraint or seclusion at will and keep him there' (Perrow 1965, p922). As demonstrated in several studies police patrolmen possess extensive discretionary power to arrest or not to arrest – a decision which has obvious immediate consequences for the individual but which may also materially affect his longer term prospects (Aaron 1966; Skolnick 1967; Wilson 1969; Grosman 1975).

Administrative lawyers in particular are concerned with the exercise of police discretion. They examine, *inter alia*, the exercise of discretion by police in terms of compatibility of discretion with the rule of law and with the ideal of justice. Goldstein, for example, focuses on the fact that the decision to arrest is a low visibility decision and discusses ways of increasing the visibility of these decisions and procedures for evaluating them (Goldstein 1960; pp543–589). Kadish argues that the judgement to arrest or not is made under a variety of circumstances, for different reasons which vary between cases. He maintains that:

> A primary issue to be faced in resolving the dilemma of making discretionary judgements in the administration of criminal justice compatible with the values of the rule of law is to determine specifically the areas of choice in which primary reliance may acceptably (or not) be vested in the discretionary judgements of public officials, and in which it need (and must) not (Kadish 1962, p929).

Concern is not, however, limited to the discretion of police patrolmen. As Bottomley's (1973) study of *Decisions in the Penal Process* systematically documents, discretion is exercised at all levels of the penal system: by prosecutors (cf Grosman 1969), magistrates (cf Hogarth 1971), parole officers (cf Dawson 1966). In these situations concern is expressed about fundamental notions of law, intent, consistency and fairness.

Furthermore, studies outside the criminal justice system attest to the presence and exercise of discretion in other organizations. So for example, Keith Lucas (1957) analyzed the decisions made in the social welfare system in the United States, while more recently

Adler and Asquith (1981) compiled a comprehensive set of papers on many facets of discretion in the social welfare system in Britain. An excellent empirical analysis is that by Zimmerman who investigated the way in which receptionists in a district office of a Metropolitan County Bureau of Public Assistance used judgement in assigning applicants for public assistance to intake caseworkers. One of his major findings was that receptionists deviate from the stated rules or procedures on the basis of their judgement but justify their actions by claiming that the particular course of action was reasonable under the circumstances and essentially satisfied the provisions of the rule despite the obvious breach of precedent (Zimmerman 1970, pp221–238). There are even a few analyses of discretion in educational organizations. So, for example, Messick (1968) analysed the delegated discretionary powers of school boards in the US, Simpkins and Friesen (1970) reported a study of the discretionary powers of classroom teachers, Manley-Casimir's (1977–78) article reported the analysis of the exercise of discretion in school discipline, while Crowson and Porter-Gehrie (1980) reported their analysis of the discretionary behaviour of principals in large city schools.

Aside, however, from the analysis by Thompson (1967) of discretion in organizations, and that by Bottomley (1973) of discretion in the penal system, the most systematic analysis of discretion and its exercise in organizations is that by Lipsky (1980) in his provocative synthesis, *Street Level Bureaucracy*. The work by Nakamura and Smallwood (1980) also documents the presence and use of discretion by officials during the process of policy implementation.

The effect of discretion: considerations of ethics and fairness

Finally, discussions in various places acknowledge the inherently problematic character of discretion as a normative concept and the practical issues of ethics and justice raised by its exercise. Pound, cited earlier, acknowledged that discretion '. . . is an idea of morals, belonging to the twilight zone between law and morals' (Pound 1960, p926). The most systematic attempt to conceptualize and offer a solution to this aspect is Davis' (1969) analysis of *Discretionary Justice* in which he not only argues the case for discretion and its exercise but also argues for the need to confine, structure and check such discretion in the interests of justice.

Re-framing educational administration for another day

Given this race through even the partial array of literature adduced here, it should be clear that there is a substantial amount of extant thought, analysis, observation and discussion about the problem of discretion in administrative life. Given also my interest in and commitment to the proposition that discretion and its exercise is an absolutely central administrative process, that it is quintessentially a human activity and hence not a property of organizations, that it provides the bridge between empirical and normative, between fact and value in decision-making, it should then come as no surprise that I agree with Hodgkinson's foreshadowing of his argument:

> In searching for the answers we shall argue that, while a knowledge of organization theory may be desirable gloss on the administrative escutcheon, and while skills in the acquisition and deployment of power are of the essence, the essential competence lies in the area of judgement. And this, it will be seen, has moral implications. (Hodgkinson 1978, p ix)

Nor is it surprising that I agree in general with Greenfield's analysis of the pathologies of the field of educational administration and proposals for redemption and re-direction (Greenfield 1986, pp71–76). In particular, I agree with Greenfield's call for a new mode of inquiry in educational administration, one that is interpretive and subjective, one that focuses on administrators as they administer – their hopes, fears, intentions, motives, both good and evil, generous and manipulative; their struggles with questions of conscience, indeed their very administrative personality – their sincerity, integrity, capability, sense of justice.

I further agree with Greenfield's call that:

> We must seek new models for administrative training – ones that acknowledge responsibility, right judgement, and reflection as legitimately and inevitably part of administrative action. Such programs would lead the field of study toward what Scott (1985, p156) has called 'revolutionary moral discourse' and away, therefore, from instruction in a putative science of organization and administration. (Greenfield 1986, pp74–75)

What, then, does all this imply for re-framing educational administration for another day? In short, it implies re-conceptualizing the field, heuristics and preparation programmes. More fully stated, such a change requires that we return to the 'road not taken' and 'take' it through the bend in the undergrowth; such a decision implies a radical re-conceptualization of the field of educational administration in normative terms, a thoroughgoing review and selection of appropriate modes of inquiry suitable for eliciting understanding of administrative life, and a fundamental re-thinking of preparation programmes.

Recently, Mintzberg and Jorgenson wrote:

> Every community of scholars has its central concept. For economists, that concept is the market; for political scientists, it is politics. For a more recently developed community of scholars called organization theorists, the central concept is organization. (1987, p214)

What, then, is the central concept of administration? I submit it is *discretion*; the calculus of decision-making. This is the beginning of the road not taken, the road we need to take.

Notes

[1] I am indebted to Professor Greenfield for his comments and suggestions on the first draft of this paper.

[2] As used in this essay the phrase 'discretionary power' merely emphasizes the discretionary aspect of power. Power appears to be inherently discretionary; that is, the possession of power confers the freedom to exercise judgement and make choices about action. Here, then, *discretionary power* is a shorthand form of *the power to exercise discretion*; they are equivalent phrases.

References

Aaron, Thomas J 1966 *The control of police discretion* Springfield: Charles C Thomas.

Adler, Michael and Asquith, Stewart 1981 *Discretion and welfare* London: Heinemann.

Barnard, Chester 1938 *The functions of the executive* Cambridge, Mass.: Harvard University Press.

Bates, Richard 1989 *Is there a new paradigm in educational administration?* Paper presented to AERA, San Francisco.

Bottomley, A Keith 1973 *Decisions in the penal process* London: Martin Robertson.

Boyer, Carl B 1949 *The history of the calculus and its conceptual development* New York: Dover.

Caroll, J S and Payne, J W 1976 *Cognition and social behavior* Hillsdale, N J: Lawrence Erlbaum.

Cross, Ray 1980 'A description of decision-making patterns of school principals' *The Journal of Educational Research, 73,* 154–159.

Crowson, Robert L and Porter-Gehrie, Cynthia 1980 'The discretionary behavior of principals in large-city schools' *Educational Administration Quarterly, 16*, 45–69.

Davis, Kenneth, C 1969 *Discretionary justice* Baton Rouge: Louisiana State University Press.

Dawson, R O 1965 'The decision to grant or deny parole: A study of parole criteria in law and practice' *Washington University Law Quarterly.*

Dawson, R O 1969 *Sentencing: The decision as to type, length and conditions of sentence* Boston: Little Brown.

Dimock, Marshall E 1936. 'The role of discretion in modern administrations, in John M Gaus, Leonard D White and Marshall E Dimock (eds), *The frontiers of public administration*. Chicago: University of Chicago Press.

Friedrich, Carl J 1958 'Authority, reason, and discretion' in Carl J Friedrich (ed), *Authority* (pp28–48). Cambridge: Harvard University Press.

Goldstein, Joseph 1960 'Police discretion not to invoke the criminal process: Low visibility decisions in the administration of justice' *Yale Law Journal, LXIX,* 543–589.

Greenfield, Thomas B 1975 'Theory about organization: A new perspective and its implications for schools' In M Hughes (ed.), *Administering education: International challenge* (pp71–99). London: Athlone.

Greenfield, Thomas B 1980 'The man who comes back through the door in the wall: Discovering truth, discovering self, discovering organizations' *Educational Administration Quarterly, 16*(3), 26–59.

Greenfield, Thomas B 1986 'The decline and fall of science in educational administration' *Interchange,* 17(2), 57–80.

Greenfield, Thomas B 1990 *Personal communication.*

Griffiths, Daniel E 1957 'Administration as decision-making' in Andrew W Halpin (ed), *Administrative Theory in Education* (pp 119–149). New York: MacMillan.

Griffiths, Daniel E 1959 *Administrative theory*, New York: Appleton-Century-Crofts.

Griffiths, Daniel E 1979 'Another look at research on the behavior of administrators' in G L Immegart and W L Boyd (eds), *Problem finding in education administration: Trends in research and theory* (pp41–62, 263). Lexington, Mass.: Lexington.

Gronn, Peter 1983 *Rethinking educational administration: T B Greenfield and his critics.* Victoria: Deakin University.

Grosman, Brian A 1969 *The prosecutor* Toronto: University of Toronto Press.

Grosman, Brian A 1975 *Police command* Toronto: Macmillan.

Gulick, Luther 1933 'Politics, administration, and the "New Deal"' *Annals of the American Academy of Political Science, 169*, 55–66.

Hammond, Kenneth R, McClelland, Gary H, and Mumpower, Jery L 1980. *Human judgement and decision-making* New York: Praeger.

Hodgkinson, C 1978 *Towards a philosophy of administration* Oxford: Basil Blackwell.

Hodgkinson, C 1983 *The philosophy of leadership* Oxford: Basil Blackwell.

Hogarth, John 1971 *Sentencing as a human process* Toronto: Centre for Criminology, University of Toronto Press.

Janis, Irving L and Mann, Leon 1977 *Decision making* New York: Free Press.

Jones, Cathaleene and Aronson, Elliot 1973 'Attribution of fault to a rape victim as a function of respectability of the victim', *Journal of Personality & Social Psychology, 26*, 415–419.

Kadish, Sanford H 1962 'Legal norm and discretion in the police and sentencing processes' *Harvard Law Review, LXXV.*

Keith-Lucas, A 1959 *Decisions about people in need*, Chapel Hill: University of North Carolina Press.

Kelley, Harold H 1973 'The processes of causal attribution', *American Psychologist, 28*, 107–128.

Landy, David and Aronson, Elliot 1969 'The influence of the character of the criminal and his victim on the decisions of simulated jurors', *Journal of Experimental Social Psychology, 5*, 141–152.

Laski, Harold J 1933, February. 'Discretionary power', *Politica, I*, 274–275.

Lipsky, Michael 1980 *Street level bureaucracy*. New York: Russell Sage.

Locke, John 1965 *Treatise of civil government and a letter concerning toleration*, edited by Charles L Sherman, New York: Appleton-Century-Crofts.

MacIntyre, Alasdair 1984 *After virtue*, Notre Dame, IN: University of Notre Dame Press.

Manley-Casimir, Michael E 1971, October 'School discipline as discretionary justice' *Administrator' Notebook, 20*(2).

Manley-Casimir, Michael E 1974, February 'School governance as discretionary justice', *School Review, 82*(2), 347–362.

Manley-Casimir, Michael E 1976 *The exercise of administrative discretion in secondary school discipline*, unpublished Ph D dissertation, University of Chicago.

Manley-Casimir, Michael E 1977–78 'Discretion in school discipline', *Interchange, VII*(1/2), 84–100.

Manley-Casimir, Michael E 1986, Fall 'Review of Peter A Sola' (ed), *Ethics, education and administrative decisions. Educational Studies, 17*(3), 355–359.

Manley-Casimir, Michael E 1989 'Conscience, community mores and administrative responsibility: A prologue, *Administrator's Notebook, 33*(4).

Manley-Casimir, Michael E and Pitsula, Pat 1988, May 'The Charter, culture and public school curriculum: Emerging perspectives and guidelines', *Education Law, I*(1), 37–69.

Maselli, Mary D and Altrocchi, John 1969 'Attribution of intent', *Psychological Bulletin, 71*, 445–454.

Messick, John D 1968 *The discretionary powers of school boards,* New York: Greenwood Press.

Mill, James 1937 *An essay on government.* Cambridge: Cambridge University Press.

Mintzberg, Henry & Jorgensen, Jon. 1987 'Emergent strategy for public policy' *Canadian Public Administration, 30,* 214–229.

Morris, Van Cleve, Crowson, Robert L., Hurwitz, Emanuel, & Porter-Gehrie, Cynthia. 1982, June 'The urban principal: Middle manager in the educational bureaucracy' *Phi Delta Kappan, 63,* 689–6902.

Nakamura, Robert T and Smallwood, F 1980, *The politics of policy implementation,* New York: St. Martins Press.

Perrow, Charles 1965 'Hospitals: Technology, structure, and goals', in James G March (ed), *Handbook of organizations* (p922). Chicago: Rand Mcnally.

Pound, Roscoe 1960 *Discretion, dispensation and mitigation: The problem of the individual special case.* N Y U L Review, 35, 926.

Scott, W 1985 'Organizational revolutions: an end to managerial orthodoxy', in *Administration and Society, 17(2),* 149–70.

Simon, Herbert 1965 *Administrative behavior,* New York: Free Press.

Simpkins, W S and Friesen, D 1970, May. 'Discretionary powers of classroom teachers', *Canadian Administrator, IX(8).*

Skolnick, Jerome H 1967. *Justice without trial,* New York: Wiley.

Stamp, Josiah 1938 *The anatomy of judgement,* Address delivered at McMaster University, February 25.

Thompson, James D 1967. *Organizations in action,* New York: McGraw-Hill.

Vickers, Geoffrey 1961 'Judgement', *The Manager,* 30–39. The sixth Elbourne Memorial lecture given to the British Institute of Management, November 2, 1961.

Vickers, Geoffrey 1965 *The art of judgement,* London: Chapman & Hall.

Wallsten, Thomas S 1980 *Cognitive processes in choice and decision behavior,* Hillsdale N J: Lawrence Erlbaum.

Wilson, James Q 1969. *Varieties of police behaviour.* Cambridge: Harvard University Press.

Zimmerman, Don H 1970. 'The practicalities of rule use'. In Jack D Douglas (ed) *Understanding everyday life* (pp221–238), Chicago: Aldine.

PART III
LEADERSHIP IN EDUCATION

3.1 Managerial Capability: What Headteachers Need to be Good At

Ernest Cave and Cyril Wilkinson

This paper presents an account of the first of a two phase research project investigating the concept of managerial capability. In this first phase the researchers were seeking to identify and distil essential capabilities which the education manager requires in order to perform effectively in key areas of the management arena.

The background

Within the area of research into managerial roles and functions, studies of what managers actually do have provided a broad delineation of managerial behaviour (Carlson 1951; Hemphill 1959; Stewart 1967, 1976, 1982, 1989; Mintzberg 1975; Kotter 1982). A difficulty with the structured observation and recording methods used in many of these studies is that they do not reveal what the intentions underlying the managerial activity may be or what abilities are needed if the outcomes are to be successful. Yet the purpose of the study of management is to improve performance and investigation of what managers do and the relationship of that action to their intentions and resulting outcomes is crucial. Another recurring shortcoming of existing research is the failure to relate what managers *actually do* to what they *should do* or are expected to do (Hales 1986; Luthans 1987). In fact, *'should do'* considerations cannot be addressed without exploration of the context, intentions or outcomes of the observed behaviour.

Attempts have been made to analyze what managers need to be good at, in order to be effective, and various categorizations have been presented. The vocabulary which has emerged includes such terms as skills, competences, abilities and capabilities (Hayes 1979; Constable 1988). Often, however, it is difficult to identify a clear empirical base for such analyses, since it is difficult to find methods of investigation that satisfy commonly accepted notions of research inquiry. Research methods which attempt to probe beneath the surface of observed managerial behaviour are likely to be based on rigorous introspection, analysis, reflection and debate, and are as yet largely undeveloped.

What headteachers do

In education, as interest in management developed, attention increasingly focused on the role of the headteacher and the need for managerial skills. A number of studies, based on empirical evidence illustrate that headship combines features of 'the leading professional' and 'chief executive' roles (Hughes 1972). These aspects of the role, and the ambiguities and confusions that arise from them are critically examined in a series of papers edited by Peters (1976). A specific account of the tasks of heads as perceived by heads themselves and other senior school staff is provided by Lyons (1976). Richardson (1973) presents a more penetrating examination of headship behaviour in the specific context of a large comprehensive school, and her perceptive analysis is an influential contribution to our understanding.

The study in education which, in its intentions and methodology, most closely parallels the investigations into private sector managerial behaviour, is that of Hall, Mackay and Morgan (1986). The project is based on observation of headteachers at work, diary completion, and interviews with school staff, LEA officers and advisers. The aim was to find out 'what heads actually do rather than what they, or theoretical analyses, say they do'. The findings closely resemble those of similar researches in the private sector. They affirm the importance of formal and informal lateral and vertical relationships (cf Kotter 1982). A significant finding is that head-teachers have considerable freedom to interpret what their job entails and what emphasis to give the various aspects (cf Stewart 1982).

The search for competence

During the 1970s the search for management competences began. In 1971, the American Management Association, a forum where the ideas of leading American companies can be shared, launched a project, based on observation and analysis of 1,800 management jobs, to discover generic competences. These were then assembled into the AMA managerial competency model. The definition of competence adopted was: 'a generic knowledge, motive, trait, self-image, social role, or skill of a person that is causally linked to superior performance on the job' (Hayes 1980). The model identifies, in addition to specific knowledge competence, four clusters of generic competences, which they identify as intellectual, entrepreneurial, socio-emotional, and interpersonal. Their conclusion is that 'the data in our study clearly demonstrates that this combination [that is, all five clusters working together] greatly enhances the manager's chance of success'. Unfortunately no attempt is made to analyze the implications of this synopsis.

In Britain, the Management Charter Initiative (MCI) is a large scale programme strongly supported by the government, now involving over 200 UK leading private and public organisations, with the intention 'to improve management standards in Britain'. It has an expressed clear commitment to the concept of competence, defined as 'the ability to perform effectively functions associated with management in a work related situation' (Consultative Paper 14 December 1988). A coherent programme is proposed for education and training, an important aspect of which is a nationally accepted three-tier qualification structure based on assessment of sets of competence benchmarks. The breakdown of a concept of competence as an overall ability to perform effectively into narrow sets of subordinate competences which represent the knowledge, skills and qualities needed is problematic.

Jacobs (1989) makes the important point that while it is possible, by obtaining and carefully analysing performance data, to identify clusters of behaviour that can be reliably and logically classified as competences, what is obtained is only a partial and fragmented view of the complexity of management. Management performance involves other activity which is difficult to isolate and describe; it involves qualities and abilities which are not easy to observe or discover, and has outcomes which defy measurement. It should be noted that within the MCI movement there are those who are not committed to the concept of separate and assessable competences.

There are doubts about the basic idea of analyzing a professional management job into elements of competence; not only are so many required, but it is held by some that management must be treated holistically. 'I usually explain this by the metaphor of getting a quantity surveyor to describe St Paul's Cathedral; it is not so much the number and shape of the building blocks that is important as the way they are put together' (Everard 1989).

Although many industrial concerns have subscribed to MCI, Mitchell and Cuthbert (1989) suggest: 'There is no commonly held concept of competence across industry.' For Constable (1988) competences are the effective performance of skills. He recognises that something else is required and lists additional attributes such as energy, judgement, integrity and resilience. One difficulty with this list is that there are qualitative differences between, say, judgement, and energy. While Constable sees a trait like resilience as an additional attribute, Boyatzis (1982) would define it as a job competence; 'an underlying characteristic of a person in that it may be a motive, trait, skill, aspect of one's self-image or social rule, or a body of knowledge which he or she uses' (cf AMA model). Burgoyne (1989) posits, but does not develop, the concept of 'meta-competences' which enable managers to use specific competences effectively. These have to do with being able to learn, adapt, anticipate, and create change.

A distinctly different approach from that of the prior specification, development, and assessment of atomised skills, has been adopted by the Far West Laboratory for Educational Research and Development, San Francisco. In 1983, a professional development programme for school principals was begun under the title 'Peer Assisted Learning' (The PAL Program). It is based on four years of intensive research to seek a realistic understanding of the principal's role. Key components of the research strategy were intensive observation of the activity and interactions of 17 principals (*shadowing*), followed the next day by detailed discussion between the principal and field officer on the context, reasons for the action, and intended outcomes (*reflective interviews*). The research instruments of shadowing and reflective interview between paired principals became a structured development technique. An important outcome of the programme is that principals develop 'higher order thinking' that allows them to connect their management actions to an overarching perspective of their school settings and their aspirations for students.

The research methodology

The choice of research methodology was crucial to this investigation as no well established, documented approaches existed to enable penetrating scrutiny of the underlying generic dimensions of managerial capability. This reflects the problems which emerge when an attempt is made to analyze the elements of managerial work, which in reality is a complex set of closely interconnected activities (Wilkinson and Cave 1987). In determining an appropriate method of enquiry the researchers were informed from three sources: their experience of peer group interaction, focus groups as a form of qualitative research, and the PAL project.

Effective peer group interaction, an integral part of the Action Research approach, is the cornerstone of the Master of Science programme at the University of Ulster. Groups are encouraged to engage in reflective enquiry which seeks to analyse and understand their own and others' practice leading to courses of action for sustained improvement. Creative thinking is also encouraged as a complementary activity by which is meant the ability to form novel associations from looking at the elements of managerial reality in an open and unconstrained way. This approach offered the possibility of uncovering, if they existed, elusive generic capabilities from complex realities. It was decided to bring together six alumni from the MSc programme who met on ten occasions from 22 June 1988. The participants had the advantage of three years cognitive development in the group dynamics described above.

The focus group as a form of qualitative research has many characteristics in common with features of the above approach. 'The hallmark of focus groups is the explicit use of the group interaction to produce data and insights that would be less accessible without the interaction found in a group' (Morgan 1988). The style of approach is exploratory rather than hypothesis testing and based on interview and interaction. Surprisingly focus groups have not been widely used in research in the social sciences or education, but the method clearly offers a valuable vehicle for group members experienced in rigorous reflective analysis.

For this research, headteachers were chosen from the primary, secondary and further education sectors and two female members were included to allow for possible gender differences in style and practice. The group was restricted to six members, as evidence suggests that larger groups require a higher level of moderation. Sessions were audio-taped, a technique familiar to the participants who had undertaken similar activities on the MSc programme. The researchers acted as moderators of what were multi-stage focus groups which met on a number of occasions to follow through topics across sessions to encourage the development and evolution of ideas and concepts. Wells (1979) calls this technique 'tracking'. The intention was to identify and capture key themes by a process of distillation. The moderators adopted a detached style allowing members to raise and explore issues but maintaining proximity to the focus of enquiry. Participants were encouraged to identify critical incidents which they felt were significant and typical of the flow of management activity in their institutions. Cue and summary were used as framing devices for sessions and, over time, members used these as self-managing techniques. Questions were used sparingly to direct the flow of interaction. Criteria were identified and applied by the moderators which governed the quality of interaction – namely, *range, specificity and depth*. Range refers to the coverage of a broad selection of issues recognised as significant in the research area. Specificity refers to precise and detailed accounts of particular aspects of management practice while depth implies rigorous, searching analysis and treatment. Time for each session was limited to a maximum of two hours to encourage concentration and to avoid dissipation. Sessions were held in the participants' own schools and colleges which gave them first hand contact with differing establishments and the incentive to offer and share their considerable and varied experience. Some problems did emerge in practice. On occasions it proved difficult for all members to attend sessions because, as principals, they had to respond to unexpected crises in their institutions. Indeed one member missed several sessions as she was granted a sabbatical to investigate education management programmes in the USA. However, a group membership of six allowed some latitude in attendance.

The focus group approach also offered advantages. The interaction between members led to an interchange and development of ideas in directions unlikely to happen during individual interview. Because of the participant-focused nature of the group exchanges, the setting is less open to control than individual encounters and, therefore, less likely to be subject to researcher prescription and bias. The researchers also became aware that the members developed both individually and as a group and there were qualitative differences in terms of the criteria of range, specificity and depth between initial and later sessions. Kaboolian and Gramson (1983) called their focus group experiences 'peer group conversations' and this description certainly captures the style and spirit of the sessions.

In the account which follows contributors are identified by sector (primary [PS], or secondary [SS], or further education [FE]), status (maintained [M] ie Catholic, or state [S]); and gender (male [m], or female [f]).

Group deliberations

The constraints of a relatively brief research paper prevent a detailed account of each of the ten sessions.[1] As decision making is the vital element in the managing task, four contrasting decision issues are selected as examples. Two emerged from one session and the remaining two from different occasions.

Example 1

During the opening session in Drumcree High School, whether or not to join Education for Mutual Understanding (EMU) was offered as an issue requiring a Yes/No decision within a short timespan. EMU is a major curriculum project in Northern Ireland and is heavily resourced and supported by the Department of Education and the present Education Minister. It seeks to encourage sympathetic and understanding relationships between Catholic and Protestant schools. However, it has been opposed by many local politicians, churches and community members who see it both as a first step towards integrated schooling and an imposed initiative from central government at Westminster. Everyone in the group regarded it as a critically important decision with clear political overtones as well as educational implications. In two schools in particular the political/community aspects dominated. One school is in a strongly Nationalist area seeking to preserve its distinctive Irish culture and identity. Nevertheless the headteacher saw his task as persuading the governors to enter the project:

> The agenda has to be handled carefully. While not appearing to be simply jumping on a bandwagon of resources the governors have to be persuaded that various benefits will come from joining in. [SS/M/m]

The other school is in a staunch Unionist area and the headteacher was well aware that her governors would oppose any political interference they perceived as emanating from London.

> My governors' initial reaction is to reject anything that comes from Stormont Castle. [SS/S/f]

The EMU issue instigated a lengthy discussion about the tactics that might be used. There was some disagreement over the question of how much direction/information should be given to a board of governors;

> I carefully filter the information and arrange the position on the agenda. My governors don't like long meetings. [SS/M/m]

All concurred that they were able to influence their boards of governors and a vital tactic was the winning of support of key figures. For example, the Chairman of the Board of Governors in one of the schools is Director of the Down and Connor Maintained Schools Ecumenical Movement. Although less striking than the example given above, all the headteachers were able to recognise the key figures in their governing bodies and stressed the paramount importance of good relationships with the chairperson. They felt it was also important to know the interests, dispositions and beliefs of all members of boards of governors. In the state primary school situated in a middle-class area of Belfast the board of governors did not rely heavily on the professional judgement of the head but in the remaining schools the governors looked to the headteacher for information and guidance.

It was also apparent in this opening session that many of the concepts and capacities identified and sharpened in later group meetings as constituting what managers need to be good at, were freely used. Having recognised EMU as a potentially emotive political issue, they saw *the capacity to read the situation* as critically important: the board of governors, teacher attitudes, community perceptions, resource implications, reactions of the Department of Education and the area boards were consequential variables in the circumstances. Concepts like balanced judgement, political acumen, judicious caution and skills like reconnaissance, persuading, negotiating and bargaining recurred in the discussion.

Example 2

Some of the literature on decision making distinguishes between 'routine' decisions (structured, certain, simple, recurring, standardised) and 'non-routine' decisions (unstructured, uncertain, complex, non-recurring, novel). In one group session the danger of assuming that routine recurring decisions are necessarily simple and certain became apparent. The conclusion was reached that the capable manager is one who has the insight to recognise when apparently simple decisions may have complex undertones.

Discussion had centred on the broad issue of the expected consequence of the new legislation which has been introduced in Northern Ireland in parallel with the Education Reform Act, 1988. One of the group, almost as an aside, posed the question, 'What do we do if a teacher asks for leave of absence to attend the wedding of a close friend and this is not provided for by the regulations?'. On the face of it this is a routine issue where agreed procedures and required information are readily available. In the case of Further Education this indeed appears to be so. The FE principal pointed out that his staff have clear contracts and 'it should just be played by the book'. He added, 'Of course, in FE the principal can distance himself from such decisions'. In the primary and secondary sectors the situation is less clear cut. Although regulations governing leave of absence exist, the primary and secondary headteachers felt that strict adherence to such a tight delineation could easily lead to staff also playing by the book. They argued that flexibility was needed but that such flexibility could create its own potential difficulties and that the exercise of judgement, tact and sensitivity was essential.

The conversation broadened into a fuller discussion of the kinds of relationships between headteacher and teaching staff that characterise effective schools and colleges. Marked differences in attitude and opinion became apparent which partly reflected differences in context but, more markedly, differences in personality and perceptions. In particular the female members emphasised the importance of close, supportive relationships. One of them made the point:

> We have introduced counselling for pupils but we seem to neglect the important area of counselling for our staff. [SS/S/f]

Once again the issue of relationships with staff seemed to hinge on balanced judgement:

> You can run the place on the basis that relationships matter most or you can be so inflexible that you give the impression that people don't matter. To what extent do you depend on good relationships and to what extent on authority? [PS/S/m]

Differences between the views of the FE principal and the headteachers in the primary and secondary sectors were revealed:

> The powers of the principal are awesome in the new situation. You are part of the employer. You cannot have a close relationship. You will have to distance yourself from the informal relationships which exist in any college. The principal may have to take a more objective administrative line in the new era. [FE/S/m]

The opposing view was most strongly expressed by a female headteacher:

> You cannot step back. You will lose the spirit of the school and its main purposes. You must win the respect of the staff. You have to build bridges and establish relationships with key figures. [SS/M/f]

When the attention of the group was directed to the focal issue of what the manager needs to be good at in establishing and maintaining cooperative relationships or, more broadly, in managing people, the usual interpersonal skills were offered – communicating, negotiating, bargaining, influencing, counselling. There were, however, many caveats expressed and there was a general consensus that more fundamental cerebral capacities distinguish the more effective manager from the less effective: thinking on your feet, balanced judgement, assessing the situation. Typical comments were:

> It's more a question of knowing when to negotiate and when not to. [SS/M/m]
> It's important to decide how big an issue you want to make of certain things. You have to know what penalties arise from taking too strong a line. [SS/M/f]
> You learn to pick up the messages in each situation. You need to know your own arena and to diagnose all the circumstances. [PS/S/m]

Examples 3/4

During one of the later sessions the Further Education principal recounted two very different incidents which had occurred that morning. They led to subsequent discussion about common capabilities which may underpin situations apparently dissimilar in character. A member of the inspectorate called in to the college to compliment the principal on the development of a successful Craft, Design and Technology programme. The programme emerged from an exercise in strategic planning which sought to establish general policies and intentions for the college and the acquiring and disposition of resources to achieve them. An audit of college activity was undertaken, followed by analysis and forecasting leading to a decision to promote and develop appropriate areas of the curriculum. Rational investigation and planning took place which had reasonably long term implications for the college:

> Key elements of this process involved scanning the external and internal environment and making informed choices in harmony with the purposes and values of the college. [FE/S/m]

A second incident, very different in kind and timespan for decision making, followed soon after the inspector left. A lecturer from the Catering section arrived in the principal's office in great agitation to announce that a girl had been injured in a scuffle during which a knife which she had been holding in her hand had been deflected into her leg. The principal had to take immediate action to ensure that the usual medical precautions were followed and the girl was despatched to hospital for further treatment. On further investigation it emerged that students were not supposed to be in the kitchens without supervision but they had infiltrated unnoticed during break-time. The principal reflected on the circumstances and identified a number of implications. The parents would have to be informed and this required sensitive handling by the staff concerned. Clearly rules had been broken and this raised the question of how watertight and tenable the regulations and working practices of the college were in relation to such a happening.

> I also had to take into account the possibility of the local press publishing a story which could harm our reputation. The good report by the inspector is unlikely to hit the press! [FE/S/m]

One of the female headteachers distinguished between immediate and long term situations and argued that different capacities were required. She felt that the long term requires 'strategic thinking and planning' and the immediate crisis demands the manager 'to be good under pressure' and tended to perceive these abilities as exclusive. Others in the group, while agreeing that strategic planning is essential, maintained that the capacities needed to put the strategy into action came down in the end to managing people. So once again it becomes a matter of reading situations, political awareness and balanced judgement. Equally the thinking on one's feet involved in the crisis situation has elements of diagnostic, analytical and synoptic abilities but these have to be exercised within extreme time constraints. The group presented an interesting management concept in response to the crisis episode. One suggested that it would be sound management practice to identify 'paradigmatic' incidents which test the effectiveness of the infrastructure and procedures of the college. The ability to handle crises of this kind depends on deliberately thought out and previously instituted structures, regulations and practices.

Summary and conclusions

The proposition which emerges from this investigation is that knowledge and skills are prerequisite tools in the process of managing a given situation. Effectiveness depends totally on how appropriately they are used in the process. The capacities identified by the group are seen as vital elements *in the process* of using knowledge and skills effectively. They are not seen as being of the same kind as skills but of a different order. In much of the competency literature a competence is presented as an outcome of using knowledge and skills effectively.

Recent writers have recognised more elusive abilities which are required if knowledge and skills are to be used effectively. Boyatzis (1982), for example, refers to meta-competences without fully exploring the processes through which knowledge, skills and meta-competences lead to effective action. Because of the confusion over differing conceptions of the term 'competence' the focus group decided to avoid its use. Thus capability is realised in effective action in which skills and knowledge are used appropriately through the exercise of higher order capacities. The group emphatically claimed that effective performance is recognisable.

> Everyone knows who the really successful headteachers are, even though they may be quite different in style. This is because they have different values and intentions. [SS/M/m]

There was prolonged discussion about two recently retired headteachers who are commonly recognised as having run highly successful schools. The group agreed that both showed great capability although there was disagreement about the relative merits of the two schools.

There is common assent on the main areas of knowledge required by headteachers: professional knowledge of educational principles and practices, knowledge of theories and models of managerial processes and knowledge of the social, political and legal contexts. Recently there have been investigations of the discrete interpersonal skills necessary for headship: persuading, bargaining, explaining, listening, reporting, informing, counselling, appraising, chairing, interviewing and team building are typical of a list which keeps being added to. Skills have also been enumerated in other key areas like organisation and resource management, and management development programmes for headteachers increasingly are predicated on the assumption that these are skills which are teachable, learnable and transferable. Fewer analyses have been made of the nature of the enabling capacities needed to apply these skills appropriately in the holistic situations in which headteachers find themselves daily.

The research intention of following topics across sessions to encourage the development and evolution of ideas and concepts was fully realised. The following key concepts were the focus of continuing discussion: reading the situation, balanced judgement, intuition, political acumen. They were identified but members found it difficult to establish relationships between them. The researchers present here the attempt to capture and clarify the ideas which emerged from intense, prolonged discussions involving complex philosophical and psychological issues.

Reading the situation

This emerged as the overriding capacity and was voiced in a variety of ways:

picking up the vibes around you;
keeping your antennae out;
being aware of other possibilities and options;
able to assess and weigh up all the factors in the situation;
being alert and receptive to what is going on.

It was also seen to apply to a wide range of decision making circumstances: long term strategic planning, handling crisis situations and recurring, daily encounters. The FE principal in particular stressed that sensitive awareness and diagnosis are important in the light of the new legislation and the growing volume of boundary management. The views expressed seemed to recognise that 'reading the situation' involves more than mere diagnosis; it includes continuous response and deliberate action to influence evolving circumstances. Reconnaissance, identification of areas requiring attention, analysis, reflection, synthesis and evaluation were seen as contributory elements many of which occur in the other cognitive activities which were identified.

Balanced judgement

The ability to exercise balanced judgement was also seen as critical. Group members saw it as related to problem solving in that, once a situation has arisen or a problem has been recognised, analysis follows and key factors are identified and evaluated in the process of choosing a course of action. It was clear that as the group distilled their thinking over a number of sessions they did not see it as an exercise in mechanical logic, 'It is not merely clinical analysis but a combination of that with intuition.'

There was considerable agreement that the kind of judgement necessary is significantly different from judgement in the legal sense:

> You have to be prepared to base decisions on much softer evidence than would be accepted in a court of law. You very rarely have time to collect all the evidence you would like and you have to exercise judgement on a partial picture. Values also can't be left out of that picture.

It is interesting that while Constable speaks about making *sound* judgements the recurring theme in the discussions was about *balanced* judgement. The group saw the examining and weighing of the advantages and disadvantages of factors in often ambiguous and conflicting circumstances as important and the testing of decisions against the priorities and values of the school. Balanced judgement was seen as particularly important in times of crisis and dilemma.

Intuition

Intuition was seen as serving judgement, following a long debate about the relationship between them. The group did not agree with a conception of intuition which has considerable currency in psychological research and literature and is given in the Oxford dictionary: 'the immediate apprehension of an object by the mind without the intervention of any reasoning process':

> Intuition is more than mere hunch or guesswork. It may start as a gut feeling but is tested against the bank of your own experience.

March (1974) hints at the cerebral aspects when he suggests that intuition 'is an alternative way of consulting our intelligence'. The group saw memory, ordered experience and feeling as playing a part in intuition. This view is in sympathy with De Bono (1982) who argues that the mind is a pattern making and pattern using system: 'we think and then store thinking'. The more well stocked and thought through the mindstore is, then the more likely intuition will offer worthwhile assistance. This more extensive interpretation of intuition is likely to mean a more ready acceptance of its use although emotions and feelings have been acknowledged as legitimate management instruments in recent times.

Political acumen

While political skills have featured prominently in lists of what managers need to be good at, the group make an important distinction between possession of political skills, like bargaining, and political acumen: 'It's not enough to know how to bargain but when to bargain. Timing is all important.'

Their notion of political acumen is closely tied in with thinking on one's feet, learning from experience, reading the situation and using intuition: 'It is about hearing what people are not saying. That's part of political awareness.' Thus political awareness has to do with sensitivity and with flexibility to take account of changing situations rather than relying simply on experience. 'You, others and circumstances will have changed.' In discussion of the new legislation the group stressed the importance of such tactics as controlling information, identifying and cultivating key parties, establishing effective networks, developing credibility and occupying public space.

Review

In an early session one group member captured the initial feelings about effective headteachers, 'You know who they are but you don't know why they are.'

In the final review session the group claimed to have come to a clearer understanding of the 'why'. They felt that while they had greater conceptual clarity it was still difficult to put the essence into words. They seem to confirm the assertion that managerial behaviour is 'something about which we can know more than we can tell'.

Equally, in the ten sessions there was much more told than can be reported in this brief account. For example, the group saw personal qualities like integrity, stamina, commitment and conviction as fundamental and greater emphasis was placed on the foundational role of value systems than appears in the account.

Notes

[1] Normally accepted procedures for presenting evidence require transcripts of tapes to be included to set the quoted extracts in context. These are available from the authors but clearly cannot be presented here.

[The researchers record their indebtedness to the members of the focus group for their vital contribution: Jim Billingsley, David Green, Raymond Harbinson, Sister Yvonne Jennings, Louis Knox, P J O'Grady and John Watson.]

References

Boyatzis, R 1982 *The Competent Manager: a model for effective performance* New York: Wiley

Burgoyne, J 1989 'Creating the Managerial Portfolio: Building on competency approaches to management development' *Management Education and Development*, Vol 20, Part 1, pp56–61.

Carlson, S 1951 *Executive Behaviour*. Stombergs. Stockholm.

Constable, C J 1988 'Developing the competent Manager in a UK Context' *Report for the Manpower Services Commission*.

De Bono 1982 Letter as appendix in Heirs, B and Pherson, B '*The Mind of the Organisation*' New York: Harper and Row.

Everard, B 1989 'Competences in Education and Education Management'. *Management in Education*. Vol 3, No 2, Summer.

Hales, C 1986 'What the Managers Do' *Journal of Management Studies* 23; January.

Hall, V Mackay, H and Morgan, C 1986 *Head Teachers at Work* Milton Keynes: Open University Press.

Hayes, J. 1979 *A New Look at Managerial competence: the AMA model of worthy performance*. Management Review, November

Hemphill, J 1959, 'Job descriptions from executives', *Harvard Business Reviews* 37, 5.

Hughes, M 1972 *The Role of the Secondary Head* PhD Thesis, University of Wales.

Jacobs, R 1989 'Getting the Measure of Management Competence' *Personnel Management*, June.

Kaboolian, L and Gramson, WA 1983 'New Strategies for the use of focus groups for social science and survey research'. Paper presented at the American Association for Public Opinion Research.

Kotter, J 1982 *The General Managers* New York: The Free Press.

Luthans, F 1987 *Real Managers*, New York: Ballinger.

Lyons, G (1976) *Heads' Tasks: A Handbook of Secondary School Administration* Slough: NFER.

March, J 1974 'Analytical Skills and the University Training of Educational Administrators', *The Journal of Educational Administration* Vol XII, No 1, pp16–43.

Mintzberg, H 1973 *The Nature of Managerial Work*, New York: Harper and Row.

Mitchell, L and Cuthbert, T 1989 'Verdict Unproven' *Competence and Assessment*, Issue 9, Summer.

Morgan, D 1988 '*Focus Groups as Qualitative Research*' London: Sage Publications.

Morgan, G 1986 *Images of Organisation*, London: Sage Publications.

Peters, R (ed) 1976 *The Role of the Head*, London: Routledge and Kegan Paul.

Pye, A (1988) 'Management Competences in the Public Sector.' *Public Money and Management*. Winter, pp62–64.

Richardson, E (1973) *The Teacher, The School and The Task of Management*. London. Heinemann.

Stewart, R 1967 *Managers and their Jobs*, London: Macmillan.

Stewart, R (1976) *Contrasts in Management: a study of different types of managers' jobs: their demands and choices*. Maidenhead. McGraw Hill.

Stewart, R 1982 *Choices for the Managers* Maidenhead: McGraw-Hill.

Stewart, R 1989 *Leading in the NHS*, London: Macmillan.

Wells, W 1979 'Group Interviewing' in Higginbotham, J and Cox K *Focus Group Interviews. A reader*, Chicago. American Marketing Association.

Wilkinson, C and Cave, E 1987 *Teaching and Managing: inseparable activities in schools* London: Croom Helm.

3.2 Effective Educational Executives: An Essay on the Concept of Strategic Leadership

Jim Guthrie

Introduction

Regardless of the significance and timelessness of conventional leadership prescriptions, by themselves they are increasingly insufficient. Today's effective executive must also understand and use a range of strategic planning components. These modern components, to be maximally useful, must be incorporated into the leadership style, into the day-to-day operational actions of an executive. In effect, these strategic planning components must become an intimate part of a manager's thinking. A strategic leader must constantly be engaged in 'strategic thinking'.

This modern management style is labelled 'strategic leadership'. This title separates it from past patterns and prosaic pronouncements. *Strategic* in this context refers to the continual need on the part of a contemporary educational leader to appraise conditions both external and internal to an organization, assess the organization's mission relative to environmental changes, and consistently assess existing organizational procedures.

In addition to the necessity of constantly evaluating and planning, a strategic executive must continue to meet the conventional, time-honored expectations of leaders and managers in complex organizations. However, strategic management should not be mistaken as an extra, peripheral, or added set of burdensome tasks which are somehow cobbled onto the core of conventional leader activities. Rather, strategic leadership is a new and enlarged executive framework into which conventional management activities fit. Strategic leadership is not what a successful leader will do instead of, or exclusive of, other leader activities. It is something that an executive does in addition to or along side of conventional management activities.

This chapter (1) describes environmental changes which are dramatically altering the context in which modern educational leaders operate, (2) defines terms and explores fundamental questions regarding leadership, (3) summarizes conventional components of executive behaviour, (4) explains the dimensions of modern strategic leadership, and (5) deduces the implications for leadership preparation.

Before embarking on these tasks, however, it is important to emphasize that the following leadership descriptions and explanations are constructed around five fundamental assumptions. These conditions render it insufficient for a leader to be a 'great' individual or to be knowledgeable about organizational dynamics alone. These conditions render strategic leadership imperative.

Fundamental assumptions

- What it is necessary to know to be an effective strategic leader for an education organization can be learned.

Effective strategic leadership is a set of skills and understandings which are *not* contingent upon an individual executive being endowed with Herculean physical and intellectual abilities.

- Big companies, big government, big universities, big school systems, big conglomerates, big multinational corporations, big bureaucracies are now a dominant fact of life.

At least since World War II, effective leadership has relied less upon isolated individual initiative and more upon the ability of a leader to mobilize and direct organizational activities. Today, one leads not only with time-tested traditional traits, but also by understanding the complexities of organizational dynamics.

- Contemporary leadership increasingly occurs less through coercion and more through persuasion.

Once upon a time, or at least once upon a simpler, less complicated, and less interdependent time, one could lead through individual intelligence and personal force of will. In recent times, the end of the twentieth century, this had changed. Modern leaders must frequently view themselves as part of a leadership team and as a component of a multi-tiered decision-making setting in which many individuals will participate in shaping an outcome.

- Global socio-demographic, economic, environmental and political currents are dramatically altering the conditions under which educational institutions and educational leaders must operate.

The primary force altering the external environment in which educators increasingly operate is international economic competitiveness. This, in turn, is promoting cultural globalization, demographic diversification, ecological interdependence, and political intensification.

- Change appears to be the only contemporary condition which is constant, and, thus, organizations and their leaders must continually adapt.

The evolving contemporary context

The following quotation from an October 1989 *Atlantic* article crystalizes the complex, intertwined, and rapidly evolving nature of international manufacturing and services industries. This quotation also captures the complexity and global nature of the new context in which contemporary leaders must operate.

> Ford, with one third of its sales from outside the United States, owns 25 per cent of Mazda. Mazda makes cars in America for Ford; Ford will reciprocate by making trucks for Mazda; and the two companies trade parts. Each owns a piece of Korea's Kia Motors, which produces the Ford Festiva for export to the United States. Ford and Nissan, Japan's No.2, swap vehicles in Australia and are planning a joint minivan program in America. Ford and Volkswagen have merged into a single company in Latin America, which exports trucks to the United States.
>
> General Motors holds a 41.6 per cent stake in Isuzu, which is starting a joint venture in America with Suburu, which is partly owned by Nissan. GM also owns half of Daewoo Motors, Hyundai's major competitor in Korea. Daewoo makes Nissan cars for Japan and Pontiacs for America; soon it will be selling cars that were primarily designed by GM-Europe to Isuzu in Japan. GM has also teamed with Japan's No.1, Toyota, to produce cars under both companies' labels in America and Australia. (Moris 1989, pp53–54)[1]

This new economic world is also reshaping other dimensions of human society. Culture is itself being transformed, populations are becoming more homogeneous, ecological fragility is ever more evident, and education is being drawn ever more intensely into the orbit of politics as a result. The following descriptions treat each contextual dimension separately. However, it should be understood from the outset that the following five conditions are intensely intertwined and self-reinforcing.

A globally competitive economy and the 'human capital imperative'

Rapid communication, expanding information, and modern organizational arrangements are transforming national economies. Economies and nations are now global in their competitive outlook, internationally interdependent, insatiable in their quest for technological innovation, and crucially dependent upon the availability of human talent. Reliance upon a narrow intellectual elite appears increasingly outmoded.

Modern manufacturing and service industry techniques demand a labour force capable of adjusting to new technologies and making informed production decisions. *Crucial resources once came from the ground. Now they come from the mind.* Educated and highly skilled human intelligence increasingly is viewed as a nation's primary economic resource, and it is needed in large amounts.

Throughout history, technological innovations have redistributed power, enabled a tribe, a people, or a nation to vie for and gain dominance. Fire, ferrous metal, farming,and firearms are historic dicoveries which transformed nations and transferred power. Modern examples include internal combustion engines, interchangeable parts, electrical energy, and electronic components.

The list is longer, but the point is the same. Significant technological revolutions formerly were founded upon sporadic scientific discoveries. Increasingly, such shifts are crucially dependent upon systematic inventions. Nations now compete to create such inventions and be the first to rush into the market with them. They believe that elevating or sustaining their standard of living depends crucially upon being competitive in this regard. This is the 'human capital imperative'.

Modern economics, however, are not simply boosting or gently nudging an already initiated notion that education systems should enhance a nation's human capital resources. Rather, competitive economic forces rapidly and intensely are reshaping the forms of schooling across national boundaries. This globalization of education is occurring primarily because nations can no longer easily protect their domestic producers from international economic forces.

Failure to respond quickly to technological and organizational inventions can rapidly jeopardize a people's standard of living and a government's political future. Increasingly, even Eastern Bloc nations find that they are no longer immune to, or can wall themselves off from, the rapid ebb and flow of international trade, monetary, technological, and financial developments.

Traditional educational values and institutions are being reshaped by government officials who, in response to the above-described economic imperatives, believe that new educational policies are necessary for their nation to become or remain competitive.

Specific educational reform tactics may differ from nation to nation, depending upon historic development patterns, contemporary politics, current resource levels, and operating structures. For example, in national systems emphasizing an elitist schooling model – eg, England, and historic members of the British Commonwealth – the clear long-run education reform goal is to expand the numbers of individuals eligible for and interested in seeking higher levels of schooling. In egalitarian-oriented systems, such as the United States, education reform is intended to elevate achievement standards such that there are larger numbers of well-educated workers.

Regardless of the variety of national tactics, the western world objective is the same. The long-run goal for policy makers is to utilise educated intellect as a strategic means for a nation to gain or retain an economically competitive position in the global marketplace.

Cultural globalization

It is not only that economic endeavours are now international in nature, so also is our culture. Pervasive electronic communication, inexpensive worldwide transportation, and international marketing of consumer products are shrinking the world dramatically. It is not simply that radio and television enable worldwide viewers to be informed almost first-hand about distant events. Ironically sometimes, such as in disasters like the October 17, 1989 San Francisco Bay Area earthquake, remote viewers and listeners actually may be better informed than many of those immediately on the scene who are deprived of electrical power and other resources. Rather, some far more fundamental dynamic is at work. It is not only news which is spreading with the speed of the electromagnetic spectrum, but it is also ideas, opinions, fears, and aspirations.

Ideas about what exists elsewhere, what is possible, what is right and what is wrong, and about who does what to whom are no longer easily restricted to a geographic locality or narrowly defined region. A global community is being constructed electronically, and the availability of rapid and inexpensive transportation is reinforcing this condition for individuals. Despotic leaders could once wall off their followers from the 'dangerous' influence of outside ideas. This is increasingly impossible. Not only is there a flourishing international market for popular consumer goods but also citizens of one nation are ever more intensely informed regarding the beliefs, hopes, and conditions of citizens of all other nations. Their own ideas and dreams are forcefully shaped as a consequence.

'Globalization' has consequences for leaders. Not only must they now be attuned and responsive to the ebb and flow of forces immediately connected with their constituents, but they must also be ever attentive to events and views throughout the world. Queen Anne learned of the Duke of Marlborough's victory over Louis IV's armies at Blenheim ten days after the event August 13, 1704. A modern nation's leader would be informed almost immediately. The new 'global dynamic' means that local conditions can rapidly be transformed by distant circumstances. Teachers in Germany now know of job openings in Greece and Georgia and parents in Madrid have an interest in school site management reforms in Miami. Worldliness and breadth of understanding are no longer simply desirable qualities. Increasingly, they are imperatives of leadership.

Demographic diversification

Global economic forces, modern transportation, wars, technological developments, and ecological disasters are triggering ever larger population movements. City populations throughout the world are increasingly heterogeneous. Cultural, racial, and religious pluralizations increasingly characterise modern industrial nations.

What are the consequences, for leaders, of increasing demographic diversity? The first response is that extreme personal views regarding cultural supremacy and any desire for individual insularity and isolation are outmoded, dysfunctional, and, ultimately, doomed.

Educational leaders must come not simply to accept demographic diversity, but must enhance their professional knowledge to cope with and take advantage of it. Eventually, well informed prospective leaders will come to understand that such diversity represents a potential wellspring of creativity and strength for their organization in particular and for nations as a whole.

Additionally, educational leaders must face the fact that added diversity may, at least initially, render it more difficult to gain consensus among stakeholders regarding goals. Additional effort may have to be expended in gaining agreement on a mission and aggressively attempting to build a community of shared values.

Ecological interdependence

The fragility of the physical environment is ever more evident scientifically, ever more apparent internationally, and ever more compelling politically. Globalized economic forces are consuming awesome levels of raw materials and sophisticated production technologies are resulting in environmental reactions previously never seen. Ozone depletion, acid rain, soil erosion, radiation leakage, pesticide saturation, rain forest destruction, hazardous waste accumulation, overfishing and overgrazing, air and water pollution, greenhouse effects, and disappearing species are no longer problems limited to a few highly industrialized nations.

Environmental problems triggered by the actions of one nation can spill over national boundaries and rapidly become a danger to the citizens of many nations, perhaps the entire world. There is a paradox involved. The previously mentioned forces, global communication and internationalized economies, exacerbate environmental problems and, simultaneously, render the world's population better informed about them.

There is little choice regarding the eventual outcome. The need for environmental regulation will become a larger part of the political agenda of virtually all nations, at least the industrialized nations. The global effects of modern production and consumption will reinforce international communication and cooperation. Education systems will be expected to intensify their instruction regarding environmental issues.

Political intensification

Increased efforts by policy makers to utilise education systems to enhance national economic productivity, and the desire by environmentalists that schools assume a larger role in sensitising students to the fragility of the earth's ecology and the trade-offs between economic development and worldwide ecological balance, are drawing education ever more tightly into the orbit of political debate.

What once were primarily the domains of professional educators and academics increasingly are subsumed into the realm of policy makers and government officials. Central government specification of curricula goals, widespread use of standardized tests for measuring the 'productivity' of an educational system, added emphasis upon science and mathematics courses, the welding of individual higher educations institutions into larger state and national systems, efforts to link higher education more tightly to business and economic development are all trends developing throughout Western nations. These are actions generally imposed on educators by public officials. They exemplify the trend toward education policy increasingly being part of the larger political agenda.

What do these changes mean for leaders?

In the opening to the book *Character: America's Search for Leadership*, Gail Sheehy (1990) writes:

> We live in a global electronic marketplace where money now moves faster than the human mind, where terrorism can now hold a whole nation hostage to an aggrieved group whose name we can't even pronounce, where missiles are programmed to lift off in a matter of minutes after the command is given. In a world so often electrified by the suddenness and the swiftness of change, a great burden is placed on our leaders (p1).

What are the consequences of these trends for educational leaders? Should all education managers strive to become walking encyclopedias of world events, ecological and technological trends, and political power? Clearly not. However, there are profound implications for the preparation and performance of future educational leaders.

Educational leaders should come to understand that the only constant may be change. External conditions will continue to shift in a kaleidoscopic manner. Only those leaders who anticipate change and possess sufficiently broad intellectual categories to make sense of it can reasonably expect to guide their organizations successfully through the almost inevitable torrent of communication and whirlpool of political and economic forces which will characterise the twenty-first century.

No longer can an educational leader assume that his or her exclusive focus is upon what transpires inside, or even in the immediate community of, a school, a college, or an education system. Henceforth, what takes place inside is as likely to be a function of what occurs outside, and throughout the world, as it is likely to be a result of internal dynamics among teachers, students and others located immediately nearby. The pace of change, and the influence of the external world are the forces which are new in the lives of educational leaders.

It is these forces which require that educational executives adopt the mode of 'strategic thinking,' that they become Strategic leaders.

What is a 'Leader'?

This is a difficult question to answer. For a first effort, suffice it to declare what a leader is not or at least what only rarely constitutes an effective organizational executive. An institutional leader is only rarely a human being possessed of remarkable genetically' endowed capabilities.

Highly visible luminaries – historic figures such as Ghengis Khan, Joan of Arc, Mahatma Ghandi, Simon Bolivar, Winston Churchill, or Martin Luther King, media stars, high level political officials, military heroes, corporate titans, religious visionaries, military geniuses, scientific wizards, and athletic notables – often shape popular perceptions of leadership.

However, the overwhelming number of organizational leaders are almost never widely known and seldom become heroes, at least not in a historic or media sense. They are otherwise quite normal individuals to be found in every walk of life who consistently perform their leadership roles with relatively quiet effectiveness. They have existed across time and across cultures, and there are no boundaries to their race or gender.

Leaders exhibit a remarkably wide range of psychological and physical characteristics. To emulate Dr. Seuss: some leaders are big and some are small; some are short and some are tall; some have a deep booming voice, and others hardly speak at all.

Now, having commented on their diversity and specified what they are not, it is appropriate to offer a first definition of what legitimately constituted leaders are.[2]

A leader is an individual who accepts the authoritative expectations of others responsibly to guide the activities and enhance the performance of an organization. *In more simple terms, leadership is motivating members of an organization to engage in actions they otherwise might not do.*

Components of this definition will be explained and expanded upon later. Suffice it to mention here that a strategic leader is one who attempts to meet these expectations for an organization by incorporating into his or her day-to-day thinking and overall management posture the constellation of practices which comprise strategic planning.

A strategic leader is one who understands that not only is change always present, but also that the external environment of an educational institution will continually change and impose new challenges for education in the process. A strategic leader is one who realizes that his or her educational organization must constantly be appraising the external world, assessing its own purposes and performance in the light of those findings, and systematically altering its procedures accordingly.

Are leaders born or made?

This is an enduring but a quickly answered question. In those few instances in which leadership requires a towering intellect or a rare gift or artistic genius or physical prowess, the prerequisites for leadership may be genetically determined and thus conferred on only a few. However, in the overwhelming proportion of organizational settings, effective leaders need not posses exotic innate abilities. No one can be a leader in every setting. However, almost everyone can become a leader in a setting appropriate to his or her talents, training, and interests.

Few persons could successfully replace Joe Montana in leading a last minute Super Bowl touchdown drive or substitute for Magic Johnson during an NBA championship game. Conversely, it is not clear that either of these two unusually capable leaders could be a sustained success as a high school principal, teacher union official, school district superintendent, or college president. Leadership is situational.[3]

Effective leadership entails the successful chronological coincidence of a constellation of individual characteristics and an appropriate institutional context in which to exercise them. Assuming that an individual is situated in an organizational setting in which he or she has a reasonable chance of being accepted as a leader, then the amalgam of individual skills, abilities, and understandings necessary to be effective can be learned. Diligence, discipline, and devotion may be necessary to comprehend and polish these characteristics, but these are traits well within the range of most human beings to acquire.

Common leadership characteristics: VISIONS

Despite their many human differences, successful modern leaders repeatedly exhibit important common characteristics and engage in common activities. Leaders:

- Possess a vision of what the organization with which they are connected should be like.
- Know how to motivate and inspire those with whom they work.
- Understand the major operational levers which can be employed to control or change an organization's course.
- Are intensely sensitive to and continually reflect upon the inter-action of external environmental conditions and internal organizational dynamics.
- Understand the fundamental components of strategic thinking that can be used to guide or alter an organization.
- Comprehend the symbolic significance involved in representing their organization to the outside world.

These activities and characteristics are grouped below in seven categories and introduced in this section. These crucial components are labelled Leadership VISIONS in order to provide readers with an easily remembered mnemonic. Each is worthy of substantial expansion. Here however, is an introduction.

Vision

If you do not know where you want to go, almost any road will take you there. Organizations are little different on this dimension. They have an unceasing capacity to consume resources and engage in self-serving activities. For example, it is only the most bumbling and inefficient operation that cannot manage to issue its own employee paycheques on time.

However, to be productive, to serve clients effectively, to manu-facture products to a high standard and do so with economic efficiency, requires a sense of purpose. One of the most important components of effective leadership is to assist all parts of an organization in acquiring such a sense. This is what is meant by vision.

Sometimes this means that leaders are advocates for change. Their organizations do not match their vision, and they want to change them. On other occasions, in other settings, leadership may necessitate advocacy of the status quo. This could be the case if there is a fundamental threat, either from outside or inside, against which a defence must be mounted. In one instance, a leader's vision may be of change; in another it may be a plan for preventing the 'wrong' change. Regardless, a leader knows, or comes to devel-op knowledge about, what his or her organization should be like, and is willing to undertake the steps necessary to achieve this vision. It is this vision which directs a leader when co-operating with subordinates in establishing organizational goals.

Knowing what an organization should accomplish and how it

should proceed is important for a leader but the ways in which he or she expresses this vision and moves to incorporate it as a component of the organization's culture are equally important. Today's worldly complexity seldom permits the unilateral imposition of goals by an authoritative, dictatorial leader. Persuading followers to accept a vision of what an organization should be like, is as important a part of leadership as having a vision itself. That leads to the next topic, inspiration.

Inspiration

Inducing members to act in a manner consistent with an organization's purposes is a major dimension of leadership. One cannot be an organizational leader without knowing or learning how to motivate followers. This can be relatively easy if the organization is small, comprised of willing volunteers, the tasks involved are generally pleasurable, and the objectives can be quickly achieved. Serving as the captain of a neighbourhood sports team might meet this test.

Conversely, being faced with large numbers of reluctant or recalcitrant participants who are expected to engage in distasteful activities over a sustained period constitutes a major motivational challenge. This is why being a great military commander or leading personnel in high risk environmental or medical endeavours is no small task. Motivational techniques must be appropriately tailored to the circumstances involved. To do so, leaders can select one, or a combination, of tactics from among principal strategies such as the following:

1. One can inspire an organization by example, by *modelling* the behavior desired of followers, eg, being brave, analytical, statesmanlike, professionally or technically competent, or whatever is appropriate given organizational circumstances.
2. One can lead by *inspiration*, elevating a goal or a cause and exhorting followers to pursue it, frequently by suggesting that personal emotional or spiritual fulfilment will result for participants as a consequence.
3. *Power* is also a tactic in the arsenal of leadership. Followers sometimes can be motivated to act out of trepidation that they will be denied something they desire, or they will lose something desirable they already possess (like their freedom, their life, physical possessions, or their reputation), unless they comply with the leader's instructions and admonitions.
4. Lastly, motivation can consist of *co-optation*, inducing followers to believe that pursuit of the institution's objectives is consistent with their individual goals. Under this scenario, followers

are motivated by the belief that organizational achievement will lead to personal enhancement.

Symbolic representation

A leader represents an organization to the variety of external people to which it must relate, and a component of his or her effectiveness is tied to the extent to which those inside the organization believe the leader to be a successful representative symbol for them. The components of success on this dimension are tightly tied to the individual history, purposes, and contemporary circumstances of an organization. What constitutes successful external representation for a baseball team is different to that for a symphony orchestra and that in turn is different to that for a school or college.

Those responsible for the selection of leaders will almost assuredly give consideration to this component. In addition, however, a leader should be mindful of the expectation held in this sphere and should strive, at a minimum, to match them. A particularly effective leader understands that these expectations can change and that his or her performance on this symbolic dimension must change, in time, to conform. Constant attention to details is important. It is almost impossible to be too good at public speaking, or remembering the names of those with whom one must deal, or selecting appropriate attire.

Integrity

An effective leader possesses at least two kinds of integrity, personal and professional.

Personal integrity

Do strategic leaders have scruples? Is there any force to guide an organization other than political expediency? Can one be a leader and not be personally or professionally honest? What is the place of integrity for an organizational leader? Can one be an effective leader in an educational organization and unfairly or cynically manipulate people, deliberately withhold the truth, or denigrate others in order to achieve the 'vision'? When, if ever, do organizational ends justify any leadership means?

Much as one might wish to offer, or receive, black and white answers to questions such as the above, they do not easily exist. It is sometimes alleged that Franklin Delano Roosevelt had prior knowledge of the Japanese naval task force which mounted a devastating December 7, 1940 'surprise' attack on U.S. military forces at Pearl Harbor. However, according to this theory, the President deliberately engaged in widespread deceit, permitted the attack to occur relatively unopposed, and tolerated the death and destruction in order to motivate the American people to engage in a war which to that point was widely unpopular and viewed as unnecessary.

The facts are nowhere conclusive regarding this conspiracy of silence. However, assuming for purposes of discussion that the charges of duplicity are accurate, was the President justified? Was the loss of thousands of lives at Pearl Harbor acceptable in order to motivate a people to oppose a force which could have altered the course of democracy for decades or centuries to come? Did the desired end justify the deployment of such disastrous means?

Questions such as these can and should provoke endless debate. Suffice it here to state that leadership of educational organizations generally poses fewer, and simpler, moral dilemmas. However, education is itself a moral undertaking. It has as its purposes the propagation of society and its ideals, and the fulfilment of the individual. Consequently, educational leaders frequently operate under an umbrella of moral legitimacy far broader and more strict than executives in other endeavours.

A principal, teacher activist, union leader, dean, college president, or government official may quickly lose credibility and legitimacy among followers if he or she as a leader is exposed as knowingly engaging in deceit. In short, the effectiveness of an education leader generally requires adherence to a high standard of ethical behavior. Strategic leaders should be no exception.

Professional integrity
Effective educational leaders know about education. They know at least two things. First, they are knowledgeable about instruction and the teaching side of schooling. They are informed about instructional and learning theories. They understand the components of curriculum construction and the fundamental importance of subject matter integrity.

Additionally, effective educational leaders are informed regarding the institution of education. They know educational history and philosophy, the economics of education, and education law. They are sufficiently informed regarding contemporary issues as to be able to elevate the quality of discourse among both professional colleagues and lay clients of their institutions.

Professional integrity not only informs the day-to-day activities and decisions of effective educational leaders, it also enhances their legitimacy among followers. Repeatedly proposals are offered for principals and superintendents to be recruited from among the ranks of business or military executives (Guthrie 1988, p36). The argument is that leadership is generic and those individuals who have proved themselves successful in other settings could just as readily succeed in leading educational institutions. On occasion this is true. Generally, however, the transfer of leadership across major institutional boundaries fails.

The prime problem to be overcome for the prospective transfer leader is professional integrity. The successful leader from another setting is usually insufficiently informed regarding instruction and the institution of education to earn credibility in the eyes of 'followers'. As stated at the beginning of this essay, large components of leadership are situational and may not transfer easily across institutional and organizational boundaries.

Organizational sophistication

Leaders must know of and learn how to use the fundamental levers that can be employed to guide or alter the course of an organization. This is a substantial challenge with schools and colleges. One imminent organizational theorist characterized the tenuous leadership linkages which exist between various levels of an education organization's chain of command as 'loosely coupled'.[4] These are not the only weaknesses, however.

It frequently is difficult for educational organizations to agree upon and specify their mission or goals. Thus, it can be difficult for a leader to know what to do, not to mention finding ways in which to do it. Schools and colleges often are collegial in nature, and heavy-handed; top down leadership may be strongly resisted. Incentive systems in educational organizations historically have been uniform and unequal treatment of employees by a leader can be strongly discouraged. Scientifically based instruction is in its infancy, and the absence of an empirically validated full educational technology makes it difficult for a leader to specify follower behaviour with precision.

The list of impediments to leadership could continue, but the point would be the same. Educational organizations are particularly difficult to command.

Regardless of such obstacles, there are effective *operational strategies* by which leaders can successfully shape the course of an educational organization. There are five of these. They are, not necessarily in order of their significance, goal setting, personnel selection and training, incentive and reward systems, resource allocation (budgeting), and evaluation and information.

Goal setting

It is increasingly difficult for a leader of any persuasion or in any circumstance to establish organizational goals singlehandedly. The complexity and interdependence of today's world renders it unlikely that followers will blindly accede to leaders. Consequently, a leader must ensure that his or her vision is incorporated in or transformed into an organization's goals. However, he or she must simultaneously ensure that followers believe in those goals. The best way to gain such an assurance is to invite widespread participation in shaping and setting the goals.

What is so important about goals anyway? The process of arriving at agreement about what an organization will attempt to accomplish has value. It bonds employees together, can cement management and workers and holds the prospect of creating a team. Greater productive energy can result.

Second, aside from the advantages of the team building process, establishing goals provides performance targets. These can be both organizational and personal in nature. Individuals ought to know, as a consequence of goal setting, what they are expected to contribute to the organization's success. Both they and the overall team have something for which to strive and if goals are properly constructed, should have objective indicators of the degree to which they have succeeded. In essence, goal setting not only establishes where an organization and its members intend to go, but assists, in knowing how to measure progress in getting there.

Personnel selection

When it comes to allocating time, a leader can spend few more productive hours than those devoted to the selection of personnel. Careful attention to the initial recruitment, employment, and induction of staff can contribute enormously to the success of an organization.

By itself, this mechanism is likely to be insufficient. It is not enough to recruit and employ able teachers and other individuals. Additionally, the expectations for their performance, resulting from the above-described goal setting, must be made clear and reinforced. They must consistently be evaluated, in light of these expectations, and when they reasonably need help, it should be forthcoming. Nevertheless, even *given* such complexities, the initial choice of people is a crucial lever for shaping an institution.

Performance incentives

Public schools and some colleges are characterised by a particularly pernicious and peverse personnel incentive system. At its most cynical view, the system rewards employees for putting distance between themselves and pupils. The conventional professional education career path is to become a classroom teacher and subsequently be promoted to positions such as counsellors or curricular specialists, into administration as principals, central office managers, and then into leadership positions such as superintendents and state officials. Few endeavours other than schools so systematically reward employees for becoming remote from the institution's main function, instruction, in the instance of schools.

An education leader must understand the potential power that praise, promotion, and punishment can have upon employees, and consciously shape incentive systems so as to reward employees for pursuing the organization's purposes. As crucial as management is to the success of an institution, instruction is what schools and colleges are expected to accomplish by society. An educational organization's reward structure should reflect this expectation and, thus, be established primarily to induce and reinforce good teaching.[5]

Becoming an administrator, or having an opportunity to assume assignments other than as a classroom instructor, should not be seen as a reward for being a good teacher. As simple and self-evident as it may seem, teaching should be celebrated in schools, and all other activities should be subordinate in importance. Becoming and being an effective administrator should be regarded as important in its own right. It should not be viewed as a reward for having been a good teacher. An organization's incentive and reward system should make this principle indelibly clear.

Resource allocation
Budgeting can be used as an incentive system for organizational subunits. Institutions can shape the performance of individuals through rewards such as pay, praise, promotion, personal fulfillment, and punishment. The performance of organizational subunits within an institution can be influenced through resource allocation decisions.

This can occur through two avenues. The first is by providing a group of employees, eg a particular school or an operational subunit such as a music department, with an increment in resources. In short, increase the budget, even if only a little in terms of purchasing power. This will make the point to employees their services are valued and they are being given more resources as a consequences.

A second avenue, even if overall resource levels remain the same, is to provide a subunit with added decision discretion. In effect, the message becomes, 'you are important and your judgement is valued'. Thus, you can have expanded discretion regarding the manner in which you utilize resources allocated for your organizational function.

Evaluation

A fifth operational lever is evaluation and information. An employee, or operational unit within an organization, which is unevaluated is out of control. Employees deserve feedback on their performance, and clients deserve knowledge regarding an entire organization's performance. Evaluation is the mechanism through which such information can be obtained.

Knowing that appraisal is going to occur systematically, and be undertaken in an equitable and accurate manner, will do much to shape the performance of employees. This is a particularly effective operational lever when employees are well informed about the objectives they are expected to accomplish and against which their performance will be evaluated. It is an even more effective operational lever when employees are engaged in establishing the objectives against which their performance will be assessed.

Nurturing

Leadership is rational, analytical, and action orientated. However, it also has an emotional facet. Effective leaders care. They want their organizations and their employees to succeed. They not only invest their time and their ideas, they invest themselves. They invest themselves in terms of commitment to the organization's goals, compassion for clients, concern for employees, and contempt for short-sighted, overly self-serving, or irrationally selfish activities which distract from the organization's effectiveness.

Strategic orientation

A strategically alert executive realizes that the need for leading never ceases. The external environment and internal dynamics of organizations are constantly in flux.

Modern organizations, particularly public sector agencies, have become deeply entwined with the larger social environment in which they operate. Consequently, an effective leader continually must scan the horizon to sense the build-up of forces which might have an effect on his or her organization.

In part this means remaining in touch with a broad spectrum of public and private agencies and actors which exert direct influence over an organization. In addition, however, it necessitates understanding broad social, demographic, economic, and political trends which, while perhaps appearing glacial, may have an equally inexorable effect. Leaders must continually be alert, and must constantly be considering new data and generating possible organization adjustments.

Thinking downstream, appraising likely external changes, regularly assessing the operating progress and functioning of an organization, aligning resources with purposes, and undertaking necessary mid-course corrections, are the essential components of strategic leadership. Each cycle of organizational events represents a window of opportunity for a leader to undertake whatever assessment or operational changes may be necessary.

An effective modern leader understands and knows how to take advantage of the rhythmic dynamics of organizational life. For example, scheduled governing board meetings, budget development, legislative sessions, academic years, prescribed personnel evaluations, state or national testing programs, contract expirations, proposal due dates, reporting deadlines, and a vast spectrum of scheduled events establish a rhythm within and for an organization. These cycles, if fully integrated into the decision structure of an organization, can serve as a framework around which to engage in strategic leadership, and provide opportunities for tactical organization intervention.

Strategic thinking applied to educational leadership

Successful leaders in the future will be distinguished by the degree to which they understand that a static world no longer exists. Organizations must comprehend and cope with the continual changes which occur in their external environment, and successful leaders will be those who are able to make sense of change and interpret it meaningfully for their organizations.

Strategic leaders engage in a constant appraisal of the external environment, and unceasingly ask, 'What does this changing condition mean for my organization?' They understand that external changes eventually permeate the internal world of organizations and promote or provoke dislocations and discontinuities which, if not recognized and rationalized, will impede the effectiveness of an organization and sooner or later render it dysfunctional.

The purpose of strategic leadership is not organizational change. Change is everywhere, and, of their own accord, organizations will change. The question is, 'Will change be purposeful, productive, consistent with the organization's objective, and to the benefit of its clients?'

Strategic leadership is characterized by a self conscious, self-initiated, self-critical, continuous and interactive cycle of appraisal and action. It involves strategic planning, but encompasses much more. Strategic planning is frequently an activity in which an organization episodically engages or arranges to have performed for it by a team of outside planning experts. Strategic leadership is built upon strategic planning and incorporates these activities into the regular rhythm of organizational life.

Moreover, a strategic organization eventually develops a planning and analytic capability internally, and for planning purposes is relatively independent of outsiders. A successful strategic organization evolves such that eventually it does not depend exclusively upon strategic *leadership*. Rather, strategic *thinking* begins to permeate the entire institution. Leaders, managers, and most of all employees come to think and act continuously in terms of appraisal, analysis, and action.

Lastly, strategic leaders come to adopt a different concept of time. They think downstream. This is not to neglect the here and now for to do so is to imperil what went before. However, immediacy is insufficient. A strategic leader must constantly be anticipating new events and their consequences. Also, quick successes are few. Generally, accomplishing an organization's goals must be viewed as a long-term undertaking. Organizational momentum will seldom permit sharp departures from an established course. However, by concentrating on an eventual goal it is possible to make consistent short-term, micro course corrections which, in time, will achieve desired objectives.

Appraisal

Strategic leadership involves a set of cyclical activities. Like all cycles, they are incomplete and eventually collapse if one phase is continually omitted or ineffective. Thus, beginning a description at this point is not meant to convey a message that appraisal is the primary or most important component of the cycle. Rather, it simply is necessary to begin somewhere and this component is a convenient beginning. Keep in mind, however, that organizations exist to accomplish purposes and doing so, ultimately, depends upon action. Thus, if one could begin with a discussion of the action phase of the cycle, eventually the question would have to be posed as to whether or not it was the right action. That is the question which most distinguishes a strategic organization from one which is moribund.

To appraise is to measure and assign a value. Strategic leadership necessitates constant measurement and evaluation of conditions both external and internal to an organization. The dimensions which should be appraised are illustrated below. Keep in mind, however, that appraisal involves more than simply applying an empirical yardstick to these conditions. It also entails placing a value upon them, rendering a judgement regarding their significance, placing them in an evaluative context, so that their significance for the organization can be determined. If measurement were all that was necessary, then the task could be performed by technicians alone. However, it is the combination of measurement and wisdom which characterizes an effective strategic leader.

The external and internal dimensions which should systematically be appraised will vary depending upon the nature of the organization. Private sector firms may be oriented more toward market conditions and public sector organizations more toward politics. Higher education may be oriented more toward state and federal governments, and public schools more toward local government. Private schools may concentrate more on philanthropy and public schools more on tax rates. One of the important responsibilities of a strategic executive is to determine and periodically review the dimensions to be appraised. However, the following list will illustrate the concepts involved.

External dimensions

Demographics
An educational organization should regularly appraise relevant demographic conditions. What are the sizes of forthcoming age cohorts? What is the ethnic, racial, and gender composition of school or college age groups? These data comprise a crucial base from which to extrapolate many other useful data such as facilities needs, financial projections, and personnel needs.

Economics
What trends are developing in an educational organization's immediate locality, region, or state? This is particularly important for vocational training institutions. However, it is also of concern for secondary schools, community colleges, and post-secondary institutions which orientate themselves toward a region. Attention should be paid to the likely effects of these trends upon the availability of future revenues and the likely consequences of the trends for employment of the institution's graduates.

Public opinion
Attention should be given to two kinds of public opinion. One is the

attitude of the general public about education. An effort should be made to develop precursors of public views; to grasp possible change in citizen outlook which might shape the expectations they hold for educational institutions. A second dimension of public opinion consists of the views of an institution's more immediate clients, pupils, parents, employees, public officials, etc, regarding the effectiveness of the organization.

Socio-political dynamics

What forces are in operation in the larger society which are likely to influence the organization? Are there technological innovations which may alter employment, leisure, or family conditions? Are demography and economics combining to shift political priorities? Are international events changing such as to influence domestic political outlooks regarding education?

Internal conditions

Finances

Projections of an organization's likely revenues and expenditures, usually employing a five year rolling horizon, should be undertaken annually. When constructed systematically and repeatedly, these projections can become sufficiently honed to provide organizational decision makers with advance knowledge of likely opportunities for growth and improvement or of the possibility of retrenchment.

Employee morale

What employees think and feel is crucial to the successful operation of an organization, and a variety of methods should be used to appraise this dimension. Leaders and managers should always be sensitive to what is developing around them, among those employees closest to them. By itself, however, such first hand opinion is insufficient. Systematic polling, under conditions which pose no threat to respondents, should also take place. Also, behaviours such as grievances filed, work stoppages, absenteeism, and turnover rates should all be recorded as possible indicators of employee morale and opinion.

Outcome measurement

An educational organization should systematically accumulate outcome data. These should include but not be limited to, student test scores, persistence or dropout rates, graduation levels, degree completions, and downstream performance (at the next level of schooling or employment).

Process measures
What are the patterns of students course enrollments; do students pursue curricular or vocational objectives by a pattern of gender, race, or socioeconomic levels; what are the time to completion rates of students and do they form patterns, what times of day or week are courses offered, what are the rates of library usage, what are tardiness and absenteeism levels, and what are participation rates in extracurricular activities?

Operational costs
What are the cost profiles of various programmes and organizational subunits? How do these profiles compare with historic trends and with the same operations in comparable institutions? For example, what are the relationships of administrative to instructional costs? Are the cumulative costs of substitute teachers climbing or decreasing over time? What about utility costs?

Organizational structure
Are the subcomponents within an organization arranged in a manner which facilitates communication, enhances accountability, and reduces unnecessary duplication? Are reporting lines clear, spans of control reasonable, and client convenience maximized?

Combining appraisal and action

Information regarding external and internal conditions should constantly be collected, compiled, and synthesized in a strategic organization. However, the uses to which such data are put are crucial. An organization easily can suffer from informational paralysis, collecting more data than can be used and incurring excessive costs as a consequence. Information for its own sake has little value, and can become dysfunctional. Thus, it is critical that a strategic executive knows the purposes for which data are collected and ensures that those purposes are met. If an information item cannot be used, then the data should not be collected.

One of the important reasons for constantly measuring is to assess the appropriateness of an organization's objectives. This is a complex set of deliberations which typically involves collaboration with public representatives and policy setting bodies. The point is to determine whether or not changes in the external or internal environments, or the interactions between the two, have implications for the organization's mission and goals and the manner in which the organization pursues its mission.

Has the regional economy changed sufficiently that the district's curriculum should be altered? Do new state-issued curriculum guidelines necessitate new testing or textbook policies? Are faculty members reaching an age profile which necessitates a major recruitment programme for new personnel? Are categorical programmes interfering with the core functions of the schooling process?

These and dozens of similar questions should regularly be posed by educational policy makers and strategic executives. The answers to such questions may suggest that the status quo continues to be appropriate. Nevertheless, the organization is the better for having asked and answered the question. The answers either dictate a change in mission or operation, or they reaffirm and reinforce what currently is being done. In either instance, at the conclusion of appraisal, the organization is more confident of its purpose than was previously the case.

Action

Strategic leadership is not all evaluation and planning. It is every bit as important to know 'what is right to do' as it is 'to know how to do it right'. A leader's principal responsibility is to determine the right thing to do and to motivate organizational members to achieve the goal. Hence the stress here upon vision, appraisal, analysis, and assessment. However, it should be remembered that organizations exist to accomplish goals, not simply to set them. Action is thus the flywheel which maintains an organization's forward momentum. A strategic leader is obligated to ensure that action is consistent with organizational goals and is as continually finely tuned as appropriate analyses and feedback can make it.

Preparing strategic leaders

What are the implications for leadership preparation? What does strategic leadership entail that requires anything different from previous admonitions regarding leader preparation? What is or will be sufficiently different in today's and tomorrow's worlds to make one think that leaders should be prepared differently as a consequence? The simple answer is a great deal.

An effective modern executive must possess the ability constantly to (1) assess a changing external environment, (2) interpret these changes and deduce their consequences for the organization, (3) cooperate with others in the determination of appropriate new directions. (4) motivate colleagues and employees in the pursuit of organizational goals, and (5) appraise the organization's progress in meeting objectives. This constellation of executive skills constitutes strategic leadership.

These are not abilities that can simply be willed to exist within individuals or that can be assumed to evolve in the normal flow of a professional career. Their acquisition must be conscious and planned. At least the following fields of knowledge are necessary in constructing a comprehensive foundation for effective executive action:

Fundamental knowledge

There is no substitute for this foundation component. Individuals devoid of a broad understanding of literature, history, political theory, physical and life sciences, economics, behavioral and social science, and the arts are handicapped in their ability to make sense of what is transpiring about them. Only a comprehension of the world's rich historical and cultural tapestry can provide a backdrop against which to make informed judgements. An effective liberal education enables a strategic executive to impart meaning to rapidly evolving events and conditions that might otherwise appear random and chaotic. A liberal education provides perspective, offers informative analogies, assists in assigning, priorities, shapes values, and enhances communication.[6]

Professional knowledge

Strategic leaders need to comprehend a body of professional knowledge for at least two reasons. First, it will inform their executive decisions and actions. Second, it will enhance their legitimacy and elevate their standing with those they lead and those who are served by their institutions. This 'professional' component has three social and behavioral science dimensions. First is an understanding of the psychological, sociological, and anthropological foundations of education. Cultural patterns, social stratification and mobility, principles of human development, and racial dynamics are illustrative of critical understandings for a strategic leader. Also, an appropriate knowledge of learning theory and instructional practice is crucial. Finally, an understanding of fundamental components of school and college curricula matters is necessary as a professional cornerstone.

Institutional knowledge

Strategic leaders are obligated to influence the direction of their institutions. Knowing where you are, and where you have been, facilitates knowing where to go. Hence the need to be fully informed regarding institutional matters such as the history of education, organizational sociology, educational law, governance, and finance.

Decision knowledge

Gathering and analyzing information about an institution's external environment and its internal performance are also critical functions for a strategic leader. Conducting these activities successfully requires an understanding of important information gathering and analytic techniques stemming from economics, statistics, survey research, testing, and accounting. Included here are knowledge on technical dimensions such as the logic of inquiry, experimental and quasi-experimental design, projection techniques, measures of central tendency and dispersion, probability theory, production functions, ratio studies, quantitative and qualitative evaluation, opinion polling, standardized testing, and psychological measurement.

There exists more than one means for acquiring the above-described knowledge base. The details of interpretation can differ from nation to nation and upon the operating circumstances in specific jurisdictions and institutions. Also, the mix of preparation experiences, eg, time allocated to classroom instruction, supervised practice, and apprenticeship, is not appropriate for debate here. Suffice it to say that while there is little about strategic leadership that restricts its practice to super heroes, there is also little about it of which one is intuitively capable of performing. Thus, regardless of the specific sequence and arrangement of experience, professional preparation of the most rigorous level will be necessary in order for education to derive full advantage of the endeavour's prospective potential.

Experiential knowledge

The preparation of strategic leaders also requires an opportunity for examining experience. A conventional internship will seldom suffice. Careful selection of an appropriate mentor and model is a good beginning. However, thereafter, training institutions must ensure than leaders-in-training are systematically encouraged to reflect upon the practices they see around them and speculate regarding the means by which they could be improved. Also, leadership preparation is enhanced by providing apprentices with multiple experiences, in private, public, and non-profit making organizations.

Conclusion

The foregoing components of preparation for educational executives differ little from what is needed for strategic leaders more generally, regardless of the organizational setting in which they are engaged. Further, it is not clear that existing programmes and institutions for training educational executives are capable of the radical adjustments necessitated by the above-described preparation proposals. Thus, it may well be that the most appropriate settings for the preparation of strategic leaders are in public policy programmes or business schools. Here the core components of preparation can be conveyed and a segment of training can be reserved for those dimensions unique to education, ie, professional and institutional knowledge.

Notes

[1] If he had been writing one month later, the author could have mentioned that Ford planned to purchase England's number one luxury car producer, Jaguar.

[2] Leadership has long been a topic for political theorists, social scientists, business advisors, worldly observers, philosophers, and others. The extent of historic and contemporary concern probably ranks leadership with politics, money, love, warfare, religion, and sex as a popular topic. For major reviews regarding scholarly, philosophical, and practical dimensions of leadership see Burns (1978), Edinger (1964), Friedrich (1961), Gibb (1969), Hare (1957), Janda (1960), McFarland (1969) and Selznick (1957).

[3] Social science studies of leadership have at times emphasized: individual traits of lenders, eg, physical characteristics and personality: and the interactions of leaders and followers, eg, group dynamics and the complexities of situational differences. These research findings and postulates are described and synthesized by Aaron Wildavsky (1988).

[4] For added explanations of the concept of 'loose coupling' see Karl Weick (1982, pp673–5).

[5] Universities are also expected to generate new knowledge, conduct research. The more prestigious the university, the less attention is probably paid to instruction.

[6] This fundamental knowledge is also intended to encompass fundamental skills such as the ability to speak, write and count in a fluid and correct manner.

References

Burns, J 1978 *Leadership*, New York: Harper and Row.
Edinger, L 1964 'Political science and political biography 1' in *The Journal of Politics*, 26, May.
Friedrich, C 1961 'Political leadership and the problem of charismatic power' in *The Journal of Politics*, 24, February.
Gibb, C 1969 'Leadership' in Lindzey, G and Aronson, A (eds) *Handbook of Social Psychology*, Mass: Addison-Wesley.
Guthrie, J 1988 'Should principals be required to have been teachers?' in *Education Week*, 8, October 9th.
Hare, P 1957 'Situational differences in leader behaviour' in *Journal of Abnormal and Social Psychology*, 55, July.
Janda, K 1960 'Towards the explicational of the concept of leadership in terms of the concept of power' in *Human Relations*, 13, November.
McFarland, A 1969 *Power and Leadership in Pluralist Systems*, Stanford: Stanford University Press.
Morris C, 1989 'The coming global boom' in *Atlantic*, 264 (4), October.
Selsnick, P 1957 *Leadership in Administration*, New York: Harper and Bros.
Sheehy, G 1990 *Character: America's Search for Leadership*, New York: Bantam Books.
Weick, K 1982 'Administering education in loosely coupled schools' in *Phi Delta Kappan*, 63 (10), June.
Wildavsky, A 1988 'A cultural theory of leadership' [unpublished paper].

3.3 Educational Leadership for Quality Teaching and Learning

Bill Mulford, Darrell Fisher and Neville Grady

The importance of educational leadership

Murphy and Hallinger (1987) talk about three conditions unfolding which demonstrate that educational leaders can exert considerable influence over the quality of education that occurs in their schools. First, there is a growing understanding that an earlier mind-set of the leader as the beleagured professional who could exercise little influence over his or her school and who was only connected distantly to important educational processes and outcomes, does not have to be so.

Second, there is a suggestion that the dark cloud that has hung over education in the recent past is dispersing gradually. Education is once again at the forefront of the public agenda with schools emerging as a major focus of attention.

A recent paper by Hughes (1988) 'Educational Leadership for Curriculum Development', highlights this latter focus in pointing out the increased acceleration in the patterns of change influencing the curriculum, patterns that reflect continued and deep contention as to desirable curriculum content and emphasis. He points to a new attitude to authority that does not just accept without question, legal, statutory or hierarchical decisions. There is a demand for wider participation in decisions, with a growing emphasis on the instrumental, technical, technological, and accountable. Hughes sees such factors reflected in the recent history of curriculum development where there is pressure to shift from the fully school-based model towards a common or core curriculum.

Caldwell (1988) in a paper entiled 'Educational Leadership for Self-Managing Schools, continues and refines Hughes' analysis. He emphasises the movement of schools to become self-managing within a framework of policies and priorities determined centrally. Concern for the economic well-being of our nation – the feeling that education should make a contribution to the general standard of living – has resulted in this move to centralization. Broad goals and expectations are set, outcomes are specified and frameworks for accountability are established by the centre. The recent book edited by Chapman (1990) reinforces this view.

Third, literature from areas such as school change, school improvement, staff development, the administrator as instructional leader, and school effectiveness, points to the sense of importance of the educational leader for improvement in organizational conditions and processes and, notably, pupil outcomes.

Hughes (1988) emphasises throughout his paper the importance for educational leaders to possess an ability to listen, assess and respond. These are skills that require a knowledge of, and a willingness to select from competing societal demands, the worthwhile goals – goals which give meaning and purpose to life. Hughes also stresses the importance of skills in co-operation, co-ordination, involvement, and mediation for those involved intimately in carrying out a school's activities. Caldwell's (1988) position is consistent in identifying the following four areas of knowledge and skill required in developing a capacity for self-management:

- capacity to work within national and state frameworks and priorities, and with teachers, students and members of the community in the design and delivery of a curriculum to meet the needs of every student;
- capacity to gain a commitment to a shared vision of excellence;
- knowledge about a wide range of approaches to learning and teaching and to the creation of appropriate environments for learning and teaching; and
- ability to design and implement an ongoing, collegial, cyclical approach to goal-setting, policy-making, planning, budgeting, implementing and evaluating.

A growing understanding of educational leadership, education's return to centre-stage and literature on effective leadership and schools all point in the one clear direction – to the importance of educational leadership for quality teaching and learning.

The response from educational leaders

Since educational leadership is, after all, meant to enhance teaching and learning, it may be somewhat surprising to find that leadership preparation programs have, in the main, tended not to focus on curriculum and instruction. This situation grows even more difficult to believe when research at every level of educational administration uncovers consistently leaders who believe they *should* devote more time to instructional issues (Murphy and Hallinger 1987).

Yet the instructional leadership role is one that most educational leaders perform neither well nor often. Murphy and Hallinger (1987, p249) argue that, '. . . in most . . . schools, curriculum and instruction are managed by default'.

Literature based on research which attempts to answer the question 'What do principals do in schools?' by actually having observers following them around and reporting on their every behaviour, reinforces this image. The principal's world is one consisting of variety, brevity, fragmentation, uncertainty, ambiguity, superficiality, control of action by others, a hectic pace, preference for the verbal, and a lack of overt feedback on, or appreciation of, their actions.

By way of illustration, these studies found that:

- the average duration of each principal's activity is about seven minutes with two-thirds of the activities being from one to five minutes;
- just over one-fifth of activities are interrupted with many (25 per cent) never being resumed;
- unscheduled meetings occupy almost one-half of the principal's time, with scheduled meetings (20 per cent), desk work (23 per cent) and 'tours' (5 per cent) taking up most of the rest; and
- three-quarters of time during the school day is spent in contacts with people, with half of these contacts being on a one-to-one basis. (Mulford 1986)

Sergiovanni (1982, p330) would not be surprised by this emphasis on what he calls the 'tactical' (day-by-day, short-term, highly focused actions or means serving a larger purpose), as opposed to the 'strategic' (enlisting and employing support for certain policies and purposes and for devising plans towards goals). The emphasis on tactical requirements of leadership, he maintains, reflects the broader management culture of western society. 'Such values as efficiency, specificity, rationality, measurability, and objectivity combined with beliefs that good management is tough-minded are part of this culture.' Attention can also be given to the tactical requirements, 'because they are easy to teach and learn, specific, easily measured, can be readily packaged for workshops, and are otherwise accessible'. Unfortunately, the essence of education – teaching and learning – would appear to have been displaced in the eyes of many educational leaders. Has it been displaced because improvement of interpersonal relationships, curriculum and instruction, calls for delayed gratification with the signs of progress being not detected easily? Has the tangible and immediate replaced the more nebulous, long-term but obviously more essential?

As our understanding of the correlations between active instructional management and student learning has grown, so must pressure to change training content to provide educational leaders with the knowledge and skills to manage curriculum and instruction successfully in their schools.

A more even balance

Two articles and a book are illustrative of attempts to provide a more even balance among the three inter-related emphases – instruction, curriculum and administration – in educational leader development.

Rogus (1988) examines the literature in the areas of school improvement, teacher effectiveness, and the nature of leadership. He explicates selected observations and findings from this literature that were helpful in reviewing and developing what he calls 'teacher-leader' programmes. He uses five categories of leader behaviour – self-deployment, empowerment, vision, communicating the vision, positioning. Bennis and Nanus (1985) provide the focal point and assist in generating the process component of programme outcome statements. School improvement and teacher effectiveness categories then serve to identify the content focus of programme outcome statements. Rogus also provides an expanded set of sample teacher-leader programme outcomes under each leader behaviour category. Two examples are:

- self-deployment with a focus on, eg an inquiry orientation toward teaching, and demonstrated through an understanding of alternative philosophical positions as they relate to teaching;
- positioning with a focus on, eg patience and persistence in carrying out an action project with selected staff, and demonstrating a high level of trust among peers and a set of ethical norms that serves as a model of professional behaviour.

Blum et al (1987) report on a programme designed to help principals apply research on leadership and school effectiveness. Based on a synthesis of research on practices of effective principals and incorporating research findings on programme implementation, change and adult learning, the 'Leadership for Excellence' programme builds knowledge and skills through a year-long series of workshops in the five content strands of vision building, school climate and culture, curriculum implementation, improving instruction and monitoring school performance.

In a year-long series of seminars and workshops, principals select one of the five content strands to pursue. First, participants in all strands meet in a cross-strand seminar for training in a 'Peer-Assisted Leadership' (PAL) process. Principals are assigned to pairs with the charge that each will assist his or her partner to improve leadership skills. Partners 'shadow' each other, gathering data, then conduct 'reflective interviews' with each other. Strand and cross-strand seminars, workshops and applications then continue over the year.

The final example of literature which aims to provide a more even balance among the three inter-related emphases in educational leader development is a book by Duke (1987). The book is based on the belief that one of the most important commitments of an educational leader is the continuous improvement in instruction. He also argues that since knowledge and needs of students are always changing, questions related to what should be taught, how it should be taught and how to determine that students have learned what has been taught, must be asked on a *continuing* basis.

The heart of Duke's book is a model of instructional leadership involving seven key functions (listed in the bottom half of Figure 3.3.1). Two of the key functions, co-ordination and trouble-shooting, cut across all of the other five, that is, teacher supervision and development, teacher evaluation, instructional management and support, resource management and quality control.

Duke's vision of instructional leadership which derives in part from recent research on school effectiveness, is tied directly to a vision of teaching excellence. He stresses that the relationship between instructional leadership and teaching excellence (symbolised by the central line with two arrows) is characterised by continuing inter-action; each influences the other constantly, and, clearly, teachers and senior personnel both have important functions to perform.

The argument so far

To reiterate the argument so far: A growing understanding of educational leadership, education's return to centre-stage and literature

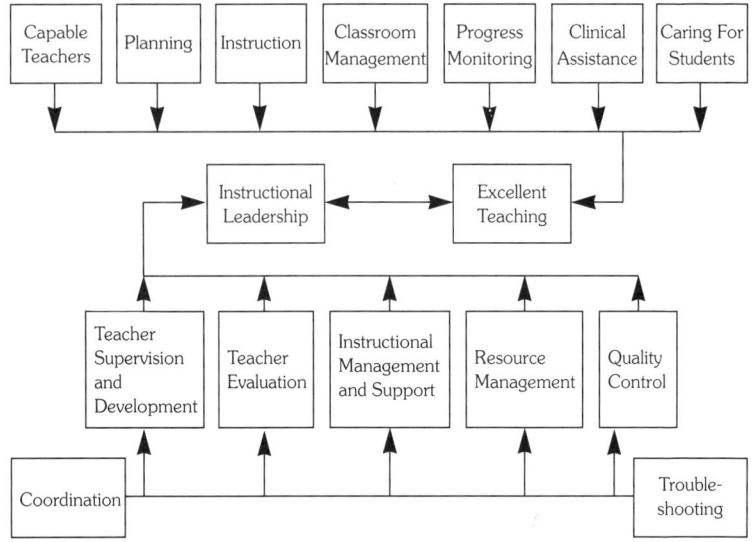

Figure 3.3.1 – a model of instructional leadership
Source: Duke (1987, p35)

on effective leadership and schools all point in the one clear direction – to the importance of educational leadership for quality teaching and learning. Yet both preparation programmes and the actual behaviour of educational leaders in their schools suggest a neglect of this essential part of education. Some recent literature has attempted to redress this situation with both curriculum and instruction featuring equally alongside administrative matters of both the 'tactical' and 'strategic' types in models of, and programs for, effective educational leadership.

Priorities for action

We now *know* not only that something needs to be done but also what this something *should be*. However it is vastly easier to know something than to achieve it. Without specific attention to making our knowledge operational, such advances in our understanding of educational leadership are not likely to move beyond the realm of rhetoric.

Most recommendations for educational reform continue to focus on what could be called the *hardware* of educational excellence:

programmes, standards and requirements. The recommendations seem to propose reform by addition. We would argue that significant change in education first requires building the bridges and roads over which educational reforms can travel. The *software* of educational excellence, called 'school improvement', builds those roads and bridges by seeking to create local capacities, or processes, for implementing and managing change.

The crux of our argument is that for better outcomes in schools there is a need to give greater emphasis to implementation aspects, and that the most important aspect of effective implementation is obtaining co-operation among teachers (and between teachers and the community). We must be clear that planning and developing improvement efforts is not the same as implementing them. Similarly, we must realise that group effectiveness is not just a matter of pushing people in at the deep end of the currently popular and profusely propounded pool of participation. *We must learn how to lose time in order to gain time.*

Awareness of, and development of skills in, group and organizational processes must be a *first* step in any effective change. Instead of others trying to insert something into a school's culture, educational leaders should be trying first to help that culture develop an awareness of, and a responsiveness to, itself.

In other words, we are arguing strongly that the way forward towards making things happen is to focus first on developing group and organizational processes.

Leithwood and Fullan (1984, p11) help reinforce this position (the emphasis is ours):

> Many schools and school systems . . . find themselves continually buffeted by proposals for change . . . lacking any keel, these organizations have little choice but to sail with the wind, whatever its direction . . . there is little certainty that such organizations will be any further ahead in ten years than they are at present. However, keels can be acquired; perhaps more accurately, they can be grown, slowly but deliberately . . . *central to this process is the building, testing, and fine-tuning of systematic problem-solving procedures.*

One proven approach to help educational leaders in this task is to have them focus on the school environment or climate. Numerous references have been made to the fact that an essential element of an effective school is a good school climate. For example, Owens (1981, p226) states that the effectiveness of schools 'is significantly influenced by the quality and characteristics of the organisational climate'. Sergiovanni and Starratt (1983), in a comment on the importance of climate, argue that a healthy climate frees supervisor and teacher to work more fully on educational matters. Other writers like Rutter et al (1980) and Halpin and Croft (1962) describe climates that allow teachers to gain satisfaction from their work and have confidence in the administrative structure of the school.

Brookover et al (1978) found that the school climate can affect the behaviour and academic performance of students. These findings were also supported by Rutter et al (1980), and Fisher (1982).

Purkey and Smith (1985, p356 – 7), in summarising the research on effective schools, stated:

> The most persuasive research suggests that student academic performance is strongly affected by school climate . . . composed of values, norms, and roles existing within institutionally distinct structures of governance, communication, educational practices and policies, and so on. Successful schools are found to have cultures that produce a climate or 'ethos' conducive to teaching and learning . . . (which) will vary, in part in response to the composition of the staff and student body and to the environment in which the school exists, leaving each school with a unique climate or 'personality' . . . Nevertheless, academically effective schools are likely to possess a cluster of similar characteristics that encourage and promote student achievement.

Thus climate can be viewed as a combination of the enduring characteristics which describe a particular school and distinguish it from other schools and the feelings which teachers have for their school.

It is our belief that the best way to improve the climate of a school is for teachers to have information about the climate which can be discussed and form the basis of school change. Aspects of the climate or work environment of the school are measured and the results interpreted. Instruments like the School Level Environment Questionnaire (SLEQ) or the Work Environment Scale (WES) provide educational leaders with a means of doing this (Fisher and Fraser 1990a, 1990b). The interpretation of these results could form the basis of staff discussions in order to promote change.

But where to next? What is the *second* step for effective educational leadership? We would suggest it is the 'keel', the 'vision', the 'mission', the 'strategic'. Emphasis here needs to be on the leader's ability to engage stakeholders in a community of critical enquiry to discover and test important values and then to seek the emergent general or common direction with eloquence, persistence and detail.

A strong and consistent educational platform is essential to this task.

As Weick (1982, p675) had pointed out in characterizing schools as 'loosely coupled systems':

The administrator's voice and vision are two of the few things that teachers share in common. Diverse ideas about the school's mission are common under conditions of loose coupling. This very plurality makes for successful local accommodations. But people also need some shared sense of direction for their efforts. This already exists in most tightly coupled systems, but it must be built and reaffirmed in a loosely coupled system. Articulating a theme, reminding people of the theme, and helping people to apply the theme to interpret their work – all are major tasks of administrators in loosely coupled systems.

Administrators must be attentive to the 'glue' that holds loosely coupled systems together...

Summary and conclusion

In summary, educational leadership for quality teaching and learning is important. Yet both preparation programmes and the actual behaviour of educational leaders in their schools suggest a neglect of this essential part of education. Recent literature has attempted to redress this gap between what is desirable and what happens in practice.

But it is vastly easier to know something than to achieve it. We have argued that if we want our knowledge of advances in understanding educational leadership to move beyond the realm of rhetoric then clear priorities for action need to be followed.

The first priority for action is a willingness to lose time in order to gain time. Awareness of, and development of skills in, group and organizational processes must be a first step. Instead of others trying to insert something into a school's culture, educational leaders should be trying first to help that culture develop an awareness of, and a responsiveness to, itself. One proven approach to help in this task is to focus on school environment or climate.

The second priority for action is the slow but deliberate growth of educational leaders' and a school's educational vision.

To conclude this paper, it is important that there be a clear understanding of our leadership focus. Such an understanding is important because, as Murphy (1988, p654) notes, 'If belief in leadership as the ticket to organizational success waxes and wanes, it is clearly ascendant at the moment.'

We see leadership as a function that can (and should) be carried out by all those engaged in the educational enterprise, including those with formally designated leadership roles. In fact, we go further to argue that, to be effective, leadership *must* be seen in this functional way.

Sergiovanni (1987, p66) states, 'The greater the density of leadership, the more successful the school is likely to be . . . .' For him, 'Leadership density means the total amount of leadership expressed on behalf of school quality by students, parents, and teachers as well as by principals'. In this context, then, the principal's leadership is understood by Sergiovanni (1987, p18), 'as an enabling process that frees, encourages, and energizes others to join with the principal in the leadership process'.

We would agree that the culture of a school will change significantly for the better when teachers stop functioning in isolation and start collectively solving problems related to students' learning. To use Heifetz and Sinder's (1987, p194) words, we see the formally designated leader's role more as one of 'guide, interpreter and stimulus of engagement'. A leader's vision, as they so poignantly point out is, 'the grain of sand in the oyster, not the pearl'. (Heifetz and Sinder, 1987, p197)

There is another reason why a functional view of leadership is important. Murphy's (1988, p655) article, entitled 'The Unheroic Side of Leadership: Notes from the Swamp', makes the point well: 'Only a relative handful of individuals possess extra-ordinary vision. Unrealistic standards make it easy to undervalue ordinary competence [and] . . . undermine conscientious administrators who think that they should live up to these expectations.' Murphy's (1988, p655) argument, as well as ours, is that in order to restore a balance in the current literature on leadership, there is a need to concentrate on the 'unheroic', that is:

> . . . developing a shared vision (as well as defining a personal vision), asking questions (as well has having answers), coping with weakness (as well as displaying strength), listening and acknowledging (as well as talking and persuading), depending on others (as well as exercising power), and letting go (as well as taking charge).

Given our functional focus on leadership, it should now be clearer to the reader why we have argued the importance of processes as the first priority for action. It also allows us to escape the possible dilemma between the concept of 'teacher leadership' and the concept of the formal educational leader, such as a school principal, as 'instructional leader'.

Our priority for effective action, processes then vision, in no way diminishes the importance of the 'building a vision' step. However, Duke's (1987, p291) assertion that this second step must be a genuine one on the part of the educational leader, one that constitutes a continuing affirmation of the value of youth, provides a fitting conclusion not only to his book but also this chapter.

If school leaders are to help others find meaning in the school experience, they themselves must be clear about what the school experience means. School leaders who, for example, try to help teachers improve instructionally at the same time that they convey uncertainty about their own level of commitment to the educational enterprise are not likely to be very convincing. School leadership for instructional improvement ultimately represents more than a concern for professional growth and career advancement. It constitutes a continuing affirmation of the value of youth. To devote time and energy to improving how and what the young are taught is to be dedicated to leaving the world not as it is found, but better.

References

Bennis, W and Nanus, B 1985 *Leaders: The Strategies for Taking Charge*, New York, Harper and Row.

Blum, R, Butler, J and Olson, L 1987 'Leadership for Excellence: Research-Based Training for Principals', *Educational Leadership*, Sept, 25 – 29.

Brookover, W et al 1987 Elementary School Social Climate and School Achievement, *American Educational Research Journal*, 15, 2.

Caldwell, B 1988 'Educational Leadership for Self-Managing Schools', CCET Commissioned Paper, Hobart: Tasmanian Department of Education.

Chapman, J 1990 (ed) *School-Based Decision-making and Management*, London: The Falmer Press.

Deal, T E and Kennedy, A A 1982 *Corporate Cultures: The Rites and Rituals of Corporate Life*, Reading, Mass: Addison-Wesley.

Duke, D 1987 *School Leadership and Instructional Improvement*, New York: Random House.

Fisher, D 1982 'Relationships of actual class environment and actual-preferred congruence to student outcomes', unpublished doctoral thesis, Sydney: Macquarie University.

Fisher, D and Fraser, B 1990a 'School Climate: Assessing and Improving School Environments', *Set*, 2, Melbourne: ACER.

Fisher, D and Fraser, B 1990b 'Validity and Use of the School Level Environment Questionnaire', ERIC document ED318 757.

Halpin, A and Croft, D 1962 'The Organisation Climate of Schools', USOE Research Project, Contract no. SAE 543 – 8639, Aug.

Heifetz, R and Sinder, R 1987 'Political Leadership: Managing the Public's Problem Solving' in Reich, R (ed), *The Power of Ideas*, Cambridge, Mass: Ballinger.

Hughes, P 1988 'Educational Leadership for Curriculum Development', CCET Commissioned Paper, Hobart: Tasmanian Department of Education.

Leithwood, K and Fullan, M 1984 'Fostering Long-Term Growth in School System Effectiveness', *The Canadian Administrator*, 24, 3, 6–13.

Murphy, J 1988 'The Unheroic Side of Leadership: Notes from the Swamp', *Phi Delta Kappan*, 69, 9, 654–659.

Murphy, J and Hallinger, P 1987 'New Directions in the Professional Development of School Administrations: A Synthesis and Suggestions for Improvement' in Murphy, J and Hallinger, P (eds), *Approaches to Administrative Training In Education*, New York: State University of New York Press.

Mulford, B 1986 Indicators of School Effectiveness: A Practical Approach, *ACEA Monograph No 2*.

Owens, R 1981 (2nd ed), *Organisational Behavior in Education*, Englewood Cliffs, NJ: Prentice-Hall.

Purkey, S and Smith, M 1985 'School Reform: The District Policy Implications of the Effective Schools Literature', *The Elementary School Journal*, 85, 3, 353–389.

Rogus, J 1988 Teacher Leader Programming: Theoretical Underpinnings, *Journal of Teacher Education*, Jan. – Feb., 46–52.

Rutter, M et al 1980 *Fifteen Thousand Hours: Secondary Schools and Their Effects on Children*, Harvard University Press.

Sergiovanni, T 1982 'Ten Principles of Quality Leadership', *Educational Leadership*, 39, 5, 330–336.

Sergiovanni, T 1987 *The Principalship: A Reflective Practice Perspective*, Boston: Allyn and Bacon.

Sergiovanni, T and Staratt, R 1983 (3rd ed), *Supervision, Human Perspectives*, New York: McGraw-Hill.

Weick, K 1982 'Administering Education in Loosely Coupled Systems', *Phi Delta Kappan*, 63, 10, 673–676.

3.4 The Arriving Principal: Self and Community Portraits

A. Ross Thomas

Towards a study of arrival

The importance of the principalship in the effective operations of schools is widely acknowledged. Evidence of this is forthcoming from research projects that investigate virtually the entire spectrum of educational issues.

Recent years have witnessed a developing concern of Australian public education systems for the quality of their school principals as they either investigate or implement revised methods of selection/promotion/appointment. The traditional 'orderliness' of the seniority-based route to the principalship is being replaced, if only slowly, and in part, by other means of selection.

The nature of the principalship has also been undergoing closer scrutiny. The literature now devotes far less space to the normative aspects of the principalship and much more to the *actual* nature of the role. In particular, the observational studies pioneered in Australia by O'Dempsey (1976) and replicated by others such as Willis (1980a, b), Thomas, Phillipps and Adamson (1981), Phillipps and Thomas (1982, 1983), Clarke (1985) and Werder (1986) have contributed significantly in this regard.

There are, therefore, grounds for confidence in predicting that the quality of Australian school administrators will improve – the recognition of the importance of the role, greater knowledge of what the principalship entails, and more demanding methods of selection would seem to guarantee this.

Missing from this equation, however, is a clear indication of improved or expanded preparation programmes for principals. All systems of education offer induction programmes of varying length, content and intensity for newly-appointed principals, but these are sometimes criticised as being too much orientated to the mechanical or operational aspects of school administration and not sufficiently illuminating of the cognitive and interpersonal components of the role. Programmes in educational administration offered by tertiary institutions (which in no State are mandatory for aspiring principals) are also sometimes criticised for being too theoretical and detached from the 'real world' of school leadership. Some attempts have been made to redress this perceived imbalance in approach through programmes like the one offered by the Institute of Educational Administration in Victoria.

The further development of improved preparation programmes – within education systems and tertiary institutions – will be facilitated by greater knowledge of the demands made of principals in an increasingly open and changing environment. The observational studies referred to above have contributed much in this regard but all have used as subjects established, experienced principals – principals who have made the transition from teacher and who have 'weathered the storm'. Missing from these studies have been arriving or newly-appointed principals assuming responsibility for their first schools. There are good reasons for a detailed, specific study of principals in this category.

For example, there is probably no more relevant occasion than during the first year of an initial appointment to ascertain (i) the adequacy of experience and formal programmes as preparation for the principalship; (ii) what are the surprises or unexpected experiences of new principals; (iii) the extent to which the goals, aspirations and intentions of beginning principals may be realised; (iv) what is the nature (and tempo) of change for beginning principals; (v) how quickly a new principal adapts to the job.

Questions such as these have been addressed by relatively few studies. Of those identified in recent years, most have been conducted in the United States. For example, newly-appointed primary school principals have been studied by Ogawa and Smith (1985), Berman (1986), Hart (1986a, b, c) and Augenstein and Konnert (1988). New secondary school principals have been investigated by Diederich (1987) while Duke et al (1984) and Daresh (1987) have studied both primary and secondary school appointees. In the UK Weindling and Earley (1987) have reported on the first years in office of secondary school principals while, in Australia, Thomas and Muscio (1984) and Thomas (1987) have reported on their interviews in which both primary and secondary principals reflected on their early days in office. Harvey (1989) has conducted a study of new primary and secondary principals in the Western Australian public school system.

Arrival within the NSW state education system

In a study supported by the New South Wales (NSW) State Department of Education, the author has pursued the following objectives:

1. To record and analyze during their first year of office the experiences of a sample of newly appointed principals in NSW public primary and secondary schools.
2. To recommend the design and implementation of preparatory procedures and continuing professional development programmes appropriate to the needs of newly appointed principals in the NSW public education system.
3. To design teaching/instructional materials appropriate to such procedures and programmes.
4. To suggest guidelines for the selection of new principals.

Accordingly, throughout the 1989 school year, the activities of newly appointed first year principals in large primary schools (19) and high schools (34) have been closely monitored.

Data relevant to the four broad objectives expressed above, and to numerous problems and issues contained therein, have been gathered through a variety of methods, times and locations. Principals have, for example, completed several questionnaires (which contain some novel approaches to the generation of knowledge); maintained audio diaries; reported on critical incidents; reflected on their roles, performance and readiness for office. They have also been interviewed frequently via telephone and, in some instances, observed while on the job.

The preceding approaches have provided information on arrival mainly through the perspectives of the principals themselves. The perceptions of the teachers and communities involved, procured through visit and interview, have provided another perspective on the phenomenon of arrival.

Presented below is a portrait of arrival for one of the schools visited – a portrait to which the principal, teachers and community members have all contributed.

Arrival from the principal's perspective

It was 'the sudden kaleidescope of jobs with which one was confronted' which was the initial challenge for this new principal. The continuous interacting with so many people took a lot of coming to terms with. 'One had to step back and try to grasp the specific functions of the various rooms and responsibilities of different people.'

In analysing the students the principal gained an insight into the community. His style was to give advice very openly. It was up to the recipients to use this as they wished. People whom the principal had met came from a wide cross-section of the community. It was the principal's intention not to become too familiar with people. His style was 'to talk to people, to get their opinions, then to leave it at that'. This principal's major satisfactions were the progress made by students and the involvement of students and staff in major displays including physical education and gymnastic work. An energy revivor for him was the one hour trip to and from school each day. The most significant achievement has been the development of a positive school tone through confidence building, a changed school uniform, the development of classroom environments and special attention being given to the school grounds and gardens. He has been at odds with one or two 'old guard' teachers who believed that punitive discipline was 'the be all and end all'.

This principal found the principalship to be rewarding, challenging, fulfilling but physically tiring. He believed that a principal had to have a wide-ranging arsenal of competencies such as sympathy, empathy, understanding, firmness, an ability to limit boundaries and give direction. In his view one also had to make a specific effort to be consistent. It was the quality of leadership which was so important. He believed that the principals's style of leadership was very much up to the individual and the principal's perception of the situation of the school at the time.

Arrival as seen through the eyes of the school community

This secondary school of attractive conventional buildings set in well-kept grounds in a small bicultural rural community has extremely well-equipped and well-designed specialist facilities. It has an excellent gymnasium; an extremely well-appointed library and well-kept outdoor sporting areas. Nevertheless, in the eyes of the community there were better educational opportunities for their children to be found in other schools in the area. The school was ready for change.

In such a small community accommodation was a major problem. The principal travelled for an hour to school each day; the deputy was living at the local hotel until suitable accommodation could be found for his family; many staff had their own small farms.

Autocratic and aloof, the previous principal only reacted to issues brought to her as she tended to work in her office all day. It had been hard for her to make an impact as she had been in an acting capacity for two years. She had been a member of the staff for several years and had followed a principal who had been in the job for 20 years. A core of the 'old guard' were happy with the status quo and uneasy about changes which were envisaged.

Establishing credibility
The principal came with clear ideas as to how to effect his influence and implement change. He appeared to be very comfortable with his position right from the start. According to staff he was like 'a breath of fresh air'. He worked positively to overcome the negative attitudes which had pervaded community perceptions. At the initial assembly the principal had discussed the meaning of the school motto and the visible symbolism in the school.

In order to familiarise himself with the situation the principal had spent a day with each head teacher to discuss faculty programmes. The role of the head teacher in the context of the school's social structures was also discussed.

It was the opinion of staff that the principal had an imposing presence. He did not allow paperwork to detract from his informal contacts with classroom interactions. Sensitive and aware of the situation, he was able to recognise pretence and unaccomplished tasks. Although he kept a tight rein on the budget, staff were kept informed and consulted. The community found the new principal very easy to talk to. They knew where they stood. The principal was prepared to become involved in discipline problems. He attended welfare meetings and took a firm stand where necessary.

Relationships with others
Good communication, both in the written and oral form, was this principal's greatest attribute. He was very professional both in his approach and in his handling of people. He had an ability to be able to calm irate parents so that they discussed problems in a reasoned manner.

Through cross-faculty representation, cultural integration of the school was being developed. Great care had been taken to select appropriate staff for the school's forward planning committees.

Already the principal had created a much more open school environment. Executive members were consulted and on occasions struggling teachers were assisted by the principal in their classrooms

The emphasis was on positive reinforcement. He was a very influential leader. In contrast to previous years, this principal had a vision for the school. His jovial, open personality meant that he found it easy to relate to people in his wanderings about the school. He was often able to solve problems as they occurred.

The principal's bulletin to parents, which sometimes contained photographs of various school activities, had been initiated in an effort to establish a positive build-up for the school. Businesses were now behind the school, supporting inter-school fixtures. Being conscious of not overloading parents, the principal himself often offered to help the Parents and Citizens' committee.

In an effort to better understand the needs of Aboriginal students and the kinship of their families, meetings with Aboriginal elders were held every week and an oral history of the area was in the planning process.

The new leader had raised staff expectations of themselves and of what they could expect from students. He had a lack of tolerance of the 'she'll be right' attitude. Administration was seen to be firm and fair, whereas previously it had been firm but not necessarily fair. Often a piece of literature was read to students in assembly. Although the principal threw discussions open at meetings he had a way of defusing conflict by making his point clearly and of not being afraid to make a stand.

Changes to be made
There had been many changes in the way that the school had been managed. It had become more centralised; staff had been expected to show initiative; there had been a redefinition of student welfare policy; and long-term planning had been instigated in
- curriculum
- assessment and reporting
- document reappraisal
- information booklets for new students and
- mandatory policy.

Students now sat on chairs in assembly. There had been an obvious improvement in staff morale. Students were proud to be achieving. Their expectations had changed academically, in behaviour and in sport. Decisions had become more school-based. Staff were consulted before ideas were taken to the executive. The deputy and the principal had a shared approach to their jobs which was different from the defined roles of the previous administration. There was a move to improve the grounds so that students could enjoy their breaks. The sign on the entrance doorway had been changed from 'Only Year 12 to enter through these doors' to 'Welcome to...High School'. A very attractive interviewing room and reception area had been made out of the 'isolation' room; and there had been a rationalising of the office staff's responsibilities.

Shifts in values

From the small changes made at the beginning more focussed, long-term planning was emerging. The principal's enthusiasm was infectious, motivating others to become more involved.

The principal's door was always open. He liaised with the school captains and encouraged even the youngest students to keep in touch. The principal's background in English was reflected in his expectation of written and oral presentations. There was an emphasis on preventative programme planning, rather than discipline, and many channels of communication had been opened. The way that the students were handled was vital to the morale of the whole school.

After reading all the students' reports the principal concentrated on the positive aspects, rewarding excellence in assembly but quietly discussing poor reports with students in his office.

One constraint appeared to be that the principal needed to be content to 'hasten slowly'.

Overall there had been a major attitudinal change by all concerned with the school. Thoughtful and caring, the principal acted as a role model for others. Students were 'talked to – not down to'; the general morale of the school had increased and dress standards, for both students and staff, had changed. Students now enjoyed coming to school.

The principal was seen to be friendly and to be aware of the needs of the community. He had worked positively to overcome negative attitudes, encouraged staff to raise their expectations of themselves and their students, and was very consistent in his relationships with people. The school was a much quieter place and those who worked and learnt there seemd to be much happier.

Summary

The preceding portrait, prepared after a visit to the school in the third term, is one of several generated from this study. Not all present such a positive, improved picture as this. For some arriving principals, even by the year's end, it was difficult to describe their schools in terms as accomplished as these; it was difficult to view their futures with great optimism. Overall, however, the majority of principals could have been labelled successful by the year's end – in spite of the great variety of experiences encountered, the largely unknown arena (especially for high school principals) in which they were to work, and the never ending demands placed upon them.

The analysis of extensive interviews repeatedly highlighted

several facets of arrival. Be they achieved in a positive or negative sense, the four issues outlined in the portrait above – establishing credibility, establishing relationships, introducing changes, and shifts in values – collectively seem to account for much of what constitutes arrival in NSW schools.

References

Augenstein, J J and Konnert, M W 1988 'Implications of Informal Socialization Processes of Beginning Elementary School Principals for Role Preparation and Initiation' Paper presented to the annual meeting of the American Educational Research Association, New Orleans.

Berman, K L 1986 'Elementary Principals: The First Year' unpublished PhD dissertation. University of Colorado at Boulder. *Dissertation Abstracts International* 47, 9. March 1987 pp3249–33250A.

Clarke K M 1985 'The Principals: See How They Run' unpublished MEd Admin thesis. University of New England.

Daresh, J C 1987 'The Beginning Principalship: Preservice and Inservice Implications' paper presented to the annual meeting of the American Educational Research Association, Washington.

Diederich, A M 1987 'Tasks While Braiding the Rainbow Stripes: The Transition from Teacher to Administrator' paper presented to the annual meeting of the American Educational Research Association, Washington.

Duke D L, Isaacson, N S, Sagor, R and Schmuck, P A 1984 'Transition to Leadership: An Investigation of the First Year of the Principalship' A Working Paper sponsored by the Educational Administration Program, Lewis and Clark College, Portland, Oregon.

Hart, A W 1986a 'Leadership Succession: Reflections of a New Principal' unpublished paper.

Hart, A W 1986b 'Attribution as Effect: An Outsider Principal's Succession' unpublished paper.

Hart, A W 1986c 'Successor Sensemaking of Leadership Change in Organisations' unpublished paper.

Harvey, M 1989 'Professional Development Needs of Newly Appointed Principals: Leadership for School Development' Western Australian College of Advanced Education and Education Department of Western Australia. Perth.

O'Dempsey, K 1976 'Time Analysis of Activities, Work Patterns and Roles of High School Principals' *Administrator's Bulletin* 7,8.

Ogawa, R T and Smith, J F 1985 'How a Faculty Made Sense of the Succession of its Principal' paper presented to the annual meeting of the American Educational Research Association, Chicago.

Phillipps, D M and Thomas A R 1982 'Principals' Decision Making: Some Observations' in Simpkins, W S Thomas, A R and Thomas, E B *Principal and Task: An Australian Perspective*. University of New England, pp73–83.

Phillipps, D M and Thomas, A R 1983 'Profile of a Principal Under Stress' *Primary Education*. 14,6. pp6–8, 31.

Thomas, A R 1987 'The Arriving Principal' In Simpkins, W S, Thomas, A R and Thomas, E B (eds) *Principal and Change: The Australian Experience* University of New England, pp195–203.

Thomas, A R and Muscio, A 1984 'Credibility, Rumour, Change: Considerations for the Arriving Principal' *The Practising Administrator*. 6,1. pp28–30, 21.

Thomas, A R, Phillipps, D M and Adamson, J N 1981 'Profile of a Principal: An Observational Study' *The Practising Administrator*. 3,2. pp12–14.

Werder, K F 1986 'Instructional Supervision by Secondary School Principals: An Observational Study of Queensland State Secondary Schools' unpublished MEd Admin thesis, University of New England.

Willis, Q F 1980a 'The Work Activity of School Principals: An Observational Study' *The Journal of Educational Administration*. 18,1 pp27–54.

Willis, Q F 1980b 'Uncertainty as a Fact of Life (and Work) for the School Principal' *The Australian Administrator*. 1,4.

Weindling, R and Earley, P 1987 *Secondary Headship: The First Years*. UK NFER: Nelson.

3.5 Future US Educational Leaders: From where will They Come?[1]

Stephen Jacobson

Over the past few years, there has emerged a growing body of evidence that challenges long-held beliefs about optimal school and school district size. Specifically, recent school-size research questions the assumption that 'bigger is better' (Coleman, 1986; Goodlad, 1984; Monk and Haller, 1986; Walberg and Fowler, 1987). Coleman (1986, p95), for example, observed that in his sample, 'The unusually successful districts were rather small'.

As a result of an emerging 'small is beautiful' orientation, important changes are occurring in the governance structures of schools. Many state policy-makers are being encouraged to allow small, usually rural, districts to explore structural and technological alternatives to consolidation. On the other hand, some of the largest districts in the US have begun experimenting with greater decentralization through the use of site-based management.

These trends should produce an increased demand for school administrators in the US over the next few years. Yet, central to its recommendations for the improvement of educational leadership, the National Commission on Excellence in Educational Administration (NCEEA 1987) urged campuses that house administrator preparation programmes to begin preparing 'fewer – better'. If implemented, the Commission's call to close the more than 300 programmes it has deemed inadequate (out of an existing 505

preparation programmes in North America) would reduce dramatically the flow of certified administrators into the available pool. A
supply-side reduction of this magnitude at a time when the field
may be expanding could produce a serious shortfall in the number
of adequately prepared educational administrators in the US.

Even if the number of field-based changes in governance proves
not to be significant, some have argued that many of the problems
currently faced by America's schools are more a consequence of
under-administration than poor administration (Heller and Pautler
1990). In their attempts to restrict the growth of school budgets
and resultant property tax increases, some communities have simply capped the size of their district's school administration, thereby
forcing incumbents to assume more responsibilities than time will
adequately allow. Therefore, even within existing governance structures, simply providing adequate administrative support could
increase the demand for certified administrative personnel, just as
reformers are seeking to reduce the supply.

The purpose of this paper is to examine administrator supply
and demand and to consider relatively untapped sources of educational leadership. The paper begins with a look at current administrator supply and demand in the US based on data from a study by
Bliss (1988). Using the State of New York as a case in point, I will
attempt to show that an apparent over-supply in administrative personnel can seriously misrepresent both the availability and distribution of qualified school leaders.

Next, the paper reviews traditional career patterns, selection processes and occupational socialization in school administration, and
examines how these factors have served to impede the entrance of
high-calibre women, minorities and non-teachers into positions of
educational leadership. As Miklos (1988, p55) observed, 'Administrators come from traditional pools of candidates even when
changing conditions support broader recruitment'.

The paper concludes with a discussion of how proposed reforms
in education might change these traditional factors and impact the
supply, demand and composition of educational leadership in the
US.

Administrator supply and demand in the US

Bliss' (1988) supply and demand study revealed a mean over-supply of 5,758 certified school administrators per state, or roughly
1.34 individuals for every administrative position. It is important to
note that the data revealed considerable variation among states,

ranging from an apparent shortage of 1,622 certified administrators in Virginia to a surplus of 45,131 in New York. Taking the most extreme case, New York's surplus yields a supply:demand ratio of 4.38 certified individuals for every administrative position. Yet, as Bliss cautions, since many if not most positions are currently filled, his data actually over-estimates demand. In other words, his figures underestimate the magnitude of New York's administrator glut.

One might argue from a purely labour market perspective that an over-supply of this magnitude could only bode well, since the size of the candidate pool should allow school districts greater selectivity. Yet many districts in New York have, in fact, experienced difficulty in attracting and retaining administrators. While the problem is perhaps most pronounced among New York's rural districts, where low pay and professional isolation produce high rates of turnover (Jacobson, 1988), the state's inner-city schools also seem to have difficulty in recruiting and retaining competent administrators (Lomotey and Swanson, 1990).

The reasons many talented individuals choose not to make themselves available when administrative openings arise are perhaps best understood by examining first the traditional routes that people follow into public school administration.

Who enters administration?

Historically, school administration has been represented almost exclusively by former classroom teachers. The fact that teachers would choose to self-select administration is not at all surprising since administration represents the logical, if not the only, step upward in public education's rather flat organizational hierarchy. The fact that others from outside the classroom so rarely find their way into educational administration is perhaps more a function of state certification and licensing requirements than of individual interest or initiative. From their examination of the evolution of administrator preparation, Cooper and Boyd (1988, p252) conclude that the present 'one best model' of administrator training effectively closes entry to all non-teachers. 'This path to the school administrator's office is so long and narrow that latecomers and outsiders are almost never welcome.'

While defending the importance of state certification requirements, Cooperman and Klagholz (1987, p2) argue that there are two basic licensing errors that need to be recognized: (1) accepting someone who is likely not to possess entry-level competence, and (2) rejecting one whose basic competence is probable. The effective exclusion of all non-teachers from public school administration represents potential errors of the second type.

Teachers choose to become administrators, or at least begin administrator preparation, for a variety of reasons, not the least of which is the fact that an administrative position provides the opportunity to increase one's overall package of benefits. As Griffiths et al (1965, p29) noted, promotion to administration '... promises greater reward in less time'.

Obviously, administration's benefits are not limited to pecuniary rewards. Recognition, respect and authority, as well as the opportunity to have a greater voice in decision-making, are nonpecuniary rewards that may play as important a role in career choice as salary for some individuals. Indeed, for many teachers, the chance to 'escape' the classroom may be the most attractive reward that administration has to offer. Nevertheless, for the 'benefits-oriented' teacher, greater monetary reward is a powerful incentive (Griffiths et al 1965), and an examination of salary differentials between administration and teaching is instructive.

Data from New York suggest that since the release of *A Nation at Risk* (NCEE 1983), the report that triggered America's educational reform movement, the once potent monetary appeal of administration may have begun to diminish. One of the top priorities of the reform movement was the improvement of teacher salaries in order to make the field more professionally competitive. Local efforts to reach that goal, such as Rochester's much-publicized contract that will pay a top salary of $57,581 in 1989–90 and reward some 'lead' teachers upwards of $70,000, have had a significant impact on classroom teachers' earning potential.

During the period 1981–82 and 1986–87, increases in teachers' salaries in the State of New York kept abreast of and even exceeded increases in salaries paid to some categories of administrators, specifically elementary assistant principals and senior high school principals. In other words, while administrator salaries still exceed teacher salaries in absolute terms, the difference between these salaries have diminished. But while improved teacher salaries may make entry into administrative *positions* less financially attractive than in the past, there continues to exist monetary incentives in many contracts that still make entry into administrative *preparation* attractive: specifically, salary differentials based upon graduate credit accumulation. Using the aforementioned Rochester contract as an example, that district offers teachers a 4 per cent differential for each 15 hours of graduate credit accumulated beyond the bachelor's degree. In New York, a master's degree is required for permanent teacher certification, while administrator certification is

usually based upon completion of an additional 30 hour preparation programme beyond the master's.

It seems likely therefore that New York's surplus of certified
administrators may include teachers who have no interest in leaving
the classroom, but enter administrator preparation simply because
of the salary differentials their education produces. If, at a later
date, these teachers decide to enter administration, they then have
the proper credentials; if they decide not to enter administration,
they still have the additional income derived from the differentials
that accrue over the course of their teaching career. The recruiting
difficulty experienced by some districts may be due in part of the
fact that their entry-level administrator salaries are lower than
salaries paid to experienced teachers holding administrator
certification. In other words, from a strictly financial perspective,
there exists a marked disincentive for an experienced teacher to
assume administrative responsibilities in return for lower pay. The
potential strength of this disincentive is further magnified if one also
considers that administrators typically have a longer work year
(eleven or twelve month contracts as compared to a standard ten
month teacher contract), *and* less job security than teachers (in
many jurisdictions administrators cannot be tenured).

School administration and teacher orientation

In addition to benefits-oriented teachers, who often seek promotion
out of the classroom, Griffiths et al (1965) identified two other categories of teachers, pupil- and subject-oriented, who typically do not
opt out of the classroom. Ortiz and Marshall (1988, p123) contend
that 'a misreading of Taylor's scientific management turned schools
into competitive bureaucracies, rather than collaborative service
organizations, emphasizing control over instruction'. As a result,
educational administration has come to be viewed as a 'technical
practice focused on efficiency and hierarchical control' (Ortiz and
Marshall 1988, p138). Therefore, if a teacher's primary orientation
is toward instruction, whether pupil- or subject-oriented, then enter-
ing administration, as presently conceived, is less attractive than
remaining in the classroom.

One of the consequences of this perception is 'the long-standing
bifurcation of education by gender [that] has routed women to
instruction and men to administration' (Ortiz and Marshall 1988,
p133). Shakeshaft (1988) contends that since woman often enter
teaching in order to be near children, the more disassociated with
learning they perceive administration, the more likely they are to
avoid it. Thus, the prevailing perception of administration appears

to make the field less desirable to women than to men. Evidence of
this bifurcation can be found in the fact that while women held
61.7 per cent of elementary school principalships in 1905, the
figure declined to 19.6 per cent by 1972–73 (Tyack and Hansot
1982). By 1988, Heller et al (1988) reported that of a sample of
more than 1100 school administrators, just 15 per cent were
women, while among superintendents only, the figure was less than
5 per cent. The figures for minority representation in this category
were even more discouraging, as only 3 per cent of the superintendents in the sample were members of a minority group.

Administrator selection

Another factor that appears to work to the distinct disadvantage of
women and minorities is a selection process that favours known
and loyal candidates. Miklos (1988) contends that local candidates,
particularly those who place an emphasis on deference to authority, have a distinct advantage when competing for entry-level
administrative positions. Ortiz and Marshall (1988, p136) argue
that the existence of this informal promotion system that
perpetuates traditional hierarchical role relationships is simply a
desire by education's predominantly white male power structure
to maintain control: '. . . the chiefs want to retain the power inherent in defining what is valuable, good, and proper'. They report
that this bias 'manifests itself in less encouragement from superiors,
less preparation and motivation . . .' (Ortiz and Marshall 1988,
p131). Indeed, Valverde (1974) reported that administrators in one
urban district actually discouraged women and minorities from pursuing administrative preparation because they felt that members of
these groups lacked the characteristics necessary for educational
leadership.

  As a result of this 'old-boys' network, whether real or imagined,
women and minority teachers are socialized to see little chance for
advancement into administration. Many highly capable women and
minorities avoid administration or simply exit education entirely
because they believe that their path to advancement will be determined more by local sponsorhip than personal merit.

Organizational socialization

For those few women and minorities who do enter administration,
their limited numbers produce problems of isolation and loneliness.
For example, minority administrators are commonly assigned to
minority schools where they often become professionally isolated

and their opportunities for further sponsorship drastically diminished (Valverde and Brown 1988). Women administrators face similar problems, as Shakeshaft (1986, p172) writes:

> Women principals and superintendents, because they are tokens and because they are not included or do not choose to be included in all-male activities, often report lack of colleagueship with male administrators and a deep awareness of 'loneliness at the top'.

Perhaps as a result of this separation from the 'male-defined' norms of their colleagues, many women administrators redefine the organizational culture within their schools. Specifically, 'female-defined' schools tend to be more child-centred, less hierarchical and allow more opportunities for shared decision-making than 'male-defined' schools (Shakeshaft 1988). Women administrators 'take a more active stance towards instructional leadership' (Wheatley 1981, p269). Pitner's (1981, p288) study of superintendents revealed that '... females used their time to visit classrooms and teachers, keeping abreast of the instructional program, while males used the time to walk the halls with principals and the head custodians'.

Shakeshaft (1986) contends that the literature on 'female-defined' schools reaffirms the conclusion reached by Hemphill et al (1962, p334) that women should be favoured over men for administrative positions:

> ... if the job of the principal is conceived in a way that values working with teachers and outsiders; being concerned with objectives of teaching, pupil participation and the valuation of learning; having knowledge of teaching methods and techniques; and gaining positive reactions from teachers and superiors.

In contrast to the prevailing perception of administration, the conception offered by Hemphill et al emphasizes collaboration over competition – instruction over control. If conceived in these terms, school administration would probably become far more attractive to pupil- and subject-orientated teachers. In other words, by redefining the role and responsibilities of the educational administrator, it might be possible to begin áttracting more school leaders from the ranks of those 'dedicated' professionals whose primary interest in instruction traditionally caused them to avoid administrative positions. An increased interest in administrator preparation by this previously untapped pool is particularly important if we begin preparing 'fewer-better', because it would enable preparation programmes to be more selective in their admissions and thereby address a second concern of the National Commission's report, ie. the lack of quality candidates for preparation programmes.

Educational reform and future school leaders

Although the first two waves of reform were relatively silent about the role of the school administrator, the recommendations of first wave reports such as *A Nation at Risk* (NCEE 1983) simply reinforced existing notions that school improvement was dependent upon technical efficiency and hierarchical control. In contrast, reformers of the second wave began to question implicitly both educational administration's present orientation and its traditional career path. Recommendations from both *Teachers for the 21st Century* (Carnegie 1986) and *Tomorrow's Teachers* (Holmes 1986) reveal a deeper concern for issues of organizational governance and offer a restructured profession in response. For example, at the pinnacle of the Carnegie Task Force's proposed teacher hierarchy would be a building-level committee of 'lead teachers' whose administrative responsibilities would include the development of curriculum instructional supervision, setting performance criteria, course scheduling and assignment, and even the hiring and dismissal of personnel. In other words, this cadre would be responsible for making decisions, particularly in the area of instruction, that in the past had been reserved almost exclusively for administrators. Under this system, traditional administrative positions would become primarily managerial, yet school leadership would no longer be divorced from the classroom. Participation would be broader based, with key individuals remaining intimately involved with classroom instruction. School administration would become a bicameral form of leadership, with one group of teacher/administrators responsible for the technical core of instruction, while another group of administrator/managers would be responsible for maintenance and control. This broadened conception of educational leadership would not only make the field of administration more attractive to instruction-orientated teachers, but could allow alternative career paths to be developed for qualified non-teachers as well.

Alternative paths to administration

The responsibilities of the school business official in the US are primarily managerial in nature, providing such service and support functions as fiscal planning and budgeting, facility maintenance, purchase and supply, food services and pupil transportation. Yet existing administrator certification in New York requires three years of teaching experience. Under existing conditions,

> ...It is possible, and likely, that a candidate can get a School District Administrator certificate and function as a chief business official of a

district without ever having completed one course in business or finance. It is also possible that a person could have two years of teaching experience, hold an MBA degree, have served successfully for three years as a civil service business manager, hold a doctorate in Educational Administration and still not meet current certification criteria. (NYSAS-BO 1988, p4)

These are examples of the two basic licensing errors described earlier, ie, inclusion of individuals lacking basic skills, and exclusion of those whose competence is probable. NYSASBO's proposed certificate for School Business Administrators seeks to address errors of the first type by requiring aspiring business officials to be trained in both educational and business administration, and addresses errors of the second type by allowing 'candidates with proven business competencies and expertise greater access to the field of public school administration' (p5). Included in this pool of non-teacher candidates would be business managers from the private sector, as well as many of the civil service employees currently working in school districts. An existing shortage of qualified school business officials will only be magnified if the movement towards site-based management intensifies. Providing competent individuals, with limited or no teaching experience, greater access to the school business office seems a reasonable approach for dealing with potential shortages in this non-instructional component of administration. More challenging, and potentially problematic, is allowing individuals with limited or no teaching experience greater access to the principalship.

As early as the turn of the century, the primary responsibility of the building principal in the US had changed from 'principal' teacher to administrative manager (Jacobson et al 1954). Issues of instruction gave way to clerical concerns such as record-keeping and scheduling, as principals were called upon to manage larger and more complex schools. Nevertheless, the currently popular effective schools literature has been interpreted to suggest that the 'effective' principal is one who is both an efficient administrative manager and an instructional leader. As a result, today's principal feels pressured to assume both roles, yet experiences frustration over the ambiguity and conflict that this dual function creates.

In its call for changes in the preparation and certification of school principals, the New Jersey State Department of Education (NJSDE 1986, p56) argues, 'The time has long passed when principals can realistically be expected to function as the 'head teachers' or 'teaching experts' of their schools. Indeed, instructional leadership must cease to be thought of as meaning personal teaching expertise'. Indeed, the Department recommends (pp67–68) that principals receive 'highly focussed training and practice, not in how to teach, but in how to observe and evaluate teaching', the assessment of which would depend upon 'generic management and leadership competencies implied by a conception of the principal as an organizational executive, rather than a teaching expert or a specialist in public school administration'. In addition to programmes in educational administration, individuals could prepare for the principalship through training in business or public administration, management science or organizational leadership. After obtaining the appropriate degree, aspiring principals would then have to 'acquire a practical familiarity with schools as organizations and with the work of teachers from the perspective of an executive' (NJSDE 1986, p78). This 'practical familiarity' would take the form of a carefully supervised administrative internship and require the aspiring administrator to 'know the business' (Peters and Waterman 1982). In other words, this approach to preparation and licensing still values the importance of exposure to the classroom and classroom instruction by the aspiring administrator. What distinguishes New Jersey's approach from traditional career routes is that it opens the door to a wider pool of non-teacher candidates.

Peterson and Finn (1988, p106) wonder, 'Would the teachers in a school allow themselves to be led by one who had not come up through the ranks?' and conclude that if two conditions are met, the leadership of non-teachers would be acceptable: (1) that teachers are themselves provided a career ladder that would allow them greater access to instructional decision-making; and (2) that non-teacher administrators become familiar with pedagogic issues so that they can provide knowledgeable support and assistance when needed.

The conceptual underpinning of New Jersey's proposal depends upon a vision of school leadership that increases both participation and the articulation between administrative and instructional responsibilities. The impact of this new vision (and the alternative career routes it creates) on the supply of high quality school administrators cannot be determined *a priori*. Nevertheless, it would be viewed as a meaningful experiment that needs to be monitored carefully.

Conclusions

There is a growing body of literature to suggest that educational leadership is a critical determinant of educational quality. Yet, just as we are beginning to consider recommendations to prepare fewer, there are structural changes occurring in the field that indicate that we will be needing more educational leaders. Educational administration has obviously reached an important juncture. If we are to prepare 'fewer-better', we must first reconceptualize what educational leadership entails and who should be involved. For even if we prepare them better, if we simply prepare fewer of the same type of candidates, ie, candidates with the same preferences and orientations as in the past, we are not likely to address successfully the challenges of the next millenium. If the field is to become more attractive and accessible to the broader range of potentially high quality candidates, then school leadership must come to be viewed as being as concerned about fundamental pedagogic and instructional issues as it has been traditionally about issues of efficiency and control. Furthermore, educational leadership and the expertise required for obtaining it must come to be viewed as residing both in and outside of the classroom. These changes would signal a redefinition of school leadership that for women and minorities, pupil- and subject-oriented teachers and non-teachers might make administration more attractive.

Proposed revisions in administrator certification in at least two states indicate that a movement towards a new conception of educational leadership has already begun. Assuming these changes make administration more attractive to a wider range of candidates, preparation programmes that chose to prepare fewer-better could then be far more selective than in the past. But with increased selectivity should come a greater responsibility on the part of institutions of higher education to help their graduates locate field placements, particularly aspiring minority and female administrators. In other words, as preparation programmes become more sensitive to market realities, they should take an advocacy role in administrator sponsorship. Marshall (1979) notes that since traditional field-related sponsorship is often more problematic for women than men, women tend to depend upon their graduate preparation in administration as an alternative source of career entry sponsorship. Unfortunately, sponsorship in many preparation programmes often means little more than posting job openings on a bulletin-board or helping students develop their resumes. Administrator preparation programmes could play a significant role in redressing the marked under-representation of women and minorities in the field through the aggressive placement of their graduates. Although there are data to suggest improvements in the proportion of minority and women educational administrators over the past decade (Jacobson 1990), these changes have come primarily in large urban districts. Through aggressive entry-level sponsorship, administrator preparation programmes could help make important inroads in other geo/demographic areas as well –

inroads that would offer minority and women candidates greater visibility and thus greater access to subsequent field-related sponsorship.

Note

[1] This paper is a revision of a chapter that appears in S Jacobson and J Conway (eds), *Educational Leadership in an Age of Reform*. New York: Longman, 1990. Printed with permission.

References

Bliss, J 1988 'Public school administrators in the United States: an analysis of supply and demand' in D Griffiths, R Stout and P Forsyth (eds) *Leaders for America's Schools: Final Report and Papers of the National Commission on Excellence in Educational Administration*. San Francisco: McCutchan, pp193–199.

Carnegie Forum on Education and the Economy 1986, *Teachers for the 21st Century*. New York: The Forum.

Coleman, P 1986, 'The good school district: a critical examination of student achievement and per pupil expenditures as measures of school effectiveness', *Journal of Education Finance*, 12(1): 71–96.

Cooper, B and Boyd, W 1988 'The evolution of training for school administrators' in D Griffiths, R Stout and P Forsyth (eds) *Leaders for America's Schools: Final Report and Papers of the National Commission on Excellence in Educational Administration*. San Francisco: McCuthan, pp284–304.

Cooperman, S and Klagholz, L 1987 *Teaching Experience and the Certification of Principals*. Trenton, NJ: New Jersey State Department of Education.

Goodlad, J 1984 *A Place Called School*. New York: McGraw-Hill.

Griffiths, D, Goldman, S and McFarland, W 1965 'Teacher mobility in New York City', *Educational Administration Quarterly*, 1(1): 15–31.

Heller, R, Conway J, and Jacobson S, 1988 'Here's your blunt critique of administrator preparation', *The Executive Educator*, 10(9): 18–21, 30.

Heller, R and Pautler, A 1990 'The administrator of the future: combining instructional and managerial leadership' in S Jacobson and J Conway (eds) *Educational Leadership in an Age of Reform*. New York: Longman, pp131–143.

Hemphill, J, Griffiths, D and Federicksen, N 1962, *Administrative, Performance and Personality*. New York: Teachers College Press.

Holmes Group 1986, *Tomorrow's Teachers: A Report of the Holmes Group*. East Lansing, MI: The Holmes Group.

Jacobson, P, Reavis, W and Logsdon, J 1954, *The Effective School Principal*. New York: Prentice-Hall.

Jacobson, S 1988 'Effective superintendents of small, rural districts' *Journal of Rural and Small School*, 2(2): 17–21.

Jacobson, S 1990, 'Reflections on the Third Wave of Reform: rethinking administrator preparation' in S Jacobson and J Conway (eds), *op cit*, pp30–45.

Lomotey, K and Swanson, A 1990, 'Restructuring school governance: learning from the experiences of rural and urban schools' in S Jacobson and J Conway *op cit*, pp65–2.

Marshall, C 1979, *Career Socialization of Women in School Administration*. Unpublished dissertation, University of California, Santa Barbara.

Miklos, E 1988, 'Administrator selection, career patterns, succession and socialization' in N Boyan (ed) *Handbook of Research on Educational Administration*. New York: Longman, pp53–76.

Monk, D and Haller, E 1986 *Organizational Alternatives for Small Rural Schools*. Ithaca, NY: New York State College of Agriculture and Life Sciences, Cornell University.

National Commission on Excellence in Education 1983, *A Nation at Risk: Imperative for Educational Reform*. Washington, DC: US Government Printing Office.

National Commission on Excellence in Educational Administration 1987, *Leaders for America's Schools*. Tempe, AZ: The University Council for Educational Administration.

New Jersey State Department of Education 1986 *The Preparation and Certification of School Principals in New Jersey*, Trenton, NJ: The Department.

New York State Association of School Business Officials 1988 *Licensing and Certification of School District Business Administrators*, Albany, NY: The Association.

Ortiz, F and Marshall, C 1988 'Women in educational administration' in N Boyan (ed) *Handbook of Research on Educational Administration*. New York: Longman, pp123–141.

Peters, T and Waterman, R 1982, *In Search of Excellence*. New York: Harper and Row.

Peterson, K and Finn, C 1988, 'Principals, superintendents and the administrator's art' in D Griffiths, R Stout and P Forsyth (eds), *Leaders for America's Schools: Final Report and Papers of the National Commission on Excellence in Educational Administration*. San Francisco: McCutchan, pp89–107.

Pitner, N 1981, 'Hormones and harems: are the activities of superintending different for a women?' in P Schmuck, W Charters and R Carlson (eds), *Educational Policy and Management: Six Differentials*. New York: Academic Press, pp273–295.

Shakeshaft, C 1986, *Women in Educational Administration*. Beverly Hills: Sage.

Shakeshaft, C 1988, 'Women in educational administration: implications for training' in D. Griffiths, R Stout and P Forsyth (eds), *Leaders for America's School: Final Report and Papers of the National Commission on Excellence in Educational Administration*. San

Francisco: McCutchan, pp403–416.

State Education Department 1982, *Public School Professional Personnel Report: New York State 1981–82*. Albany, NY: The Department.

State Education Department 1987, *Public School Professional Personnel Report: New York State 1986–87*. Albany, NY: The Department.

Tyack, D and Hansot E 1982 *Managers of Virtue*. New York: Basic Books.

Valverde, L 1974, *Succession Socialization: Its influence on school administrative candidates and its implications on the exclusion of minorities from administration*. Washington, DC: National Institute of Education Project 3-0813. ERIC ED 098 052.

Valverde, L and Brown, F 1988, 'Influences on leadership development among racial and ethnic minorities' in N Boyan (ed), *Handbook of Research on Educational Administration*. New York: Longman, pp143–157.

Walberg, H 1989, 'District size and student learning', *Education and Urban Society*, 21(2): 154–163.

Walberg, H and Fowler, W 1987 'Expenditure and size efficiencies of public school districts', *Educational Researcher*, 16(7): 5–15.

Wheatley, M 1981, 'The impact of organizational structures on issues of sex equity' in P Schmuck, W Charters and R Carlson (eds), *Educational Policy and Management: Six Differentials*. New York: Academic Press, pp255–271.

PART IV
THE DEVELOPMENT OF EDUCATIONAL LEADERS

Management Development in Education and Elsewhere: Three Overviews

4.1 Management Development for Today and Tomorrow

Rosemary Stewart

Good management is a mix of knowledge and skills. Developing good managers is like developing good doctors in that apprenticeship and practice are essential. However, management development is unlike the development of doctors in that it is possible to be a good manager without any formal education in management. Teachers of management like myself, always need to remember that. It stops us from having too unrealistic a view of what one can contribute and should encourage us to consider more carefully why one thinks one can contribute anything!

For an audience of educational managers it is sobering to remember that most managerial learning takes place on the job. Formal education in management will not make a man or woman a good manager, although it should help in planning, in understanding the environment, in the recognition and analysis of problems, in identifying the most likely solutions and in understanding and using management tools. Variety of experience and of challenges and a boss who is a good coach are more important for developing managers than what we educationists can provide. However, we can help managers to learn from experience and to recognize what new competences they need.

One of the enduring characteristics of managerial work is getting work done and achieving objectives through other people. A manager is dependent upon others to achieve his or her objectives. This contrasts with purely professional work where you rely upon your own skill. The more senior you are the more your work is done by influencing others. Management development can help managers to become more effective in achieving their objectives through others.

Managing subordinates is the traditional form of people management, but many managers have to learn to achieve their objectives by influencing people who are not responsible to them. There are people in other departments whose co-operation may be essential. There are also people outside the organization upon whom the manager may also be very dependent. In seeking to get your subordinates to do what you want you have the support of some position authority, and probably of some expertise authority as well, but in seeking to influence your peers and people outside the organization you have to rely more upon your understanding of the other person's situation and upon your personality. Often you will need, too, an understanding of politics – both internal organizational politics as well as party politics. Managers who are very good at managing subordinates may not have the understanding, sensitivity and sometimes even political guile, to be good at the other types of influencing. Giving them early experience of jobs where they have to learn the art of influencing people who are not their subordinates is a necessary part of the development of potential senior managers.

Developing managers to be more effective in their ability to influence others should be done in two ways: one is by providing job experiences that require different skills in influencing people; the other is by teaching about organizational behaviour so that managers have the necessary knowledge to understand why people are behaving in particular ways. The latter can usefully be done both academically and experientially. The social sciences provide the basis for the academic education. There exist handbooks of experiential exercises that have been developed to help managers to extend their understanding of their own and other people's behaviour. The basis for these exercises is the recognition that managers can often learn more by experiencing than by being told. Managers, for example, may learn more about leadership and team management by spending some days tackling a variety of physical challenges together, such as climbing a mountain, than they will by lectures. They can then be helped to reflect upon what they can learn from the experience of their own emotions and behaviour and that of others.

Much of management development today is designed to prepare potential managers for changes in management and to help existing managers to understand them and learn to manage them. Management today is in many ways different from management yesterday and management tomorrow is likely to be different again. Hence we need to understand the changes that are taking place, and those we can reasonably predict will take place, before we can talk about management development for today and tomorrow.

Changes affecting managers

The people aspect of management is changing with the changes in managerial jobs. It is becoming more important and this is also true in many professional and technical jobs. Managers are now often dependent upon a more complex set of relationships. They have to enlist the cooperation of more people both within and outside the organization.

The other changes affecting many management jobs, and hence the skills and competences needed, are:

- a greater vulnerability to changes from outside the organization, which are often unpredictable;
- greater responsibility for a wider range of activities because many managers are now responsible for several functions. This is one of the results of the move to greater decentralization which has taken place in many different kinds of organizations;
- increased span of control because the number of management tiers have been reduced in many organizations as part of a general drive to improve efficiency;
- increased accountability because greater delegation has been accompanied by clearer accountability;
- more rigorous and faster performance assessment;
- greater use of information technology.

Managers are under more pressure, work longer hours, and need to have the skills and competences to cope with their new roles.

The new or enhanced competences needed to cope with these changes are usefully summarized by Gareth Morgan (1988) in his book, *Riding the Waves of Change: Developing Managerial Competences for a Turbulent World*. He addresses himself to managers in companies but most of what he has to say is relevant to managers in the public service in general and to educational management in particular. He identifies nine competences. These focus on competences to cope with the changes taking place, not on the traditional competences. I shall use his list of competences but give my own explanation of them.

1. *Reading the environment*. Although this is more important in a competitive business than in educational management, it applies to any manager whose work is vulnerable to external changes and this is certainly true of education. Reading the environment means recognizing the social, political, economic and technical changes that are taking place that are affecting, or may affect, one's own organization.

2. *Managing proactively*. The word 'proactive' has still not entered many of our dictionaries although it is common in American and now in much British management discussion. Times of rapid change require the manager to be active in advance of anticipated threats not just reacting to them once they have arrived. It is closely related to the first competence, for the proactive manager who, to take an obvious example, recognizes demographic changes in countries with a declining proportion of young people, will start to take actions to cushion the effects of this upon the organization, whether it is a school, university or a company.

3. *Leadership and vision*. Because of all the changes that are taking place managers today need to be leaders as well as good managers. They should point the way forward and encourage others to follow. The word 'vision' is now often used to encourage leaders to think boldly about what they want to accomplish. In Shell they talk of 'visioning'. I have recently written about this for the health service Stewart (1989), but the same general steps described in that book also apply to leadership in educational management. The first step is determining what is the ideal that one should strive for and being committed to achieving it; the second is analysing the difficulties in the way and the third is deciding on the practical steps to be taken towards achieving the ideal. Leadership can be developed, it is not just innate. Leadership is more difficult in the public service than in the private sector because of the temptation to yield to the 'if

only' culture which may often prevail: 'if only we had more money', 'if only the politicians would be reasonable', 'if only . . .'.

Leadership was most associated with the military and with politicians, but many books are now being written about the need for leadership in business. Less in heard about leadership in the public services, but I believe that the development of leadership abilities is even more important in the public sector because of the need to encourage people to think positively about what can be accomplished, rather than to bewail the failings of politicians and senior civil servants.

4. *Human resource management.* Because managers are now often involved in managing change and because of the pressures to be more effective and efficient they have to become better at using human resources effectively. They can no longer leave it to personnel managers (establishment officers) but have to be more involved themselves, for example, in appraising the performance of their staff. One danger in much of the public service, and perhaps in educational management too, is to think of oneself more as a professional who carries out a distinctive role than as a manager of others whose main justification for having a managerial job is the ability to make the best use of their abilities.

5. *Promoting creativity, learning and innovation.* In a company this is important because of the rapidity of product change in many industries, but even in education there are new products, new teaching technologies and a need to be innovative in coping with economic pressures.

6. *Skills of remote management.* This is included because many people now work *for* organizations rather than *in* them, as sub-contractors or for a service fee. These relationships also need to be managed and the output assessed. The growth of information technology is making it easier for some people to do much of their work from home. Studies of these new home workers show that managers have to learn new skills in managing them.

7. *Using information technology as a transformative force.* Again Gareth Morgan was primarily thinking of the way in which information technology can radically change some industries, such as banking, and the relationship between customer and supplier. But learning to use information technology innovatively in education should also be transforming.

8. *Managing complexity.* I spend much of my time teaching experienced managers at Templeton College. When I was first there many of the managers considered that they had been

sent by their companies but that there was little that they needed to learn. They saw themselves as being good managers because they had reached their present position. Now, because most managers have to deal with much more complex relationships and problems they are anxious to learn and eager for help.

9. *Broadening contextual competences.* The context of business is more complex, particularly of global business, but educational managers, particularly those in universities where less of their income will come from public funds, need to have a better understanding of their environment so that they can position themselves in it as successfully as they can.

Management development

Before I discuss the changes affecting management development in the UK you may find it helpful to hear about some of the common aspects of management development in the private sector. There are great variations in the amount and the nature of management development in different companies. However, some generalizations can be made that you may find relevant. One, is that there is a boom in post-experience management education and all the main providers are fully booked well ahead. This is because more top managers recognize that their managers need to be equipped to meet the changes affecting their company. The concept of continuing education for managers now has some support, so that managers in some companies, for example IBM, are expected to have some educational opportunity each year. More common, however, is the idea of key stages in a manager's career when education is necessary. Three main stages are recognized:

1. *The first managerial appointment* with particular attention to supervisory skills but also to understanding how the job fits in with related departments.
2. *The manager of managers.* The importance of this career transition is that the manager can no longer rely mainly on his or her technical expertise as the way of exercising authority. In the first managerial post there will still often be a fair amount of technical/professional work, at the next level it is more purely managerial. A further complication in some organizations is that the manager may now have some subordinates who are geographically remote.
3. *Preparation for general management* where an understanding of the organization's environment and of other functions

becomes more important together with the need to think strategically.

Additionally, many organizations give their managers specialist training in particular management techniques or updating courses. Many of the larger companies, particularly those in the service industries, also develop – either in their own training centre or in collaboration with a management education centre – special programmes to meet new needs. A famous example is the course on customer relations run for British Airways of which many customers may have noticed the benefits. Another is the programmes we, at Templeton College, Oxford, have been running for some time for Thames Water Authority to help to equip its managers to make the transition from public utility to public company.

Changes in management development

The main changes taking place in management development in the UK are the following.

There is greater emphasis on self-development, which has implications both for the individual and for the approach of those responsible for management development. Self-development means that the aim should be to encourage individuals to take responsibility for their own continuing management development. Providing money for education and giving time off for it really leaves the development to the individual, particularly if there are no, or only very broad, criteria about the subject of the training, and decisions about how and where it takes place are left to them. One problem for top management is knowing how far one is willing to leave the judgement of development needs to the individual. It may be those who are most in need of development who do not recognize the need. Another problem is deciding what, if anything apart from providing money and time, should be done to facilitate the individual's self-development.

There is more concern with learning by doing. Action learning, initiated by Reg Revans in 1945, continues to have an active following here and a greater one than in the past (Revans 1982). The focus is on learning by doing, where managers 'learn with and from each other by mutual support, advice and criticism during their attacks upon real problems, intended to be solved in whole or in part'. An example of action learning is for a number of managers to form a learning group and to work together to tackle a problem in one of their organizations.

There is greater interest in management qualifications following several surveys of management education in the UK which said that there was too little of it. There has been a rapid expansion in the number and type of MBA courses; and a debate about whether it is appropriate to have a chartered manager, just as one has a chartered engineer, which is one aspect of a concern for identifying the competences that are needed both by managers in general, and in particular organizations.

There is more distance learning and more use of information technology.

More attention is being given to people management, strategic thinking and financial and computer skills.

An important idea, which has been around for some time, but is getting more attention now, is that of the learning organization. This is important because it means that managers have to adopt a different attitude to their work and to relations with colleagues and subordinates. It is common, particularly in public services, to criticize mistakes and not to seek to learn from them unless forced to do so by a public enquiry. The idea of a learning organization is that participants seek to learn from mistakes rather than to focus on identifying blame. This means that it is the responsibility of all managers to treat successes, failures and on-going problems as opportunities for learning. It also means seeking to learn from other managers rather than to score off them. So for some organizations, including I suspect many educational ones, to become a learning organization would mean a radical change of approach.

Conclusion

The changes affecting most managers, whatever the organization, require them to have new and enhanced competences. They need, therefore, to continue to develop themselves and to encourage their staff to do so too. In the UK at least it is becoming easier for them to do so because of the growth of a wide variety of short management courses and of MBAs, including distance-taught MBAs that can be taken while still working.

The growth of management development programmes, which differ both in content and in process, provides a wider variety of opportunities for managers to be developed and to develop themselves. Yet educational programmes are still only a minor aspect of management development. It is what happens within the organization that matters most: the variety of job experiences that individuals are given, the contribution of superiors who are good coaches and actively interested in encouraging their staff's development and the existence of mentors who can take a more detached, and possibly more objective, interest in an individual's development. The culture of the organization will also be important, whether, for example, it is one that recognizes that mistakes will be a necessary aspect of learning. However, development does not only take place within the organization, hence some managements that take development seriously arrange secondments to other organizations and/or encourage their staff to participate in community activities.

The fashionable phrase for those who recognize the need for all in the organization to learn to meet current and future challenges is 'the learning community'. Does this phrase accurately describe the culture even of those organizations which are dedicated to education?

References

Morgan, G 1988 *Riding the Waves of Change: Developing Managerial Competences for a Turbulent World*, San Francisco: Jossey-Bass.

Revans, R 1982 *The Origins and Growth of Action Learning*, Bromley: Chartwell-Bratt.

Stewart, R 1989 *Leading in the NHS: A Practical Guide*, London: Macmillan.

4.2 Developing Educational Leaders: An International Perspective

Ron Glatter

Introductory Note

This chapter, which was a source document for IIP '90, is an edited and adapted version of the final chapter of a book which drew on ten national case studies of school leaders (headteachers, school principals and others with formal responsibilities) and their professional development. The chapter was drafted by the author on behalf of an editorial group consisting of members from the Netherlands, Sweden, the United Kingdom and the United States (Stego et al 1987). The national case studies, from Australia (Victoria), Canada, England and Wales, France, Italy, Japan, the Netherlands, Sweden, Switzerland and the United States, were reported in Hopes (1986).

This activity was part of the International School Improvement Project (ISIP) of the OECD's Centre for Educational Research and Innovation (CERI). ISIP was a wide-ranging project which has produced and stimulated many publications relating to the process of planned school improvement. Of these, Glatter (1986), Hopkins (1988) and Blum and Butler (1989) are perhaps the closest to the theme of IIP '90, along with those referred to in the last paragraph.

Although what follows focuses explicitly on *school* leadership, the analysis and proposals seem applicable to management in other educational contexts as well.

The chapter falls into three sections. First, it makes some observations on the requirements of school leadership for educational improvement, then it suggests some implications for policy arising from the work done and finally it indicates topics on which the editorial group felt that further collaborative work within and across national boundaries would be valuable.

These reflections and suggestions are offered as a stimulus to further debate. How relevant are they to the educational world of the 1990s? What other factors need to be taken into account? Do they apply at all to the contexts of developing countries?

Leadership requirements

Here we wish to draw out just a few points about the practice of leadership for improvement that appear to us to be especially important. The first is encapsulated in the following comment based on a study of Swedish school leaders:

> The results of this study indicate that it is essential that the head should have the opportunity to develop his or her pedagogic outlook and his or her personality. It is extremely demanding to have to lead an organization which has inherent conflicts and where indeed there is often great antagonism between rival groups and interests. Without a 'compass', the head all too easily gets into difficult waters (Stalhammar 1986).

This statement points towards the first three of the main conclusions about leadership for improvement that seem to have emerged from our work and that have not received enough attention in the past.

School leaders need to possess or develop a well-thought-out and consistent view of their social and educational task as a whole, to provide them with a frame of reference as they deal with the myriad specific problems which arise during the improvement process. The four major tasks for effective leaders of improvement identified in our work were: taking a long-term view; setting a direction; achieving integration and balance; managing the external context. These all imply the need for a 'compass' to guide their actions. This is reinforced by the increasing evidence of the pressure-laden and fragmented existence of many school leaders (Hall et al 1986) and the consequent risk of improvement plans being blown off-course if problems are dealt with on a purely *ad hoc* basis. We do not yet know enough about the dimensions of the required 'helicopter quality' (Foy 1979), but it certainly includes educational, organizational and personal components:

- a coherent view of a desirable educational direction for the school;
- an awareness of appropriate organizational means for achieving this;
- an understanding by the school leader of his or her own characteristics and impact upon the school.

By itself, however, this quality may amount to no more than dogmatism, insensitivity and inflexibility, and can lead (as we saw in some of our studies) to severe difficulties during the improvement process. *School leaders need, in addition, to possess or develop a close understanding of the social character of their schools, without becoming imprisoned by it.* Schools are staffed to a large extent by professionals, who expect a considerable degree of autonomy and who are often able to defend personal and group values and interests in a powerful, persuasive manner. Proposals for improvement, from wherever they arise, are likely to threaten some values and interests. The process of setting and agreeing priorities that, especially in a time of severely constrained resources, is likely to be a central part of any plan for improvement, will also disturb the existing deployment of power and values. Achieving consensus, therefore cannot be an over-riding aim of leadership for improvement. On the contrary, leaders preoccupied with such an aim tend not to take initiatives or to promote significant improvement processes. Conflicts are likely to arise during attempts at improvement and leaders must be prepared to handle them and turn them in a constructive direction. This gives rise to our third observation.

Leadership for improvement requires not only courage and judgement, but also the skills connected with the leadership of individuals and of small and larger groups. These skills include praising and emphasizing achievements, enabling everyone to make a contribution, listening closely and managing conflicts. (It is noteworthy that such skills are also usually associated with effective teaching!) Teambuilding and team leadership skills of this kind are vital requirements for people involved in promoting or facilitating improvement. They must be based on a genuine respect for colleagues and students, even where disagreements exist.

School leaders need to have a close working knowledge of their external context and to be able to use that knowledge imaginatively in support of improvement objectives. This includes an understanding of external support facilities and of how relevant knowledge and skills available outside the school can be harnessed to the improvement effort. In our case studies, it was striking how rarely school leaders appeared to call on, or even consider using, such facilities (we shall return to this point later). Other features of the external context, such as the surrounding community, local government bodies and so on, need to be understood and their resources drawn upon creatively.

School leaders need to be able to work in a wide variety of modes as they guide improvement processes. These include analytical, collegial, political and cultural modes, and there are distinctive sets of capabilities associated with each.

These are broad, general observations which arise from our work, and they obviously need to be interpreted in relation to particular working contexts. For instance, they will have a different significance in a school that has 80 teachers compared with one that has only three or four. The quality of the leadership task will be different in these two situations. There will be much greater formality in the larger school, and several teachers are likely to have formally defined leadership responsibilities: the requirements for leadership implied by our observations can then be shared among a group of people, not vested solely in one person. In the smaller school, there may well be much greater involvement by classroom teachers in leading the improvement process, but all the formal responsibility is likely to be borne by a single person – the headteacher.

Nevertheless, despite the wide variety of working contexts in which leadership for school improvement may be exercised, our observations point to some common factors: in particular, the difficulty and complexity of the task, and the fact that, although some skills of a fairly specific nature are involved in being a successful leader, a great deal depends on less tangible, even elusive qualities such as judgement, sensitivity, courage, imagination, perseverance, personal stability, practical sense and professionalism. There can be no doubt that school leaders need a supportive environment to help them promote and facilitate improvement in their schools. Equally, there can be no doubt that the help needed to perform the kind of task we have portrayed cannot be reduced to a narrowly defined concept of 'training' in a specific range of skills. A varied, sophisticated and well-considered set of arrangements for development and support is called for. In developing this theme, we turn now to consider some of the policy implications arising from our work.

Policy implications

Enabling school leaders to be more effective as leaders of improvement will require policy changes at the level of school systems. Policy-makers are invited to consider the following suggestions.

School systems should develop comprehensive policies for the recruitment and development of school leaders, in full recognition of the significant resource requirements of these strategically important activities. We have included recruitment as part of such policies, because we believe that some of the qualities referred to in the previous section need to be present and identifiable at the point of selecting an individual for a vacancy. Concern has been expressed in some countries (Hopes 1986) about the lack of systematic procedures and clearly defined criteria for selection. The need for selectors to be provided with training in selection methods and with more focused and relevant information about the particular vacancy and about the candidates has been stressed (Baltzell and Dentler 1983; Morgan et al 1983).

Policies for the development of school leaders focused on improvement should take account of the key requirements for effective development programmes. We concluded that, in brief, these are:

- an adequate period of time for learning;
- scope for reflective learning;
- a focus on concrete situations;
- application of learning in collaboration with colleagues.

These requirements suggest that: development programmes must be closely related to the actual work and functioning of the school; they need to extend over a considerable period of time; preparation and follow-up are crucially important; they should foster a 'team development' approach by involving as many other members of the school's personnel as is feasible; they should make considerable use of experience-based methods (such as peer consultation, investigative school-based projects, job exchanges and so on), rather than simply relying on formal 'courses'.

Policy-makers should give careful consideration to the forms of development appropriate for different stages of a school leader's career. Ideally, there should be a 'lifelong' approach. This would include provision for school leader roles other than that of headteacher. The resource implications of such an approach may be too great for many countries to contemplate, but they should at least bear in mind the career 'profiles' of their school leaders when determining their priorities. For instance, our work suggests that heads often become involved in leadership for school improvement almost as soon as they take up the position, when they are least prepared for the complexities and pitfalls involved. This challenges the conventional assumption that preservice and induction programmes should concentrate on providing heads with a 'survival kit' focusing mainly on administrative matters and basic managerial skills, and that development related to improvement, and to the crucial requirements identified earlier in this chapter, can safely be left to later. Some of the less satisfactory outcomes recorded in our case studies seem to have been due in part to the lack of appropriate support arising from this mistaken assumption. This leads directly to our next suggestion.

Policy in this area should be based on a detailed understanding of the actual work patterns and behaviour and the development needs of school leaders, and school leaders and their representative organizations should participate in the design of policies and programmes. The detailed understanding referred to here must be gained partly through research and evaluation, about which we shall say more later. Regarding the involvement of associations of school leaders, we note with interest that these are among the bodies which actually provide programmes in Japan (Arai et al 1986), in the State of Victoria, Australia (Moyle 1986) and in the USA where the programme is linked to a sophisticated selection process based on an 'assessment center' approach (Rutherford et al 1986). At the level of the individual school leader, the complexity of the leadership task and the need for maximum involvement and motivation in relation to development argue for a considerable degree of individualization and 'negotiated content' to be available if the school leader desires this.

School systems should reconsider their expectations of school leaders: if they wish school leaders to be active supporters and promoters of improvement they might reduce the administrative burdens involved in the job to allow school leaders to devote more time to educational development. This could involve:

- examining the administrative tasks currently required to see whether all are necessary and, if they are, whether they are done in the most efficient and effective manner;
- providing more administrative staff support to school leaders;
- encouraging school leaders to place their professional leadership tasks uppermost in their priorities.

This does not apply only to heads. Handy has commented that the deputy head in many English secondary schools 'is in fact a rather expensive and under-trained bursar' (Handy 1984, p35).

When introducing larger-scale educational reforms aimed at improvement, school systems should ensure that adequate training, support and resources are given to school leaders to enable them to lead the implementation of the changes within their schools. Schools are currently expected to adopt many changes decided upon by education authorities. The quality of their implementation and institutionalization will depend on the extent to which school leaders are equipped with the understanding and resources to turn the authorities' intentions into reality at the level of the school. This is particularly important when several significant changes are expected to be implemented within schools more or less simultaneously, as is often the case currently. Such attempted reforms often fail because of the lack of a realistic strategy for system-wide implementation. When proposing a particular innovation of this kind, policy-makers should assess whether the system currently has the capacity to carry it out: school leadership capacity is an important component of this.

School systems should consider how well equipped external support agencies are for providing help to school leaders and what improvements are needed. The lack of use of external support agencies by many school leaders could be due to any of several factors: lack of perceived need; limited knowledge of what is available; non-availability of help at the time it is needed; a poor opinion held by school leaders of the suitability and/or competence of the external support staff; a sense that calling in help would undermine the perceived status of the school leaders among the rest of the staff; a view that relevant support agencies are too closely identified with the formal structure of authority; straightforward insecurity or lack of confidence about laying one's leadership open to inspection. The reasons should be investigated and, if necessary, more appropriate or acceptable support systems developed, or existing systems brought into closer contact with school leaders. It may be, for instance, that some support provision for school leaders should be quite separate from the formal hierarchy, and that, in view of the relative isolation of the headteacher's position and the stresses involved in leading attempts at improvement, there is a need for confidential advisers. These might be experienced professionals who are not in a hierarchical relationship with 'their' head/principal and who are perhaps linked with an agency not connected to the management structure.

Topics for further consideration

We have identified a number of topics on which further consideration and investigation are urgently needed. It is only in the past few years that the importance of effective leadership at school level has come to be recognized in many countries, and our knowledge base in this area, in consequence, is still very limited. The development of policies at national and other levels is now proceeding rapidly and, to ensure that these are soundly based, there is a major need to tackle the many unresolved questions. The country case studies, as the authors often admitted, made clear how much work remains to be done and how little knowledge there is about the effectiveness of present arrangements.

We are convinced that international collaboration in this area can be particularly useful. Many of the issues that we raise below could be most helpfully explored through international co-development activities of various kinds, involving the exchange and joint evaluation of experience. We consider that such activities are critically important: their outcomes may not seem as direct and tangible as those taking place *within* countries, but we believe that they enable a wider range of options to be explored, circulated and tested, and that they can produce more powerful and resilient models than those developed in only one national context. Clearly, a number of conditions are needed for work of this kind to be effective and valuable: in particular, support from a range of national authorities, including a willingness to evaluate the work over a reasonable time-span, and efficient arrangements for disseminating the outcomes within, and considering their implications for, individual national contexts.

Should participation in school leader development be compulsory or voluntary? From all the evidence obtained during the course of our work, it is clear that school leaders should be provided with and should take part in extensive high quality development programmes. The task of school leadership, whether at principal or other levels, is challenging, complex and demanding and the content and nature of schooling as well as the expectations placed on school leaders are changing rapidly in all countries. We were tempted to conclude that participation in development programmes should be compulsory, but we are concerned that compulsory participation might adversely affect motivation and hence the quality of learning, and could run counter to the approach of 'development' rather than 'training' to which we adhere. So this remains an open question for us. It should be explored further and experience of different approaches, including compulsory participation, should be compared and assessed. There is, however, at the least, a clear case for strong incentives to encourage school leaders to participate in professional development, by, for instance, providing extra remuneration and/or giving recognition for promotion.

How might external support systems become more responsive to the needs of schools and school leaders attempting improvements? We have already referred to this problem. There is a need to consider:

- how school leaders can be better informed about what external resources exist and their potential input;

- how shool leaders can relate expertise and resources existing within the school to those that are available externally, so that each can complement the other;
- how the style and modes of external agencies can be adapted to suit the needs and 'rhythms' of schools attempting improvements;
- what part school systems and their staff can play in promoting these connections, and in co-ordinating the activities of the various agencies involved.

What is the role of 'external' school leaders in school improvement and what are their needs for development in this regard? Several groups external to the school have important roles in promoting and facilitating school improvement. In some countries, as our case studies reminded us, school system personnel such as inspectors have a pivotal role: in all countries it is a significant one. The case studies also showed that in several countries the school leadership role of parental and other community representatives is becoming increasingly significant, for instance through participation on school boards and councils. There seems an urgent need to consider what kinds of development and support members of such groups should receive in connection with their roles in school improvement, and how this help might relate to the kinds of school leader development that we have been discussing here. There might well be benefit in some 'cross-functional' forms of development, involving both 'internal' school leaders and, as appropriate, inspectors, administrators, politicians, parents, community representatives and others. The ways in which community and parental representatives in particular can make an effective contribution, and what help they need in order to be able to do this, are very poorly understood, and these questions should perhaps be given priority attention.

By what modes and in what formats can school leaders be most effectively helped to develop their capabilities for leading school improvement? We have given a good deal of attention to this question in our work (see Stego et al 1987, Part III; and Blum and Butler 1989). Further attention should be paid to developing methods of evaluating existing programmes, and we also need a much clearer understanding of the settings and styles that are most likely to promote learning in this area. For instance, how can school leaders be helped to learn reflectively from their own day-to-day experience as well as from more formally structured development activities?

How can a range of employment policies relating to school leaders contribute to school improvement? School leader development should be viewed, as we have already argued, in the context of the school leader's career profile as a whole. In terms of promoting effective leadership of school improvement, we must recognize that policies on selection, placement, transfer, work requirements and expectations, leadership development, levels of remuneration and career and personal rewards generally all have a part to play. Although this is a difficult area and one in which international comparisons tend to be particularly misleading because of contextual differences, it is important to consider the total impact of the full range of employment policies and practices. For instance, if there is little competition for the position of head/principal because the rewards are thought to be too limited, it is likely to be difficult to attract and select heads committed to leading school improvement. Studies are needed to examine the relative effects of different employment policies on school leadership for improvement, to identify those which have a particularly constraining impact, and to suggest alternatives.

Could policies and programmes be informed by a better understanding of the actual situation of school leaders and of their behaviour? We believe that both school systems policies and development programmes should be rooted in a clear awareness of school leader behaviour and of the factors that affect it. We therefore think that school-based research, including observation of school leaders at work, ought to be given great importance in shaping ideas about the issues that we have considered here. Several research programmes of this kind are under way in various countries. Syntheses should be made of the main outcomes of these studies and their implications should be carefully considered. Studies are also needed of the expectations placed on school leaders by teachers and other staff in school, by students, and by parents, authorities and others outside the school, and the ways in which school leaders perceive these expectations and accommodate and respond to them. Work of this kind will help to ensure that our attempts to develop effective leadership for improving the quality of schooling are firmly grounded in the real circumstances of school life.

Notes

The author wishes to acknowledge the key contributions of his collaborators on this project – Shirley Hord (USA), Kees Gielen (the Netherlands) and Eskil Stegö (Sweden) – to developing the ideas and proposals in this chapter.

References

Arai, I, Maki, M, Makita, A, Nakatome, T, Okuda, S and Takahashi, S 1986 'Japan', in C Hopes (ed) 1986 op cit.

Baltzell, D C and Dentler, R A 1983 *Selecting American school principals: a sourcebook for educators*, Cambridge Mass: Abt Associates.

Blum, R E and Butler, J A (eds) 1989 *School Leader Development for School Improvement*, OECD-CERI International School Improvement Project, Leuven (Belgium), Acco.

Foy, N 1979 'Management education: current action and future needs', *Journal of European Industrial Training*, 3(2).

Glatter, R 1986 'The management of school improvement' in E Hoyle and A McMahon (eds) *World Yearbook of Education 1986: the Management of Schools*, London: Kogan Page/New York: Nicols.

Hall, V, Mackay, H and Morgan, C 1986, *Secondary school headteachers at work*, Milton Keynes: The Open University Press.

Handy, C 1984, *Taken for granted? Understanding schools as organizations*, York: Longman.

Hopes, C (ed) 1986, *The School Leader and School Improvement: case studies from ten OECD countries*, OECD-CERI International School Improvement Project, Leuven (Belgium): Acco.

Hopkins, D 1987 *Improving the Quality of Schooling: Lessons from the OECD International School Improvement Project*, London/New York: the Falmer Press.

Morgan, C, Hall, V and Mackay, H 1983, *The selection of secondary school headteachers*, Milton Keynes: The Open University Press.

Moyle, C 1986, 'Australia, The State of Victoria' in C Hopes (ed) 1986 op cit.

Rutherford, W L, Murphy, S C and Hord, S M 1986 'United States of America: Parts A, B and C' in C Hopes (ed) op cit.

Stalhammar, B 1986, Personal communication with the author.

Stego, N E, Gielen, K, Glatter, R and Hord, S M (eds) 1987 *The Role of School Leaders in School Improvement*, OECD-CERI International School Improvement Project, Leuven (Belgium): Acco.

4.3 The Preparation of Educational Administrators: Is a Division of Labour the Answer?

Kevin Wilson and Alan Macintosh

Discourse about the preparation of educational administrators[1] seems to be never-ending. Perhaps more has been said and written about it than many would care to know. The topic is constantly revisited probably because of its importance, but mostly because the practices at any one time fall short of the potential, people believe or perceive should obtain. Even a cursory review of the extant writings on this topic would show that, although it has been thoroughly if not exhaustively covered, satisfaction with past and current practices seems insufficient to let the matter rest. The purposes of this paper are first, to review some of the major criticisms of preparation programmes, and second, to suggest a rapprochement.

Reports and commentaries about training programmes have not been too positive or laudatory. The kinder ones have suggested that:

> Growing specialization in the field of educational administration resulting from new knowledge (for example, operations research) is one reason for program change. Another is the continuing search for more effective

patterns of field experience, instructional method, and content in preparatory programs.[2]

Recently, in the United States, more strident voices have been heard which decry the evolution of a model of mandatory preparation that is shaped by certification requirements imposed by the state. At worst, such 'training programmes' consist of a mixture of weekend 'how-to-do-it' courses, at best, some university-based programmes have retained most of the *bona fide* features of graduate study.

A number of disparaging assertions about preparation programmes surfaced in papers and submissions to the National Commission for Excellence in Educational Administration (Griffiths et al 1988). Some noted the lack of integrity in current programmes. They are said to have become so customized to attract and suit the convenience of part-time students, that any logical structure or orderly sequencing of course content has been overlooked or completely ignored. In addition, it was claimed that graduate students enrolled in the same course differ so markedly on such matters as prior knowledge, previous courses taken, degree sought, administrative experience, and career aspirations, that attempting instruction in common is foolish. Apparently, in some programmes, PhD, Masters' and Diploma students are enrolled in the same course. Others suggested that entry, continuation and exist standards are too low.

Many criticisms refer to the discontinuities between the formal study of educational administration and its practice; this particular issue seems to be voiced more often and fervently than before. While concern about it is attributed mostly to practitioners, even professors have queried the relevance of their formal studies to the role of a practising administrator: 'I was head of a department and the difficulty, the stress of acting on behalf of the organization... was not something that any of my previous studies had prepared me for' (Greenfield, cited in Gronn 1983, p14).

Bridges (1977) built a case for concluding not only that graduate training is unlikely to prepare students to cope effectively with managerial work, but that the result of most programmes is 'trained incapacity'. How did Bridges justify such a conclusion? He identified the following as sources of differences in the 'lifestyles' of graduate students and practitioners: time cycles and horizons (graduate students have some weeks to review cases and prepare papers; practitioners' work is characterized by fragmentation and brevity); communication styles (the success of graduate students is measured by how well they can communicate in writing, the practitioner's success is measured by the quality of verbal communication); interpersonal status and its effect on things like conflict resolution; and the emotional-cum-psychological differences between the university *milieu* and the workplace of the practitioner. He then argues that because the academic study setting is so dissimilar to the workplace setting, the period of formal training is dysfunctional. Bridges can count as adherents to his position any number of practitioners who have taken formal preparation programmes. This view may have some credence, but it may also be a wrong view.

What Bridges and others have described, quite rightly, are two distinct cultures. This should not be too surprising given our understanding of how cultures are formed. That they go on to use this distinction to imply that the two cultures should be made as similar as possible, is surprising. The logical extension of this position would be to move all preparation to the workplace. If this were done, it probably would not be long before some would criticize the disjointed nature of 'learning-on-the-job', its shallowness, and its trial-and-error basis. Still others might be moved to regret the lack of time to read, contemplate, and assimilate some of the insights about organizations.

But there is also a climate of opinion among associations of practitioners that favours a much greater emphasis on field-based practice. In fact, a recent publication of NASSP (1985) sets out a framework for the preparation of principals that is predicated on the apparent failure of a university-dominated approach to preparation. In the introduction to the report, the following comments appear:

> The coming of systems approaches, failure of the 'theory-based' [emphasis added] movement, accountability pressures, and the introduction of new technologies into a labor-intensive field (along with some sound curriculum development work) have rekindled interest in performance-based approaches. (p1)

While noting that the central weakness in preparation programmes is the failure to bridge the gap between the classroom and the field, the report recognizes that the best programmes will be those that achieve a well-articulated continuum of activities throughout both settings. To facilitate this, a case is made for the establishment of a one-semester practicum, prior to an internship. The purposes of the practicum, conducted under university supervision, are seen as developing, demonstrating and receiving feedback on administrative skills. Under such a scheme, students would spend time working in schools and have regularly scheduled debriefing seminars with peers and supervisors.

In the light of these reviews, are there no general overall considerations that could make training programmes become progressively better? Almost thirty years ago, Lortie (1962) addressed this question and noted that 'professional preparation in such fields as medicine, law, engineering, and architecture is similar in one key respect – the division-of-labor established between university and profession in the induction of new practitioners' (p77). He went on to describe how this division-of-labour has worked well for the older professions, and to suggest that those concerned about the preparation of educational administrators might do worse than to adopt similar procedures. The most fundamental shift following from a division-of-labour model is

> the recognition that the education of the young practitioner is not complete when he graduates from professional school. Receiving the diploma is but the beginning in a series of major turning points in the learning career of the doctor or lawyer. The man who wants professional recognition faces several subsequent junctures where he must show his competence and face either acceptance or rejection by those judging that performance ... law partnerships or major hospital appointments are not assigned to men with minimal credentials. Such credentials merely define the pool from which candidates for major responsibility will be selected. The specific arrangements for teaching and testing young practitioners vary from field to field, but they are of crucial importance in all the older professions. (Lortie 1962, p77).

If Lortie's premise, outlined above, is applied to the preparation of educational administrators, there might be quite a different assessment of the work of university departments from that which is currently reported. The thesis in this paper is, in part, about such a division of labour, or what might be called a separation into spheres of interest, but the major premise developed here is a little more involved than a discussion of the theory/practice debate. What will be argued is that the critics of the study of educational administration, of the practice of educational administration and of the preparation of educational administrators seem to develop their criticisms from a point of view which sees, or wants to see, educational administration as monolithic. That is, until all the pieces of knowledge about theory and practice fit nicely together, preparation programmes are likely to fall short of the mark. In this paper, we will suggest that this view is questionable and is not particularly helpful in shaping preparation programmes for practitioners.

There are several ways in which one could argue against the monolithic nature of 'educational administration'. One is to reflect on the different kinds of people who have an interest in the 'stuff' of educational administration. Let us list some of the 'stakeholders': administrators-in-training, practitioners, consultants, researchers, teachers and scholars. Sometimes personal predilections may blur the distinctions among these people, but we will argue that, for the most part, the separate interests they represent are distinguishable and reasonable. They each have a vantage point which makes them interested in matters which may be quite disparate. Scholars and practitioners are compared as an example.

Scholars are attracted to matters epistemological and metaphysical and wax eloquent about them: and so they should. Practitioners have insights about effective and efficient ways of leading and managing organizations. Some of their insights may be so good that they are just waiting for a theory to embrace them. There is nothing wrong with each group going its separate way; the sky will not fall if their interests are not always coincidental. Scholars should continue their musings and skirmishes about the merits of this or that paradigm. Practitioners have to get on with the reality and immediacy of their work situations. The distinctiveness of interests among the various stakeholders should not be seen as a source of disillusionment or consternation about the state of educational administration. Practitioners for the most part are unlikely to become involved in a discourse about the merits of phenomenology; most scholars may not be particularly enthusiastic about the minutiae of the practitioners' world. But those with different vantage points can co-exist and occasionally they may inform each other's actions.

What import does this kind of separation of spheres of interest have for the preparation of educational administrators? One matter implicit in the above discussion is the question of whether differences in students' perspectives need to be taken into account. Students are supposedly administrators-in-training; but do they come to their formal training with the perspective of researchers, practitioners or scholars? Their teachers probably expect them to be all of these at various times. But if they are only considered as one or several of these, there may be something very important that has been missed. Perhaps those who conduct preparation programmes should pay some attention to the 'person' who comes to graduate school.

If development of the person is seen as important, a number of other programme ingredients might be worthy of consideration. One of them may be the importance of the imagination. British poet Ted Hughes (1988) says that 'since this is the basis of nearly everything we do, clearly it's very important that our imaginations should be strong rather than weak' (p35). Hughes goes on to point out that those with an accurate and strong imagination are often regarded as 'something more than human' (p36). In educational administration we usually classify these people as possessing some unteachable knack, when in fact the knack may be a competent imagination, something we could teach.

Canadian literature scholar Northrop Frye (1963) would be likely to support Hughes with the observation that since we use our imagination all the time, in all our conversation and practical life, 'we have only the choice between a badly trained imagination and a well trained one' (p57). Frye, indeed, would go further: 'Everything man does that's worth doing is some kind of construction, and the imagination is the constructive power of the mind set free to work on pure construction, construction for its own sake' (p50). Do our departments consist of badly trained or well trained imaginations?

We hear a lot about the division of labour in preparation between ourselves in the university department and practitioners in 'the firing line'; indeed the trend seems to be towards the field, towards internships and in-service training, and away from the university. But the university must retrieve some of its lost ground; and the opportunity for 'the power of the mind set free', for reflection, for imagination to be strengthened and honed is what the university offers best. The university department cannot reproduce a microcosm of the usual workplace of the educational administrator, nor should it try to do so. Declarations which encourage departments to make their programmes 'more practical' are knee-jerk reactions to shortcomings that ought not to be solved in the university context. Such urgings also do a disservice by denigrating the proper role of the university department, which is to attend to the conceptual and analytical skills of administrators-in-training.

Lortie (1962) suggests that what the university department can and should do well bears, 'on the creation and transmission of general, systematic knowledge relevant to the profession' (p77); and, we would add, on the development of the person, a thoughtful, reflective person. Many have written about such a component. Schon's (1987) work on reflection and the practitioner/administrator are well known and rightly influential; Achilles (1981) and Popper (1982, 1985) among others, are notable advocates of using materials from the humanities to promote reflection in preparation programmes. Macintosh (1989) found that an increasing number of professors in Canada appear to be making use of short stories, novels, documentaries and their visual derivatives as a means of introducing some form of human, reflective element into their classes.

If the humanities approach is seen as a daunting prospect, Hughes (1988) offers another alternative, the study of comparative educational administration. He downplays the purpose leading to direct transfers to concepts or procedures from the foreign country into the home country, and rather promotes the notion of reflection, the element missing from traditional educational administrator preparation. Hughes further includes in his definition the idea of bringing together the sub-disciplines of Comparative

Education and Comparative Administration, a merger that cannot help but further the practice of reflection as students strive to relate intellectually their knowledge of administrative and organization theory with their knowledge of education in a philosophic sense.

The university department should not claim that the formal study programme equips candidates for immediate assumption of an administrative role. But the department may serve a unique function in readying men and women for the next stage in preparation, which might involve induction into the practice of administration under the auspices and control of the practitioner group.

Is there a case for the internship as the culminating activity of pre-service preparation? In large part, support for the internship seems to rest on strong advocacy. 'The internship is so important that it is the sine qua non of a modern programme of preparation of educational administrators', (AASA 1960, p82) is a sentiment that is often endorsed and seldom questioned. Not a great deal has been done formally to assess the validity of such claims, although some evaluations of the internship, as a distinct activity, have been reported. Some 'field experiences' might be helpful, but their major purpose should be to explicate ideas, theories and understandings dealt with in formal courses, and not to replace them. Briner (1963) was moved to write: 'At present the state of meaning associated with the internship typically involves operational definitions and associated indicators, a first level of meaning only' (p8); and it is likely this is still true.

There is quite a lobby, perhaps even a bandwagon, in educational administration for experience; experience is valued increasingly, it seems, over theory; experience, it is said, takes place outside the university seminar room and quickens the rush towards practical, hands-on, real-life arrangements for prospective school administrators. We said earlier that the university must discourage this rush: Frye (1963) gives us a reason. He reminds us of what Marcel Proust says about those events we call experience, 'where everything dissolves into the past and where we never know what's coming next, [which] can't give us any sense of reality, although we call it real life' (p32). Proust believes that when it comes to 'ordinary experience we're all in the position of a dog in a library, surrounded by a world of meaning in plain sight that we don't even know is there' (cited in Frye, pp32–33). Frye adds that, 'no matter how much experience we may gather in life, we can never in life get the dimension of life that imagination gives us' (p42).

Where does all this leave us? If we are true to our theme, we have to be circumspect in drawing this discussion to a close. The discussion has treated the matter of preparation programmes in a general way by positing that different stakeholders are differentially interested in 'the stuff' of educational administration, and that this difference does not mean that the field is in chaos. However, our premise implies that account should be taken of the kinds of perspectives administrators-in-training have or need to experience. We conclude by making two major points. First, preparation programmes should address the perspectives of the practitioner, the researcher, the scholar, and perhaps most important of all, the person. Second, the true worth of a preparation programme is to be found in the living memory of those who experience it. Perhaps many versions of interests and ideas can serve those memories. The quality is not merely a function of the mix of theory and practice, of the social sciences and the humanities, or any other dichotomy for that matter; the excellent programmes are likely to be an unusual mixture of many of these. Some learning may be contrived, some may be through observation, some may be by trial and error; but some should be through personal discoveries and insights. If more attention is paid to the development of the person, our departments may get a new lease on life, and a renewed purpose as the evolution of our field continues.

Notes

[1] Educational Managers is the more common term in Europe.
[2] These comments were made by Piele and Culbertson in the foreword to the ERIC/CEM-UCEA Series on Administrator Preparation.

References

American Association of School Administrators 38th Yearbook 1960, *Professional Administrators for America's Schools*, Washington, DC: AASA.

Achilles, C 1981, *Quo Vadis? Some Approaches to the Use of the Humanities in Leadership Preparation Programs*, paper presented at an AERA Invited Symposium, Los Angeles (ERIC Document Service No. ED 202 166).

Bridges, E 1977, 'The nature of leadership' in Cunningham, L, Hack, W and Nystrand, R (eds) *Educational Leadership: The Developing Decades*, Berkeley: McCutchan.

Frye, N 1963, *The Educated Imagination*, Toronto: CBC Publications.

Griffiths, D E, Stout, R T and Forsyth, P B 1988, *Leaders for America's Schools*. Berkeley, C A: McCutchan.

Gronn, P 1983, *Rethinking Educational Administration: TB Greenfield and his Critics*, Geelong: Deakin University Press.

Hughes, M G 1988, 'Comparative educational administration' in N J Boyan (ed), *Handbook of Research on Educational Administration*, New York: Longman.

Hughes, T 1988 'Myth and education' in K Egan and D Nadaner (eds) *Imagination and Education*, New York: Teachers College Press.

Lortie, D C 1962, 'Complexity, specialization and professional knowledge: overall strategies in the preparation of school administrators' in J Culbertson and S P Hencley (eds), *Preparing Administrators: New Perspectives*, Columbus, Ohio: University Council for Educational Administration.

Macintosh, A A 1989, *Humanities: Content in preparation programs for educational administration: a Canadian perspective*, unpublished master's thesis, University of Saskatchewan, Saskatoon, S K, Canada.

National Association of Secondary School Principals 1985, *Performance-based Preparation of Principals – A Framework for Improvement*, a special report of the NASSP Consortium for the Performance-Based Preparation of Principals, Reston, VA: NASSP.

Popper, S H 1982, 'An advocate's case for the humanities in preparation programs for school administration', *Journal of Educational Administration*, 20(1): 12–22.

Popper, S H 1985, *Pathways to the Humanities in Preparation Programs for Educational Administration*, Tempe, A Z: UCEA.

Schon, D 1987, *Educating the Reflective Practitioner*, San Francisco: Jossey-Bass.

4.4 A Regional On-site Administrator Programme from the USA

Glen Earthman

Introduction

During the past decade, educators in the US have been confronted with a great number of reports on education, most of which have been critical of what is being done in the public schools. Among those reports have been some that have also been critical of the manner in which educational administrators are prepared by the colleges and universities. It has not been a secret that the best the institutions of higher education can do to prepare administrators is to involve prospective candidates in a series of course work which is state certification mandated, but which may or may not be relevant to the job to which they aspire. This is to say that the vast majority of administrator preparation programmes simply give a person a licence to obtain a job; the programmes do not really prepare them for the challenges and problems they will face in that position.

Reform background

The reports on the condition of education in the US that were issued during the decade of the 1980s impacted heavily upon the method of preparing educational administrators by citing the inadequate training these professionals were receiving at the colleges and universities. The University Council on Educational Administration issued a report on the status of programmes for training administrators in the US, and stated that present programs were characterized by:

Lack of a definition of good educational leadership.
Lack of leader recruitment programs in the schools.
Lack of collaboration between school districts and Universities.
Lack of minorities/women in the field.
Lack of systematic professional development for school administrators.
Lack of quality candidates for preparation programs.
Lack of prepration programs relevant to the job demands.
Lack of sequence, content and clinical experiences in preparation programs.
Lack of a licensure system which promotes excellence.
Lack of a national sense of co-operation in preparing leaders.
(1987)

This rather dismal assessment of the existing programmes is, however, accurate without exaggeration. But in all honesty, the present state of preparation programmes is not a result of indolence or lack of caring, but rather a result of not keeping up with the times. All programmes reflect the certification requirements of the respective states and these requirements were set sometimes as much as twenty years ago. The school organizations have changed considerably in that period of time as have the problems administrators face in the schools. This is simply a matter of the certification requirements not keeping step with the changing conditions of the schools, and, as a result, the preparation programmes reflect the out-dated certification requirements, not the present conditions.

Restructuring of preparation programmes

In keeping with the demands for reform of the programmes that prepare educational administrators, many states initiated efforts to restructure them. Most efforts attempted to incorporate the more recent research findings on preparation that have been generated from such sources as the research on effective schooling and national reports on leadership training, such as *Leaders for America's Schools, A Progress Report and Recommendations on Educational Improvement in the SREB States,* and *Preparing Virginia School Administrators: An Analysis of Policy Options.*

Components of a restructured programme

Most efforts to restructure the administrator preparation programme suggest certain components that should be in existence to meet all of the demands of a programme that will prepare administrators for the schools of the future. Some of the more salient components are: a co-operative effort between the local school system and university staff, the programme administered off-campus and located within the local school system, revision of the existing course work to make it more relevant to the job, a full-time internship, use of a mentor, adequate assessment of candidates, individualization of the educational programme and follow-up support. These components make up the Regional Principal Preparation Program.

Co-operative effort

The certification regulations promulgated in Virginia mandate that the university staff work co-operatively with the personnel in the local school system to develop the entire programme. This means that considerable planning effort must take place in order to deal with all the issues and aspects. A committee is composed of representatives of the university and interested local school systems to provide the governance and guidance for the project. This committee serves as a steering group to make the decisions regarding all phases of work. The method of identifying, selecting and admitting students is co-operatively decided by the steering committee, for instance. The procedure must account for university regulations regarding admission of students and also for local school system concerns and personnel need. Likewise, the content and experiences that comprise the programme must be jointly decided. This is based upon both the knowledge-base of administration which the university staff can bring and what the local school system believes a school administrator does while on the job. These two sources then determine the content of the coursework. The actual teaching of the course work still remains primarily with the university teaching staff because of the course credit and degree requirements, but is greatly augmented by local school system personnel who serve as adjunct professors. This effort becomes a team teaching arrangement between the two groups who share responsibility for the instructional programme. The co-operative effort continues in decision making regarding the places where the internship will be held, who will be responsible and what kinds of experiences the students will have. Finally, the method of assessment of the students is also decided upon by the steering committee. This group solves problems that may arise during the course and becomes the governing body.

Off-campus/on-site programme delivery

One of the major shifts in orientation in the restructured programme is the aspect of delivering all coursework at the local school system site rather than on the campus of the university. This geographical shift is more than just a physical move, for it represents a shift in emphasis from a research-based degree to a practitioner degree. Although this shift may appear subtle, it is of major importance to the contributing organizational bodies. This plan takes the professor away from the university confines and into the scene where the student will perform as an administrator. This is significant and it also reinforces the co-operative nature of the entire programme. If the programme were conducted on campus, it would necessitate all school personnel and students going to that location and would not represent much of a change in either orientation or substance. In addition, the local school setting can serve as a laboratory in which students can practice the art and science of educational adminstration, and professors can be involved as contributors to that laboratory experience. The setting also serves as a place where university staff can obtain some in-service practical experience about the administration of the school building. The setting also provides for a better tie-in with the experiences of the internship.

Recruitment of students

Under the old programme of principal preparation, students made the recruitment decisions in as much as they were the ones who would pay for it through tuition payments. It was a market driven programme, based upon the free enterprise of each student. In addition, most programmes were the basis of an economic model designed to support doctoral programmes in educational administration. Because of this, universities enrolled large numbers of students in the certification level courses to generate funds to support other parts of the institution's degree programmes. Entrance requirements for such courses were usually minimal to enable large numbers of students to enroll.

Under the restructured preparation programmes, recruitment of students is more structured, systematic and quality driven. There are still sufficient means for all students to either be nominated by their peers or superiors or for self nomination to occur. All personnel in the local paricipating school systems are notified of the possibilities for nomination and are given forms to complete either for themselves or others. It is important that a large pool of applicants be secured in order for the best candidates to surface. Minorities of all types are encouraged to apply. The self nomination process encourages minority persons to apply, but, in addition, notices are sent out specifically requesting such nominations. In some cases, minorities are identified by former graduates of the university who are contacted for names of possible candidates. A positive recruitment programme is necessary not only for meeting the demands for equal employment opportunity directives, but also to obtain superior candidates who will reflect the population to be served.

Coursework relevant to the job

The coursework taken by a student under the previous certification programme does not reflect the changes in society and schools that have taken place over the past ten years. Under most programmes, the certification component consisted of a certain number of courses that were not related to each other nor to the local school building organization. Courses such as school finance which dealt with the theory of financing public schools were included in the certification requirements. The contents of this course, although relevant to higher level course work, is not the kind of knowledge a principal of a school building needs to secure and allocate resources. In the restructured programme, the content to be studied by the prospective administrators must relate directly to the job expected of principals. Selection of the content may seem like an easy task, but first of all there has to be agreement by both university staff and local school system personnel on what a principal does. When that is determined, relevant knowledge, skills and even attitudes that are used on the job can be identified. This is not a replication of what the principal does presently on the job, but rather what the principal of the future may need in these areas.

In the Regional Programme for the Preparation of Principals, the school building principal was defined as one who is primarily a creator and implementor of educational programmes for students at the building level. The principal leads a group of educators within the constraints of a larger system but endeavours to enlarge those constraints. The person is an educational scholar, leader and manager who knows that schools exist to produce individual learning.

As the school executive, the principal must be a learner at all times. The person must have a broad knowledge of disciplines and be exposed to the philosophical bases of education. The principal must study the theory and research on learning. The successful person must have a comprehensive knowledge of how students learn.

The principal is a visionary leader who possesses good human relations skills. The person must possess vision for the organization, and this is gained by a thorough understanding of the goals of education; theories of learning; family life and development; curriculum; governance and technology of education. The vision is then communicated to teachers, parents, central administration and the community at large. The principal empowers these people to implement the programme of the school. The thrust is one of high expectations, and, at the same time, the person has the confidence to be an informed risk-taker who permits and accepts change.

In addition to scholarship and leadership, the prospective principal must possess good management skills essential to the efficient operation of the school building. These skills are used by the principal to allocate the resources of the organization to accomplish set goals in an effective and efficient manner.

In order to assist a prospective principal to gain the skills, knowledge and attitudes necessary to perform at a high level of effectiveness in accordance with the above definition, the curriculum and other instructional activities of the programme must provide experiences through which to gain them. Certain skills, knowledge and attitudes will be gained from the internship while others will be gained from both formal instructional activities and individual experiences. The curriculum designed for this programme accommodates all three instructional thrusts.

The curriculum will be delivered over 24 months. The content and time requirements in hours and semester credits follow:

	Minimum hours	Semester credits
Experiential activities	600	12
Formal instruction	360	24
Individual study	360	—
Total hours expected	1320	36

The experiential activities will be covered through the fulltime internship each candidate will have.

Direct instruction on foundations of education, theories and practices in education and administration and related studies will be provided in the formal instructional component of the programme. The specific areas of instruction will be:

	Minimum hours	Semester credits
Leadership/administration	120	8
Child development	60	4
Programme/curriculum development	60	4
Instruction/learning supervision	60	4
Nature of education	30	2
Liberal arts studies	30	2
Total formal instruction	360	24

The specific content of each of the broad areas of formal instruction have yet to be determined; however, the content will be derived from the definition of what a principal does as outlined above. The subject matter content of the programme will, however, be couched within the framework of university courses to comply with the degree requirements of that institution. The course timetable is as follows:

	1989–90	1990–91
Fall	EDAE 6914 Problems: The Principalship — Leadership Skills	EDAE 5604 Seminar: Legal, Financial and Personnel Issues
Spring	EDAE 6014 Administration of Instructional Programmes & Support Services HUM 555 Order & Chaos A Liberal Arts Perspective	EDAE 5054 Administration of Special Needs Programmes EDCI 6914 Problems: Teaching & Learning in the Curriculum
Summer	EDAE 5614 Internship: Principalship — School Site Leadership I EDAE 5604 Seminar: The Context of Education	EDAE 5614 Internship: Principalship — School Site Leadership II EDRE 5404 Foundations of Education Research and Evaluation

The total semester credits accumulated under this plan is 36. The prospective principals will complete the internship experiences during the school year, but register for the internship credit during the summers to equalize the financial tuition burden of the entire programme.

Full-time internship

A very important component of the restructured principal preparation programme is the full-time internship for each prospective principal. Full-time has been defined as being a minimum of 90 days in the school during the two year period. The internship is further defined as being conducted during the time when the school is in session or when a significant activity is being conducted such as an evening meeting of the school board. The internship is objective-driven so that the experiences provide direct learning in the operation of the school. The internship is not an opportunity for the prospective principal to follow the principal around looking over the shoulder of the practitioner. The intern is intimately involved in the decision-making life of the school organization. The objectives defined for the internship must be completed within the time frame of the programme. There are 62 objectives that the intern can work to achieve; however, the precise objectives are identified by the intern, mentor, faculty advisor and the advisory committee. The objectives chosen are then identified in the Individual Education Programme for each intern. Some common objectives must be met by all interns, but the majority are selected to fit the needs of each individual.

The internship is conceived as an opportunity for the prospective principal to actually administer portions of a school programme under the watchful eye of a trained practitioner in much the same way that a medical intern practices under the supervision of a fully licenced physician. At the beginning of the internship, the prospective principal will get to know the school organization by examining many documents and sources of information. This will give the person a good knowledge-base upon which to base future work. Gradually, the intern will take on more responsibility for certain jobs. The intern will supervise students and teachers in a variety of settings, both formal and informal, and will make some classroom observations of teachers, then conduct follow-up conferences with teachers. This will occur after the intern has gained observation skills and knowledge through training by the mentor. The intern will also be assigned responsibility for other segments of the operation of the school. For example, the intern may be assigned the responsibility of organizing and conducting a staff development programme for the teachers in the school. The intern could also assume responsibility for developing the annual school improvement plan for the building. These and other significant experiences are the proper format for learning the practical administration of the school and for putting into practice theory that is taught in formal course work.

The 90 day internship can be accomplished in one of two ways. One way would be for the intern to spend 90 consecutive days in the school. This would provide for the total immersion of the intern into the life of the school and provide for a sustained effort at administering the school. On the other hand, there are some experiences that the intern should have that may not fall within the 90 day span of time. For instance, before actually having that full responsibility, prospective principals should experience the opening of school in the fall and the closing of it during the spring. These activities do not fall within a 90 day time frame. In a compressed period of time, there may not be sufficient time to reflect upon experiences they have had and to discuss them in a didactic manner with a mentor, thereby learning the reasons behind certain actions or decisions. Because of this, the Regional Programme for the Preparation of Principals decided to spread the 90 days over two years and have the intern spend 45 days each year in the schools. In this manner the intern can have a variety of experiences that cover two years, yet work on some long term projects. The intern can also develop a long-standing learning relationship with the mentor.

In order to obtain a broad understanding of administration in a number of settings, the interns in the Regional Program are required to spend the equivalent of at least six days interning in an organization outside of the field of education. These experiences could be held in a hospital, insurance company, newspaper or government office. The objective in having the interns complete this experience is to help them understand the similarities and differences in administration in non-educational institutions.

Mentorship

Each intern is assigned to a mentor who serves as the first line supervisor of activities while that person is in the school building. The mentor also helps the intern identify and achieve the objectives of the internship and at the same time provide some direct instruction in how to administer organizations. Over the two years, the mentor will provide emotional as well as professional support to the intern during the learning phase of the programme and this will continue through the follow-up activity.

Mentors are chosen for their exceptional leadership qualities in the local school system and are approved by the school administration. They are principals who more closely exemplify the definition of a principal stated for this programme. These persons are ones who have been rated as superior by those above them in the organization. Furthermore, the principal chosen as mentor must have shown a good deal of commitment to the programme and a willingness to serve in the capacity of a mentor.

Advisory committee

Each prospective principal is assigned an advisory committee composed of the university faculty professor, mentor, and a representative of the local school system. The university faculty member will serve as the chair of the committee. The role of the advisory committee is to develop a close and caring relationship with the prospective principal. The prospective principal and committee is viewed as a team working together to maximize the prospective principal's chances of success. The specific responsibilities include:

- Assess the participant's entry-level skills, knowledge and attitudes; assist the prospective principal in preparing an Individual Educational Plan (IEP); and approve the plan.
- Meet periodically with the participant to evaluate progress of the prospective principal.
- Receive feedback from the participant and provide counsel on both personal and professional matters.
- Select 45 days annually that will be used by the participants in an internship or practicum and provide logistics for time away from the work situation of the prospective principal.
- Provide a strong network with the central office staff and all components of the local school system.
- Ensure that the prospective principal receives comprehensive and rich experiences in preparation for success in the position of principal.
- Assist the prospective principal in preparing to take an administrative position in the future.
- Assist the prospective principal in locating a suitable position after finishing the programme.
- Provide follow-up assistance when the prospective principal leaves the programme.

Each member of the advisory committee also has a unique role. The university faculty representative will ensure that the prospective principal has an academically sound and acceptable programme which includes content in leadership, student development, instruction, curriculum, the nature of education and liberal studies. The local school system representative will establish and co-ordinate time schedules for the participant. The mentor will serve as the on-site director of field experiences throughout the prospective principal's two-year programme. The mentor will also ensure that the prospective principal has appropriate on-site experiences in a school building setting.

The Advisory Committee will be responsible for the prospective principal being involved in the following activities in a school setting while serving as an intern:

- Curriculum development;
- Staff development,
- Interviewing, selecting and assigning personnel;
- Preparation and administration of a school budget;
- Supervision of bookkeeping and accounting procedures;
- Developing an annual school improvement plan;
- Coordination of student scheduling and orientation;
- Developing a master schedule;
- Supervision and evaluation of student activity and athletic programmes;
- Positive student discipline;
- Preparation of local and state reports;
- Work experiences with other principals, supervisors and administrators within and outside of education that will broaden the person's conception of schooling, its environment and its administration.

Formal meetings of the advisory committee are called by the chair, but any member of the committee can request a meeting. These meetings are used for reviewing assessment data, identifying intern experiences, reviewing and improving the IEP and evaluating the progress of the prospective principal at the end of each semester.

Development of an Individual Education Plan (IEP)

Each prospective principal prepares an IEP which is presented to the Advisory Committee for review and approval. The contents of the IEP are based upon assessment data derived during the initial sessions of the semester courses. The IEP looks very much like those used in the public schools throughout the United States. Each IEP contains the following information:

1. A summary of assessment data.
2. Courses to be taken each semester.
3. Description of internship or practicum experiences.
4. Extra-curricular activities.
5. A schedule of dates set for the practicum, courses and other activities.

Although the coursework may be the same for each participant, individualization will be accounted for through both the internship experiences and the extra-curricular activities. Identification of these experiences and activities will result from review of assessment data. Appropriate experiences and activities will be prescribed by the advisory committee to remedy or strengthen any area as necessary. The IEP will serve the prospective principal during the two years of the programme and will be revised when appropriate.

Assessment of prospective principals

One of the more important aspects of the restructured principal preparation programme is the reliance upon assessment of all candidates. The assessment is a continuous activity beginning with the selection procedure and continuing to the time when the prospective principal exits from the program. A variety of assessment practices and instruments will be used. During the initial sessions of the instructional modules, several instruments were used to give the participants some idea regarding their leadership potential. The following instruments were used at that time: FIRO-B, California Psychological Test, and Myers-Briggs Inventory. The results of these instruments were shared with the participants and discussed with the idea of helping them to evaluate their leadership potential and to identify any areas on which they wished to improve. Assessment also occurs during the formal coursework throughout the two year period of study, and this is augmented through the periodic review of the work of the participant by the advisory committee. The prospective principal is also assessed by the mentor through the internship experiences.

The final assessment will be through the Assessment Center of the National Association of Secondary School Principals. The Southwest Virginia Regional Assessment Center is located on the campus and will be used to assess all of the prospective principals that complete the programme. This experience assesses twelve dimensions which are considered essential for success in the position of the principalship. These dimensions are: problem analysis, judgement, leadership, organizational ability, decisiveness, sensitiveness, stress tolerance, range of interests, personal motivation, educational values, oral communication and written communication. Assessment experiences in this Centre consist of leaderless group activities, in-basket responses, interviews and problem-solving activities all of which contribute to an overall assessment of the candidate. A final report detailing strengths and weaknesses is given to the local school system to use in helping the candidate work on whatever weaknesses were identified through the assessment activities.

On-the-job follow-up

A formal programme of follow-up activities has been formulated to assist the prospective principal to succeed when placed in an administrative position. These activities are designed to provide support, to help in making adjustment to the position, to provide assistance in any particular problem and to give feedback on the quality of work that is being done. Principals will be visited by the university faculty member as the first line contact between the advisory committee and the graduate of the programme. The purpose of the visit will be to maintain the bonding that has been set during the programme and to provide whatever technical assistance the person might need. Further, the other members of the advisory committee — mentor and central office staff member — will conduct supevisory visits where desired and necessary. In fact, the advisory committee as a group will provide follow-up activities to the graduate where appropriate.

Graduates will also be brought together as a group to share experiences, to continue the bonding within the group, to identify resources that may be needed by the individual graduates and to extend the knowledge base of the group. Group experiences will be both formal and informal to meet the needs of the individuals. Some of the get-togethers will be of a social nature to further the bonding, whereas other sessions might be formalized enough to have a presentation and discussion of a specific topic. The specific nature of the group sessions will depend to a great extent upon the needs of the graduates, but the mechanism is in place to be used in the manner that will assist the new principal to the greatest extent.

Evaluation

The project that is now underway will be evaluated at the end of the first year and again at the conclusion of the programme for this group of individuals. Further, evaluation of the graduates will take place following the end of the first year of their work as an administrator. This evaluation will be conducted jointly with the university faculty and school system personnel. An evaluation of the entire programme will be made using external and internal evaluators. Universty personnel from neighbouring institutions of higher education and school system personnel will be used to help conduct the evaluation. Evaluative methodologies and instruments are being developed, based upon the goals of the programme and the description of the type of principal to be trained. This two pronged effort will allow both the process and product of the programme to be evaluated. Data derived from these evaluations will serve as the basis for further principal preparation programmes that will be developed in other parts of the state.

References

Astuto, T A, Wagoner, J & Yeakey, C 1988, *Preparing Virginia School Administrators: An Analysis of Policy Options*, Charlottesville, VA: Virginia Educational Policy Analysis Center.

National Commission on Excellence in Educational Administration 1987, *Leaders for America's Schools*, The Commission.

Southern Regional Education Board 1987, *A Progress Report and Recommendations on Educational Improvements in the SREB States*, Atlanta, GA: SREB.

4.5 Educational Administration: Internship Programmes in Canada

Edward Hickcox and John House

Background

The notion of internships as component parts of professional training programmes is a familiar concept. Most often associated with formal training programmes in medicine, internships of various kinds have been utilized in education in various ways, including training programmes in Educational Administration.

Internships in Educational Administration involve, generally, placing the student in some administrative position in an organization for a period of time. Under supervision, the individual performs tasks and works with a supervisor or mentor, observing what the practice of administration is like in a real situation. Internships exist, also in non-university based training programmes, typically programmes run by school systems to identify, train and socialise future administrators within the system.

Internships in Educational Administration have been around for a long time. In the early 1960s, for example, the Ford Foundation poured massive funds into a prototype administrative training programme in New York State known as the Ford Foundation Internship Programme (Hickcox, 1966). This programme involved a co-operative effort by four upstate New York universities, Cornell,

Buffalo, Syracuse and Rochester, to provide intensive on-site experiences in real administrative positions for a year. While judged successful during the four year funding period, the programme did not survive when the costs had to be carried by the participating organizations. Even today, however, New York State requires an internship experience of some sort for those wishing certification for central office administration.

The internship has been an important component of the doctoral programme at the Ontario Institute for Studies in Education (OISE) for more than 15 years. In Ontario, a Ministry commissioned study on supervisory officers (Fullan, Park and Williams 1987) recommends internship experiences as a qualification for senior administrative positions.

The original impetus for this chapter was to report a survey of internship programmes in Canadian universities and school systems. As will be documented presently, the survey indicated mainly that neither universities nor school systems in Canada have highly developed internship programmes as part of professional preparation for administration, with a very few exceptions. Further, a review of published papers in the field yields a paucity of serious work.

The purpose of this chapter, therefore, is to report the survey results and to discuss what publications there are. From this, we will attempt to offer some clarification of the general notion in terms of models of the internship, and finally we will suggest issues surrounding the development and use of internships and make some evaluative comments.

The survey

A letter was sent to 18 universities across Canada which have graduate programmes in Educational Administration, either at the masters level or the doctoral level. Replies were received from 11 institutions. Except for OISE, whose programme will be discussed in more detail later, none of the institutions had made an internship experience central to the programme. Only at OISE was the programme connected to the EdD degree. Other institutions which indicated partial use of the internship approach in training programmes included the following:

University of Saskatchewan. In its Master of Education programme Saskatchewan had a fairly highly developed practicum programme as one course option. In this approach, the emphasis was definitely on having the students pursue quite a sophisticated project on-site in a school system, or, in fact, conduct a regular research project. While gaining a sense of what an operating school system is like, there is little doubt that the main intent is experience in carrying out research and projects and reporting on them. Supervision focuses on planning the project, and there is unlikely to be any on-site supervision.

McGill University. McGill has an internship program designed to orient its overseas students to school organization and culture in Quebec. To this end, students from abroad are placed in school situations for a period of weeks during which time they carry out administrative tasks, shadow administrators, and in general attempt to gain a perspective to assist them in adjusting to graduate study in administration in Canada.

Simon Fraser University. Although Simon Fraser does not have an internship component in its programme, Professor Norman Robinson of the Department of Educational Administration there indicated that one particular school district, the Kamloops School District, had run an in-house internship training programme, for more than 20 years. Otherwise, a recent study by Professor Robinson indicated that internship and clinical experience were not common in personnel practices in British Columbia.

Memorial University. Memorial University reported that it had an internship option as part of its Masters level programme in Educational Administration. Only a few students availed themselves of the opportunity, however, and there was no description of the programme.

Brandon University. While there is no internship programme as such at Brandon, there is a practicum type experience where students at both the BEd and MEd levels can have on-site experiences for a period of six weeks and receive course credit. An attempt is made to identify the needs of the student prior to placement and to place him or her in an appropriate setting. There is on-site supervision. Since the MEd program at Brandon is not yet fully operational, it is too early to tell whether the clinical aspects of the programme will be an integral aspect of it.

The Ontario Institute for Studies in Education. As indicated at the beginning of this chapter, the internship component of the EdD programme has been an important element since its inception in 1973. For a period of 10–12 weeks in the spring of the residence year, students are placed on a full time basis in some organization under supervision. A variety of organizations are used, including school systems, provincial organizations, and non-educational organizations such as IBM. There is a university supervisor and an on-site supervisor. The internship assignment is an administrative task which must have an element of risk for both the organization and the intern. The nature of the specific assignment is negotiated among the on-site supervisor, the university supervisor and the intern, and is specified in a form of contract. All interns meet once a week at the university for a seminar at which experience and ideas are shared. At the conclusion of the internship, the performance of the intern is assessed in separate written reports, which include grades by both the on-site supervisor and the university supervisor. The assessment reports are shared with the intern. Course credit is given for the internship.

The other responding universities reported no internship programmes and no school districts with developed in-house internship type experiences. In Ontario, however, it is known that some school boards have fairly sophisticated in-house administrator training programmes. These, in general, have not involved internship type experiences, however.

In general, there seems to be little activity and little interest in internships among Departments of Educational Administration in Canada. In no case, with the exception of OISE, was there a perception that the on-site experience is or should be central to administrative training. At the conclusion of the chapter we will attempt some analysis of why this is so.

Literature review

A recent review of the literature on the topic of administrative internships has revealed little in the nature of specific research studies which evaluate the effectiveness of internship programmes for administrators in practice (see Hickcox and Power 1989). Only one of the twenty-seven US studies examined actually reported results on the effect of internships on practice or attempted to measure effectiveness with any sort of product emphasis.

Each item, however, reported very positive experiences. In fact, in terms of evaluation, the overwhelming impression was that those who had undergone well organized internships had enjoyed them immensely and often regarded them as the most valuable aspect of their training programmes.

Some major characteristics of the internship programmes were gleaned from the descriptive items and can be summarized as follows:

1. Administrative internships range in length from two days to two years. The most acclaimed seem to be those which last for a full year.

2. Internship may be either full-time or part-time. The part-time ones generally occur within the school system where the intern has a full-time job.
3. Internships sometimes carry stipends equivalent to a teacher's salary.
4. Descriptions of internship programmes usually emphasise the importance of selecting good candidates. In one of the few general discussions of internships, McIntyre (1979) poses the problem in a way that only the most secure of us can accept. He documents that in terms of standardized tests, such as the Miller Analogies Test, graduate students in Educational Administration score significantly lower than any other group, including students in other areas of education. Without engaging in arguments about the validity of these tests, and recognizing that there are many outstanding students in our programmes, we must still acknowledge that the chances of bringing marginal people into the profession are greater in Educational Administration than in other fields. For an internship programme to be effective, McIntyre argues, the participants must be of high calibre. Unfortunately, while these articles emphasize the importance of good selection of candidates for internships, they don't generally offer much in the way of creative or innovative approaches for achieving this purpose. A move by some universities into assessment centre approaches for the selection of interns may alleviate this problem somewhat.
5. Most internship programmes described involve a combination of on-site experiences and university seminars. There is very little information provided, however, on the content of the internship experiences – that is what the interns actually do. The general intent seems to be to provide them with a 'real job' rather than providing them with trivial experiences.
6. Internships generally are cooperative efforts between university departments of Educational Administration run as part of a degree training programme and on a cooperative basis with school systems. The term "partnership" is often used in describing these programmes, meaning partnership between the intern, the university, and the school system.

What is worthy of notice with respect to the partnership concept is that there are responsibilities as well as benefits involved for all partners. Obviously, the intern gains the greatest benefits in that he or she is provided with practical administrative experience. Since lack of experience is often cited as a problem for those aspiring to administrative positions, the internship is recommended as an appropriate way to gain such experience.

Posey, Carlisle, and Smellie (1988) suggest that the internship is best undertaken at the end of a university programme, so that interns have already acquired a sound theoretical base on which to build in the practical field. Bialac and Wallington (1985) point as well to the opportunities provided in the internship programme for increased self-confidence, marketability, and clarified career goals. As well, interns get practical experience in developing an under-standing of the dynamics of a real organization, particularly with respect to the independent and interdependent roles, functions, and responsibilities of its members.

In terms of responsibilities, they suggest the intern must be will-ing to comply with the routines and structures of the organization, participating in all institutional and professional development ses-sions as assigned, so that he or she will achieve maximum benefits from the experience.

Bialac and Wallington elaborate on the responsibilities of the intern, listing a variety of activities such as producing a product, sharing knowledge, and so on. Obviously, the responsibilities of the intern as well as the benefits accrued will vary with the nature of the assignment.

Mann (1987) and Goodlad (1987) outline the responsibilities and benefits involved in the internship experience, not only for the intern, but for the university and organization as well. The universi-ty, they suggest, benefits in relation to the opportunities which are provided through the internship to enable their students to link the-ory with practice. As well, the internship programme provides for collaborative inquiry into problems within the school system and feedback regarding how university programmes can be refined to train school administrators to address these problems more effec-tively.

University supervisors, Mann suggests, have a responsibility to place students in suitable settings so that sufficient overlap exists between school or school board agendas and university training programmes.

The organization within which the intern is placed has benefits and responsibilities associated with its partnership role as well. Goodlad points to the benefits to the organization resulting from its participation as a partner in internship programmes. These benefits include a pool of qualified personnel for future hiring as well as opportunities to act as a resource base to assist university personnel in evaluating and revising their programmes. Mann likens the partnership in the internship programme to a symbiotic relationship where each partner shares not only in the responsibili-ties but in the benefits as well.

As indicated previously, these characteristics were outlined in articles which were not research-based but merely descriptive in nature. One study only, Sweeney, Huth and Engle (1981) attempted to assess the effectiveness of internship experiences. The researchers administered an instrument to about 60 secondary school principals who had internship experience and to about 60 who had not had such an experience.

The results are discouraging for those convinced of the significance of internships in preparation programs. Essentially no significant differences could be found between the two groups in terms of administrative practices in use. Interns ranked their own performance higher than did non-interns, but there was no significant difference in perception relative to the ability to discharge responsibilities for office management, staff relations, community relations, providing a favourable climate, inspiring confidence and overall administrative performance. The interns overwhelmingly, however, stated that the internship was a very valuable experience.

A recent paper by Cynthia Jackson of Nova University (1989) describes an 'active intervention model' (AIP) which purports to develop problem-solving skills in students through the identification of organizational problems in school districts and on-site efforts to solve them. She also refers to recent discussions in the US about the need for praticum type experiences for administrators (Runkel 1989; Griffiths, Stout, and Forsyth 1988).

Since the literature is so sparse in the research dimension on this topic, the findings as outlined above should be viewed with caution. Further study about the effectiveness of internship programmes along a number of dimensions seems to be necessary before any worthwhile conclusions can be drawn. Until this happens, educators should tread lightly when referring to the effectiveness of internships in practice. While acknowledging their popularity, it should be noted that effectiveness and popularity are terms which are not always synonymous.

Internship models

We can identify at least three basic internship models. By internship, we mean a component of an administrative training programme involving on-site experience in an organizational setting where the student becomes a part of the organization for a period of time. It includes supervision from within the organization and external to the organization.

In the first model, the internship is carried out as part of a degree programme at the university level, either a masters programme or a doctoral programme. The student is appointed to the staff of an organization, preferably at the organizational level, for a period of time ranging from several weeks to a year. During this period, the student works at tasks assigned by the organization, and he/she observes the operation of the organization from the participant observer point of view. He/she meets on some kind of regular basis with a university supervisor, and he/she also has an on-site supervisor. Some sort of end product is expected, either in terms of a report or a study or a seminar presentation. Course credit goes with the experience. The programme at OISE would be an example of this model and variations would include the project-orientated programme at the University of Saskatchewan. Another example[1] is found at Syracuse University in up-state New York (Sage and Blumberg 1988). In this programme, a small group of doctoral students take their resident year in the doctoral programme while serving an internship, usually in their own system. They must be involved in some major project for change, and they must provide a major report on this by the end of the year. The group meets on a regular basis during the year.

In the second model, a school district will organize an internship experience for members of its own staff for purposes of identifying and training future administrators within the system. A teacher, for example, might spend half time in the principal's office for a year, carrying out vice-principal duties. The group of interns might meet on a regular basis, perhaps once a month, to share experiences and to hear presentations from exprienced administrators and outside educational figures. The programme in the Kamloops, British Columbia school district is an example.[2]

In the third model, an outside organization, for example an administrator's organization, may organize an 'internship' programme for prospective or incumbent administrators in a jurisdiction. An example is the programme run in Ontario for several years by the Ontario Association of Education Administrative Officials and currently by the Ontario Council for Leadership in Educational Administration. In this programme, newly appointed central office administrators may undertake an intensive training programme which has an internship component. For a period of time, perhaps two weeks or a month, the participant works in a district other than his/her own, perhaps a situation with a particular programme of interest. There is no direct supervision, as such, but the participants attend various seminars and conferences as a group over a two year period.[3]

Issues

Internship programmes in general and each model in particular has pluses and minuses in terms of usefulness in administrative training. Some of these issues are outlined below. In general, we believe that the right kind of internship has immense potential for influencing individuals towards better administrative practice. There are two factors, at least, however, which should guide the administration of internships. The first is to ensure that the mentor, or on-site supervisor, is absolutely first rate. Ideally, there should be some sort of reputational survey done among participating systems to identify principals or central office administrators who are excellent role models. Most of us do not have the time, energy or resources to do this well, but we should. The second is to think through, with the on-site supervisor, the content of the experience. This involves knowing the intent of the training programme itself. Are we looking to train instructional leaders, organization managers, administrator scholars, research-oriented administrators, or some combination? It is more than a matter of finding a place that will take the particular individual.

An important issue is whether there should be a university connection or whether other organizations can develop viable experiences. Our position is that the rounding effect provided by the university connection provides the proper balance between the 'hands on' experience often requested by practitioners and the more general understandings often thought to be the result of academic exposure. The university connection, also, has some possibility of negating the tendency of perpetuating past practices by placing individuals in mentoring situations with practicing administrators.

A major concern with those involved in sophisticated internship programmes is their cost. They are labour intensive from the point of view of the university supervisor, without any accompanying academic payoff. An offshoot of this is that probably those actually engaged in intern supervision are the less academic staff members. This might tend to defeat the very purpose of university involvement.

Finally, most internship programmes are not subject to sufficient evaluation of their effectiveness in any kind of rigid way. Further, we need to find ways to promote research of a systematic nature into what sorts of clinical experiences really result in better administrative behaviour on the job.

Notes

[1] Information about the Syracuse program was obtained in several conversations between E Hickcox and A Blumberg of Syracuse.

[2] This judgement is based on dialogue with officials of the Kamloops District by E Hickcox in November of 1988 at a conference in Vancouver, British Columbia.

[3] Based on conversations with Peter Angelini, Executive Director of the Ontario Council for Leadership in Educational Administration.

References

Bialac, C and Wallington, J 1985 *Staff Development Leadership Institute for Principals*, Raleigh: North Carolina State Department of Public Instruction.

Fullan, Michael, Park, Paul, and Williams, Thomas, 1987 *The Supervisory Officer in Ontario*, Toronto: Queen's Printer for Ontario.

Goodlad, J 1987 'Schools and universities can, and must, work together', in *Principal* 61(1), pp9–15.

Griffiths, D, Stout, R and Forsyth, P 1988 (eds) *Leaders for America's Schools*, Report of the National Commission on Excellence in Educational Administration, Berkeley: McCutchan Publishing Company.

Hickcox, Edward S and Power, Mary, 1989 'Preparation Programs and Internship', paper presented at the Annual Meeting of the Canadian Association for the Study of Educational Administration, Quebec City, Quebec.

Hickcox, Edward S 1966 'An Administrative Internship in a Suburban School System' unpublished Field Study for the Interuniversity Ford Foundation Project II, Cornell University.

Jackson, Cynthia L 1989 'The Active-Intervention Practicum (AIP) Model', paper presented at the 3rd annual conference of the University Council for Educational Administration, Phoenix, Arizona.

Mann, D 1987 'Business involvement in public school improvement,' *Phi Delta Kappan* 69(2), pp123–8.

McIntyre, Kenneth. 'Training Programs for Principals' *Theory Into Practice*, Vol 18, No 1, Feb 1979, pp28–32.

Posey, L Carlisle, G and Smellie, N 1988 'An internship case study', in *Training and Development Journal*, 42(2), pp59–64.

Runkle, J 1989 'The Practicum in Educational Administration: still useful but major changes are needed', University of North Carolina at Greensboro Report.

Sage, D and Blumberg, A 1988 'The study of practice: A field based EdD residency program' Paper presented at the 2nd annual meeting of the University Council for Educational Administration, Cincinnati, Ohio.

Sweeney, Jim, Huth and Engle 1981 'Principal Internships – A Look at the Facts'. *Education*, Vol 102, No 2, pp151–153.

4.6 School Leadership Development for the Twenty-first Century: an Australian case

Ann Clark

Introduction

Local context

This chapter is in the context of an education system based in Parramatta some 20 kilometres west of Sydney, Australia. It is a system operated by the Catholic Church and as such, has a freedom in the direction it takes within the constraints of the educational and funding policies of the New South Wales (State) and the Australian (Federal) Governments.

The Paramatta Catholic Education System consists of a group of schools under a Board of Education. The Chief Executive Officer is responsible for the conduct and operation of all the schools in the system. The *system* is recognized by the State and Federal Governments as one of many such systems throughout the country. Each system receives capital and recurrent funding from both levels of government. Each system is responsible for the administration of the government money and other finances received from school fees and other sources. It is responsible for the employing of teachers and the appropriate allocation of resources with the co-operation of the schools within the system.

Currently the Parramatta system of schools (the Parramatta System) operates 50 primary and 22 secondary schools with 37,000 students. The projection for the year 2001 is 90 schools and 60,000 students. A small number of independent Catholic schools relate to the system flexibly and utilize some of the services the system provides.

The area covered by the Diocese of Parramatta, of which the Parramatta System is its educational arm, is the fastest growing area in Australia in terms of population, with all the social problems inevitable in a place of rapid and artifically contrived growth. The Parramatta System became autonomous only three years ago with the establishment of a new Diocese. It was cut off from the much larger Catholic Education system of Sydney. Parramatta enjoys the strengths of a young, growing, vibrant system seeking to build on the part of the inheritance it received from Sydney and to establish its own identity and traditions.

The global context

The schools of the Parramatta Diocese, of course, are sensitive to and significantly affected by the kaleidoscopic changes in the social and educational environment worldwide. Its schools are required to face issues of quality, excellence and equity, devolution of decision making, rationalisation of services and frequent and radical restructuring. There is every indication that these, and other issues as yet only dimly perceived, will demand an increasing amount of time and energy of all education systems into the next century. At the same time, the economic imperatives and the expectations of a community increasingly more sensitive to educational questions will have a decided impact on public policy, with a corresponding impact on the availability and utilization of education resources.

Philosophical context

In seeking to identify the challenges that face our future leaders it is necessary to keep in clear focus the primary function of our schools. This has been articulated by the Parramatta System in a *Corporate Vision Statement*. This states that:–
— our schools will be centres of human excellence,
— centres of learning which strive towards excellence, in all areas of human growth,

— agents of change which take a leadership role on moral and values issues,
— places where young people experience the rich heritage of Catholic teachings, culture and tradition.

The key group in the pursuit of excellence, of quality teaching and learning in a school, is the staff. Schools become 'excellent', 'effective' or 'successful' (Sergiovanni 1987) through the efforts of staff. Parents can contribute effectively in school life only if the staff allows that development to occur. Individually, and collectively, staff fashion excellence in a school. Principals, and to a lesser extent systems leaders, can only establish the conditions which permit and encourage the pursuit of excellence by staff.

The *Corporate Vision Statement* expresses the ideal of what the System wants its students to be. It is a statement of the ideal of what kind of person the graduate should be at graduation.

Educational sociologists are predicting that those who are students now may expect to be retrained three times during their working life. This demands a flexibility on the part of schools and students for which neither is adequately prepared at present. The Parramatta System has as its vision to train its students to be independent thinkers with well established skills of reasoning and critical analysis, including an understanding of the fundamentals of research. School leaders must be given the capacity to bring together the human and material resources entrusted to them, and to manage and to lead so that the ideal as portrayed in the *Corporate Vision Statement* is achieved.

Vision for the twenty-first century

The Parramatta System has concluded that a crucial factor in implementing plans for the future is the effective development of leaders of its system. Leaders for the future must be able to identify the challenges facing education and specifically in this context, the challenges facing the Parramatta System. They must be able to address these challenges appropriately, be able to comprehend their implications and be able to contribute to the development of appropriate responses.

The Parramatta System has identified seven issues that it considers to be the primary challenges for the year 2000.
1. To ensure the identity of the Catholic school.
2. To articulate the profile of the "ideal" graduate and to achieve that ideal.
3. To identify and develop future leaders.

4. To assist teachers and leaders to cope with the demands placed on them by the unrelenting pace of change.
5. To involve parents more actively in the development and education of their children.
6. To promote the professional and religious development of teachers in Catholic schools.
7. To ensure the consistent pursuit of excellence in teaching and learning.

These seven challenges relate to all levels of the education system and they inter-relate and impinge one upon the other.

To ensure the identity of the Catholic school

This identity must be reviewed and probably restated. The vision and goals of a Catholic school in the past were embodied in the religious men and women who led and taught in Catholic schools. Their obvious and tangible religious presence has been replaced by another just as strong and obvious a religious presence but in a different form. We need to ensure that the new form is maintained in quality and that it is *seen* to be maintained.

To have an authentic Catholic school requires leaders with a vision and a clear sense of purpose, with a capacity to apply Christian values as appreciated in the Catholic tradition. Such leaders will provide a vibrant and optimistic call to Catholic schools to bring them into the twenty-first century with their fundamental mission and goals intact.

To articulate the profile of the 'ideal' graduate and to achieve that ideal

The ideal graduate of a Catholic school of The Parramatta System as set out in its *Statement of Understanding and Vision* is one who will:–
1. Search for truth.
2. Be responsible for his or her own learning and decision making.
3. Be able to think, research, reason reflect and act in the light of Gospel values.
4. Strive for excellence in all areas of human growth.
5. Gain knowledge, skills and competence necessary to participate in and contribute to society.
6. Learn from a curriculum which is academically rigorous and relevant to his/her life experiences.

7. Determine a set of personal values which will form a framework for life decisions.
8. Be convinced of the concept of learning as a lifelong process.
9. Have a commitment to the Christian faith and practise it in the Catholic tradition.

To move from a simple statement of an ideal to an achieved reality demands a rigorous process of dynamic school and curriculum development followed by evaluation and further modification.

To identify and develop our future leaders

This system has as its goal to develop strategies and processes to find its future leaders and to provide them with systematic, on-going development.

Development processes will be systematic and on-going. Co-operative ventures between systems, schools and tertiary institutions are being developed. Development will be linked to accreditation and based on a praxis model. As well, the developers of relevant courses will have as their aim a multi-skilling of their participants. This will be a prime need for a leader of the future.

To involve parents more actively in the development and education of their children

The need for a partnership with parents and the basis of that partnership is urgently demanded in schools. Developing that partnership is a very slow process and involves a mutual giving and receiving. Current school principals do not come from a culture which sets high store by parental participation however much they proclaim its value. That participation is still very limited, not so much because of neglect but rather a consequence of the way the system evolved.

To promote the personal, professional and religious development of teachers in Catholic schools

Robert Newton (1984) has pointed out correctly, I believe, that all teachers in Catholic schools contribute to the religious development of students. Staff are essential to this development because of the *modelling* they provide, the *climate* they create and the *culture* they support.

We know since the research of Fowler (1984), Flynn (1985) and others that religious growth is an idiosyncratic phenomenon. Staff are at a variety of stages in their personal, professional and religious development and so a variety of mechanisms is needed to assist them to grow as people and as professionals.

To ensure the consistent pursuit of excellence in teaching

The pursuit of excellence has to respect the human person with all the talents and limitations that each person brings to the school and classroom. The student has the right to experience excellence in every contact with the school. This assumes that all school activities will be sensitive to the capacities, expectations and social context of the student.

The pursuit of excellence has direct implications for the methodologies used in the classroom and for the development of curriculum that will reflect both broad educational policies and the special needs of each local community.

Practical application – development of school leadership

In giving a high priority to developing its leadership for the future the Parramatta System has set down six operational goals for the development of leadership.

1. To achieve a general perception of leadership which is collaborative, positive and conducive to growth.
2. To raise the understanding and level of skills of school staff in human resource management so that staff and indirectly students are seen to be valued and supported.
3. To establish planning processes which permit responsible and broad parent and community involvement and produce three or five year plans for the development of schools and of the system as a whole.
4. To assist designated leaders and potential leaders to understand the leadership role in the context of church, state and school.
5. To encourage the wider participation of teachers in personal, professional and religious development.
6. To develop a use of critical reflective practice in the pursuit of school and system development.

As a means of achieving these goals the system is gradually introducing practical programmes as the major strategies in leadership development. These programmes are:–

- total school development process,
- inservice programmes,
- extension of the use of appraisal of senior school and system staff,
- a carefully defined process for recruitment and selection of executive staff.
- executive exchange.

These are expanded briefly below.

Total school development

The Parramatta System is now using a longer planning perspective of from three or five years so that school communities can engage in worthwhile and purposeful development. *'Planned change* and not *organizational drift'* (Owens and Steinhoff 1976) must be the determining influence in the directions to be taken in this decade especially in developing leaders. Our leaders must learn to become reflective practitioners (Starratt 1986).

The Action Development Cycle (D'Orsa 1990) in Fig 4.6.1 sets out the planning strategies for the system and individual schools.

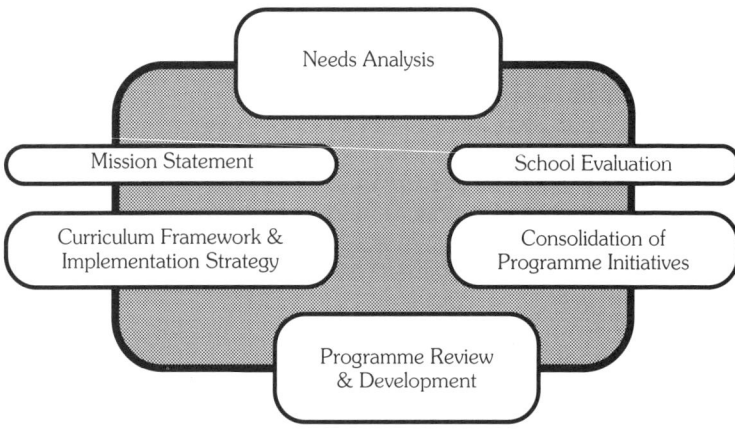

Figure 4.6.1. – The action development cycle

The logic of the model indicates that schools start at the Needs Analysis phase and work in an anti-clockwise direction around the six components. Practical experience indicates that schools have been working at each of these levels in a rather haphazard manner most of the time. The proposed key change is the thorough coverage of the cycle within a pre-determined period of time.

To assist leaders to think in terms of a strategic model along the lines of the one shown above, the system is developing processes, resources and training programs to support them in understanding and implementing the model.

Inservice programme

The Parramatta System currently runs six levels of training programmes for staff to assist the leadership to meet the challenges identified elsewhere in this chapter. Figure 4.6.2 outlines the six levels.

Executive Development Programme
- Master of Educational Administration
- Graduate Diploma in Educational Leadership
- Certificate in Education Leadership
- Professional Development for Principals

Religious Development Programme
- Graduate Diploma in Religious Education
- Spiritual Formation Programme for School Staff.

Middle Management Training
- Facilitator skills for Studies Co-ordinator
- Facilitator skills for Guidance Co-ordinators

Network Programme
- Administrators' networks
- Subject specific networks

Classroom Teachers Programme
- Subject specific courses
- Managing classroom diversity
- Programmes with a whole school focus, for example:
    gifted and talented children,
    personal development,
    special education

Induction Programme
- Orientation days
- Classroom management

Figure 4.6.2. – Levels of training for staff in the Parramatta System

The programmes offered in 1990 will broadly reflect what has been planned for the next ten years. However, as different needs emerge due to government legislation, societal expectations and the like, the overall programme will be sensitively reviewed to take these into account.

Many of the courses are planned to provide practising administrators and aspiring leaders with the skills, knowledge and critical understanding needed to be effective in an educational setting.

Other courses reflect directly the goal to ensure that professional development of teachers will lead to school improvement.

*Extension of the use of appraisal of senior school and
system staff*

The process of systematic appraisal has been operating for approximately two years and is being used for all principals after the two
years of their appointment. The experience so far has been successful but it is clear that the potential for difficulties is considerable
and that the success of this instrument is by no means automatic.
The difficulty is to provide a mechanism that is a successful mix of
providing affirmation of the staff but also providing direction and
realistic critique that permits and encourages healthy growth.

The appraisal process operates on two levels. Minor appraisal is
an organized process which takes place over the course of one year
between a colleague and a supervisor. The focus is on a professional dialogue between two colleagues with a shared mission, walking
together in mutual collaboration. This leads quite naturally into the
second level. Major appraisal involves the whole school leadership
and development process. It takes place approximately every three
years. The focus is on the community aspect of our schools, the
relationship among all members of the school executive team and
the principle of shared leadership.

*A carefully defined process for the recruitment and
selection of executive staff*

The system is moving towards a more sophisticated approach to
selection and recruitment of executive staff but has not yet achieved
a totally successful system. The process already involves the principles of equal opportunity employment and the careful use of well
balanced interviewing panels with representation of appropriate
other staff, parents and local church representatives. The process
remains under constant review.

Executive exchange

Many of our current and likely future leaders have never actually left
school. They progressed from pre-school to primary, to secondary,
to tertiary and then back into the classroom. We are exploring
experiences other than the narrow, although valuable time, spent
in educational institutions as a means of broadening the experience
base and the horizons of our future leaders.

A programme is being developed of interchange with senior business personnel and school and senior office personnel. This results
in periods of up to six months being spent by principals and other

school and system executives working in a setting outside the education arena.

Conclusions

The Parramatta System has concluded that the development of its leaders for the present and the future is crucial if it is to achieve its avowed aims. The programmes of development of leaders are still very much in the experimental phase, and it is yet to be demonstrated conclusively that the programmes implemented will be able to achieve all that is expected of them. One fundamental question is the extent to which the system can rely on on-the-job training and part-time courses for working teachers. This question has two related parts. 'Can the courses be developed to sufficiently quality standards?', and, 'To what extent can the busy teacher learn and grow in such an environment?'

The courses are therefore being monitored very carefully and attempts are being made to develop performance indicators that will give more precise definitions of training needs and the extent to which potential leaders can acquire desired knowledge and skills.

It is clear that even with the best designed courses and developmental work experience more is required in the effective development of leaders. Also, the whole system must work conscientiously and coherently to ensure the professional and personal growth and development of all staff whether or not they have leadership potential. The system and each part of it must ensure that staff are affirmed, supported, trusted and liberated. If the system is unable to ensure that its teachers develop personally and professionally, then it would be ludicrous to expect that they could allow, let alone contribute to, a corresponding growth in their students.

Attempts are being made to develop varied and enriching career paths so that all teachers but particularly the potential leaders of the future may develop and retain a sense of challenge with fresh fields to conquer.

Developments in Australia at state and national level in questions of teachers' salaries and conditions, are contributing to the development of the teaching profession here. It is becoming easier to remain in teaching without loss of status or salary and it can be assumed that there will be a greater growth in the leadership skills of teachers and administrators as a result.

The Parramatta System is facing the problems of all systems with the shortage of applicants and particularly of applicants with the special qualities demanded in a modern education system. This has led us to explore the sensitive areas of recruitment from outside the education profession, the development of executive cadetships and the specific training and employment of administrative leaders at what, in the past, would have been seen as too early a point in the career path.

In conclusion, the question before us is how can a school best prepare tomorrow's child for tomorrow's world. Tomorrow's child will be called on to renew the society and the church of the twenty-first century. It appears that together we also have the knowledge about what should be done to educate tomorrow's child. What may be lacking is the wisdom and the will to use that knowledge and to act imaginatively and effectively to prepare educational leaders who will ensure that tommorrow's school is appropriate for tommorrow's child.

References

Fowler J 1984 *Becoming Adult, Becoming Christian: Adult Development and Christian Faith*: New York: Harper and Row.

Flynn M 1985 *The Effectiveness of the Catholic School Sydney*: St Paul Publications.

Owens R A and Steinhoff C R 1976 *Administering Change in Schools* Englewood Cliffs: Prentice Hall.

D'Orsa J B 1990 'School Development in Practice': *Catholic School Studies* October.

Newton R 1984 'A Systematic Approach to Faculty Religious Development' *Living Light* Fall.

Parramatta Diocesan Schools Board 1990 *A Statement of Understanding and Vision* Catholic Education Office. Parramatta.

Sergiovanni T 1987 *The Principalship: Reflective Practice Perspective* New York: Allyn and Bacon.

Starratt R J 1986 'The Principal and Reflective Practice', Lecture given Fordham University, New York.

Starrat R J 1984 '*The Religious Development of the Catholic School Teacher*', Paper delivered to Conference of Catholic School Superintenents, New Orleans.

4.7 Developing Educational Managers in Australia: Guidelines for Tertiary Courses

Neil Johnson

The training of educational personnel in management has captured the limelight in Australia. In many states, current and aspiring educational managers now have two obvious incentives for obtaining tertiary qualifications in educational management. First, employers are beginning to treat certification in management as an important criterion for selecting executive personnel. Secondly, in line with recent developments overseas (eg Coopers and Lybrand 1988; Lange 1988; Beare 1989), the control of many educational decisions is being transferred to schools and regional offices (Beazley 1984; Scott 1990) and principals and other local personnel are being called upon to accept new responsibilities. Accordingly, politicians, management consultants, bureaucrats and educators alike are asserting the need for management training at all levels.

While this pressure for merit promotion and decentralisation of power has had much to do with the growing interest in tertiary courses in educational management, the efforts of universities themselves have acted as a third incentive for many practitioners. Over the past few years, some tertiary institutions in Australia have striven to make their offerings in educational management relevant to practice, more flexible as well as intellectually challenging.

One such course has been the Master of Educational Administration (MEdAdmin) course offered by the University of New South Wales to current and aspiring educational managers in Sydney. The procedures used for a recent course review and redesign in that instance will serve as a case study and context for discussing three major issues that designers of educational management courses will need to consider in the 1990s. While the case discussed here is typically Australian, the implications are unlikely to be limited by geography.

Reviewing courses: an Australian case

The MEdAdmin course at the University of New South Wales was established in 1979. By the beginning of 1988, this was still the only post-graduate course for educational managers in Sydney, a city of 3.5 million people (other courses specialising in educational management have been created since). All instruction had been carried out part-time by lecturers from other areas of education and by practising educational executives. The course had never been comprehensively reviewed since its inception, and the curriculum lacked coherence. The duration of this course was longer than most equivalents in Australia. The total enrolment in 1988 comprised about 80 students, most of whom were primary and secondary teachers – some quite junior teachers. The first full-time lecturer in educational management was appointed in mid-1988.

In the course review that was conducted in the second half of 1988, three main strategies were used. A meeting was convened of an *ad hoc* advisory committee comprising interested members of the faculty concerned, a visiting academic from overseas, and leaders in the local education community. Related literature and information about parallel courses at other institutions in Australia, Britain and North America were reviewed. In addition, past and present students, and a group of prospective students, were surveyed to identify students' perceived needs.

The review resulted in substantial restructuring of the course. A new curriculum was developed to provide for the progressive development of knowledge in key areas of educational management. The course length was brought in line with other programmes (although the imposition of more rigorous and uniform assessment requirements meant that expectations were not reduced). A minimum period of three years of professional experience was prescribed for admissions. A summer programme was instituted to allow students to pursue a portion of their studies full time during the long academic/school vacation in January. Several other changes were also made.

Following the restructuring, which took effect from January 1990, the number of applicants for this course grew rapidly: the total enrolment increased to 142 students, with 97 being admitted in 1990. With a similar intake in 1991, the enrolment is expected to exceed 200 students. (An early deadline for applications is also being imposed for the first time in 1991, to permit greater selectivity in offers of places on the course).

There is little doubt that this course has attracted interest partly on account of government initiatives to transfer educational management responsibility to schools and introduce merit selection and promotion of staff (Scott 1989, 1990). Judging from students' coursework evaluations and informal comments, however, perceived interest and relevance of instruction have also contributed to the interest in this redesigned course for developing educational managers.

Arising from the review outlined above, three major course design issues are proposed as crucial for the preparation and development of educational managers in the 1990s. Attention will turn now to (a) the importance of conducting regular reviews of courses, (b) clarification of the purpose of a course as the initial step in design and development, and (c) the content of instruction.

Periodic reviews of courses

Courses that are not reviewed regularly soon become outdated. As lecturers' research interests change, redundancies appear in the curriculum. Lecturers with little direct expertise in the field attempt to introduce subjects that sometimes are of doubtful worth for educational managers. Assessment requirements for individual subjects begin to vary markedly. And the changing needs of students are neglected.

If educational managers are to be adequately prepared, such drawbacks need to be remedied. Courses for preparing educational managers need to be reviewed and reorganised periodically.

Of course, political as well as academic considerations need to be kept in mind when conducting such a review; and the three strategies mentioned earlier can be helpful in both respects. When defending plans for course reform to institutional committee members who have little knowledge of educational management issues and current needs, the results of a survey of student and expert opinion can be particularly advantageous. Expressed preferences of the clientele can give university committees confidence in the marketability of a course. Recommendations by prominent writers in the field and leaders in the profession provide evidence of academic substance and practical relevance. Information gleaned from a survey of student opinion or comments by professional and academic experts about the relevance of specific content can also be useful for persuading lecturers to change existing content and methods; for example, a list of student's remarks given to a lecturer can be both informative and persuasive. Of course, the political importance of extensive support from current literature, a clear rationale for the proposal, and an articulate well informed oral defence also cannot be underestimated.

Apart from inevitable changes in content and approach, the mere fact of scrutinising the course can be therapeutic and energising for all involved. Lecturers are prompted to examine and revise old practices, to read in new areas, to adopt new teaching procedures. Students are motivated by the opportunity to contribute to change and are stimulated by more up-to-date material and amended teaching practices.

To this end, the MEdAdmin course at the University of New South Wales will be assessed on a continuing basis by the co-ordinator, and more formally every two years. A 'Course Review Committee', comprising personnel from the school, faculty, the profession and student representatives, will be established to examine and advise on all aspects of the course: the relevance and organisation of individual subjects; appropriateness of handbook descriptions; quality and breadth of advertising; consistency and adequacy of evaluation across the range of subjects; coherence and usefulness of the course overall; potential for including new subjects; as well as staffing. Lecturers will be asked to aid in this process by obtaining anonymous evaluation reports regularly from students.

A clear purpose

When contemplating management preparation in tertiary institutions, the intent of the course needs to be decided at the outset. Traditionally, many university courses for developing educational managers have focused on academic learning and research, acting on the principle that graduate studies should develop students' conceptual and analytical skills; thesis-only doctoral courses represent the extreme. As Walker (quoted by Duignan and Teather 1985) has indicated, educational management preparation in Australia started this way: 'No "pretence" was made of training administrators: the thrust of the [University of New England] program was to widen horizons, to provide a range of theoretical constructs from which administrators might choose and to force candidates to carry out research . . .' (p37).

Thesis requirements arguably do more than develop higher order skills: they prepare candidates for further research. Proponents of coursework degrees consider that, in terminal masters degree courses, it is unnecessary for those who intend to remain in professional practice to conduct their own research.

Towards the other end of the spectrum, some commentators (eg Guthrie and Clifford 1989) now advocate a reorientation away from academic issues towards problems immediately confronting schools. According to Murphy (1989), educational management courses can survive only by emphasising practical training and furnishing practitioners with checklists of desirable behaviours. Seemingly further towards the extreme still are practices used in experiential courses such as that at Butler University (Smith 1989) to develop 'fifty-two proficiencies for educational excellence' (p491).

Interestingly, in response to governmental pressure (Higher Educational Council 1989), several Australian institutions are now looking to the North American idea of offering professional doctorates in educational management. As doctorates, the degrees will be expected to involve study of equivalent standard and length to the research doctorate, although, as the only coursework-plus-thesis doctoral degrees, EdDs are unlikely to encounter the US problem of becoming indistinguishable from some PhDs (Rowell 1989). (A distinction between EdDs and some MEdAdmin degrees, however, may prove more difficult to sustain). The intention of these professional courses will be to allow educational managers to proceed to an expert level in a way that is directly relevant for practice. In common with North American procedure, the emphasis should be on 'application of research findings instead of discovering new truths about education through research' (Rowell, p8). Doctor of Education courses are expected to be popular among practitioners – although it may be some time before they can be recommended as a prerequisite for principalship in Australia! (cf National Policy Board for Educational Administration 1989).

Ultimately, each institution has to make its own judgement about the purpose of its course, and an awkward balance has to be struck between theoretical education and more instrumental professional development. Perhaps a balanced position involving some integration of theoretical knowledge and practical skills might be academically legitimate as well as attractive and immediately useful to students. The main point here, however, is that a conscious decision ought to be made on such a fundamental issue.

Appropriate content

The third major issues in the design of instruction for educational managers relates to the content of courses. In this regard, the University of New South Wales investigation revealed some important opportunities and issues that have resulted in significant additions to the programme offering. Two new subjects, about women in educational management and 'supervised fieldwork' in management, have been established in response to student demand and perceived need. In the near future, a subject focusing on financial issues will be introduced; this topical dimension of educational management rarely receives detailed attention in courses in Australia.

The issue of women in educational management enjoys a growing theoretical and research literature, and is beginning to take hold in international preparation courses. There is, however, much institutional reluctance to teaching women's issues in educational management (Shakeshaft 1987), despite government pressure (eg Higher Education Council 1989) and continued claims (eg Jayne 1989) that training courses which neglect gender-fair literature and case studies exacerbate women's under-representation in management. The argument for introducing a subject of this kind is therefore substantial. The University of New South Wales subject is proving attractive and informative to both female and male students. It deals with feminist scholarship and androcentric bias in educational research, expectations of and constraints on women educators, equity in the classroom and gender differences in management. It is taught by an educational executive with a research background in this area. Certainly, such a subject is just one of several options (see Shakeshift 1987) for improving gender equity in and through management training courses; but it is a beginning.

Fieldwork (a concept which has much in common with the notions of 'internship', 'clinical experience', 'residency' and 'practicum') is not a new idea in business management. As Pye's (1988) British research revealed, supervised experience on the job is regarded by many business executives as 'the best form of training any manager can have' (p84). Nor is it a new idea in educational management, at least not in North America. There is a long history of writing about educational management internships (eg Hencley 1963; Hickcox and House in this volume; Hughes and Ubben 1970; Lutz and Ferrante 1972; Peper 1988) culminating

recently in major policy commitments to promoting clinical education as part of all educational management preparation courses
in the United States (Griffiths et al 1988; National Policy Board
for Educational Administration 1989; University Council for
Educational Administration 1990). Indeed, the writer has had valuable personal experience as the intern to a university president in
Canada. However, the notion of supervised fieldwork seems a
novel one for countries such as Australia.

As an illustration of the way fieldwork could be organised in locations unaccustomed to educational management internships, a
fieldwork placement has been conceived at the University of New
South Wales to provide on-the-job management training under
joint supervision by a practising manager and an academic supervisor. It has been justified to institutional committees of approval on
the grounds of helping the student to relate knowledge of theory to
practice and develop practical intuitive management skills, assist in
future screening for employment and promotions, and provide service to the field. Each placement is arranged individually to give the
student experience in a new managerial context; the student's
needs and interests and the availability of a suitable location are also
important. In contrast to the school-oriented supervised practice
advocated elsewhere (eg Griffiths 1988), however, students in the
Sydney course may be placed in school systems, universities, businesses or other environments. This view accords more with the
principle behind the early practice at the University of New England
of arranging visits to several governmental and commercial organisations (Duignan and Teather 1985).

The nature of the experience should be determined in advance,
or at least at the outset, of the placement. The student might be
expected to carry out a number of assigned managerial tasks which
should be instructive for the student as well as assisting the supervisor. (Peper (1988) has furnished an extensive list of likely tasks.)
Before commencing each activity a preliminary discussion of the
work context, problems and other issues should occur; after completion the supervisor and student should review the student's performance in handling the task. On other occasions, the students
might be invited to observe the supervisor in meetings or engage in
other activities which the supervisor considers informative for the
student. In general, the placement for a University of New South
Wales student is expected to occupy 15 days of full-time work in a
single setting. The placement is conducted either in a three-week
block (for a part-time student, during a vacation) or in two or more
shorter blocks; as a last resort, it could involve fieldwork for one or
two days per week for several weeks. The student normally should
be in attendance at the supervisor's workplace throughout the

K

period of the placement. Because the fieldwork is undertaken for the purpose of a masters degree, no remuneration need be involved. The scheme also depends on voluntary participation by supervisors and their employers. Following the placement a written report of, say, 5,000–7,000 words should be submitted for assessment by the academic and fieldwork supervisors. This report requires the student to discuss agreed aspects of the managerial experience and to relate learning to knowledge gained elsewhere in the masters course, thereby emphasising the connection between theory and practice.

Subjects designed in conjunction with educational authorities can also give tertiary courses a direct connection with the practice of educational management. To this end, the management preparation courses at the University of New South Wales and seven other universities in the state now include an optional coursework subject which is approved by the academic institutions but taught by suitably qualified members of the profession. This 'joint course' is a co-operative arrangement between the state education authority and the institutions. The Department of School Education pays $750 towards the total $1,800 MEdAdmin course fee for each participating student. It also funds casual relief for two days so students can attend an introductory symposium and allows up to two hours per week of release time for students to travel to 5pm classes if necessary. Students in external courses also receive one week of release time for attendance at vacation residential schools. While the cost for the employing authority is high, the scheme gives its personnel a strong incentive to obtain managerial knowledge and qualifications. Students benefit from financial assistance, training related directly to their own school systems, and an incentive to continue with higher degree studies. From the institution's viewpoint, the joint subject provides a valuable link with the profession, enhances the connection between theory and practice, and provides an additional source of enrolments.

At the same time, system-specific schemes should occupy only a limited portion of higher degree offerings. As research by Licata and Hack (1980) has disclosed, educational managers rarely transfer from one district to another over the course of their careers. A resulting '"inbreeding" tendency, apparently applicable to the principalship at all levels' (p93) can lead ultimately to a loss of creativity in school management within the system. Arguably, exposure to perspectives outside the school systems and school sector may provide much needed stimulation for school executives.

Graduate education is also the rightful responsibility of tertiary institutions, and the certification that recognises high intellectual attainment as well as acquisition of information should not be devalued by trading certification rights for enrolments. Tertiary institutions therefore need to retain the primary role in educating the students who will receive their degrees. At the University of New South Wales the position is being strengthened rather than relaxed in this regard: at least 75 per cent of the MEdAdmin course must now be academically-orientated content taught by full- or part-time staff of the university.

One avenue for broadening the educational programme within the confines of the university is by exposing students to management studies in other departments. Informal discussion and personal experience have shown that subjects taken in other disciplines (and other areas of education) stimulate students to think in new ways, challenge their accepted theories and approaches to decision making, and introduce new perspectives on research and management. As Swift (1970) remarked, such a view was influential in the early development of educational management courses at the University of Alberta:

> The study and analysis of organizational structure had long been pursued by other persons both within and without universities, by private funding agencies, by schools of business administration, by economists, by political scientists, by social psychologists and sociologists. Dr. Reeves and his staff were convinced that there was much to be learned from these other sources and disciplines. Hence, there was an early declaration that an interdisciplinary approach would be pursued . . . students may choose as part of their formal program courses offered in other faculties and departments of the University . . . in law, in economics, in business, in mathematics, in psychology, in political science, in sociology . . . depending upon . . . interest of the student and . . . thesis interest . . . (pp45–46).

As Pye (1988) recently observed, business managers also value interaction with colleagues from 'completely different organisational backgrounds and cultures' (p79). Students of educational management may be well served by encouragement to enquire about opportunities for study in related disciplines; cross-listing of subjects in faculty handbooks is a good start.

Beyond encouraging students to broaden coursework options, there is scope for developing interdisciplinary subjects and instructing in co-operation with other departments and faculties. At the University of New England, for example, professors in educational management and two other fields have developed jointly a subject on public policy (Harman 1988). At the University of New South Wales one multidisciplinary subject has been developed to expose managerial personnel in education, librarianship, health professions and social work to research procedures used in the social sciences; illustrations will be drawn from each realm. A second subject explores professional ethics in these four areas of management. In other circumstances, it may be appropriate for law lecturers to teach school law to educational managers, for commerce lecturers to provide a business perspective on management, for sociology and anthropology lecturers to contribute to instruction in social research, and so on.

As Hannah (1980) has observed, interdisciplinary instruction capitalises on specialist knowledge from a variety of disciplines. It also broadens the perspectives of practising educational managers by taking them beyond their own field of experience and expertise to consider techniques and modes of thinking and managing that prevail in other disciplines. From an academic viewpoint, interdisciplinary cooperation can also create potential sources of interdisciplinary research, enhance collegiality across the campus, and highlight the important work and so improve the reputation of the institution's educational management unit.

Conclusion

This chapter has argued for regular, comprehensive review and reform of courses for preparing educational managers in Australia. There are practical as well as political benefits in using educational managers' expressed interests, experience from comparable courses, and expert advice from academics and educational executives to construct courses that are both stimulating and relevant for educational managers today. Attention has been given to the matter of deciding on theoretical understanding and/or practical knowledge as the basis of course design. With regard to the content of instruction, suggestions have been made for including in curricula emerging areas such as women in educational management and financial management preparation, and for incorporating a fieldwork component. Alternative teaching arrangements have been advocated, such as joint teaching with staff from local education authorities, interdisciplinary instruction and encouragement of students to enrol in individual subjects in other disciplines. In each of these ways, the intellectual stimulation and practical contribution – and so also the appeal – of tertiary courses for educational managers can be enhanced.

References

Beare, H 1989 *Educational administration in the 1990s*, Paper presented at the Annual Meeting of the Australian Council for Educational Administration, Armidale, New South Wales.

Beazley, K E 1984 *Education in Western Australia*, Report of the Committee of Inquiry into Education in Western Australia. Perth: Western Australian State Government.

Coopers and Lybrand 1988 *Local management of schools*, Report to the British Department of Education and Science, London: HMSO.

Duignan, P A and Teather, D C B 1985 'Teaching educational administration externally at post-graduate level at the University of New England' *Distance Education*, *6*(1), 34–55.

Griffiths, D E 1988, April. 'Educational administration: Reform PDQ or RIP', invited lecture to the Annual Meeting of the American Educational Research Association, New Orleans.

Griffiths, D E, Stout, R T and Forsyth, P B 1988 *Leaders for America's schools: The report and papers of the National Commission on Excellence in Educational Administration*, San Francisco: McCutchan.

Guthrie, J W and Clifford, G J 1989 'A brief for professional education' *Phi Delta Kappan*, *70*(5), 380–385.

Hannah, W 1980 'Administrative studies in education: Programmes vs. needs', *Journal of Tertiary Educational Administration*, *2*(1), 41–50.

Harman, G S 1988 personal communication.

Hencley, S P (ed) 1963 *The internship in administrative preparation*, Columbus, Ohio, University Council for Educational Administration/Committee for the Advancement of School Administration.

Higher Education Council 1989 *Review of Australian graduate studies and higher degrees*, initial report for the National Board of Employment, Education and Training, Canberra: AGPS.

Hughes, L W and Ubben, G C 1970 'New leadership for the secondary school' *NASSP Bulletin*, *54* (September), 61–69.

Jayne, E 1989 'Women as leaders of schools: The role of training' *Educational Management and Administration*, *17*(3), 109–114.

Lange, Rt Hon D 1988 *Tomorrow's schools: The reform of educational administration in New Zealand* Wellington: Government of New Zealand.

Licata, J W and Hack, W G 1980 'School administrator grapevine structure' *Educational Administration Quarterly*, *16*(3), 82–99.

Lutz, F W and Ferrante, R 1972 *Emergent practices in the continuing education of school administrators*, Eugene, OR: University Council for Educational Administration.

Murphy, J 1980, October, Keynote address to the Annual Meeting of the Australian Council for Educational Administration, Armidale, New South Wales.

National Policy Board for Educational Administration 1989, 'Improving the preparation of school administrators: An agenda for reform, *UCEA Review*, *30*(3), 11–15.

Peper, J B 1988 'Clinical education for school superintendents: The missing link', in Griffiths, D E, Stout, R T & Forsyth, P B (eds) *Leaders* for *America's schools: The report and papers of the National Commission on Excellence in Educational Administration*. San Francisco: McCutchan.

Pye, A 1988 'Management training: Acts of faith, scenes of competence', *Journal of General Management*, *13*(4), 74–87.

Rowell, C G 1989 'PhD in education: Making it different from the EdD – A case in point, *UCEA Review*, *30*(2), 8–9.

Scott, B W 1989 *Schools renewal: A strategy to revitalise schools within the New South Wales state education system*, interim report of the Management Review: New South Wales Education Portfolio, Sydney: Government of New South Wales.

Scott, B W 1990, *School-centred education: Building a more responsive state school system*, Report of the Management Review: New South Wales Education Portfolio, Sydney: Government of New South Wales.

Shakeshaft, C 1987, *Women in educational administration*, Newbury Park, CA: Sage.

Smith, J M 1989, 'Preparing principals for the future: Experiential learning in educational administration' *Education*, *109*(4), 490–493.

Swift, W H 1970, *Educational administration in Canada: A memorial to A W Reeves*, Toronto: Macmillan.

University Council for Educational Administration, 1990 'The preparation of educational administrators: Statement of purpose', *UCEA Review*, *31*(1), 2.

4.8 The Professional Development Needs of Newly-appointed Principals: Lessons from the Western Australian Experience

Arthur Schwartz and Michael Harvey

Introduction

The appointment to a first principalship is both a demanding transition from earlier roles and a turning point in an educator's career. The fledgling principal, who may have only a limited knowledge of school and community, staff and students, faces a new and complex set of pressures and expectations in the context of an unaccustomed degree of social distance from those who would previously have been colleagues and equals. He or she can only draw upon knowledge and experience gained in past roles and different settings to meet the pressure for quick decisions in the new environment.

Role statements typically do not distinguish between first-time and experienced principals. While some newly-appointed principals will find that their schools have been well run, others will find themselves scapegoats for inherited difficulties and resentment. Some may have support and mentors nearby, while others will feel personally and professionally isolated, alone in the principal's office and believing that to ask for assistance will be taken as a sign of weakness.

Whatever may be the situation of individual new principals, the appointment of a cohort of new principals is an important step in the process of school system maintenance and renewal. The collective success or failure of each group of new principals is a determinant of the organizational and educational health of the system. The school effectiveness literature indicates the importance of principals in creating and maintaining school environment and culture conducive to learning (eg, Department of Education and Science 1977; Purkey and Smith 1983; National Institute of Education 1985; Mulford 1986). It may be argued that the progress of a school system is related to the rate at which each cohort of new principals becomes able to make educationally effective decisions.

Little is known about minimal levels of competence required of beginning principals and how long it may take new appointees to reach acceptable levels of effectiveness and comfort. Their situation received relatively little attention in the research literature prior to the mid-1980s. Despite a growing number of reported studies, many questions remain about transition from teacher to principal. Just what is it which confronts new principals as they open *their* schools for the first time, and what are the more common coping strategies in use? What combination of knowledge and skills is necessary for their survival and success? What in the operations of a larger school authority helps and hinders their confrontation of new responsibilities?

The first year in office of ten newly-appointed principals in Western Australia was studied in an attempt to answer these and similar questions, and in the belief that examining the situations faced by new appointees, their interpretations of those situations, and their consequent actions, will indicate the professional development needs of prospective principals as well as those already in office.

Design of the study

Conceptual framework

The study examined issues of management, school culture, instructional leadership, and the practical politics of school administration, along with the importance of principals' discretionary decision-making as a factor in effective management and maintaining good working relationships within the school and with its external environment (Schwartz 1981; Morris et al 1984).

The concept of 'organizational culture' refers to the deeper-level basic assumptions, values, and beliefs which are collectively learned and shared by participants (Schein 1985). Modifying school culture thus becomes an important part of the principal's 'instructional leadership'. Effective leaders are able to focus attention on critical aspects of organizational culture and thus reshape it, although the literature on organizational culture and writings on the culture of schools uncritically derived from it have been criticized for promoting manipulative and exploitative management (Bates 1987).

Leadership in the school situation becomes effective when a principal succeeds in shaping a climate in which there is agreement on fundamental values and practices, and such agreement constitutes a shared view of the school's nature and objectives. Among the characteristics attributed to principals of effective schools are the ability to exemplify and promote such educational values as a climate of high expectations and a commitment to learning-related goals in the school.

There are, however, likely to be a number of leaders or potential leaders in any staffroom, reflecting a political reality of multiple centres of power within a school, each competing against the others for influence and territory. Thus the internal micropolitics of the school may be a barrier for any principal attempting to re-shape school culture or to change the direction and characteristics of a school and its programmes (Ball 1987; Hoyle 1987).

It is in this context that a principal attempts to influence the direction in which the school is moving. Since a new principal will at best only partially understand the interpretations which others in the school give to actions and events, the influence of principals was defined here to accommodate both intentional and unintentional interventions by them.

The principal is thus seen as an actor who applies knowledge, experience and understanding to a perceived image of the school and its situation, generating decisions out of the interaction of those factors. As the principal's experience and knowledge accumulate, however, that image of the school and its context will change. Thus reflective consideration of one's actions and their consequences after the fact has the potential to modify the perspective which will then be applied to future situations. With experience in their schools, principals should be able to modify their situational analyzes, their preferred styles of operation, and the image of themselves they attempt to project.

The context

The 1980s were a period of extensive change for public education in Western Australia. New policy opened government schools to community participation to an unprecendented degree; changes in secondary curriculum were intended to increase retention rates, broadening the range of students staying on to complete full secondary programmes; administrative decentralization and reorganization of the central bureaucracy were intended to increase the autonomy of schools (and principals). This was accompanied by increased financial accountability and responsibility for planning at the school level, and growing expectations for collaborative styles of school management. These trends and others, along with the rhetoric of 'instructional leadership', have changed the formal responsibilities and informal role expectations for principals, but without traditions of local control and parent and community involvement. Despite indications that centralized control is being reasserted (Birch and Smart 1990), the reality for principals has been an expectation that they develop at least the framework, if not the fact, of increased staff consultation and community and parent involvement in schools.

School development

One manifestation of these changes in Western Australia has been the policy of 'School Development', an official euphemism for school improvement. School Development policy requires individual schools, under the principal's direction and with some consultative assistance, to assess the state of their own programmes and practices, to systematically plan and implement efforts to increase their responsive to community needs and concerns, and thus to raise their overall educational effectiveness (Harvey 1987). These expectations contrast with the previous pattern of centralized control, in which each principal was to operate as 'an overseer whose main function is to monitor actions and ensure compliance to established policies and standards' (Murphy 1990).

School Development policy was a significant factor in the work of principals examined in this study. It required the new principal to begin what in some schools would have to be dramatic changes both in operating patterns and the organizational culture underlying them, starting literally on the first two days of the school year, pupil-free days known officially as 'School Development Days'.

These changes occurred at the same time as the promotion criteria in a system centralized at the state level (without local education authorities or school boards) were changed from seniority to 'merit promotion'. This change was implemented over a two-year period including our data-gathering phase, with initial uncertainty in the field about how 'merit' was to be defined. In Western Australian state schools, promotion and competition for desirable teaching posts frequently involves transfer from one community to another. The consequent levels of staff turnover and relocation at intervals has created a culture of transience among school staff, especially outside the Perth-Fremantle metropolitan area. It was a period of uncertainty and conflict in education, in particular for new principals moving into first appointments, with ill-defined and unexpected new responsibilities and challenges.

Research design

A year-long study was undertaken of ten newly-appointed principals across the range of primary and secondary school categories and sizes in both metropolitan and country areas of the state. Data were gathered by observation of principals interacting with their deputies, teachers, students, parents and others in and around their schools; through multiple interviews of the principals and those in contact with them; and through analysis of relevant records and documents.

Findings

This statement of findings covers some of what we found new principals experience as difficult and crucial elements in their new role. From deficits revealed in the knowledge and skills of a group of teachers representative of those selected for promotion to the principalship, inferences can then be made about professional development needs both prior to, and in the initial stages of, that first appointment. The findings are organized according to a number of themes which emerged in the course of the study.

Anticipation

The interval between announcement of the new appointment and its effective date may provide the only chance for a principal-designate to see the new school in operation and gain an idea of its characteristics, its community and population, and the outgoing principal's style. The latter will be the key to expectations held for the new principal. In particular, the principal-designate should at this point pay attention to the culture of the school, and the role played in it by the outgoing principal. Providing time for visiting the new school while in session and the outgoing principal still in office, and assistance with the cost of travel where necessary, would be an investment by the school system towards smoothing the transition from one principal to another. Such visits should be considered part of both the administrative transition process and jurisdictionally-supported professional development for new principals.

Induction programmes provided for principals-designate by higher authority are too often examples of information overload. Far more important is a guided focus on problem-solving for particular types of schools. The mass of information on the school system and its internal procedures, which is typically provided as the major element of induction programmes for new principals, could much better be put in writing, where it can be consulted by new appointees as they find necessary. The most important single piece of system information for principals-designate may be an up-to-date list of whom to call on for what kinds of information.

Principals-designate often begin their new appointments largely uninformed about their new school's operations. They lack basic data on everyday matters such as timetable, timetabling constraints, staffing and finance, but they will be called on from the first day with the expectation that they have such details at their fingertips. Only once on the scene and with the school in operation will they encounter the dynamics of staff and student relationships, for example. Thus from the very beginning they require an analytical framework for systematic scanning of the school and its environment in order to choose their style of operation for the new school year. They must also have the ability to modify decisions they have already made, as their familiarity with the school, its setting, and the expectations for it increases. With time, and perhaps very little time, they will become aware of deficits in their own professional knowledge and skills, and the possible lack of fit of their preferred operating style with the new setting. Despite this, they must be able to decide realistically such things as the suitable degree of delegation versus control, and the acceptable degree of social distance to maintain from staff.

Opening days

Many jurisdictions begin a new school year with pupil-free days when staff alone are present in each school. In Western Australia, these are labelled 'School Development Days': occasions for group analysis of the state of the school and exercises in overall staff development, under the principal's leadership. For the new principal, these days provide both an arena in which they will be expected to prove themselves and an early opportunity to establish credibility. Such days should be planned in consultation with continuing staff in order to ensure that activities are relevant to staff concerns and that the incoming principal is an integral part of proceedings. Principals must be able to focus the attention of staff on school-wide issues, and involve them in group problem-solving focussed on those issues. Inevitably, what can be accomplished by such exercises will be hindered by the fact that many teachers would prefer to use the time in their own preparations for the coming year.

Developing a network of influence

Principals are surrounded by the rhetoric of 'instructional leadership' – the expectation that they are able to keep the attention and efforts of staff and students focussed on teaching and learning. By consulting (and being seen to consult) with staff about teaching practice, curriculum development and the quality of student learning, the principal may be able to develop shared thinking about the state of the school, and to demonstrate a concern for staff views. A consequence of these joint activities will be an increase in staff understanding of the principal's views, and consequent growth of the principal's credibility in the school.

Staff will be reluctant to accurately convey their views of the new principal until after a certain amount of trust has been accumulated and a perception of mutual respect has developed. New principals must expect a 'false honeymoon' period at the start, during which they will receive little if any negative feedback. Lack of critical response by staff, however, does not necessarily indicate their support or approval of the principal's actions and policies.

Especially during a time of devolution, principals must examine the *de facto* policy process within the school to determine whether or not it has sufficient legitimacy. Existing processes may promote the tendency towards dependence in staff, rather than involvement (or even interest) in school-level policy and decision-making.

Principals require frameworks for analyzing the nature of working relationships among staff. New appointees must be able to quickly develop sensitivity towards the existence of self-defined territories among the staff of even a small school, and a feeling for the internal politics of their schools. Strategies must be available for resolving the inevitable conflicts and difficulties in working relationships. In large schools, and secondary schools with subject-based department structures, close working relationships among senior staff may not develop easily. Principals should be prepared to deal with senior staff who defend sectional interests rather than share a concern for the whole school programme.

Confronting administration

The beginning of a school year will bring a complex mass of administrative details. Principals must get beyond reactive management and day-to-day administration, in order to think about the medium and long-term future of the school. Time management skills and coping strategies are required to handle the details, and for sorting and filtering the large quantities of associated information. Delegating tasks and establishing clear priorities will ease the burden of things to be done and raise the new principal's comfort level with the brevity, variety and fragmentation of a principal's day.

Managing external relations

External relations include contacts with the school system and school community. The complexity of relationships within school systems and the depth of principal involvement in them are not often visible to teachers. Thus development of the requisite boundary maintenance skills is a major learning experience for new principals. In dealing with the community, principals must develop the public relations skills to systematically promote an image of the school which will generate and maintain community support. They must also become aware of how the image of a model school and its practices which develops at the system level may coincide or conflict with the character of their particular school, and the consequent implications of that image for the support they can expect to receive from senior management for their schools and for what they are trying to accomplish in those schools.

Coping with change and stimulating school improvement

Effective school change is most often planned change. Such planning must be strategic (long-term and concerned with relationships between school, school system, and community), and must allow for the readiness and willingness of staff to undertake the process. New principals thus require the conceptual skills to undertake strategic planning of school-level change, and the human resource skills to assess staff willingness and capabilities and then, at least, to initiate a process intended to develop the attitudinal changes which may be required. Merely developing a time-line is, by itself, inadequate planning for change. The instructional leadership skills referred to above are critical elements in the change process, which cannot begin to be effective without agreement among staff on the need for change, and their support for and perception of ownership of the change in question.

Principals also require the ability to establish and maintain effective working relationships with external change facilitators, and the confidence to encourage the emergence of second change facilitators (Hord and Hall 1987) from within the school.

Accommodating system-level reform

In many parts of the world, more and more specific responsibilities and greater and more complex expectations are devolving upon individual principals. It is no longer adequate for principals to depend solely on their intuitions in dealing with such issues as staff development, staff supervision and appraisal, school change and improvement, and programme evaluation. Whether new or experienced, principals cannot afford to remain with knowledge frozen at the end of their last period of formal training. Simply put, they must somehow find the time and energy to keep up-to-date.

Especially during periods of extensive educational change, principals must maintain awareness of the social, economic, and political contexts in which their schools operate. Only thus can they fulfill their task of interpreting the school to its system and community, and vice versa. Failure of staff to understand both the context of changes imposed upon them from higher authority, and the changing expectations of the community for its schools, can lead to the strife associated with resistance to change, or to the less painful coping strategies of withdrawal, or lip-service to externally-imposed policies seen as irrelevant or destructive. Agencies with responsibility for the supervision and professional development of school administrators should be undertaking their own strategic planning in order to keep ahead of the implications of such social, economic, and political changes for the schools and those who run them.

Planning professional development

In many places, professional development for newly-appointed principals is a matter of last-minute cramming shortly before taking up the first appointment. There is a lack of prior structured training and experience. Where this is the case, there is a need to alter the professional culture of the jurisdiction to make continuous upgrading of knowledge, experience and competency for the principalship a part of the normal working lives of aspirants to it. The path might be eased through early identification, career planning, and incremental specification of the additional skills required for each successive promotional position. For a school system, such a scheme would prove an investment whose return comes in the form of smoother school transitions from one principal to another as well as smoother transitions by neophyte principals from previous roles into their first appointments.

Experience as deputy principal would be a key element in such a structure. In recognition of the practical skills element of school-level leadership and building management, responsibility statements for incumbent principals should include the task of systematically preparing their deputy or assistant/vice principals for promotion. This could be accomplished in part by consciously exposing them to the entire range of a principal's tasks. The analogy here is to a master-apprentice model of training. Specifically included should be those aspects of the principalship not normally visible to teachers in their classrooms. For example: dealing across school boundaries with the school system and school community, and with those governmental and private agencies whose child-related mandates bring them into contact with schools; negotiating for staff and other resources at the system level or with managing boards; and long-term and strategic planning for the individual school in the context of school system and community.

First-time principals, cast into a new setting virtually on their own devices, will tend as would anyone in a similar situation to fall back on a mental image of what a school 'should' be, and that image is most likely to reflect past settings in which the individual recalls feeling personally and professionally secure. This is likely to be a deficit model, in which the recollected image serves as a frame of reference against which the new school is compared and found wanting. That image *may* be of an effective school where concerns for learning and the quality of student experience predominate, but this will not necessarily be the case. Individuals may be bound up in their previous schools and the jurisdiction's standard routine to the extent that they are unable to appreciate the context or situation-bound differences which distinguish their new school from previous settings. Thus a significant element in a professional development programme for prospective as well as newly-appointed principals (and indeed, for all school personnel) would be to provide them with images of an *effective* school and the learner within it which are not place- or jurisdiction-bound to use as their implicit frame of reference. This would better enable them to get beyond direct comparison of that which is new and unfamiliar and therefore uncomfortable, with that which is familiar, comfortable and secure, albeit ineffective.

Just as the neophyte principal will see the new school in the reflection of recollected past experience, so too will the school and community perceive and judge their new principal in terms of expectations based upon the characteristics and style of previous incumbents. This will be the case especially where the previous principal had been long in office, and the locally-held image of a 'good' or even 'real' principal reflects that individual's personal characteristics and operating style. The newcomer's credibility in the role, whether that newcomer be neophyte or experienced elsewhere, will at least initially be a function of the extent to which he or she is perceived to reflect or share the positively-recollected characteristics of the previous incumbent.

Ironically, it may be necessary at the beginning for a new principal whose preferred style differs from local expectations to meet those expectations at least in part, in order to establish the very credibility which he or she must have in order to eventually be able to change those same expectations. Thus new principals must be able to recognise and understand their own levels of comfort with what they encounter in new settings: the policies, practices, expectations, implicit self-definitions and things taken-for-granted already in place in their new schools. They must then be able to recognize what might be called the 'strategic moment' – that point at which they have achieved or established sufficient credibility as an individual rather than as a reflection of their predecessors – at which to begin the process of change. There will be an element here of developing and monitoring the degree of confidence which school and community develop in oneself, regardless of how wrongly, in terms of one's own preferred self-image in the role, that confidence may be based. There may be a Machiavellian or manipulative element here; the process is one of managing the politics of one's own credibility. Newly-appointed (as well as experienced) principals require the habit of reflection and self-monitoring of their own performance in a regular check on the state of their own credibility and of the readiness of their school and community for changed ideas and practices.

New appointees may require the advice of a consultant or mentor who is outside the jurisdiction's hierarchy to assist in setting their professional development agendas, especially in cases of professional isolation. We have emphasised that a mentor be outside the hierarchy to eliminate the element of threat in being required to discuss one's perceived needs for improvement with an actual or potential superordinate or rival.

Whatever delivery structures or sponsoring agencies may be involved, meaningful professional development requires that people undergo experiences which meet their own perceived needs. Individuals appointed to the principalship or aspiring to it must come into the habit of reflection upon their own practice, experience and needs, and then establishing their own agendas for future development in consequence. A looseness of professional development structure, which allows individuals to choose from among a range of options and which supports them in ventures outside the system, would meet this requirement.

References

Ball, S J 1987 *The Micropolitics of the School: Towards a Theory of School Organization*, London: Methuen.

Bates, R J 1987 'Corporate culture, schooling, and educational administration', *Educational Administration Quarterly*, 23, 4, pp79–115.

Birch, I and Smart D 1990 'Economic rationalism and the politics of education in Australia', in D E Mitchell and M E Goertz (eds), *Education Politics for the New Century*, 20th Anniversary Yearbook of the Politics of Education Association. Philadelphia: Taylor and Francis.

DES 1977 *Ten Good Schools: A Secondary School Enquiry*, London: HMSO.

Harvey, M J 1987 *School Development as a Contextual Factor Influencing Principals in Western Australia*, Perth: International Institute for Policy and Administrative Studies.

Harvey, M J 1988 *The Professional Development Needs of Newly-Appointed Principals: Leadership for School Development*. Perth: International Institute for Policy and Administrative Studies.

Harvey, M J 1989 The Newly-Appointed Principal: Accommodation to the Culture of the School. Unpublished paper, Western Australian College of Advanced Education.

Hord, S M and Hall, G E 1987 'Three images: What principals do in curriculum implementation' *Curriculum Inquiry 17*, 1, pp55–89.

Hoyle, E 1987 *The Politics of School Management*, London: Hodder and Stoughton.

Morris, V, Crowson, R, Hurwitz, J and Porter-Gehrie, C 1984 *'Principals in Action: The Reality of Managing Schools'*, Columbus, Ohio: Merrill.

Mulford, W 1986 *Indicators of School Effectiveness: A Practical Approach*, Australian Council for Educational Administration, Monograph No. 2.

Murphy, M 1990 'State administrator policy in seven states', *Politics of Education Bulletin, 17*, 1, pp6–7.

National Institute of Education 1985 *Reaching for Excellence: An Effective Schools Source Book*, Washington, DC: NIE.

Purkey, S C and Smith, M S 1983 'Effective schools: A review', *The Elementary School Journal, 83*, 4, pp427–452.

Schein, E H 1985 *Organizational Culture and Leadership*, San Francisco: Jossey-Bass.

Schwartz, A M 1981 *The Principal as Boundary Administrator: A Field Study of Inner-City Schools*, unpublished PhD dissertation, University of Toronto.

4.9 Towards 2000 and Beyond: Preparation of Educational Managers in India

Chaman Sapra

Introduction

Tasks facing educational managers in India, as in other developing countries, have become complex over recent decades and their complexity is likely to increase further in the future. This can be partly attributed to a phenomenal expansion of the education system to fulfil the educational needs of the growing population and increasing social demand for education, as well as to meet the requirements of trained manpower for the growing economy. It is also due to new requirements arising from the rapid changes that are taking place in social, cultural, economic, political and technological spheres.

Any long-range consideration of the educational sector requires a clear statement of the direction in which a society wishes to move. Thus it is necessary to visualize the type of society we would like to have in India in the year 2000 and beyond. The other related questions which merit consideration are: What type of educational changes will need to be brought about to meet the anticipated societal changes? What will be the nature of challenges that educational managers will have to face in restructuring the education system? And finally, What type of professional preparation will be required for managers in education, both at the system and institutional levels, to equip them to meet those challenges?

The social scenario for the year 2000 and beyond

Three national goals of socialism, secularism and democracy have been enshrined in the preamble to India's Constitution. Without commitment to these goals no new vision of Indian society can be reformulated. What is needed, therefore, is a reinterpretation of these goals in the light of our past experiences.

Starting with socialism, a number of programmes and projects were launched in the industrial and agricultural sectors during the successive five-year plans, each of which aimed at reducing inequalities of income and wealth, balancing public and private sectors, and creating employment opportunities. But they failed to create a socialist pattern of society. On the contrary, the end result of our 40-year long experience in planning for socio-economic development has been that the rich have become richer and the poor have become poorer. Efforts were also made to provide equal educational opportunities to all, irrespective of caste, creed, colour, sex, economic condition or social status. In the initial phase of planned development, it was hoped that linear expansion of educational facilities would automatically reduce inequities in education. While substantial expansion of education did take place at all levels, the objective of equality in education could not be achieved to any appreciable degree. On the other hand, the existing inequalities became further accentuated.

With respect to secularism, the necessity to strengthen it in India arose from more than one consideration, including the historical fact of partition. Rashpal Malhotra (1988) has reported a major study, the conclusions of which are:

(a) Sources of secularism on the one hand and communalism on the other run parallel, notwithstanding the Constitution's commitment to the former;

(b) Secularization processes have become weaker over the years;

(c) So far, it has not been possible to structure a relationship of secularism with nationalism or with ethical and moral values;

(d) Economic development, educational expansion and democratic experience have not strengthened the secular forces: in particular the hope of achieving secularization through modernization and industrialization has been belied by experience.

After Independence the third national goal, democracy, was accepted in India as a form of government based on a multi-party system. There have been nine general elections so far; the ninth was held in November 1989.

While initially some very good traditions were established (such as fair elections, regard for others' points of view, etc) there have been certain negative developments during the last two decades. Distrust and political intolerance among politicians have been steadily growing. The uncivilized behaviour of politicians (reflected through vulgarity, shouting and even use of physical force within the legislative bodies of the centre and states) is another disquieting development. 'Mud-slinging' and character assassination during elections have become commonplace. Caste and communal gangsterism, drug, liquor and arms smuggling have become directly or indirectly linked with the electoral and political processes. Muscle and money power were used during the last election with impunity and booth capturing, rigging and other malpractices were used on such a large scale across the country that the Election Commission had to order a re-poll in as many as 1605 polling stations in different constituencies – this surpassed all previous records.

Both the successes and failures of the past have forced the government to focus on political institutions at the levels of the district and below. The previous central government came forward with amendments to the Constitution which aimed at decentralizing power to the *Panchayats* in rural areas and the *Nagar Palikas* in urban areas respectively. While the proposals were passed by the *Lok Sabha* (Lower House), they were rejected by the *Rajya Sabha* (Upper House). The new central government also proposes to introduce modified versions of constitutional amendments on decentralization of power to the people at the grassroots.

So even after 40 years, we in India are far from achieving the goals of socialism, secularism and democracy.

These concepts have been kept vague and so have degenerated into mere slogans and rhetoric. One major lesson from our past experience is that if education is to play its mediating role in promoting socialism, secularism and democracy in the future, educational planning will have to fulfill two conditions:

1. it will have to build up people's confidence through democratic decentralization; and
2. it will have to be an integral part of a general plan for socio-economic development.

The lesson from poverty-alleviation programmes such as the Integrated Rural Development Programme and others is that no programme by itself and isolated from others can succeed. Provision for health, sanitation, drinking water, housing, education, etc, is part of the people's life and hence must be treated as parts of integrated planning. If there is new awareness that all this cannot be achieved without the people becoming partners with the government, it will be as promising as it is logical.

The educational scenario for the future

National Policy on Education (NPE) 1986 provides direction for developing the educational scenario of the future in India. It has stressed the importance of education in every walk of life and has echoed continuation of efforts to achieve the national goals of socialism, secularism and democracy in these words:

> India's political and social life is passing through a phase which poses the danger of erosion to long-accepted values. The goals of secularism, socialism, democracy and professional ethics are coming under increasing strain.... Life in the coming decades is likely to bring new tensions together with unprecendented opportunities. To enable the people to benefit in the new environment will require new designs of human resource development. The coming generations should have the ability to internalize new ideas constantly and creatively. They have to be imbued with a strong commitment to humane values and to social justice. All this implies better education.

The policy document sets forth the future tasks by insisting that the National System of Education should be designed to promote values such as: India's common cultural heritage, egalitarianism, democracy and secularism, equality of the sexes, protection of the environment, removal of social barriers, observance of the small family norm, inculcation of scientific temper and national integration, with a clear expectation that the educational programme will be carried on in strict conformity with proclaimed values. The policy thrusts of the NPE include the universalization of primary education by 1990 and of elementary education (to age of about 14) by 1995; eradication of illiteracy among adults of the 13–35 age-group by 2000; diversion of 25 per cent of students at the upper secondary level to vocational courses by 1995; improvement of quality and standards at all levels of education through upgrading of infrastructural facilities and competencies of teachers; expansion of non-formal education, including open learning systems, etc.

Based on demographic, social, cultural, economic, political and technological trends and perspectives in education as envisaged in NPE, some salient features of Indian education of the future can be visualized:

- Because of demographic pressure, large-scale expansion of education will continue.
- Micro planning and target-group-oriented strategies will have to be adopted to ensure universal enrolment and other policy targets.
- Education will become a continuing life-long process blending formal and non-formal education with greater emphasis on open-learning systems.

- More stress will be laid on value-oriented education.
- Technological developments will call for a smaller quantity and a higher quality of labour input, with more time being available for education and training.
- Technological developments will also lead to reduced number of working days per week and working hours per day; advancements in medical science will increase longevity of life so that the number of senior citizens will go on increasing; both of these developments will call for greater attention to education for leisure.
- Because of continued degradation of the environment as a consequence of economic development, education will have to pay more attention to environmental matters.
- Education will have to lay greater emphasis on the improvement of quality and standards.
- Education will make greater use of the mass media, particularly radio and TV.
- Education will have to keep in view the common school and neighbourhood school concepts.
- Education will have to shift emphasis from teaching to self-learning by the learner.
- Education will lay greater stress on multi- and inter-disciplinary approaches.
- Education will have to become strongly rooted in the world of work.
- Efforts to make education more relevant to the needs, aspirations and lives of the people will have to be continued.
- Education will have to lay special emphasis on the promotion of national integration and international understanding.

Challenges for managers in education

The challenges that managers in education will face in making the educational system responsive to the anticipated societal needs towards 2000 and beyond will be manifold indeed. To manage quantitative expansion of education at all levels, which will continue unabated, will be the first and foremost challenge. While educational managers in India have long experience in managing formal education, managing non-formal education and assuring its quality to be comparable with that of formal education will be a challenging task. Connected with this will be the challenge of withstanding social and political pressures for opening new educational institutions and upgrading the existing ones. This will imply undertaking of school mapping exercises and making the results of these exercises public.

Continuing large-scale expansion is likely to dilute the quality of education, and to maintain quality in education in the face of declining resources will be another challenge. This will have to be met through innovative devices such as granting of autonomy (with built-in accountability) to a large number of schools and colleges; the introduction of an all-India test for initial recruitment of teachers for colleges and universities; launching of a national testing service; and developing norms for accreditation of educational institutions. All these measures have, in fact, been suggested in the NPE, and their implementation will be a challenge to educational managers.

To achieve the unfulfilled goals of socialism, secularism and democracy through the instrumentality of education, provision of mass education to all, irrespective of caste, creed or colour, will be yet another challenge. Managers in education will have to adopt non-traditional and innovative approaches and new strategies to bring about equity in education through mass education, both in terms of access and success.

One of the major challenges for educational managers dealing with adult education will be to convert adult education programmes into a mass movement under the national Literacy Mission. This will necessitate involvement of a large number of voluntary agencies, school/college/university students and teachers, retired persons from civil and military services, educated unemployed youth and non-student youth, in the implementation of adult education programmes. Two other challenges in the context of removal of adult illiteracy will be to establish effective linkages between adult education programmes and programmes of other development departments, particularly those related to poverty alleviation, as well as between public library networks and continuing education/post-literacy centres.

Providing justice to the talented among the deprived, introducing discriminatory pricing to level off inequities in higher education, curbing the capitation-fee menace, implementing the concepts of common school and neighbourhood school, are some other challenges which educational managers will have to face to promote equity in education. Changing the attitudes of teachers to the first generation learners through appropriate training will be yet another challenge for equity promotion. Equity implications intended in the 'quantum jump' in technology will also have to be fully understood by educational managers.

Bringing about suitable changes in the curriculum to promote socialism, and democracy will pose another challenge to managers of education. Changes in the curriculum in this context will include, among others, value-oriented education, moral education and education for citizenship. Educational managers will have to ensure that curriculum renewal is a continuous process in keeping with changing societal needs.

Managers will also have to face a number of challenges in the process of using communication technology for educational purposes. The challenges will be in the form of making hardware available to all educational institutions in the country under a phased programme; arranging for their repair and maintenance; persuading the media to provide sufficient time for extensive use of radio and TV for formal and non-formal education; creating appropriate support structures; arranging for the development of software; and organizing training programmes for personnel connected with the production of software and also for those who will be engaged in imparting distance education through different media.

Even today managers of Indian education are faced with the dilemma of ever-expanding education systems and ever-diminishing resources for education. The situation is likely to worsen by the turn of the century. To deal with this dilemma, mobilization of additional resources for education and ensuring optimal utilization of available resources will be a serious challenge to educational managers.

The challenges identified above are by no means exhaustive. There is no gainsaying the fact that the success of educational managers to face these challenges with confidence will depend largely upon the professional preparation that they will receive during the course of their career.

Professional preparation of educational managers

The primary responsibility for managing education in India lies with 25 states and seven union territories. Education being a subject of national concern, the central government (which has a separate Department of Education within the Ministry of Human Resource Development) also plays an important role in the financing and administration of education. Management of education in India therefore can be seen as a partnership between the centre and the states.

Projections for the year 2000 in respect of education managers who will need professional preparation have been made. About 1,770,000 managers in education will be working in the Indian system at that time, of which 610,000 will be at the system level and 1,160,000 at the institutional level.

Professional preparation of such a huge number of educationists will indeed be a gigantic task when we consider the existing woefully inadequate institutional arrangements for training of such persons, and the variety of training that will have to be provided (ie pre-entry, pre-induction, pre-promotional, pre-service and in-service), for different target groups. Out of 176 universities, at present only 36 offer educational planning, administration or management in MEd or MA (Education) courses. The National Institute of Educational Planning and Administration (NIEPA), as an apex institution at the national level, is one of the few institutes which organize in-service training programmes, some of which are cadre-based and some thematic, for a variety of managers from the central and state governments, as well as from the university and school systems. The duration of these courses varies from one week to six months.

State Councils of Educational Research and Training (SCERTs) in some states also conduct in-service training programmes of short duration. While the annual coverage in NIEPA's programmes is about 1,000, the coverage in programmes organized by SCERTs does not exceed 1,500, the focus of the latter's programmes mainly being on teachers.

Analysis of current provision in relation to projected needs justifies the creation of a network of institutions in the country. Many more universities will have to launch pre-service courses in education management; a state Institute of Educational Planning and Administration on the pattern of NIEPA will have to be founded in each state and union territory; SCERTs will have to strengthen their units providing in-service training for managers in education; and District Institutes of Education and Training as envisaged in NPE-1986 will have to be established in each district on a priority basis. Special units for education management will also have to be set up in the Indian Institutes of Management and the Faculties of Management Studies of various universities.

Each manager in education (whether he/she is working at the system or institutional level) will have to undergo an in-service training programme of professional enrichment of at least one week's duration preferably every three to five years, depending upon the availability of resources. Looking at the projected number of managers requiring professional preparation in the year 2000, it will be well nigh impossible to cover all of them even after strengthening the existing institutional arrangements and creation of the proposed new ones. Alternative methods which are cost-effective will therefore have to be designed. Thus, in-service programmes can be started by Universities which are opening at the state level such as the Indira Gandhi National Open University.

The training needs in education management (in terms of knowledge, skills and attitudes) can be identified for different target groups depending upon (1) their general and professional backgrounds, (2) the positions and responsibilities they hold, (3) the roles and functions they are required to perform and (4) the problems and difficulties they have to face while discharging their responsibilities. A clear appreciation of these four factors in the perspective of changing situations and future developments is essential for getting a realistic picture of training needs.

At present the training needs are not being identified systematically by any of the institutions conducting in-service professional training for education managers in this country. The training needs are assessed (as for example by NIEPA) on the basis of job charts of various categories of educational managers, or through face-to-face discussions or correspondence with the managements of the organizations to which the participants of the training programmes belong. The result is that the training programmes are omnibus in nature and fail to meet the individual needs of the people concerned.

Systematic exercises will have to be undertaken in the future to assess the training needs separately of key level and operational level educational managers, at the system level as well as of school and college principals at the institutional level.

The course content will depend upon the roles and functions assigned to each category of educational manager. The key level educationists are, and will continue to be, mainly responsible for the decision and policy-making function, for which they will have to make greater use of quantitative methods with the help of computers. To enable them to perform effectively, those who do not have professional qualifications and experience in education will have to be fully acquainted with the existing system of education, the latest trends in educational development, the new education policy, innovative ideas in education, the use of computers in educational management, and the application of modern management techniques to educational administration. Most of the professionals holding key level and operational level positions in the education ministries/ departments, both at the centre and states, will possess professional qualifications in the field of education. Since the roles, functions and responsibilities of a manager in education are entirely different from those of a teacher, it will be imperative to provide pre-promotional/pre-induction training of two to three weeks' duration for the promotee operational level managers in the fundamentals of education management. Similarly, the promotee key level educational managers will need training of at least one week duration to upgrade their professional competencies so as to enable them to discharge higher level responsibilities. The training will have to be both in the theory and practice of education management. Greater emphasis will have to be laid on practicums in the case of operational level officers. Apart from pre-promotional training, it will also be necessary to arrange in-service training programmes and refresher courses for those officers on a continuous basis.

Most school and college principals will be promoted from the ranks of teachers. The main responsibility of these personnel is to run their institutions as efficiently and effectively as possible. The training content for this target group will include orientation to the latest developments and future trends in the field of education, departmental rules and regulations, curricular reform, general principles of management, the management of change, innovative practices in institutional management, institutional planning, budgeting, the management of resources, school/college-community relationships, etc. Practicums as a part of their training will undertake practical exercises in the preparation of plans for institutional evaluation and renewal.

It will also be necessary to organize in-service training programmes for the trainers in educational management who will be spread over the university departments of education, faculties of management studies, specialized institutes of management and other bodies conducting in-service courses. Their in-service training assumes greater significance in view of the continuous research that is being undertaken in different parts of the world.

The content areas for training of village community leaders will include micro level planning and management with emphasis on conducting house-to-house surveys to determine educational needs of persons of all age groups within the community, assessing resources, fixing priorities; and developing, supervising, monitoring and evaluating various programmes and projects concerning the universalization of elementary education (both formal and non-formal), adult and continuing education.

Instructional methodologies, now being adopted for training of educational managers of different categories in India, largely consist of lecture-discussions and panel-discussions. Though the future methodologies for training of key level educational managers will continue to consist mainly of these, increasing use of new methodologies will have to be made, including group work, case method, syndicate method, simulation exercises, role play and in-basket simulations. Films on appropriate themes also will have to be used. In long-term training programmes, project work will form an important component of training.

At present, textual and other instructional materials produced mostly in the USA, the UK and other advanced countries, and which have little relevance to the Indian situation, are being used by various universities and training institutions. Training modules and other instructional materials on different aspects of education management, as well as other content areas, will have to be developed in the Indian context and updated from time to time.

Each training programme will have to be evaluated by the trainees with a view to getting feedback from them for improvement of the programmes. Evaluation will be in terms of the extent to which pre-conceived objectives of the training programmes are achieved, suitability or otherwise of the themes selected for the programmes, handling of various themes by the faculty, physical aspects of the programme, etc. In a long-term training programme, formative evaluations will be necessary at regular intervals, to be followed by a summative evaluation towards the end of the programme. In addition, follow-up impact evaluation of the training, which at present is conspicuous by its absence, will also have to be undertaken.

Conclusion

Clearly the task facing those concerned with the development of the quality of the management and administration of Indian education during the next decade and beyond, is challenging in the extreme. But I am optimistic that all concerned, governmental and non-governmental agencies, will rise to the occasion and contribute, to the best of their capacity, to the professionalization of education management in India. Professional managerial competence will be the single most important factor to help them prepare their countrymen, through the medium of education, to enter the 21st century with a certain amount of confidence.

References

Government of India, Ministry of Human Resource Development, Department of Education (1986), *National Policy on Education*. Delhi: The Controller of Publications.

Government of India, Ministry of Human Resource Development, Department of Education (1986), *National Policy on Education – Programme of Action*. Delhi: The Controller of Publications.

Government of India, Ministry of Law, Justice and Company Affairs (1977), *The Constitution of India*. Delhi: The Controller of Publications.

Government of India, Planning Commission. *Five Year Plans*. Delhi: The Controller of Publications.

Malhotra, Rashpal 1983 'Nation building development process and communication: some basic issues,' *Man and Development*, 10(4), p13.

4.10 Developing Educational Managers for the Year 2000: the Nigerian Case

Stella Olatunji

Introduction

Political, economic, religious, and socio-cultural developments will have a significant influence on Nigerian education over the next decade. Developments within education itself will interact with these to bring further changes. This paper explores likely changes in Nigerian society and education over the next ten years and considers their implications for the preparation of educational managers.

Likely developments within the next decade

On the political front, there will be greater awareness of political rights and, hopefully, of political responsibilities. This greater awareness will be brought about partly by the generally emerging emphasis on a 'grass roots' approach to politics; but politics in education specifically will also be attended to with greater interest. A prominent issue here is the claiming of rights by teachers, parents and students. Certain activities in the school sector and of student organizations, which unfortunately often end in disaster (such as the forced participation of students in riots and demonstrations which has resulted in death), have not been questioned in the law courts. The next decade will also see parents more alive to their rights, and the grass roots approach will also see them more actively involved in educational decision making.

On the economic front, recent difficult experiences tend to suggest continued revisions of the curriculum at secondary and tertiary levels. Education will increasingly be directed away from mere acquisition of knowledge or information towards a focus on practical results, such as equipping students with saleable skills and the development of initiative so that school leavers, and in turn the nation, become more self-reliant.

Furthermore, in spite of the commitment of the federal and state governments to formal education and the large amounts budgeted for it, resourcing levels are still inadequate. Government expenditure on education will need to increase and parents will have to augment these resources if an adequate quality of education is to be ensured.

In the religious arena, enough lessons must have been learnt to make tolerance of others and their points of view a welcome relief. The educational system will be expected to provide an environment for the development of such tolerance and to nurture it. The lesson of tolerance will also be extended to the socio-cultural front, as the tolerance of socio-cultural groups different from one's own will help to achieve the objective of unity which the nation desires so much. The encouragement of a conscious interest in other Nigerian languages, music, drama, artifacts and other aspects of culture will cement the different ethnic groups together. The educational system, as usual, will take the lead in developing justifiable pride in the various sub-cultures, in researching into them and discovering similarities and differences, and in improving aspects of culture that require refinement. Continued interest in culture implies an area of increasing co-operation between communities and the schools, as the latter need the former to provide a base of information and knowledge in this area.

There will be developments deriving more directly from the changes in the educational system itself. One is the increase in school population. The recent past has witnessed tremendous increases in primary, secondary, and tertiary school populations, and this trend is likely to continue. Increasingly parents are committed to the education of their children and so are not waiting for the compulsory stage of the free primary education scheme. As the system expands school organization and management will become more complex and more facilities will be required.

Another development within the educational system is the increasing level of qualification of its workers. At one time an elementary school leaver (standard six) could be a teacher; then the minimum requirement was raised to Elementary Teacher or Teachers' Grade III Certificate. Next it was raised to Higher Elementary Teachers' Grade II Certificate. Now the minimum qualification is the Nigeria Certificate of Education (NCE). This upward trend is likely to continue.

The rate of growth of knowledge is also increasing, with a continuing sub-division into more branches of learning. The implications for curriculum, teacher specialization, student guidance and facilities are apparent.

Educational administrators for the next decade

Given these varied and complex developments, what are the requirements that an educational administrator should fulfil to the year 2000 and beyond? It seems that an overall qualification is *adequate preparation*. According to Ukeje (1989, p7), school administrators need to be '. . . able and capable persons who in addition to good teaching experience, have had the opportunity of serious study of the science and practice of educational administration, together with a breadth of educational knowledge'. Such a preparation programme, Ukeje argues, will equip the prospective administrator with technical, human, and conceptual skills. Quoting Katz, Ukeje describes technical skill as the ability to use knowledge, methods, techniques and equipment necessary for the performance of specific tasks; human skill as the ability and judgement in working with people, including an understanding of motivation and an application of effective leadership; and conceptual skill as the ability to understand the complexities of the overall organization.

Other requirements, according to Adaralegbe (1989) include knowledge and competency in the areas of public and corporate policies, human resource management, financial management, methods and systems management, laws and regulations, effective decision-making processes and implementation, and effective communication skills. He also argues that tomorrow's educational managers must have insight into modern management theories that deal with humanistic problems, the management of change, organizational motivation, and group dynamics among others. In addition, the modern administrator should be able to read research findings and understand their implications for the improvement of the system he or she is paid to sustain and develop.

These general requirements can be seen to match the needs implied in the background picture already given of developments in the Nigerian society and their implications for education. For instance, there is no doubt that educational organizations are complex and will become more so. Therefore an understanding of such organizations is important, as are the human skill requirements associated with this. The use of politics to muster support for education is also a skill to be studied and practised, as is familiarity with the law, especially as people become more aware of their rights. The ability to handle research – conduct it, read results, and apply findings – is a most vital one, especially in this scientific and technological age. Each of the requirements outlined above can be explained similarly.

Finally, attention must be paid to the proper utilization of the modern educational administrator if the most is to be made of their preparation in improving the system.

Current efforts

Against this idea, how has Nigeria fared? Generally, experience as a teacher is considered more important than pre-service specialized training for educational administration. Thus, promotions are made to duty posts (principal and vice-principal at the secondary school level, and head teacher at the primary school level) from a carefully prepared seniority list. And in the Ministries of Education only a few officials would have received formal preparation in educational administration.

Faculties and Institutes of Education in Nigerian Universities have started to make conscious efforts to correct this situation. Thus generally, with two or three courses in educational administration offered at the undergraduate level, students receive *an exposure* to administration as part of their preparation for teaching through courses on the Nigerian Educational System, Introduction to Educational Administration and School Administration.

Some institutions (the Universities of Ibadan and Ilorin) offer some specialization at the undergraduate level. However, the desirability of specialization at this level has been questioned. The general view has been that in order to administer education one has to know education. The undergraduate student is just coping with education – the foundations, methodology , tests and measurements, the educational system, and classroom management – and may not be able to accommodate specialization in the true sense of the word. Besides, these graduates cannot be employed as principals or vice-principals straight away as the over-riding policy is to promote practising teachers to duty posts from a seniority list.

Specialization at the postgraduate level occurs at a number of Universities. At these institutions students work for their masters and doctoral certificates. The achievement has been modest. For instance at the University of Benin, about 114 MEd and PhD holders in educational planning and administration have been produced between 1982 and 1989 (Aghenta 1989). Other institutions may have produced more or less.

Utilization of graduates of the programmes

Tradition still holds sway and graduates who have specialized in educational planning and administration have not been preferred over long-serving and experienced workers who do not have the specialisation. Of the 114 graduates of the Benin programmes referred to above, 11 are reported as working in a State Ministry of Education, two in a Ministry other than education, two with Education Boards, 56 are teaching in secondary schools and 12 teaching in colleges and universities (Aghenta 1989). This suggests that the graduates are not being appropriately utilized.

The only bright spot in this discouraging picture of under-utilization is that many practising administrators enter the postgraduate training programmes. For them it is in-service training, but they usually retain their jobs and will be better administrators and planners for the training received.

To aid such trainees, some faculties and institutes of education are mounting part-time programmes, for example the Headmasters Institute of the University of Benin, and the postgraduate diploma programmes of many universities, and also their masters and doctoral programmes are offered on a part-time basis. Elsewhere workshops and seminars are mounted by the universities, Ministries of Education and professional organizations. Important examples include the annual seminars on school administration provided by the former University of Ife (now Obafemi Awolowo University) and the efforts of UNESCO, through BREDA.

The content of these programmes are generally suitable for their objectives, but more options may have to be offered in the light of emerging needs cutlined earlier. Current programmes encompass fundamentals of educational administration, politics of education, education policies and laws, economics of education, educational financing, research in educational administration, advanced statistics, and cases in educational administration. Sub-specializations are also available in educational administration (for general practitioners and researchers), higher education administration, and educational planning. In all the various programmes, a healthy component is the internship requirement, as is research which leads to the production of a thesis.

Conclusions and recommendations

This paper has attempted to provide a scenario of general developments in Nigerian society within the next decade which have implications for education and its management. Attention has been drawn to the quality of the educational administrator who will guide such a system and a brief description has been given of the efforts in Nigeria to prepare, improve or update such administrators. This concluding section provides some recommendations for improving the quality of Nigerian educational administrators and for their appropriate utilization.

Training programmes

It is suggested that more Departments of Educational Administration and Planning be created because there is a clear need for well prepared administrators to produce a well-run educational system. Offering part-time and sandwich programmes is more economical because this enables prospective educational administrators to remain in their jobs; but it is equally true that first degree holders prefer to continue studying, say for postgraduate certificates, rather than continuing to wait for jobs that are very difficult to obtain. Departments of Educational Administration and Planning need to be created to cater for both groups.

A next step would be to undertake an evaluation of current programmes to see whether they are fulfilling current needs and those envisaged for the coming decade and beyond. Such evaluation should involve a critical examination of content and methodology. For instance, a department that offers politics of education may not be sufficiently up-to-date if it does not address the effects of the wider politics: for example, greater awareness of rights, education laws and the laws of the land.

Revision of content and methods is bound to affect the quality of staff required, as well as the facilities and materials needed for teaching and learning. University teachers, interested in working in the area, therefore need to be identified and given re-training or improvement courses themselves.

For the general run of practising or prospective administrators, attendance at workshops, in-service courses, seminars and such other opportunities must be required. And when obtained, atten-dance and performance on the programmes ought to be assessed for the purpose of awarding incremental units for promotion. The co-operation of Ministries of Education will need to be sought and obtained over this proposal as they will rightly be concerned about the additional salary costs that promotion signifies.

Utilization of educational administrators

It will continue to be discouraging for well-trained educational administrators not to be appropriately placed or utilized. One option is for educational administrators and their professional organisations subtly to influence policy decisions, such as those determining who can practice as an educational administrator. The change cannot be drastic because attitudes are engrained in the Ministries, Teaching Service Commissions and Boards, and the administrators themselves; all have been used to the practice of ele-vating workers from a seniority list. The aim will have been achieved when appointments to administrative posts go to profes-sionals. It must be stressed that much depends on the professional associations such as the Nigerian Association for Educational Administration and Planning (NAEAP) and the All Nigeria Conference of Principals of Secondary Schools: they simply must take the initiative.

These recommendations may need further examination, and there may be more, besides. Their central purpose is to produce educational administrators of quality who can help to ensure improvements in the system as a whole.

References

Adaralegbe, A L 1989 'The need for trained educational planners and administrators in Africa' a lead paper presented at the *West African Regional Conference on Educational Administration*, Owerri, Nigeria, December 4–8, 1989.

Aghenta, J A L 1989 'Utilization and deployment of educational planners and administrators in Africa' a lead paper presented at the *West African Regional Conference on Educational Administration*, Owerri, Nigeria December 4–8, 1989.

Ukeje, B O 1989 'The facilities, resources and strategies for the preparation of educational planners and administrators in Africa' a lead paper presented at the *West African Regional Conference on Educational Administration*, Owerri, Nigeria, December 4–8, 1989.

4.11 Preparation and Training of Educational Managers for the South Pacific: Problems and Prospects

T. Velayutham

Introduction

The preparation and training of educational managers for the South Pacific countries present certain problems and offer prospects that are in some respects comparable with those in other countries and in other respects distinctive and peculiar to the region. The discussion will be largely based on my experience in the preparation and upgrading of present and prospective educational managers at the University of the South Pacific and my involvement in certain consultancy and outreach activities in the region. Therefore, the presentation may project a rather narrow but in depth view of the problems encountered and prospects foreseen in the preparation and training of educational managers in the region, particularly in the eleven English-speaking countries served by the University of the South Pacific. These are Cook Islands, Fiji, Kiribati, Nauru, Niue, Solomon Islands, Tokelau, Tonga, Tuvalu, Vanuatu and Western Samoa.

Background

The South Pacific as a region has received a great deal of attention from academics, aid donors, researchers, business concerns, environmentalists, diplomats and every conceivable agency and interest group from various parts of the world. It can be predicted that this interest and involvement will continue and even accelerate. The countries in the region display an array of differences and, at the same time, share many common issues, problems and prospects. Therefore, they are increasingly trying out not only national strategies, but also joint and common programmes of action and development to deal with these issues and to take advantage of prospects presented to them.

The last two decades or so have seen enormous changes in the social, political, cultural and educational spheres, following decolonisation, and the advent of independence in these countries. The faith they have in education and training as tools for national development is seen in the high proportion of their national budgets allocated and the high priority accorded, to education. As much as 25 per cent of national budgetary allocations are devoted to education by some South Pacific nations. Their governments regard this outlay on education and manpower training as an investment in human resource development and a lever for modernisation.

Training programmes for educational managers

The preparation and training of educational managers take the form of pre-service courses, in-service education programmes and some *ad hoc* courses. These are offered by Ministries or departments of education, teachers colleges and institutes of higher education of some of these countries and universities.

Pre-service teacher education programmes of teachers' colleges and institutes of higher education generally include an optional course in school organisation and/or educational management. They are designed to give a general appreciation and understanding of educational organisations, relationships with community and policy implementation. Over the years, courses with some units on school organisation have been replaced by entire courses on school management, as in the case of Tonga's Secondary Teacher Education Programme (STEP).

In-service programmes not only include courses on school organisation and management, but specialist programmes in educational administration leading to a diploma and a major in the BEd degree are now offered by the University of the South Pacific. More recently higher degrees such as MA, MPhil and PhD specialising in Educational Administration are being offered by the University of the South Pacific. Each of these programmes incorporate two major inter-related strands of study: namely institutional with an organizational focus and a system strand with a multi-level system focus.

Project-mode delivery of specialist in-service programmes has been an innovative approach developed by the Institute of Education of the University in association with its Department of Education. Solomon Islands and Kiribati have taken advantage of this provision. In addition, self-financing non-credit tailor-made courses have been organised by the Continuing Education Unit with the assistance of Education Department Staff.

In various ways the University's Department of Education, Institute of Education and Extension Services Unit have responded constructively and imaginatively to the 'development needs' as urged by one of its former vice chancellors. (Maraj 1976)

The governments in the region have also mounted their own training programmes, sometimes enlisting the staff of the University of the South Pacific and/or the universities or government agencies of Australia and New Zealand. Also senior Ministry and department staff undertake study visits, postgraduate studies and specific training programmes under various bilateral aid programmes with foreign governments.

Some problems

Some of the problems described below are almost universal and therefore you may be familiar with them. Others are rather specific to some countries in the South Pacific, being determined by cultural contexts, developmental stage, comparative size, and so on.

Even now it is not uncommon to find educational managers who feel that administration and leadership in schools are unproblematic and who take them for granted as simple day-to-day operations which could be tackled as they need action. Hence many of them would not actively seek avenues for upgrading their professional competence through appropriate training programmes or courses.

Related to this issue is the view that preparation or training programmes for educational managers is a 'one-shot' or 'once in a lifetime' process in professional preparation. Very often the need for continuity, follow-up, and recurrent training is not recognized and valued by the educational managers themselves and/or by their employers. A solution to these two problems could be partly found by making available a variety of training programmes, publicising their availability and usefulness, and more importantly demonstrating their effectiveness to the target groups and their employers.

There is an urgent need to know more about those leadership and administrative variables that are amenable to improvement and distinguish them from those that are not so amenable. Sometimes a system approach to training may be necessary when appropriate changes in related groups or role-sets have to be also considered. Further research is needed in these two areas before more durable and significant benefits could be expected from our training efforts.

Preparation and training efforts should take good account of the organisational contexts and constraints within which the educational managers will be operating or working. In addition a thorough knowledge and appreciation of the social, economic, cultural and political factors that impinge on these organizations are necessary before meaningful and adaptable training or preparation can be given. Sometimes the trainees and their employers complain about the lack of these perspectives in courses and training programmes offered to their educational managers in metropolitan institutions, or on in-country training programmes offered by overseas experts and consultants with inadequate knowledge of local conditions. Some aid donors may not perceive correctly the local development priorities of small states.

Some of the countries in the South Pacific receive offers to prepare and train their educational administrators from more than one aid donor or international organisation, and still worse sometimes offers come from more than one institution within a country. Under these circumstances the authorities responsible for accepting and/or soliciting foreign aid find it difficult to decide on the sources from which they would profit most or profit at all. It may be worthwhile for the institutions which have the capacity and resources to offer such programmes to get together and discuss ways and means of co-ordinating their efforts and maximizing the benefits for the recipients. Otherwise these institutions may well be duplicating or overlapping in their inputs and creating a bewildering situation for the recipient country. This situation is likely to worsen with the adoption of a commercial/marketing approach to educational provision by some metropolitan countries (Tupeni 1989).

The classical problem of bridging the gaps between theoretical frameworks offered in preparation and training programmes on the one hand, and the practical situations on the other is still with us. Closer and continuing contact of the trainers with the practising or operating environments, and opportunities for the trainers to work for specific periods in schools and Education Offices would help to resolve this problem partly. Another approach is to integrate as much as possible the theoretical positions and the practical realities in a truly interactive manner. Such attempts to integrate theoretical aspects and practical implications should be undertaken at the preliminary planning stage itself and continued through programme delivery, evaluation and feedback. Theory-practice integration should be supported and reinforced by research and development.

Prospects for the future

Though a small proportion of educational managers feel that the administrative process is a simple and unproblematic one, there is a growing body of opinion that educational managers need to be upgraded and exposed to conceptual frameworks and theoretical propositions if the educational administrative system is to execute, and support developmental and implementing phases of innovations designed to modernise their educational systems. Hence one sees a surge in expressed demand for more and varied training and professional development of teachers and administrators.

As a result of a long history of partnership between the state and the community in education, one finds community involvement in educational development and provision an important element in the South Pacific. This aspect of managing education could be reinforced and extended by stressing the role schools and the educational system could play in assisting and supporting communities in their initiatives and development efforts, and could be a worthwhile learning experience in itself (Velayutham 1986). Otherwise community involvement would tend to be a one-sided affair, especially in the South Pacific societies which are characteristically 'caring and sharing' in their attitude to life. The programmes for preparing and training educational managers should also stress the need for the community to play a more assertive and constructive role in educational management and community development (Bhindi 1988).

The human resource development model of management is coming to the fore in many parts of the world. Some of the small South Pacific countries, too are trying to adopt certain aspects of human resource development in their educational training programmes. Those of us who work in the areas of preparing and training educational managers find a ready social laboratory in which to experiment with this new approach. For instance the leaders and senior officials subscribe to the notions of 'investing in people' and 'people-centred development' that are important considerations in human resource development. Another significant variation of approach to human resource development is the emphasis on developing 'generalist' or polyvalent or multiple role managers rather than managers with unitary specialist roles. Some of the small South Pacific countries cannot afford the luxury of specialist managers and professionals for each and every task area. Hence these countries, like small states elsewhere, are trying to create a cadre of managers who can fit into multiple roles in a flexible manner, a system that differs from the 'generalist' cadre of the public service of some developed countries (Bray and Fergus 1986).

Traditionally policy-making, planning, and implementation have been regarded as separate and unrelated functions of administration. In most small South Pacific countries these functions cannot be performed as separate functions by officials functioning at different hierarchical levels. The sheer force of operating circumstances such as distance, isolation and small-scale demand, necessitate that these functions which are traditionally conceived as separate functions are really performed together in an interactive and integrative manner. The wisdom of not neatly separating these functions among officials in the educational hierarchy is already evident in more developed and larger educational systems.

The need for bureaucracies, including educational organisations, to effect speedy implementation of their programmes and ensure greater public visibility of their performance is acutely felt in development administration. The smaller South Pacific countries present suitable environments in which to try out these two principles. Speedy implementation is usually hampered by the lack of readily available resources, trained manpower, and sometimes the general attitude of taking matters less hurriedly.

The formal aspects of bureaucracies such as hierarchical structure and impersonal relations are criticised as impeding developmental efforts of administration. In some of the smaller South Pacific countries most people know each other and usually maintain strong personal ties and close group affiliation (Bacchus and Brock 1987). This can lead to patronage and nepotism which are usually avoided in a western bureaucratic style of administration. On the other hand, knowing those administering and those administered may introduce an element of informality and accessibility thus reducing some of the evils of bureaucracy.

The decision-making structure and process of some of the South Pacific States may be rather different from those in hierarchically oriented western bureaucracy. Schahezenski (1990) suggests that the consensual administrative decision-making employed in some of the Pacific States may be more efficient in accomplishing development goals. As noted by Murray (1985), consensual decision-making in these societies takes place in less formal face-to-face situations and a general agreement is arrived at in a manner that preserves social harmony and an obligation to act upon the decision once made. Besides, even if there were disagreements, resistance or tensions in educational debate, these do not have a negative effect on educational decisions but have a positive effect and productive outcome. As Hindson (1989) reports:

> The existence of these tensions in the educational debate was not in itself negative because it often led to positive action to resolve difficulties, thus generating new educational goals. This often occurred outside the formal planning process and, given the complexities of rapidly changing socio-political conditions in the South Pacific, there are no grounds for assuming that Western-oriented planning model would have achieved any more desirable outcomes (p103).

Regional co-operation

Most of the small South Pacific countries would find it difficult to mount on their own a comprehensive preparation and training programme for their educational managers. On the other hand they increasingly find that some of the Western theoretical models and the training offered to their nationals in metropolitan institutions do not closely correspond to the local realities and conditions. The University of the South Pacific assists the countries in the region, through on-campus courses, distance education programmes, summer schools, continuing education programmes, attachments, special project programmes and consultancy visits, in their efforts to prepare, train and retrain their staff. Increasingly regional organisations such as the South Pacific Commission, Unesco's Regional Office of Education in Asia and the University of the South Pacific have mounted programmes to train educational managers and professionals. Apart from these, the South Pacific countries co-operate among themselves on a regional basis, and sometimes on a sub-regional basis, to train and prepare the educational managers and professional staff of each other's countries. Strengthening regional cooperation in this area and in other social economic and cultural development spheres has been advocated and accomplished in a large measure. A balanced approach of this regional cooperation together with some judicious selection of input from international and metropolitan sources in specially identified areas would be productive.

Conclusion

Multi-mode, multi-level and continuous professional development of educational managers in the South Pacific has been possible through the in-service, distance mode educational administration specialism offered by the University. Some overseas universities and training institutes have supplemented these efforts together with intra-regional and national efforts.

Some problems that are encountered in preparing educational managers in the South Pacific have been highlighted. Many of these may not be peculiar to the region alone. An examination of the prospects and possibilities has been undertaken in the hope that these would generate new and relevant ideas. The educational managers and professionals are being prepared to respond to and facilitate change in their organisation and systems. However, it is time that we move to the stage of preparing leaders who do not merely respond to and facilitate change, but also anticipate future trends and needs and are able to shape the future, helping to fulfil the dreams for the future of their people. The hopes expressed by a team of international experts in developing future educational managers as leaders is a suitable reminder for those of us involved in this important and complex task: 'School leaders and those responsible for training should develop programs that prepare leaders who can create tomorrows and enrich today' (Leithwood et al 1984 p191).

References

Bacchus, K and Brock, C 1987 'Editorial Introduction' in Bacchus, K and Brock, C (eds) *The Challenge of Scale: Educational Development in the Small States of the Commonwealth*, London: Commonwealth Secretariat.

Bhindi, N 1988 'The community as an educational resource and the role of the educational administrator' in *Directions: Journal of Educational Studies*, 10 (2).

Bray, M and Fergus, H 1986 'The implications of size for educational development in small countries: Monserrat, a Caribbean case 'study' in *Compare*, 16 (1).

Hindson, C 1989 'An approach to the study of educational development in small-island states with particular reference to the South Pacific' in *Education Research and Perspectives*, 16 (1).

Leithwood, K, Rutherford, W and Van Der Vegt, R 1984 'Conclusions: looking ahead' in Leithwood, K et al (eds) *Preparing School Leaders for Educational Improvement*, London: Croom Helm.

Maraj, J 1976 'Statement to the University of the South Pacific' in *Pacific Perspective*, 5 (1).

Murray, D 1985 'Public administration in the microstates of the Pacific' in Dommen, E and Hein, P (eds) *States, Microstates and Islands*, Dover: Croom Helm.

Schahezenski, J 1990 'Development administration in the small developing state: a review' in *Public Administration and Development*, 10.

Tupeni, N 1989 'Australia's involvement in the Pacific' in *Directions: Journal of Educational Studies*, 11 (2).

Velayutham, T 1985 'Success or failure', *Keynote address at the Ninth Regional Symposium of Educational Supervisors in South East Asia and the Pacific*, in Porta Vila, Vanuatu, September.

Velayutham, T 1986 'Decentralization of educational administration as a strategy for achieving equity and providing diversity' in *Directions: Journal of Educational Studies*, 8 (1 and 2).

4.12 Developing Educational Managers: a Response to the Seventh International Intervisitation Programme of 1990

David Styan

I am particularly grateful for the opportunity to respond to the deliberations of the Seventh International Intervisitation Programme, and in particular, the working groups which played so important a role in the whole enterprise. It is an opportunity that anyone involved in education management and administration would surely relish. It enables me to connect up the deliberations of the conference and its working groups with the recently published report of the School Management Task Force (1989), a Government unit set up by the Secretary of State to advise him on the most appropriate action to be taken to develop the quality of School Management in England. In outlining the Task Force approach, and commenting upon the reports from the working groups, I can re-enforce the central messages that we all see to be so vital to those presently working in education management.

The Task

Before launching upon these issues, I would like to make clear just what I mean by 'response' and to say what I do not think it means. I see a 'response' as a personal reaction to all that I saw and heard, underlining what were particularly telling comments and broad thrusts; I do not see the task as presenting a summary of all the events and ideas, or a conclusion that attempts to synthesise or resolve all the issues which were raised. Each will take their own choice of memories away with them, and introduce them into the many different contexts from wherever they came. Each has different needs, and each is pre-occupied with particular issues, and has a different agenda. In addition to friendships initiated and strengthened, each will have gained a perspective, on the education scene in North West England, and, perhaps more importantly, a new perspective on their home environment. It is often by seeing the ways others tackle issues that we can see more clearly our own predicament. It is this process of travelling to other situations in order to more precisely recognise where you are at home that is so often the value of such international conferences. It is less the 'short stay' knowledge of others than the insights that illuminate the 'long stay' when you return that are their true value. And so, this is my response to the ideas of the groups, not a precis of experience, nor a ready-packaged souvenir to take home.

So cleared of the impossible task of interpreting the conference in the context of each participant's normal working environment, I feel encouraged to share with you the thinking of the Task Force, and my personal reaction to the working groups. To enable you to more readily understand my point of view, a brief reference to my background and experience may be useful, if only to show where my prejudices come from.

Background experience

1990 marks my thirty years as a teacher. After 10 years as a subject teacher, I became Deputy Head in a large East Midlands comprehensive, and in 1973 was appointed, at the age of 35, to be Head of the newly-formed Marple Ridge High School, another 11–18 mixed comprehensive school. Housed in old, but refurbished buildings formerly belonging to separate boys and girls schools, it grew over 15 years to over 1,550 students. The school staff of nearly 100 readily responded to a participative style of management, with, for example, all key decisions being made at meetings of the Board; a group consisting of all the senior and middle managers, and as many of the rest of the staff, teaching and non-teaching who chose to attend. I also had the enormous personal advantage of being invited, shortly after taking up headship, to become a consultant tutor at the North West Educational Management Centre, where I am now Director. Like so many others who are asked to help on management courses, and with consultancies, I was the chief beneficiary from the experience. What it also helped me to do was to reflect upon and articulate the experiences at the school, adding a dimension difficult to achieve in the daily routines of a large and busy school.

A secondment for one year to become Director of the Centre for the Study of Comprehensive Schools, then based at York University, also proved crucial in extending my experience, especially in the field of school-industry links, and enabled me to get a clearer picture of what schools were achieving. Shortly after that I was elected to the National Council of the National Association of Headteachers. Here, in addition to a wide range of work including support for colleague heads in serious professional trouble, I chaired a working groups on School Management, which produced a short report in early 1988, later endorsed by a National Conference in May of that year. Which particular experience was responsible for attracting the attention of the DES I am not sure, but I am now seconded part-time from my post as Director of NWEMC to lead the School Management Task Force. With four other part-time colleagues we have been given three years to produce a report and to take whatever action we can to promote its conclusions. Thus I come to this post from a lengthy background as head of a school, with some knowledge of the demands of other heads and senior staff, the problems that beset them, and the support they need. Mine has been practical experience of managing, overlain by the chance to acquire a perspective beyond a single school, and with the opportunity to reflect upon those experiences, largely in the company of other heads.

The School Management Task Force

The particular remit of the School Management Task Force, is to seek to improve school management in England (and, by invitation, in Wales also) by:
- surveying the pattern of existing provision;
- identifying gaps and variations in the provision of support, course provision and quality;
- harnessing the support of public and private sector providers;

- helping Local Education Authorities (LEAs) establish practical strategies;
- assisting LEAs to set quantified targets;
- ensuring that LEAs make best use of the training grant money available.

My colleagues, one each from primary school, secondary school, higher education and industry, share a wide experience of management as a practical activity, and also a considerable measure of theoretical knowledge and understanding. What my experience, largely confined to schools, has taught me is the wealth of opportunity available to all adults in schools to manage, the high calibre of much of this management, and the vitally important process of reflecting upon this experience in order to improve future action. Practice of management comes first, and continues to do so. Theoretical study explains and illuminates, but never replaces the actual process of managing as the most effective way of learning about management. It follows that the best way of developing as a manager is to manage.

The remit outlined above was agreed by the then Secretary of State, Kenneth Baker, the Task Force was launched in November 1988, and work began in January 1989. Early work involved urgent consultations with individuals and groups, the commissioning of rapid surveys on the current state of management training, distance learning, consultancy and profiling, extensive reading and eventually, the drawing together of a position statement, and extended agenda for more formal and extensive consultancies. These latter points were contained in an Interim Report, published by the DES in April 1989. Inspite of some press comment that we had failed to produce 'quick fix' answers, there was general support for the process of getting the education service to discuss the agenda we had set, and then offer approval, modification, dissent or even new items for our consideration. We held four residential seminars with individuals drawn from, though not representatives of, chief education officers and chief advisers, headteachers both primary and secondary, providers of training from both higher education and private firms, and from industry and commerce. We then held eight one-day regional conferences throughout England and Wales. These were attended by every LEA, generally by chief officers, chairs of education committees, chief advisers, and a secondary and primary head. Additionally we met teacher unions, associations representing officers, advisers, LEAs, examining and training bodies, as well as many individuals. We then reviewed and discussed these experiences, and wrote our main, though not necessarily final, report in the latter part of the year. This report endorsed by a new Secretary of State, John McGregor, was published and personally launched by him in March of 1990, and we are now engaged upon promoting its contents, encouraging those with the power and responsibility to act in the light of its recommendations and undertaking further research and monitoring. We expect to be in a position to comment further on specific matters, eg selection for senior management, profiling (upon which there is an extensive trial going on in the North West) and the role of accreditation. We aim to complete our contribution to this on-going development by the end of three years, by which time the context, we hope, will have changed, and some other more appropriate body will be set up to continue the work.

In framing our report, and undertaking our programme, we are very conscious of the current climate in Education in England and Wales. A climate in which, as a result of the radical reforms of the 1980s, allied to the strident tendency to vilify teachers, using them as the scapegoats for the ills of society in general and the economy in particular, morale is low. The Task Force has been keen to emphasise that its very creation is not yet another condemnation of those who manage schools. It is, however, true that such changes as the devolution of decision-making, especially financial decisions, to schools has concentrated the minds of ministers and DES officials alike on the haphazard preparation currently offered senior staff. We are aware also that there does not really exist a service-wide approach to management. Differences, often unintentional, in salary scales and conditions of service inhibit individuals from moving throughout their careers from managing in schools to managing in LEAs, and vice versa, and from and to management education and training. Much preparation and development remains strongly segregated, rather than integrated. Recent nationwide initiatives to prepare school governors for their new role have concentrated on separate training experiences, and hence have had the predictable consequence of making good working relations with heads and staff more rather than less difficult. At the same time, we sensed that a service-wide approach achieved by central government dictat was wholly unacceptable. There was no appetite for a nationalised approach on behalf of the Department itself; nor did professionals call for such moves. Yet, having set the reform agenda, central government clearly has some considerable responsibility for creating the conditions for success. Pointing direction, and ensuring resources seem the two most favoured, rather than centralised training and assessment systems.

A further tension underlying our work is the competing aims of providing practical help to those managing change here and now, and the longer term goal of an approach that makes sense over a generation. Urgent immediate action may, so easily, promote the very opposite of what is seen to be the preferred long-term approach. Of course, the Task Force recognised from the outset that to have in place a thorough training and development programme for, say the 1988 Education Reform Act would mean starting work five years before the implementation of the reforms, not at the same time. Structuring long-term programmes to ensure better quality for the next century may be laudable, but does little or nothing for those struggling with present problems. Finally, we felt we had to bear in mind always that management, and its improvements, whilst clearly important, is not an end in itself. Every child and adult working there deserves to be in a well-run school, but it is all too easy to see management as a process distinct from, rather than crucial to, the central purpose of schools. Emphasising financial management, marketing, public relations, staff development or strategic planning is understandable, but there lurks the real danger that these are seen as purposes in themselves. Balancing the books is important, but if achieved at the expense of the learning of the young people in the school, it signifies not successful management, but failed management. A contented staff, and second-rate learning means disaster in educational terms even if the manager receives frequent plaudits from those colleagues. We are, therefore, frequently reminding ourselves that better management can only be judged by the learning that takes place, and no other criteria will do.

Against the background of such concerns, we have articulated in *Developing School Management – The Way Forward* (School Management Task Force 1990) what we perceive to be an approach which is relevant, practical and widely supported, both throughout education, and incidentally, amongst those leading companies whose search for better management is taking them along parallel paths. Our analysis begins by distinguishing between management and managers. We are most comfortable with the definition of management development used both by the Local Government Training Board in England, and also IBM UK that it is '...about the development of managers...the development of management and...the development of organisations and their purposes.' Crucial though individuals are, and important though their personal competence can be, it is not enough to train managers. To be effective the organisation need also sound management contexts in which managers can manage, and all activity has to be directed to the effectiveness of the school organisation. In other words, (a) the task must be manageable, often the result of setting sensible attainable tasks, resourcing them, and working in realistic timescales; (b) the team must be productive, which means far more attention to structure appropriate to modern needs; and

(c) the individual must be confident and capable, which means well-supported experiences, recognised, praised, credited and enjoyable. To single out the manager, apply more and more 'training', and do little or nothing about management processes, or realisable institutional targets, is to misdirect effort, intensify feelings of inadequacy, and ultimately to find few willing and able to take on the key roles with any prospect of success.

Thus the report concentrates on those measures which will, in the short-term as well as further ahead, enable the average and ordinary to succeed where only the exceptional ventured before. It emphasises that all schools need to be well managed. Consequently it highlights simple, but often ignored truths. One such is the assertion that all teachers, as well as many other adults in the education service, are managers. Far from management being the prerogative of heads, deputies and senior staff, it is a vital part of being a teacher. All teachers, as part of their conditions of service in England and Wales are required both to 'manage' and to 'administrate'. From the first day in the classroom, teachers manage the learning of the class – setting targets, motivating, allocating resources and monitoring performance. They manage by their contribution to the overall effectiveness of the school, via formal staff meetings, informal discussions and the myriad initiatives they take. Schools where teachers subside into being passive 'operators', obeying orders and working to instructions are not true learning institutions at all.

This being the case, we recognise that the way teachers, like other adults, learn to do their job, which includes managing is by doing it. Experience of managing, and learning by reflecting upon it, is the key dynamic to improvement. If, however, most early experience is unpleasant, frustrating, ineffective and unrecognised, future action will be cautious, defensive, evasive and resentful. What then becomes vital is ready access to support services that make all the difference between success and failure.

In our work, we were forcefully struck by the support on immediate offer to managers in the leading companies and not to those in schools. Information services, instant, reliable and intelligible expertise in matters legal and professional – covering issues such as employment legislation, health and safety – support services in staff recruitment both permanent and short-term, consultants prepared to come to school, self-help groups of senior and middle managers, access to basic training for junior staff, rather than those already promoted to senior positions, are all vital. Above all, we saw the need for understanding that serious educational change takes time, cannot be willed by exhortation, but needs patience, is not cheap, and requires the whole-hearted commitment of enthusiastic and optimistic staff. Much has been successfully achieved in English education in recent years by such people, but evidence of demoralisation means that, this time, successful implementation of the reforms and their maintenance and the valuing of that which is already there, is in doubt.

Current emphasis		Redirected emphasis
tutor-directed courses	→	support for self-directed study by individuals, school teams, peer groups
off-site training	→	in-school and near-to-the school training
predetermined times	→	flexitime study
oral presentations	→	distance learning materials, information packs and projects
provider-determined syllabus	→	school-determined agenda
knowledge acquisition	→	performance enhancement

Figure 4.12.1

The Task Force report envisages, therefore, a shift from training the individual to support for the institutions. It further sees training itself undergoing significant change, as is already evident in some places, from tutor dominated, offsite, didactic, simulated and passive learning to school-based, team, interactive, activities (see Figure 4.12.1). The report recognises the special demands made upon the senior managers of the service as reform gathers pace, but rejects the notion of the separate cadre of heads, with their own 'staff colleges', separated from colleagues, and treated differently at every turn. It sees merit in the effort going into pre-preparation, and especially induction, for all assuming new responsibilities, rather than exclusive treatment for those already appointed to headship or deputy headship. It urges a career-long approach, with every teacher, and every member of the support staff in a school entitled to be treated as a manager and encouraged to widen their experiences and deepen their understanding of management at every stage.

To promote this approach, the Task Force has launched upon a programme of action, in collaboration with the whole service. It is providing cash support for a consortium of LEAs to survey their regional resources, determine new support structures, develop processes and extend provision. It is publishing its message to schools, and encouraging each one to incorporate practical commitments to the school development plan. Working with teacher

associations, and those representing officers and advisers, it is disseminating examples of more effective structures for schools than
those inherited from the past and it hopes that these associations
will argue for the necessary salary structures to underpin these proposals.

The Task Force is working with school governors to re-accent
governor training and encourage a supportive attitude in governing bodies towards the managerial development of all staff, with
industrial firms to get them to share strategic thinking with education, with higher education to shift training styles and accredit experience, and with Her Majesty's Schools Inspectorate to monitor and
evaluate management along the lines advocated in the report. It has
left itself room to issue further reports, including a final one, commenting on specific issues, and pointing the way forward after its
own demise. Thus, the Task Force sees the need to re-enforce
confidence and to offer, from initial training to retirement, a career-
long coherence and high quality support for individual, team and
school. To date, the response to that aim has been most encouraging.

The working groups

Turning from the Task Force to the working groups, it seems that
each one, distilling the experiences of participants from very different contexts, reflected three overwhelming factors; the first is that
the educational world is acutely aware of *tensions* that, from time
to time, and in particular places, threaten to damage its growth and
development. The second is that, partly as a result of these tensions, but also because of an impatience with the capacity of education to meet the needs of society, these are common *concerns*
about the immediate future. And thirdly, there is a marked degree
of consensus, at least among delegates to the Seventh International
Intervisitation Programme, about what needs to be done to ensure
a *healthier climate*. Before elaborating on each of these, however,
it is worth highlighting an underlying worry about what one group
described as 'the managerial myth'. There can be no doubting the
fact that managerialism, imported from business without due regard
for the fundamental character of teaching and learning is a matter
of great concern. Some governments, notably in Britain, proposed
the view that such a concept is long overdue. They talk of bringing
business methods, training and personnel into schools, at present
in the form of governors drawn from business, but in future, perhaps as heads of schools. However, these real fears about manage-

rialism do not justify a hostile reaction to management. Schools need to be well run institutions if they are to deliver rich and stimulating learning opportunities for their students, and staff members and others employed in them have a right to expect well-managed environments. This is not anti-educational but a necessary condition wherever learning is institutionalised. Further, to be an effective teacher, it can be argued that the skills of the manager are essential alongside other professional skills such as knowledge and understanding of the subject, and of children and young people. For a school to be effective in achieving its purposes, it needs good managers; without them, anarchy, chaos and disintegration occur. The art is to use managerial techniques to enhance education, but not to use them to replace teaching and learning as the key activities for each school.

Tensions

The syndicate groups were all, in their own way, eager to throw up a bewildering variety of tensions that in many ways describe the context. One clear example is the tension between the tendency to centralise the educational systems on the one hand, and, on the other, the attempts to move decisions closer to the point of impact. It is not that this move to localise is going on in different societies, but simultaneously within the same society that espouses centralisation that causes the tension, not to say confusion and bewilderment. Closely related is the tension between control and creativity, where systems seek both to constrain in the name of quality and empower in the name of dynamic, imaginative growth. Further such tensions emerge from the group reports. The perceived dichotomy between educational and business models of delivery is another, and that also is closely related to what can be loosely seen as a tension between a values driven approach, and one that is essentially mechanistic.

The conference clearly recognised that these tensions, real though they are to those working with the uncertainties that they so often give rise to, are not the only ones. Many gave witness to the changing and competing roles of politicians and professionals. Generally speaking, a move from ownership by professionals to more direct intervention by politicians was perceived, and this lack of ownership is made more disconcerting by the constant 'shifting of the goal-posts'. The political world, with its premium on new ideas and initiatives, headlines and instant solutions operates in a different time frame from successful educational reform and so tensions intensify. A further dimensions was the tension between those who take an instrumental, utilitarian view of learning, emphasising skills and competencies related to the world of work, and those pursuing a liberal civilising path, emphasising personal growth, concepts and attitudes. The growing list of tensions is not yet exhaustive. Education systems were seen to be grappling with conflicting pressures to be international in orientation or else to serve national goods and, again, there was presented the tension between formal institutional education and informal, even 'deschooling' approaches.

Perhaps the most common of all the conflicting themes exposed at the conference was that of the debate between a planned, centrally resourced approach and the market-dominated, competitive approach. Closely related to notions of the pupil as client, or the pupil as product, this was perhaps seen as the most powerful of the tensions in education at the present time. Certainly, the profound impact of moving further towards a market culture when coupled with pressures to peg or even reduce expenditure in education is seen as a threat to the very existence of many institutions, and is proving unpalatable to many of those working in them.

Concerns

There can be no denying the strength of the concerns being expressed about these unresolved tensions, and each would have his or her own preferred resolution. It is worth observing, however, that these tensions arise in part from a growing recognition of the vital role that education has to play in society world-wide and in part from honest attempts to seek new and better solutions to questions of quality, democratic power, community interests and ways of organising things. It is also the case that many of these tensions, for instance the centralisation versus localisation debate, serve to keep in balance actual practice. In other words, resolving such tension in favour of one or the other would probably produce a clear, but less appropriate situation for education. Tensions imply forces acting against each other, and can serve to achieve near-equilibrium. Education solely in the hands of either politicians or professionals is likely to be a far less healthy activity than when there is a constant questioning of the role of each, and one acts to restrain the other.

Desirable as such dynamic tensions may be, there is no doubt that they serve to intensify the pressures upon those who are delivering education. Nowhere is this more apparent than amongst school leaders, and the conference highlighted the key effects that this heightened pressure was having, alongside the very real pressure on resources coming into the service. The most obvious effect of intense questioning about what makes for a better education system is that policy changes occur, often with dramatic speed. This change scenario, especially when it is pursued in several different directions at the same time, is difficult to manage. It becomes even more so when those managing it are not, by their previous experience and training, prepared for the consequence of such wholesale change. That is not to argue that education managers are unable or unwilling to manage change – many have done so with distinction, and will again – but rather to say that massive simultaneous change challenges everyone, and is particularly threatening when imposed by others. To the sheer scale of change can be added the breakneck timetable of change. Most reformers, but especially politicians geared to an election cycle, predict changes can be accomplished and have their effects on far too short a timescale. To reap the benefits of worthwhile change in education, ten years is often a more realistic timescale than two. Yet much is expected immediately, and evaluation, a reflex-action now deeply ingrained in education, is frequently applied judgementally long before meaningful results can reasonably be expected.

Thus the scale and pace of change is producing stress on the managers of schools and the service. Heightened by scarce resources, intensified by what in some countries seems an orchestrated campaign to undermine public confidence, low status and reward, the education manager, living in such high drama, can be forgiven for thinking that only the most god-like of heroes could hope to succeed. Clearly any service that relies for its model of leadership on recruiting the superhuman is destined to disappointment.

Other very important worries emerged in the conference discussions. There is the worry that in the politicization of education, utilitarian, measurable and expedient considerations will outweigh more substantial and worthwhile values. The ethics of education seem to many to be relegated to a low priority in the current debates and there is a danger that 'valueless' systems may result. Further, very real concern emerged that what was being lost sight of was the purpose of education, the fundamental activity of learning and the crucial interface between teacher and student. In the hectic rush to systematise, evaluate, analyze and inspect, the essential joy of discovering more about yourself and the world, the thrill of exploring the meaning of living, and the satisfaction that comes from achieving beyond your expectations may be threatened. Teaching and learning are at the heart of the matter, and no manager should ever forget that. Learning can and should be helped by good organisation, planning, preparation and professional skills, but it will also remain spontaneous, incidental, lateral, explosive and unpredictable, and there are real fears that in trying to regiment and assess, this vital dimension can be in jeopardy.

Towards a healthier climate

For me, therefore, some very clear messages emerge from the Seventh International Intervisitation Programme, and though they can be simply distilled and stated, they are very important indeed.

The first is that education, above all, must learn to value the people who work in it, cherishing them, especially through a time of intense change. If follows that the rest of society, wherever in the world it be, should avoid denigrating their work as a vital part of the system. Rather, they should be valued, supported and helped to improve.

To promote such a sense of being valued, there is an urgent need to consider the career-long development of teachers, offering entitlement to active guidance and support from initial training to retirement. Careers in the education service need to have more shape and coherence, without however resorting to the direction of labour commonly found in large companies. The introduction of personal profiles and plans would facilitate such an approach.

Teachers and schools and colleagues need far more ready access to the kind of support services regarded as commonplace in business to enable them to manage change more successfully. Central and local government dedicated to making management easier rather than more difficult would also help enormously.

Management must not be regarded as separate from the crucial business of teaching and learning. Nor must management be equated with administration, if that term is used to mean bureaucratic routines. Rather it must always contain a major element of leadership. The need for leaders with vision and values is always acute, and needs constantly re-enforcing. In this context, we should be wary of a competencies approach which may be guilty of seeing school leaders as the amalgam of definable skills rather than human beings, varied in ability and performance, but especially adept at motivating others.

Finally, management, though an essential part of a successful education service, should not be seen as the only important component, and the teaching and learning process should always be regarded as more important than administration. The appropriate management style for schools is a corporate one, and the key development unit is the school rather than the individual. More and more industrial and commercial companies are seeking such an approach: there is deep irony in schools moving towards a hierarchical, in-line system just as this is being rejected elsewhere.

Thus, for me, the Task Force, and for many who contributed to the Seventh International Intervisitation Programme in the North West of England, three key factors for the development of more effective schools in the future are:

- share power with all the participants;
- collaborate for the good of the students;
- above all, values are at the heart of any system; managers must identify and exemplify values, or they are mere cogs in a machine.

References

School Management Task Force 1989 *Interim Report,* London: DES.
School Management Task Force 1990 *Developing School Management: 'The Way Forward'*, London: HMSO.

List of Contributors

John Abbott is Director of Education 2000. Formerly Head of Alleyne's School in Stevenage, UK, he now describes himself as an educational marketer and entrepreneur.

Ray Bolam is Director of the National Development Centre for Educational Management and Policy, School of Education, University of Bristol, UK. He is a former Editor of *Educational Management and Administration*.

Ernest Cave is a Lecturer in the Education Management Unit, Department of Public Administration at the University of Ulster, Northern Ireland. He was a Group Rapporteur at IIP 1990.

Benjamin Chan is Chairman of Educational Administration and Policy in the School of Education of the Chinese University of Hong Kong.

Ann Clark is the Director of Education of the Catholic School System of the Diocese of Parramatta in New South Wales, Australia.

Glen Earthman is Associate Professor of Educational Administration in the Division of Administrative and Educational Services, Virginia Polytechnic and State University, United States.

Colin Evers is a member of the Faculty of Education of Monash University in Melbourne, Australia.

Ron Glatter is Professor and Director of the Centre for Educational Policy at the Open University, United Kingdom. He is a former Chairman of BEMAS and a founder member of the European Forum on Educational Administration. He was responsible for the organization of group work at the IIP 1990.

Jim Guthrie is Professor in the Graduate School of Education, University of California, Berkeley, United States. He is Co-Director of Project Policy Analysis for California Education. He has been a Special Assistant to the Secretary of the Department of Health, Education and Welfare and Education Specialist for the United States Senate.

Michael Harvey is a member of the Department of Education Studies in the Western Australian College of Advanced Studies.

Mark Hewlett is currently the Principal of Rawlins Community College in Loughborough, UK. Before that he was the Head of Heart of England School in Solihull. He is attracted by the idea of Education 2000 and is involved in promoting it in Loughborough. He has been Treasurer of BEMAS and is its current Chairman.

Edward Hickcox is a Professor in the Department of Educational Administration at the Ontario Institute for Studies in Education,

Canada. He is a member of the IIP Standing Committee and is to Co-Chair IIP 1994.

John House is a Professor in the Department of Educational Administration at the Ontario Institute for Studies in Education, Canada.

Meredydd Hughes is Emeritus Professor of Education at the University of Birmingham, UK where he was Head of the Department of Social and Administrative Studies in Education and Dean of the Faculty. He has been the Head of a secondary school, Chairman of BEMAS and Editor of its journal, President of the CCEA and Chairman of the IIP Standing Committee.

Stephen Jacobson is Assistant Professor in the Department of Educational Organization, Administration and Policy at the State University of New York at Buffalo, USA. He is a member of the IIP Standing Committee and is to Co-Chair IIP 1994.

Neil Johnson is a Lecturer in the School of Education at the University of New South Wales in Australia.

Tilokasundari Kariyawasam is a State Secretary for Education in the Ministry of Education, Cultural Affairs and Information and Director General of the National Institute of Education, Sri Lanka. She has held many senior posts including Deputy Director General of Education, Director of Educational Planning and was for many years a school Principal.

Gabriele Lakomski is a Senior Lecturer in the School of Education at the University of Melbourne in Victoria, Australia.

Alan Macintosh is a Doctoral Student at the Department of Educational Administration in the University of Saskatchewan in Canada.

Michael Manley-Casimir is Professor of Education in the Faculty of Education at Simon Fraser University, British Colombia, Canada.

William Mulford is Dean of the Faculty of Education and Humanities at the University of Tasmania in Australia. He is a member of the IIP Standing Committee and is currently President of CCEA.

Stella Olatunji is a visiting Professor of the Faculty of Education at Ogun State University in Nigeria.

Ken Rae is a Senior Policy Analyst in the Management/Organization Section of the Ministry of Education in Wellington, New Zealand. He played a major role in the organization of IIP 1986 and is National Secretary of NZEAS.

Peter Ribbins is Reader in Educational Management, Centre for Educational Management and Administration Studies, University of Birmingham, UK. He was Programme Convenor for IIP 1990 and Executive Editor of *Developing Educational Leaders*. He is Editor of *Educational Management and Administration*.

Chaman Sapra is currently a Consultant in Education. Before that he was a Professor at the University of Delhi in India. He is an Honorary Vice President of CCEA.

Arthur Schwartz is Associate Professor in the Department of Educational Policy and Administrative Studies at the University of Calgary in Canada.

Tim Simkins is a Principal Lecturer and Head of the Centre for Education Management and Administration, in the School of Education, Sheffield City Polytechnic, UK. Currently, he is a member of the Council of BEMAS and was Secretary to the Programme Committee of IIP 1990.

Rosemary Stewart is a Fellow of Templeton College (Oxford Centre for Management Studies) where she teaches organizational behaviour to senior managers and graduate students. For many years she was Dean of the College. In 1982 she co-directed the Seventh Biennial Leadership Symposium.

David Styan is Director of the North West Educational Management Centre in the United Kingdom. He leads the Government Task Force on School Management Development and Training. He has been Head of a large secondary school and was Director of the Centre for the Study of Comprehensive Schools.

A Ross Thomas is Associate Professor in the Department of Administrative, Higher and Adult Education Studies, University of New England, Australia. He is the long serving Editor of the *Journal of Educational Administration*.

A Velaythuam is Reader in Educational Administration at the University of the South Pacific in Fiji.

Len Watson is Professor of Education Management and Administration in the School of Education, Sheffield City Polytechnic, UK. He was Chairman of the Planning Committee for IIP 1990. He has been Chairman of BEMAS and is currently a member of the Executive Committees of CCEA and IIP.

Cyril Wilkinson is Director of the Education Management Unit in the University of Ulster, Northern Ireland.

Kevin Wilson is Professor and Head of Department in the Department of Educational Administration at the University of Saskatchewan, Canada.

Author/Subject Index